Myanmar in Crisis

The **ISEAS – Yusof Ishak Institute** (formerly Institute of Southeast Asian Studies) is an autonomous organisation established in 1968. It is a regional centre dedicated to the study of sociopolitical, security, and economic trends and developments in Southeast Asia and its wider geostrategic and economic environment. The Institute's research programs are grouped under Regional Economic Studies (RES), Regional Strategic and Political Studies (RSPS), and Regional Social and Cultural Studies (RSCS). The Institute is also home to the ASEAN Studies Centre (ASC), the Singapore APEC Study Centre, and the Temasek History Research Centre (THRC).

ISEAS Publishing, an established academic press, has issued more than 2,000 books and journals. It is the largest scholarly publisher of research about Southeast Asia from within the region. ISEAS Publishing works with many other academic and trade publishers and distributors to disseminate important research and analyses from and about Southeast Asia to the rest of the world.

Myanmar Update Series

Myanmar in Crisis
Living with the Pandemic and the Coup

Edited By
Justine Chambers and Michael R. Dunford

First published in Singapore in 2023 by
ISEAS Publishing
30 Heng Mui Keng Terrace
Singapore 119614

E-mail: publish@iseas.edu.sg
Website: http://bookshop.iseas.edu.sg

All rights reserved. No part of this publication may be reproduced, translated, stored in a retrieval system, or transmitted in any form or by any means, electronic, mechanical, photocopying, recording or otherwise, without the prior permission of the ISEAS – Yusof Ishak Institute.

© 2023 ISEAS – Yusof Ishak Institute, Singapore

The responsibility for facts and opinions in this publication rests exclusively with the authors and their interpretations do not necessarily reflect the views or the policy of the Institute or its supporters.

ISEAS Library Cataloguing-in-Publication Data

Name(s): Myanmar Update (2021 : Canberra, Australia) | Chambers, Justine, editor. | Dunford, Michael R., editor.
Title: Myanmar in crisis : living with the pandemic and the coup / edited by Justine Chambers and Michael R. Dunford.
Description: Singapore : ISEAS – Yusof Ishak Institute, 2023. | Series: Myanmar Update Series. | Papers originally presented to the Myanmar Update 2021 held at the Australian National University, Canberra, from 15 to 17 July 2021. | Includes bibliographical references and index.
Identifiers: ISBN 9789815104387 (softcover) | ISBN 9789815104394 (hardcover) | ISBN 9789815104400 (ebook pdf)
Subjects: LCSH: Myanmar—History—Coup d'état, 2021. | COVID-19 Pandemic, 2020- —Myanmar. | Myanmar—Politics and government—21st century—Congresses. | Myanmar—Social conditions—Congresses. | Myanmar—Economic conditions—Congresses.
Classification: LCC DS530.4 B972 2021

Cover photo: Artwork entitled "Untitled" by Shwe Thin Moe, who painted it with these reflections:

> This artwork is from my inner soul. It is not painted to be sold. I painted it because I was requested to paint. I painted it, because I want to do as I like and to paint as I like. Someone does not have to like it. All that matters is that I like it. I painted it based on what I felt in my heart. Artworks are a window into our soul. This painting is built from all the emotions and feelings I poured in it, including a deep motivation and desire to be free and peaceful. It also reflects my feelings of suffocation, sadness and poor physical and mental health. I poured all those feelings into this painting.

Copyedited and indexed by Justine Chambers and Michael R. Dunford
Typeset by Naing Oo
Printed in Singapore by Mainland Press Pte Ltd

CONTENTS

Acknowledgements vii
Contributors and Editors ix
List of Figures xi
Abbreviations and Key Terms xiii

Part I Introduction

1. Myanmar in 'Crisis' 3
Justine Chambers

Part II: On Crisis

2. Myanmar's Post-coup Crisis: Reflections on a History of Failed Nation Building 31
Khin Zaw Win

3. The 2021 Military Coup: Causes and Consequences 41
Morten B. Pedersen

4. Covid, Coup and Prisons: Exploring Crisis as Context in Myanmar 69
Tomas Max Martin and U Win

Part III: A State in Crisis

5. Myanmar under Contested Military Rule 95
Nicola S. Williams

6. Contested Political Authority in Post-Coup Myanmar 125
Kim Jolliffe

7. The CDM and its Allies: Myanmar's Heterogeneous Anticolonial Public(s) 159
Michael Dunford

Part IV: An Economic Crisis

8. The Myanmar Economy, Covid-19 and the Military Coup: Issues and Prospects for Recovery   185
Linda Calebresi, Maximiliano Mendez-Parra and Laetitia Pettinotti

9. Pandemic Challenges of Fishers at Kyauk Myaung Segment, Irrawaddy River, Myanmar   213
Mie Mie Kyaw

10. The Destabilization of Myanmar: The Coup and its Impact on Economic Conditions and International Business Investment   235
Htwe Htwe Thein and Michael Gillan

Part V: International Relations in Crisis

11. Neutralism or Non-Alignment: Myanmar's Recurring Foreign Policy Dilemma   261
Andrea Passeri and Hunter Marston

12. The Nature, Scope and Limits of International Responses to Myanmar's Coup   289
Nicholas Coppel

Part VI: Epilogue

13. On Disappointment and Hope: Myanmar Studies and the Multiple Crises   323
Michael Dunford and Dinith Adikari

Index   339

ACKNOWLEDGEMENTS

In July 2021, the Australian National University's Myanmar Research Centre (MRC) hosted the bi-annual Myanmar Update. The conference brought together academics, researchers, policymakers and active members of Myanmar's NGO and civil society sector under the theme of 'Living with the Pandemic and Coup', the contents of which are the subject of this volume.

The Myanmar Update is a major venue at which to present cutting-edge scholarship on political, social and economic affairs in Myanmar. Now in its third decade, it is one of only two longstanding, regularly held international conferences on the country and has consistently produced high-quality publications since the 1990s. We thank the conference speakers and participants and encourage everyone reading this volume to forge ongoing connections with local scholars that will further enhance our knowledge and understanding of Myanmar, especially as it transforms during this revolutionary period. We also acknowledge the bravery of all the conference participants who spoke from inside Myanmar in 2021, despite the hostile climate against academics and researchers collaborating with foreign institutions.

International conferences such as the Myanmar Update require tremendous collective effort and we thank all the members of the MRC who supported both the conference and preparation for the volume. The MRC was launched in 2015. Since then, the Centre has served as the university's academic hub for Myanmar activities and a thriving hub of international scholarship. The Centre provides a flexible and inclusive structure to maintain its activities, build relationships with our Myanmar partners, and create new opportunities for ANU staff and students. The strength of these partnerships is reflected in the growing attendance of Myanmar scholars in this volume series and our ongoing commitment to supporting research on the country.

We want to thank the ANU for their ongoing financial and institutional assistance for both the conference and the volume series. We are especially grateful to the College of Asia and the Pacific and its Department of Political and Social Change for their ongoing enthusiasm and support for our work. Special thanks to Dorothy Mason, whose assistance with copy-editing helped to ensure the volume's high production standards. We also thank Naing Oo for his excellent work putting the volume together as a cohesive visual product. We also acknowledge the generosity of the Myanmar studies community whose ongoing support and scholarly reviews provided critical feedback and commentary on each of the papers.

Thanks also to the collective efforts of our amazing contributors. The strength of the analysis in each of the chapters is testament to your hard work. We appreciate all of the time and effort you have put into developing these chapters and for your patience and collegiality throughout the publication process.

Finally, thanks go to the ongoing support of Ng Kok Kiong and Rahilah Yusuf at the ISEAS-Yusof Ishak Institute in Singapore. Once again, it has been a pleasure working with you on this volume and we look forward to doing so again in the future.

CONTRIBUTORS AND EDITORS

Dinith Adikari is a PhD candidate in anthropology at the Australian National University.

Linda Calabrese is a Research Fellow at ODI and a Leverhulme Doctoral Fellow at King's College London.

Justine Chambers is a Postdoctoral Researcher at the Danish Institute for International Studies (DIIS) and a Research Fellow at the College of Asia and the Pacific, Australian National University.

Nicholas Coppel is an Adjunct Associate Professor (Practice) at Monash University and the former Australian Ambassador to Myanmar.

Michael R. Dunford is a PhD candidate in anthropology at the Australian National University.

Michael Gillan is an Associate Professor of Employment relations, Department of Management and Organisations, UWA Business School, at the University of Western Australia.

Htwe Htwe Thein is an Associate Professor in International Business at the School of Management and Marketing, Curtin University, Australia.

Kim Jolliffe is an independent researcher and educator who has been working in Myanmar's conflict-affected areas since 2009 with a range of local and international organisations.

Khin Zaw Win is the Director of the Tampadipa Institute Myanmar, working on policy advocacy and capacity building since 2006.

Hunter Marston is a PhD candidate in the Department of International Relations at Australian National University and an Adjunct Research Fellow at La Trobe Asia.

Tomas Max Martin is a senior researcher at DIGNITY – Danish Institute against Torture, in Copenhagen, Denmark.

Maximiliano Mendez-Parra is a Principal Research Fellow at ODI.

Mie Mie Kyaw is an independent freelance researcher and lecturer.

Andrea Passeri is a senior lecturer in International Relations at the Department of International and Strategic Studies, University Malaya.

Laetitia Pettinotti is a Senior Research Officer at ODI.

Morten B. Pedersen is a senior researcher at the University of New South Wales Canberra and the Australian Defence Force Academy.

U Win is a pseudonym. He is a Myanmar national and experienced researcher on prisons.

Nicola Williams is a PhD Scholar at the Australian National University's Crawford School of Public Policy, a board member at the ANU Myanmar Research Centre, and an international development professional with over 14 years of experience.

LIST OF FIGURES

Figure 7.1: A police officer gives engine repair advice to a Yangon motorist participating in "Taxi CDM," also known as the "why you break down, car?" protest. In this protest action, motorists stopped their vehicles in crucial intersections and pretended to have broken engines. 169

Figure 9.1: Percentage of households facing challenges. 223

ABBREVIATIONS AND KEY TERMS

AA	Arakan Army
ASEAN	Association of Southeast Asian Nations
CCP	Chinese Communist Party
CDM	Civil Disobedience Movement
CERP	COVID-19 Economic Recovery Plan
CMEC	China–Myanmar Economic Corridor
CNF	Chin National Front
CRPH	Committee Representing the Pyidaungsu Hluttaw
DSSI	Debt Service Suspension Initiative
ERO	Ethnic Resistance Organisations
EU	European Union
FDC	Federal Democracy Charter
FDI	Foreign Direct Investment
FTA	Free Trade Area
GAD	General Administration Department
GDP	Gross Domestic Product
GoM	Government of Myanmar
GSC	General Strike Committee
GSCB	General Strike Coordination Body
GSC-N	General Strike Committee of Nationalities
ICC	International Criminal Court
IUU	Illegal, Unreported and Unregulated (fishing)

IMF	International Monetary Fund
ICNCC	Interim Chin National Consultative Council
JICA	Japanese International Cooperation Agency
KIO	Kachin Independence Organisation
KIA	Kachin Independence Army
KSCC	Karenni State Consultative Council
Kyat	Myanmar's local currency
KNU	Karen National Union
LDF	Local Defence Forces
MERRP	Myanmar Economic Resilience and Reform Plan
MNDAA	Myanmar National Democratic Alliance Army
MOGE	Myanmar Oil and Gas Enterprise
MEC	Myanmar Economic Corporation
NCA	Nationwide Ceasefire Agreement
NUCC	National Unity Consultative Council
NUG	National Unity Government
NLD	National League for Democracy
NRC	National Registration Card
ODA	Official Development Assistance
OECD	Organisation for Economic Co-operation and Development
PDF	People's Defence Forces
PRC	People's Republic of China
RCEP	Regional Comprehensive Economic Partnership
R2P	Responsibility to Protect
SAC	State Administrative Council
SDG	Sustainable Development Goals
SEZ	Special Economic Zone
Sit Tat	Myanmar state military forces
TNLA	Ta'ang National Liberation Army
UEC	Union Election Commission
UN	United Nations

USDP	United Solidarity and Development Party
UWSA	United Wa State Army
VTWA	Village Tract and Ward Administrator
YUG	Yangon Urban Guerrillas

I
Introduction

1

MYANMAR IN 'CRISIS'

Justine Chambers

On 11 March 2020, the World Health Organization (WHO) declared that COVID-19 was a global pandemic. Neighbouring the world's two most populous countries, many feared the potential impacts to people in Myanmar with its limited public resources, health infrastructure and hospitals. Initially, there was some cautious optimism, as the country was able to avoid the high case-positive loads seen in nearby India, Indonesia and the Philippines. However, with its high levels of poverty and associated inequality, concerns about the economic repercussions of the global pandemic, as well as the impact of lockdown restrictions on ordinary people's livelihoods, soon became a more paramount concern.

Amidst the global health and economic crisis, Myanmar's people were gearing up for a general election, the second held since 2011 when the military junta begun to make space for a period of social and political change (Cheesman et al. 2014; Egreteau & Robinne 2015). While the country's State Counsellor Aung San Suu Kyi campaigned on her unique ability to see the country through the pandemic as the 'mother of the nation', many people did not view the election or the government as playing a significant role in influencing their survival of the pandemic. The government's COVID-19 Economic Relief Plan (CERP) was widely criticised for its inability to reach the most vulnerable households, especially those in rural areas and the large number of people who work in the informal sector (see Mi Chan 2020). And yet, despite these criticisms and ongoing concerns about the difficulties of holding an election in the midst of a global pandemic, more than seventy per cent of the population came out to vote. While more than ninety parties competed in the election, people overwhelmingly endorsed Suu Kyi and the NLD in a landslide victory that was even greater than 2015 (Lidauer & Saphy 2021).

Less than three months later, on the day that Suu Kyi and other parliamentarians were to take their seats for a second term of government, Myanmar's democratic process and era of reform was brought to an abrupt end by a military coup d'etat. In the early dawn hours, security sector personnel arrested the State Counsellor Aung San Suu Kyi and President U Win Myint, as well as other incoming Members of Parliament, civil society activists and other critical voices. Citing unfounded allegations of voter fraud in the November elections, an official military statement declared a one-year state of emergency, transferring authority to the commander-in chief, Senior General Min Aung Hlaing, and establishing a "caretaker government", the State Administration Council (SAC).

Despite their shallow attempts to convince people in the country that this was a legitimate constitutional takeover and promises to a return to representative rule after elections (Crouch 2021), resistance to the coup was spontaneous and erupted across all corners of Myanmar. As people across the country woke to the news in the early hours of 1 February 2021, some rushed to the morning market to stock up on basic goods in fear of the unknown, while others stayed at home, in a deep sense of shock. But within a matter of days, people came out en masse, growing by the tens of thousands every day, demanding the restoration of democracy and the release of elected leaders and political activists. Led by healthcare workers, educators and labour unionists, a powerful Civil Disobedience Movement (CDM) soon emerged, effectively shutting down most government services, including from education, transportation and healthcare. A series of sham charges aimed to discredit and delegitimise Aung San Suu Kyi and the NLD showed how the military's leaders saw her removal from public office as the death of the pro-democracy movement.[1] However, led by the tech-savvy Generation Z, women activists, ethnic civil society leaders and labour unionists, protestors soon galvanised around more revolutionary goals: including calls to abolish the 2008 Constitution, to create a constitution for a genuine federal democracy and to end all kinds of authoritarianism, including discrimination against women and other marginalised groups (see Jordt et al. 2021).

Building off a deep history of creative acts of resistance including both "old and new repertoires of contention" (Egreteau 2022), the initial days of the protests had a hopeful, carnival-like atmosphere. From the busy streets of Yangon and Mandalay, to the distant hills of Naga and Shan state and down the coast line of Mon and Tanintharyi, live coverage from citizen journalists showed tens of thousands of young men and women coming out in various kinds of costumes and dress to represent different identities. From symbolic gestures like the coordinated beating of cooking pots at 8pm every night to ward off evil spirits,[2] to the three fingered salute of the dystopian Hunger Games movies, to the htamein protest on International Women's Day in symbolic defiance of the patriarchal values of the military establishment (Malar, Chambers & Elena 2023), social creativity flourished in ways which aimed to "ridicule and expose the weakness of the regime" (Egreteau 2022, 5). While 1988 revolutionary slogans and songs and Gandhian-inspired 'silent strikes' persisted, access to digital and social media also allowed for the diffusion of new and more global forms of contentious collective action, both documenting #whatshappeninginMyanmar and declaring the people's collective desire for a 'Federal Democracy' and 'Self-Determination' (Egreteau 2022; Ryan & Tran 2022).

What began as peaceful, popular demonstrations soon shifted, as the military began to mobilise age-old tactics of violence to quell the peaceful demonstrations. On 9 February 2021, Mya Thwe Thwe Khaing, a nineteen-year-old university student, was shot dead at a protest in Naypyidaw when a bullet pierced her motorcycle helmet. Violence against protestors soon escalated with the security sector opening fire on mass demonstrations, leading to a series of massacres in hot spots of the resistance. A State of Emergency was imposed — cellular service and the Internet were shut down intermittently to prevent community mobilisation, night curfews imposed and licenses for independent media revoked. Reports of night-time raids by security forces increased and disturbing videos started to circulate online too of mounting violence and torture (Cheesman 2021), providing snapshots into war crimes and crimes against humanity (see Fortify Rights 2021; HRW 2021). Houses were burnt down, people shot at point blank range, and hundreds of Generation Z protest leaders, long-time civil society and democracy activists, journalists and CDMers were arrested and detained, dragged out into the streets and beaten in front of onlookers livestreaming to the outside world.

Despite the escalating violence, the anti-coup movement responded by mobilising themselves with body armour, sling shots, improvised airguns and Molotov cocktails as well as knowledge of how to clean tear gas, build barricades and tend to gunshot wounds. As the number of anti-junta resistance actors were killed, some started to flee to the countryside to take up arms — joining small, local armed resistance groups, with support from long-established ethnic resistance organisations (EROs) (Fishbein et al. 2021). The Karen National Union, the Kachin Independence Organisation, the Karenni National Progressive Party and the Chin National Front (CNF), groups who have long fought for ethnic autonomy and federalism amidst decades of state violence, soon came to shelter tens of thousands of young resistance fighters, providing them with logistical, operational and political support. Urban warfare broke out in Yangon and other cities with bombings, arson and targeted killings, mostly on police, administrative offices and other facilities or informants connected to the regime. Beginning with guerrilla-style acts of resistance, by May these self-styled People's Defense Forces (PDF) grew in number and sophistication, bringing the country's brutal civil wars to encompass large parts of the central Bamar heartland and areas which hadn't seen conflict in decades, including Sagaing and Magwe Regions.

Coalescing around the military as 'common enemy' (in Burmese, *bone yan thu*), a groundswell of solidarity helped to unite different communities across the country. New revolutionary political groups and movements flourished as part of what became popularly referred to as the "Spring Revolution". Shortly after the coup, NLD MPs-elect from the 2020 election formed the Committee Representing the Pyidaungsu Hluttaw (CRPH). In addition to the powerful CDM movement which helped to bring the functioning of basic state administration functions to a halt, more radical groups emerged such as the General Strike Committee (GSC) and the General Strike Committee of Nationalities (GSC-N), calling for a more radical restructuring of Myanmar's politics. In March, representatives from EROs, strike committees, labour unions, activist networks and civil society groups formed the National Unity Consultative Committee (NUCC). This began to build a consensus-based platform for dialogue on the design of a Federal Democracy Charter and a political roadmap towards a genuine federal democracy, with a high degree of decentralisation and recognition of collective ethnic rights, customs and ownership of resources (Ardeth Maung Thawnghmung and Khun Noah 2021).[3] In April the cabinet of the National Unity Government (NUG) was constituted by the CRPH, made up primarily of deposed members of the ruling NLD party, but also a more revolutionary set of ethnic and civil society actors, with aims to overthrow the junta through both dialogue and, importantly, armed resistance. With the growth in armed PDF movements across the country, in September 2021 the NUG declared a 'defensive war', breaking with Aung San Suu Kyi's age-old principle of non-violent struggle against military authoritarianism (Selth 2021).

More than two years after the coup, the military is yet to consolidate power and it lacks control over much of the country. On the one year anniversary of their 'defensive war' in September 2022, the Acting President of the NUG, Duwa Lashi La, claimed that the resistance has effective control over more than half of the country, including those areas controlled by EROs (Irrawaddy 2022). An analysis from the Special Advisory Council for Myanmar (SAC-M), a group of independent human rights experts, also echoed claims from the NUG that they have "effective control" over more than fifty percent of the country (SAC-M 2022). While these claims are based on unreliable estimates, even the military itself admits it has lost control in large parts of the country, with its planned 2023 election postponed due to issues regarding voter registration and a surge in 'subversive activities' by the resistance. Even though the military is far-better equipped with modern weapons and aircraft from Russia and China, recruitment is falling and soldiers continue to defect (Kyed & Ah Lynn 2021; Thinzar Shunlei Yi 2022). Access to drone technology has also enabled the growing number of local PDF groups to step up resistance against the military (Kyi Sin 2023) and alliances with EROs are expanding and deepening.[4]

Even in areas where the military maintains a modicum of control, members of the resistance continue to carry out random, creative, guerilla-style protests in the streets, as well as other creative acts of protest (see Frontier 2022a). Despite efforts from the regime to censor and block acts of protest on the Internet, artists, graphic designers, writers, poets, cartoonists, musicians and filmmakers also continue to use their work to express dissent to the coup and highlight the injustices of the brutal security personnel, with social media abound with illustrations, poetry and protest music (PEN 2021). Despite a lack of money, equipment and training, the armed resistance too is still strong and expanding its control, withstanding some of the most ruthless counterinsurgency campaigns ever conducted by the military (Nachemson 2022). However, as part of the military's response to the resistance, civilians are bearing the brunt of atrocities in both rural and urban areas.

As of February 2023, regime forces have killed more than 2900 anti-coup activists, including at least 377 children (AAPP 2023). Nearly 18,000 people have been arbitrarily arrested, with more than 13,000 still in prison, and many subject to torture (Ibid.). Drawing on age-old scorched-earth tactics used against ethnic nationality communities, more than 55,000 homes have been destroyed in arson attacks by junta forces since the coup (Irrawaddy 2023; see also Kelly et al. 2021). Large areas of paddy have also been occupied and destroyed by the military as part of their counter-insurgency missions in traditional rice-growing regions like Sagaing (Frontier 2022b). With military support from Russia and China, air strikes too have become one of the deadliest weapons of the military, targeting both resistance strongholds and civilian areas including an elementary school, hospitals, churches and a music concert in Kachin State.

Analysis of satellite imagery, eyewitness accounts and military planning documents reveal the devastation inflicted on communities, with hundreds of thousands forced to flee to neighbouring India and Thailand amid raids, air strikes, arson, massacres and countless other atrocities (Kelly et al. 2021). Ethnic communities living in resource-rich frontier states are further made vulnerable by a growth in armed groups and resource extraction activities. Following historical processes of "dispossession, enrichment and violence" (Sarma et al. 2022: 3), the violent reimposition of military rule has drastically undermined the civic space for environmental and climate justice actors (Chambers & Kyed 2023), which during the 2011–2020 reform period provided some degree of protection to customary lands and the environment (CAT 2022; Sekine 2021). In the absence of oversight mechanisms, civil society organisations report a rapid increase in unregulated mining, which is polluting waterways, decimating forests, destroying mountains, and causing landslides and changes to fragile ecosystems (ABIPA 2023). In addition to threatening local land rights and livelihoods, junta-led plans to revive controversial hydropower dams and palm oil plantations will heavily disturb important riverine ecosystems and destroy natural forests (Ibid.; see also Suhardiman et al. 2017).

Like former military leaders, the junta has also "armed itself with new repressive laws", including removing "basic protections of freedom of expression, freedom of assembly and association, and privacy" (Strangio 2021). For those that remain in areas controlled by the SAC, it remains extremely dangerous to speak out for fear of imprisonment, torture, or death. As Penny Edwards, Kenneth Wong and Ko Ko Thet (2022: 179) write in the introduction to a recent literary collection:

> In Myanmar today, the simplest utterance is punishable as the defamation of the state. A song, a poem, a music video, an elegy are all open invitations to a cowardly regime to pursue their authors with impunity.

Official retribution for political and expressive acts builds off British-era codes and laws, including imprisonment without trial, torture and unlawful detention as part of a historical tradition of what they describe as maintaining 'rule of law' (see Cheesman 2016). Many of those who have stood trial have been denied access to lawyers and relatives and the death toll of people in custody is also rising, with at least 300 people killed in formal detention settings. In a move that shocked the world, the application of the death penalty has also been invoked for the first time in decades. In July 2022, long-time political activists and former parliamentarians, Ko Jimmy and Ko Phyo Zeya Thaw, were executed, alongside two others for their participation in the revolution and also denied funeral rites (Seinenu M. Thein-Lemelson 2022).

On the two year anniversary of the coup, more than one million people are internally displaced and an additional one million refugees and asylum seekers are living in neighbouring countries (UNHCR 2022), the majority of which remain in a precarious legal limbo often at risk of arrest, detention and deportation, and unable to return home, access services or resettle to other countries. As highlighted by the new Yangon Stories website, violence also takes other forms, including through forced evictions and arson both as a form of collective punishment, but also (re)territorialisation.[5] The humanitarian crisis is also compounded by the ongoing economic impacts of COVID-19 and the war in Ukraine. Myanmar's currency continues to depreciate and prices for food, fuel, fertilisers and basic household goods have skyrocketed, forcing many into poverty (Soe Nandar Linn 2023).[6] In this context, where more than seventy per cent of people rely on the agricultural sector for their livelihoods, farmers are taking on more debt and reducing the amount of spending on food consumption and other everyday living costs, including education and health (Aung

Tun 2022; Griffiths 2022). Wealthy cronies and medium-sized businesses are transferring their assets outside of the country and people are leaving the country in droves, desperate to find jobs elsewhere.

Despite the escalating and intersecting forms of crisis, the international response to the coup has been disappointing, focused primarily on repeated condemnations of violence and calls for a return to democracy. As the political and humanitarian crisis deepens and atrocities against civilians increase, in December 2022, the United Nations Security Council adopted its first resolution on Myanmar in 74 years, denouncing the military's ongoing use of violence and rights violations and urging for the release of political prisoners. In the same month, President Biden signed the US government's National Defense Act (NDAA), which allows for non-lethal American assistance and technologies to be delivered to ERO, PDFs and the NUG. In February 2023, a new round of sanctions targeting members of the junta and its economic entities was imposed by the United States, the European Union, Canada and the United Kingdom. Australia too, announced its first round of sanctions, targeting sixteen members of the SAC and the military conglomerates Myanmar Economic Holdings Limited and the Myanmar Economic Cooperation. Despite the significance of these symbolic gestures, they remain largely that — symbolic and performative, with little effect on the military. Indeed, despite the courage shown by the revolutionary actors in Myanmar, they receive little support from foreign governments (in stark contrast to the well-funded Ukranian resistance). Instead, the international community is relying on the Association for Southeast Asian Nations (ASEAN) to push forward with dialogue with the regime and calls for a 'return to democracy'.

While it appears that the military has not changed much over the last decade, the country and its people certainly have. The opening of political space afforded by Myanmar's changes over the 2010's saw a blossoming of civil society networks around various issues, which have become core causes of the pro-democracy movement — including the need for gender equality, labour rights, environmental protections and better representation for ethnic nationalities and indigenous communities. Indeed, for many people now guiding the discussions on the federal charter there is no returning to the 'status quo'. Spearheaded by strike groups, ethnic activists, EROs and other known critics of the NLD, one of the more interesting dynamics to emerge out of the coup is that the fight against the military has become a revolutionary struggle for a more democratic, united and inclusive

Myanmar — establishing a genuine federal democratic union where all people, regardless of their ethnicity or religion, are treated equally. Not only has the coup highlighted the fragile nature of the previous power-sharing arrangement between the civilian government and the military, but it has brought to the fore the work of the many activists that the NLD government also tried to silence and ignore.

In the midst of the current political crisis, it is sometimes easy to look at the ten years prior to 2021 with rose-tinted glasses. However, scholarship written in the period immediately before the pandemic and the coup already began to identify and analyse political and social problems that endured through the so-called "transition" years. While there were many things changing in Myanmar over this period, the legacies of military rule and their ongoing role in politics continued to stymy reforms in multiple and complex ways. As explored in our previous volume, *Living with Myanmar* (Chambers et al. 2020), ordinary people faced significant challenges in their everyday lives, and reform in key sectors, such as around land rights, education and gender equality, faced an uphill battle (see e.g. Khin Khin Mra and Livingstone 2020). While much of the former censorship regime was lifted, allowing for an era of critical journalism and literary creativity, both the military and the NLD government continued to use colonial-era laws to silence activism and dissent. The economy did indeed open up and change life for many. However, Myanmar remained one of the poorest countries in the world and the majority of people continued to rely on everyday "survival tactics" in order to get by (Thawnghmung 2019: xvii). As access to mobile, phones, electricity, and clean water steadily increased, there was also greater inequality and debt remained a significant issue for many households. In this way, the potential to enact aspirations and ideals continued to be determined by unequal access to resources, the claims and actions of "moral authorities" (Chambers & Cheesman 2019), the consequences of intersectional inequalities, as well as different histories of personal and community struggle.

Other important scholarly works that have been released since the coup also document the trends outlined above. Underpinning the structural changes occurring in Myanmar, there remained deeply entrenched structural inequalities, especially for women and girls (Hedström & Olivius 2023). After decades of brutal civil wars, the peace process too, was also falling apart, hampered by the military-designed 2008 Constitution, which effectively preserved a strong central state and provided very limited powers to ethnic states, leaders or their goals of federalism (Bertrand et al. 2022, 2). Indifferent to the plight of ethnic nationality communities and the ongoing violence inflicted on them by the military, after getting into power Suu Kyi and her party failed to promote and consolidate a common national identity. In Kachin and Shan states, armed conflict intensified, and in Rakhine state, decades of state-based persecution against Muslims and the Rohingya culminated in a genocide (O'Brien & Hoffstaedter 2020). Even in areas where ceasefires were in place, resource rich frontier areas experienced "increased militarisation and new forms of depletion and dispossession" (Hedström, Olivius & Zin Mar Phyo 2023, 180; see also Sarma et al. 2022), showing how Myanmar's transitionary era was "never uniform or entirely progressive" (Frydenlud & Wai Wai Nu 2023, 118). And yet, there is no denying that the effects of both COVID-19 and the coup have been profound, unleashing new forms of instability and crisis in all aspects of life.

MYANMAR IN CRISIS: VOLUME CONTENTS

This volume is centered around the theme of crisis. Each chapter focuses on one of three interrelated themes: on the concept of crisis, a state in crisis, an economic crisis and international relations in crisis. In Chapter Two, Khin Zaw Win reflects on the language of crisis and what it means to live in Myanmar within what outside political analysts often refer to as a 'post-coup crisis'. He helps to bring to light both the tragedy of the situation and its possibilities. He also situates what he refers to as a "state of flux" within an historical arc of ongoing crises and a failed nation-state building process. From Khin Zaw Win's view, this process goes back to the colonial era, was entrenched under decades of military rule and continued under the NLD. He reflects on 'what went wrong?' in the lead up to the coup and argues that in light of both the violence inflicted on Myanmar by the military junta and the revolutionary movement itself, "the country will never go back to the pre-coup state of affairs" and that we must instead prepare "for an entirely new landscape".

In Chapter Three, Morten Pederson examines Myanmar's post-coup crisis in politics, including the face of the new junta, the response from the people, the displacement of the NLD from the political field and the resurgence of EROs. Pederson argues that the armed radicalisation of the grassroots resistance, coupled with a growing alliance between younger leaders and EROs fundamentally decenters Aung San Suu Kyi and the NLD, towards a more revolutionary politics with "potentially far-reaching consequences for the future of the Burmese state", including a more inclusive, just and tolerant society. He also reflects on the causes of the coup and prospects for a resistance victory, arguing that while the military has a range of tactical advantages, including superior weapons technology, the widespread popular support for PDFs and EROs allows for a more hopeful analysis. Indeed, in the absence of support from the international community, the resistance continues to operate largely with material support from various diasporic communities and a vast network of underground sources of funding from people within the country.

Reflections on the longue-duree of crisis in Myanmar continue in Chapter Four by Tomas Martin & U Win, who argue that the multiple crises affecting the country are "neither unique nor exceptional". Through an examination of prison life under COVID-19 and the coup, they argue that "the experience of crisis is not aberrational, but rather a condition of everyday life for prison actors" that has been ongoing for many decades. Drawing on Henrik Vigh (2008), who argues that scholars should understand the countless struggles that structurally vulnerable people faces as "crisis in context", Martin & U Win's focus on prisoners during the COVID-19 pandemic highlights the immense brutality of the Myanmar state justice system which has always used tactics of violence to inflict fear and rule the population.

Section II focuses on the theme of a 'state in crisis', examining the impacts of the coup and the diverse set of revolutionary stakeholders that have come out of the Spring Revolution. In Chapter Five, Nicola Williams examines the contested nature of state authority in the post-coup context and ongoing deliberations and tensions around nation building amongst the pro-democracy movement. Williams argues that revolutionary groups' ongoing efforts to design a federal democratic system have potential to set the stage for a more inclusive Myanmar. However, born off the back of decades of centralised military rule, civil conflicts and long-running divisions between Bamar elites and ethnic nationality communities and leaders, she suggests that the current conversations led by the NUG, NUCC, EROs and other revolutionary groups, also run the risk of further entrenching "identities and relational dynamics shaped during military rule". She suggests that while the military may be capable of winning tactical-level battles and has consolidated control over the central state apparatus, subnational and local authority has become more complex and contested than ever before, including in the Bamar heartland.

In Chapter Six, Kim Jolliffe takes a deep dive into some of these emerging governance dynamics as different revolutionary groups secure control over newly-won territories. Jolliffe shows that where the SAC has lost control in large parts of the country, old and new revolutionary groups are not only focused on armed resistance, but also expanding and establishing critical governance functions, including education, healthcare, police, municipal and justice services. He contends that in the context of long-running civil wars and a military state that has always treated services and inclusion "as an afterthought", the implementation of non-state administration systems and social services has the potential to "address the root causes of Myanmar's protracted conflicts and human rights crises". Further, in putting a model of decentralised governance into practice he argues that these emerging governance dynamics from below could be the "seeds" of a more "peaceful and democratic future".

In Chapter Seven, Michael Dunford looks at the heterogenous nature of the revolutionary movement, examining the enormous repertoire of non-violent resistance tactics embedded within the Civil Disobedience Movement (CDM). In addition to examining well-known CDM actors like teachers which have helped to bring the functioning of basic state administration functions to a halt, Dunford draws attention to the 'tactical creativity' of the CDM and how, in the early weeks after the coup, this helped to allow a space for less radical anti-coup actors to "operate and contribute to the resistance". While much of the political commentary and analysis of Myanmar's current political crisis focuses on the armed resistance and their ability to compete with the junta, Dunford highlights the important role played by the CDM as part of a 'three-part strategy' to defeat the military. Drawing on the concept of "the politics of domination" (Chakrabarty 2007; Foucault and Ewald 2003), Dunford argues that the heterogeneous nature of the CDM movement "has helped to solidify an anticolonial public politics of resistance" which ultimately has the potential to displace the military, and its enduring "politics of violent domination".

Section III is focused on the theme of 'economic crisis' and looks at the role played by both the COVID-19 pandemic and the coup in wreaking havoc on people's lives and their ability to make a living. In Chapter Eight, Linda Calabrese, Maximiliano Mendez-Parra and Laetitia Pettinotti from the Overseas Development Institute (ODI) examine the 'issues and prospects for recovery' in Myanmar, as a result of the impacts of the global pandemic and the coup. Providing an overview of how Myanmar's economy changed over the course of the 2010's, they give a detailed analysis of how the pandemic, affected formal and illicit trade, foreign investment, migration and remittances and development assistance and finance, as a result of travel bans and border controls, supply chain disruptions and other factors. Exploring Myanmar's potential for 'Building Back Better' in the wake of the global economic slowdown, they argue while the former NLD government's COVID-19 Economic Recovery Plan (CERP) had the potential to "kickstart the economy", it fundamentally lacked an explicit environmental and gender-sensitive approach, which undermined its goals for inclusive growth. The authors argue that in the context of the military takeover, "the potential for recovery after the COVID-19 pandemic is now severely limited", ultimately leaving Myanmar's people extremely vulnerable.

In Chapter Nine, Mie Mie Kyaw gives an intimate portrayal of the impacts of the global pandemic through the lives of fishing communities, exploring the negative effects of various lockdown orders to try and curb the spread of COVID-19. Building off in-depth qualitative and survey-based research in Kyauk Myaung, a fishing community on the Irrawaddy river on the border of Sagaing and Mandalay Regions, she highlights the devastating impacts of restrictive measures, which "effectively cut off the incomes of local fishermen overnight". She shows that the COVID-19 control measures in these communities led to significant food shortages in the majority of households, with female-headed households disproportionately affected. She argues that the growing livelihoods crisis also resulted in an increase in Illegal, Unreported and Unregulated (IUU) fishing, which have much longer-term consequences for the fragile ecosystem of the Irrawaddy river and therefore, the future of local fishing communities country-wide.

In Chapter Ten, Htwe Htwe Thein and Michael Gillan take a closer look at the impacts of the coup on Myanmar's economy and the response of international investors and the business community. From tourism to foreign investment and agricultural production, they show how the violent imposition of military rule has impacted all sectors of the economy and effectively ensured the "rapid disintegration" of reforms put into place in the 2010s. Given the degradation of the business and investment environment under the SAC and the fact that military still fails to maintain control over much of the country, they argue that foreign investment is only likely to decrease in the coming years, with increasing reliance on China. They suggest that while widespread calls for international economic and trade sanctions are important and do put pressure on the regime, ultimately Myanmar's economic prospects will be shaped by the conflict between the military and the people, and their demands to finally rid the country of the barbarous leaders and their hold over the economy.

Section IV is devoted to 'international relations in crisis', exploring the interaction between the Myanmar military, foreign governments and regional and international bodies. In Chapter Eleven, Andrea Passeri and Hunter Marston, provide an in-depth historical examination of the Myanmar's military and civilian leaders commitment to a "neutral and non-aligned foreign policy" since independence and how this shaped the country's international relations over the course of the 2010's and now since the coup. They argue that under President Thein Sein (2011–2016) there was a definite shift in foreign policy, which sought a progressive reintegration in the international community through emphasis on regional and global multilateralism and a diversification of economic partnerships. By contrast, in the wake of the military's brutal 'clearance operations' against the Rohingya in 2017, the resultant actions of the NLD government, Suu Kyi and the military, helped to fuel a "siege mentality", effectively bringing an end to "this proactive era of global diplomacy". They argue that the international response to the brutal military coup has only further entrenched the general's resolve towards a reactive and inward-looking form of negative neutralism as they "prioritise efforts to eradicate domestic unrest".

In Chapter Twelve, Nicholas Coppel examines the diverse range of responses from foreign governments and international and regional bodies in response to the coup. Coppel draws on his long-term experience working for the Australian government's Department of Foreign Affairs and Trade (DFAT), including as Ambassador to Myanmar from 2015–2018, highlighting the challenges for foreign ministries in navigating the deteriorating political situation and the "tensions between contact and legitimation". Coppel argues that despite repeated calls from the resistance movement to 'save Myanmar' and for more targeted support such as seen in Ukraine, foreign ministries and international institutions outside of ASEAN do not realistically expect to "produce change within Myanmar". Rather, most foreign governments and international bodies are deeply constrained by the international system, and ultimately unable to do much beyond issuing statements, targeted sanctions and providing humanitarian assistance. He further agues that "channels of communication with the military council are necessary" and that, despite concerns that it confers legitimacy on the regime, the international community will likely continue to call for dialogue with the regime, especially through ASEAN.

ON CRISIS

I want to conclude this introduction by reflecting on language and the implications of using certain kinds of terminology. Language is important and the way we describe things matters. As noted by political analyst Matthew Arnold (2022), in comments on the junta's ongoing preparation for what they call an 'election': "this isn't just about semantics. It is about establishing the factual basis for what is transpiring in reality". And indeed, as Arnold argues, if we use the term 'election' to describe the military's sham political event through which they are planning to try and legitimise their actions, then we allow them to co-opt the language of democracy and to undermine the revolutionary goals of the Myanmar people. The chapters in this volume also reflect changes in language, such as the use of 'ethnic resistance organisations' by most authors over the use of 'ethnic armed organisations' — a term which fundamentally ignores both the history, governance mechanisms and institutionalisation of many of these politically armed ethnic groups, mobilised around the protection of ethnic nationality peoples' rights. Some of the authors have also chosen to use the term 'Sit Tat' to refer to the military, rather than 'Tatmadaw' which directly translates as 'royal armed forces' (Aung Kaung Myat 2022) — a term which neither reflects ordinary civilians' views of the military, nor how they are refer to it in common parlance (see also Desmond 2022).

We have titled this volume *Myanmar in Crisis* to reflect the various and intersecting forms of crisis that have come out of both the global COVID-19 pandemic and the coup. In 2022, Collins Dictionary declared 'permacrisis' word of the year — "An extended period of instability and insecurity, especially one resulting from a series of catastrophic events" (Bushby 2022). Given the scale of human tragedy, this term seems relevant to Myanmar. Indeed, since the coup, headlines about Myanmar often use the language of crisis to convey the serious of the situation and to compel a response. In an attempt to put pressure on regional and international leaders to do more while efforts are focused on the war in Ukraine, opinion pieces often reflect on Myanmar as a "neglected" or "forgotten" crisis (Jones 2023; Kamal et al. 2023). In the context of the ongoing violent campaigns of terror targeting civilian areas there is also a "healthcare and humanitarian crisis" (Nora 2023; Su Myat Han et al. 2021) and a growing "mental health crisis" (Artingstoll 2023).

Myanmar people too, use the language of crisis. As one of my friends commented on Facebook in August 2022:

Pandemic
Coup d'etat
Civil Wars
Economic collapse
Natural disasters
Food shortage and the coming of famine
...
Any more crisis??
You name it, we've got it...[7]

This reflection captures the sentiment of many people both from and living in Myanmar. Environmental activists talk of the four kinds of 'C crises' facing Myanmar's people — COVID, Coup, Conflict and Climate Change. For Generation Z, there is also a crisis in the education system and a crisis of opportunities. As Michael Dunford and Dinith Adikari capture in the concluding chapter, there is a deep sense of sadness and disappointment for the lives of young people and for what has been lost in the last two years as a result of the multiple and extensive crises that are now plaguing the country.

A crisis is also reflected in Myanmar's academic community and in the contents of this volume. In my work as a co-convenor of three Myanmar Update conferences at ANU and as an editor of its resulting series since 2017, I have fundamentally seen the volume as a way to celebrate and support the voices of Myanmar's academic and scholarly community. This mission is also reflected in the growth in contributions from Myanmar scholars over time and in the diversity of subject matter since its inception in 1990 (see Chambers et al. 2018, 2020; Cheesmen et al. 2012, 2014; Cheesman and Farrelly 2016; Skidmore and Wilson 2007, 2008). Such a change was especially pronounced from 2011 onwards, where after decades of censorship and heavy restrictions, research partnerships and outputs flourished, "contributing to the development of a vibrant and resilient research sector" (Chambers & Galloway 2020, 18).

In these circumstances, I want to acknowledge the limited number of Myanmar voices in this volume, as a reflection of this crisis. In the wake of the brutal violence inflicted on Myanmar's scholarly and activist community, many of the researchers who had initially signed up to participate in the 2021 Myanmar Update had to pull out of the conference. University lecturers and students joined the Civil Disobedience Movement, while other scholar activists became involved in armed resistance and/or went into hiding. While some were unreachable and in danger, many became engaged in revolutionary politics, for which an academic conference was not a priority. To make matters more difficult, the conference was held in July 2021, right when a deadly wave of COVID-19 hit Myanmar households country-wide, leaving many people caring for loved ones, as the military continued to hold back on supplies to oxygen. Of those who were able to participate in the conference, many did not have the time, energy or capacity to focus on an academic piece of writing, as they concentrated on other more pressing demands, with one contributor forced to pull out as she went underground and sought a way out of the country. However, the language of crisis, while helps to convey the devastation inflicted on different communities in Myanmar, does not solely capture the diversity of people's experiences. As Dunford and Adikari relate in their concluding reflections, "amidst the chaos and despair caused by the coup", there is also "generative potential", including within the Myanmar-focused academic community.

The terminology of 'crisis' is contentious, and scholars have critiqued how and when crisis narratives are deployed, by whom, and with what effects (Roitman 2013). Labels such as 'political crisis' and 'economic crisis' both highlight the urgency of the situation and can expose the internal dynamics and contradictions of social formations (Watts 1983: 33). The language of crisis, however, also flattens the plurality of people's experiences and the multiple set of crises that people have experienced historically and over the course of their lifetimes, as well as in the current period. What, does it mean to experience a crisis in Myanmar, when crisis is not a state of exception, but rather a permanent reality? The crisis narrative embedded in this current moment of Myanmar's history conjures up an oppositional state of normality. And yet, this is not the first coup in Myanmar, and cycles of repression and protest have been at the centre of local politics since time immemorial.

While social and political reforms over the 2010s resulted in significant and tangible changes for some, the legacies of colonialism, military violence, territorialisation and civil conflict remained a constant feature of many people's lives. Indeed, the impacts of the COVID-19 pandemic and the coup cannot be viewed as a bounded period of instability, which can be contrasted with 'normal life'. As anthropologist Megnaa Mehtta (2020) argues in an article on quotidian care in the Sundarbans of Bangladesh, states of crisis are never objective, but are intimately shaped by one's social emplacement and the intersection of multiple identities. In Myanmar, deeply rooted systems of structural and symbolic violence mean that for many people, different forms of crisis have always been an everyday state of reality — a position which is only amplified by one's ethnic and religious identity, gender and class.

But what does it do to a people and a country when their lives are reduced to crisis and a constant narrative of crisis — what anthropologist Joel Robbins (2013) refers to as "the suffering subject"? What does it mean to live amidst a crisis or multiple crises? What kind of life is possible? Is any kind of life possible? Is there still room for hope, for joy, for laughter and light? Or does crisis, as the term implies, reduce life to merely a state of survival?

This edited volume helps to capture some of the dynamics of crisis affecting people in and from Myanmar, particularly in the wake of the military coup. But with many of our authors writing from safe and privileged positions outside the country, we cannot even begin to imagine nor capture what it means to *live with* these crises, as we pose by the title of this volume. For some people, this current state of crisis is interpreted through a Buddhist cosmological lens and calls for a return to the foundations of living through the dharma, to counter the natural consequences of having an immoral leader in charge of the country (see Frydenlund et al. 2021). For Pentecostal communities, there is also talk of the coming Christ amidst the rapture (Edwards 2022). For many, the multiple crises facing the country also hold revolutionary potential. The storm before the calm of a more hopeful, aspirational and, most importantly, equitable future.

In the conclusion chapter, Dunford and Adikari reflect on the direction that Myanmar-focused scholarship might take out of this conjuncture of crises. They consider how disappointment can lead to hope — not as an abstract affect or emotion, but a means to guiding action and practice.

They also emphasise the growing importance of the decolonial turn in Myanmar research (Chu May Paing and Than Toe Aung 2021; Tharaphi Than 2021). Indeed, even though the military is trying to instil a permanent sense of crisis to justify its own existence and rule, Myanmar's people and its academic community continue to resist in a multitude of ways. As documented in the chapters of this volume, opposition to the junta across the country remains strong, with many civilians, including women and other marginalised groups, vowing to keep fighting the military "until the bitter end" (HI Burma 2022). Amongst the Burma studies academic community too, a revolution has taken root, forcing conversations on power dynamics, positionality and attention to ethical and methodological risks. In the words of one Burmese poet, Pandora, people's ability to survive and adapt also gives cause for hope:

> I get delicate / Each time I shed my skin / Don't you dare think / I am soft / If I change colors / I only want to adapt / To the shifting sand / To the strange waters" (Pandora (translated by Ko Ko Thett) 2022).

Indeed, Myanmar and its people might be living amidst crisis — but it does not define them, nor determine their lives or the revolutionary potential of this particular moment.

Notes

1. At the time of writing in February 2023, Aung San Suu Kyi is facing a thirty-three year prison sentence after a series of closed-court trials including for sedition, corruption, breaching COVID-19 restrictions and breaches of the Official Secrets Act.
2. For a longer discussion on the symbolism and significance of the pots and pans protests see Phyu Phyu Oo (2021).
3. Members of the NUCC have made significant progress, constructing the most democratic and equitable roadmap in Myanmar's history for a future federal democratic state. However, building a shared vision of the future has faced significant obstacles, as historical grievances and ideological fissures re-emerge. Notably absent from these negotiations has been the United Wa State Army (UWSA) and the Arakan Army (AA), two of the strongest armed groups in Myanmar, who have instead sought to unilaterally expand their territorial control and administrative autonomy. Indeed, despite the front of unity amongst divergent stakeholders of the Spring Revolution against the junta, there are still serious questions about the commitment of political Bamar elites to the equality and unity of all peoples in Myanmar.

4 In February 2023, the Ta'ang National Liberation Army (TNLA) and the Myanmar National Democratic Alliance Army (MNDAA) announced that they were providing training and weapons support to PDFs, as they seek to recover lost territory and build up their own systems of administrative control (Frontier 2023).
5 See https://www.yangonstories.com/ (accessed 10 February 2023).
6 The United Nations Office for the Coordination of Humanitarian Affairs estimates that at least 17.6 million people are in need of dire humanitarian assistance (UNOCHA 2023).
7 Credit Khin Zarchi Latt, August 2022.

References

AAPP. 2023. "Two Years Since the Failed Junta Coup." *Assistance Association for Political Prisoners*, 1 February. Available at https://aappb.org/wp-content/uploads/2023/02/English_Statement-on-Two-years-of-the-Coup-1-Feb-2023.pdf (accessed 1 March 2023).

ABIPA. 2022. *Caught between the Coup and Climate Change: Indigenous Communities in Burma Continue their struggle for Justice amid Unprecedented Pressures*. Chiang Mai, Thailand: All Burma Indigenous Peoples Alliance.

Ardeth Maung Thawnghmung. 2019. *Everyday Economic Survival in Myanmar*. Wisconsin: University of Wisconsin Press.

Ardeth Maung Thawnghmung and Khun Noah. 2021. "Myanmar's Military Coup and the Elevation of the Minority Agenda?" Critical Asian Studies (April): 1–13.

Arnold, Matthew. 2022. "Myanmar will not hold an 'Election' in August 2023. *The Irrawaddy*, 17 November. Available at https://www.irrawaddy.com/opinion/guest-column/myanmar-will-not-hold-an-election-in-august-2023.html (accessed 18 November 2022).

Artingstoll, Charlie. 2023. "Myanmar's Mental Health Crisis Needs and Inclusive Fit." *Frontier Myanmar*, 14 January. Available at https://www.frontiermyanmar.net/en/myanmars-mental-health-crisis-needs-an-inclusive-fix/ (accessed 20 February 2023).

Aung Kaung Myat. 2022. "Sit-tat or Tatmadaw? Debates on What to Call the Most Powerful Institution in Burma." *Tea Circle Oxford*, 3 October. Available https://teacircleoxford.com/politics/sit-tat-or-tatmadaw-debates-on-what-to-call-the-most-powerful-institution-in-burma/ (available at 20 Feb 2023).

Aung Tun. 2022. "Agriculture in a State of Woe Following Myanmar's 2021 Military Coup." *Perspective*, 2 March. Singapore: *ISEAS- Yusof Ishak Institute*.

Bertrand, Jacques, Pelletier, Alexandre and Ardeth Maung Thawnghmung. 2022. *Winning by Process: The State and Neutralisation of Ethnic Minorities in Myanmar*. Ithaca, NY: Cornell University Press.

Bushy, Helen. 2022. "Permacrisis Declared Collins Dictionary Word of the Year." *BBC News*, 1 November. Available at https://www.bbc.com/news/entertainment-arts-63458467 (accessed 27 February 2023).

CAT. 2022. *Tanawthari Landscape of Life: A Grassroots Alternative to Top Down Conservation in Tanintharyi Region*. Conservation Alliance Tanawthari.

Chakrabarty, Dipesh. 2007. "'In the Name of Politics': Democracy and the Power of the Multitude in India". *Public Culture* 19 (1): 35–57.

Chambers, Justine and Cheesman, Nick. 2019. "Coming to Terms with Moral Authorities in Myanmar." *Sojourn* 34 (2): 231-57.

Chambers, Justine, Galloway, Charlotte, Liljeblad, Jonathan. 2020. *Living with Myanmar*. Singapore: Singapore: ISEAS Yusof-Ishak Institute.

Chambers, Justine and Galloway, Charlotte. 2020. "Introduction: Living with Myanmar." In *Living with Myanmar*, edited by Justine Chambers, Charlotte Galloway and Jonathan Liljeblad. Singapore: ISEAS-Yusof Ishak Institute, 3-26.

Chambers, Justine and Kyed, Helene Maria. 2023. "Climate Change Action in Conflict Affected Contexts: Insights from Myanmar after the Military Coup." *DIIS Policy Brief*, February.

Chambers, Justine, McCarthy, Gerard, Farrelly, Nicholas and Chit Win (Eds.). 2018. *Myanmar Transformed: People, Places, Politics. Singapore:* ISEAS Yusof-Ishak Institute.

Cheesman, Nick. 2016. *Opposing the Ruke of Law: How Myanmar's Courts Make Law and Order*. Cambridge: Cambridge University Press.

Cheesman, Nick. 2021. "State Terror and Torture: The Hatred of Politics in Myanmar." *ABC Religion and Ethics*, 23 July. Available at https://www.abc.net.au/religion/state-terror-torture-and-anti-politics-in-myanmar/13270932 (accessed 1 March 2023).

Cheesman, Nick, Farrelly, Nicholas, Wilson, Trevor (Eds.). 2014. *Debating Democratization in Myanmar*. Singapore: ISEAS.

Cheesman, Nick and Farrelly, N. (Eds.) 2016. *Conflict in Myanmar: War, Politics, Religion*. Singapore: ISEAS-Yusof Ishak Institute.

Cheesman, Nick, Skidmore, Monique, Wilson, Trevor (Eds.) 2012. *Myanmar's Transition: Openings, Obstacles and Opportunities*. Singapore: ISEAS.

Chu May Paing and Than Toe Aung. 2021. "Talking Back To White 'Burma Experts.'" *AGITATE! Journal*. Available at https://agitatejournal.org/talking-back-to-white-burma-experts-by-chu-may-paing-and-than-toe-aung/ (accessed 16 March 2023).

Crouch, Melissa. 2021. "Myanmar Coup has No Constitutional Basis." *East Asia Forum*, 3 February. Available at https://www.eastasiaforum.org/2021/02/03/myanmar-coup-on-the-pretext-of-a-constitutional-fig-leaf/ (accessed 20 February 2023).

Desmond. 2022. "Guest Column | Please Don't Call Myanmar Military Tatmadaw". *The Irrawaddy*, 25 May. Available at https://www.irrawaddy.com/opinion/guest-column/please-dont-call-myanmar-military-tatmadaw.html (accessed 10 December 2022).

Edwards, Penny, Ko Ko Thett and Wong, Kenneth. 2022. "To Write a History," *Manoa*, 34 (2): 179-185.

Edwards, Michael. 2022. "Graeber, Leach and the Revolution in Myanmar." *Focaal Blog*, 27 January. Available at https://www.focaalblog.com/2022/01/27/michael-edwards-graeber-leach-and-the-revolution-in-myanmar/ (accessed 1 March 2023).

Egreteau, Renaud. 2022. "Blending Old and New Repertoires of Contention in Myanmar's Anti-coup Protests (2021)." *Social Movement Studies*. DOI: 10.1080/14742837.2022.2140650.

Egreteau, Renaud, and François Robinne. 2015. *Metamorphosis: Studies in Social and Political Change in Myanmar*. Singapore: NUS Press.

Fishbein, Emily, Vahpual & Nu Nu Lusan. 2021. 'Our Only Option': Myanmar Civilians Take up Arms for Democracy." *Aljazeera*, 15 June. Available at https://www.aljazeera.com/news/2021/6/15/our-only-option-myanmar-civilians-take-up-arms-for-democracy (accessed 24 October 2022).

Fortify Rights. 2022. *"Nowhere is Safe": The Myanmar Junta's Crimes Against Humanity Following the Coup d'État*, 24 March. Available at https://www.fortifyrights.org/mya-inv-2022-03-24/ (accessed 24 October 2022).

Foucault, Michel, and François Ewald. 2003. *"Society Must Be Defended": Lectures at the Collège de France, 1975-1976*. Allen Lane.

Frontier. 2022a. "Protests Continues Despite Deadly Consequences", *Frontier Myanmar*, 21 March. Available at https://www.frontiermyanmar.net/en/protests-continues-despite-deadly-consequences/ (accessed 26 April 2022).

Frontier. 2022b. "War Zone Farmers Suffer Disruptions and Despair", *Frontier Myanmar*, 27 April. Available at https://www.frontiermyanmar.net/en/war-zone-farmers-suffer-disruptions-and-despair/ (accessed 4 May 2022).

Frontier. 2023. "'We will Win': Northern Alliance Doubles Down." *Frontier Myanmar*, 30 January. Available at https://www.frontiermyanmar.net/en/we-will-win-northern-alliance-doubles-down/ (accessed 7 February 2023).

Frydenlund, Iselin, Pum Za Mang, Phyo Wai and Susan Hayward. 2021. "Religious Responses to the Military Coup in Myanmar." *The Review of Faith & International Affairs*, 19 (3): 77-88.

Frydenlund, Shae and Wai Wai Nu. 2023. "From Mutual Aid to Charity: Violence and Women's Changing Interethnic Relationships in Rakhine State." In *Waves of Upheaval: Political Transitions and Gendered Transformations in Myanmar*, edited by Jenny Hedström and Elisabeth Olivius, 200-220. Copenhagen: NIAS Press.

Griffiths, Michael. 2022. "Cohort Study of 1500 Households in Post-Coup Myanmar." Paper presented at the International Conference on International Relations and Development at Chiang Mai University, 22-23 July 2022.

Hedström, Jenny and Olivius, Elisabeth. 2023. *Waves of Upheaval: Political Transitions and Gendered Transformations in Myanmar*. Copenhagen: NIAS Press.

Hedström, Olivius & Zin Mar Phyo. 2023. "Troubling the Transition: Gendered Insecurity in the Borderlands." In *Waves of Upheaval: Political Transitions and Gendered Transformations in Myanmar*, edited by Jenny Hedström and Elisabeth Olivius, 1-26. Copenhagen: NIAS Press.

HI Burma. 2022. "Women vow to rise from ashes to defeat Myanmar Regime", *Myanmar Now*, 11 March. Available at https://www.myanmar-now.org/en/news/women-vow-to-rise-from-ashes-to-defeat-myanmar-regime (accessed 14 March 2022).

HRW. 2021. *Myanmar: Coup Leads to Crimes Against Humanity*, 31 July. New York: Human Rights Watch, New York. Available at https://www.hrw.org/news/2021/07/31/myanmar-coup-leads-crimes-against-humanity (accessed 24 October 2022).

Jordt, Ingrid, Tharaphi Than and Sue Ye Lin. 2021. *How Generation Z Galvanised a Revolutionary Movement against Myanmar's 2021 Military Coup* . ISEAS Trends No 7. Singapore: ISEAS.

Jones, Evan. 2023. "Are we Forgetting the Myanmar Crisis?" *Bangkok Post*, 4 February. Available at https://www.bangkokpost.com/opinion/opinion/2498610/ (accessed 7 Feb 2023).

Kamal, Adelina, Naw Hser Hser and Khin Omar. 2023. "Myanmar's Neglected Crisis Demands a Different Response." *The New Humanitarian*, 1 February 2023. Available at thenewhumanitarian.org/opinion/2023/02/01/Myanmar-coup-Ukraine-cross-border-aid (accessed 20 February 2023).

Kelly, Meg, Mahtani, Shibani & Lee, Joyce Sohyun. 2021. '"Burn it all down": How Myanmar's Military Razed Villages to Crush a Growing Resistance' *Washington Post*, 23 December. Available at https://www.washingtonpost.com/world/interactive/2021/myanmar-military-burn-villages-tatmadaw/ (accessed 5 January 2022).

Khin Khin Mra and Livingstone, Deborah. "The Winding Path to Gender Equality." *Living with Myanmar*, edited by Justine Chambers, Charlotte Galloway and Jonathan Liljeblad. Singapore: ISEAS-Yusof Ishak Institute, 2020. Pp. 243-264.

Kyed, Helene Maria and Ah Lynn. 2021. *Soldier Defections in Myanmar: Motivations and Obstacles Following the 2021 Military Coup*. Copenhagen: Danish Institute for International Studies.

Kyi Sin. 2023. "Resistance Force in Myanmar: Changing the State of Play with Weaponised Drones." *Fulcrum*, 10 February. Available at https://fulcrum.sg/resistance-forces-in-myanmar-changing-the-state-of-play-with-weaponised-drones/ (accessed 11 February 2023).

Lidauer, Michael and Saphy, Gilles. 2021. *Running Elections under Stringent Covid-19 Measures in Myanmar*. Stockholm: International Institute for Democracy and Electoral Assistance.

Marlar, Chambers, Justine. & Elena. 2023. "Our Htamein, Our Flag, Our Victory: The Role of Young Women in Myanmar's Spring Revolution." *Journal of Burma Studies* 27 (1): 65-99.

Mehtta, Megnaa. 2020. "A New Crisis and an Old Conversation: Reflections on Quotidian Care in the Sundarbans." In Intersecting Crises, edited by C. Dowler. *American Ethnologist*, 12 October. Available at https://americanethnologist.org/features/pandemic-diaries/introduction-intersecting-crises/a-new-crisis-and-an-old-conversation-reflections-on-quotidian-care-in-the-sundarbans (accessed 10 December 2020).

Mi Chan. 2020. "Myanmar's Economic Relief Plan Risks Excluding Vulnerable Populations." *New Mandala*, 12 May. Available at https://www.newmandala.org/myanmars-economic-relief-plan-risks-excluding-vulnerable-populations/ (accessed 10 December 2020).

Nachemson, Andrew. 2022. "In Myanmar, the Tatmadaw's Frustration Fuels a Cycle of Violence," *Foreign Policy*, 27 September. Available at https://foreignpolicy.com/2022/09/27/myanmar-military-tatmadaw-violence-coup-resistance/ (accessed 7 Feb 2023).

Nora. 2023. "Myanmar Regime Restrictions Spark Health and Humanitarian Crises in Kayah." *The Irrawaddy*, 27 February. Available at https://www.irrawaddy.com/news/burma/myanmar-regime-restrictions-spark-health-and-humanitarian-crises-in-kayah.html (accessed 1 March 2023).

O'Brien, Melanie and Hoffstaedter, Gerhard. 2020. "'There we are Nothing, Here we are Nothing'": The Enduring Effects of the Rohingya Genocide." *Social Sciences*, 9 (11): 209.

Pandora (translated by Ko Ko Thett). 2022. "The Venomous." *Manoa*, 34 (2): 227.

PEN America. 2021. *Stolen Freedoms: Creative Expression, Historic Resistance, and the Myanmar Coup*. Available at, https://pen.org/report/stolen-freedoms-creative-expression-historic-resistance-and-the-myanmar-coup/ (accessed 20 December 2021).

Phyu Phyu Oo. 2021. "The importance of Myanmar's pots and pans protests." *The Interpreter*. Available at https://www.lowyinstitute.org/the-interpreter/importance-myanmar-s-pots-and-pans-protests (accessed 10 February 2023).

Robbins, Joel. 2013. "Beyond the Suffering Subject: Towards an Anthropology of the Good." *The Journal of the Royal Anthropological Institute*, 19 (3): 447-62.

Roitman, J. 2013. *Anti-crisis*. Durham: Duke University Press.

Ryan, Megan and Tran, Mai Van. 2022. "Democratic Backsliding Disrupted: The Role of Digitalized Resistance in Myanmar." *Asian Journal of Comparative Politics*. Available at https://doi.org/10.1177/20578911221125511.

Sarma, Jasnea, Faxon, Hilary Oliva & K.B. Roberts. 2022. "Remaking and Living with Resource Frontiers: Insights from Myanmar and Beyond." *Geopolitics*, DOI: 10.1080/14650045.2022.2041220

Seinenu M. Thein-Lemelson. 2022. "Killing the Funeral in Myanmar." *Anthropology News*, 2 September. Available at anthropology-news.org/articles/killing-the-funeral-in-myanmar (accessed 4 September 2022).

Sekine, Y. 2021. "Emerging 'Agrarian Climate Justice' Struggles in Myanmar." *The Journal of Peasant Studies*, 48 (3): 517-540.

Selth, Andrew. 2021. "Myanmar and a New Kind of Civil War." *The Interpreter*, 13 May. Available at http://www.loweinstitute.org/the-interpreter/myanmar-and-new-kind-civil-war (accessed 23 December 2022).

Skidmore, M. and Wilson, T. (2007) *Myanmar: The State, Community and the Environment*. Canberra: ANU E Press.

---------- (2008) *Dictatorship, Disorder and Decline in Myanmar*. Canberra: ANU E Press.

Special Advisory Council-Myanmar (SAC-M). 2022. "Briefing Paper: Effective Control in Myanmar", 5 September. Available at https://specialadvisorycouncil.org/wp-content/uploads/2022/09/SAC-M-Briefing-Paper-Effective-Control-in-Myanmar-ENGLISH-2.pdf (accessed 8 September 2022).

Soe Nandar Linn. 2023. "Myanmar Plunges Deeper into Economic Crisis." *East Asia Forum*, 24 January. Available at https://www.eastasiaforum.org/2023/01/24/myanmar-plunges-deeper-into-economic-crisis/ (accessed 20 February 2023).

Strangio, Sebastian. 2021. "Myanmar Junta Arms Itself with Repressive New Laws," *The Diplomat*, 15 February. Available at https://thediplomat.com/2021/02/myanmar-junta-arms-itself-with-repressive-new-laws/ (accessed 5 April 2022).

Su Myat Han, Kaung Suu Lwin, Khin Thet Swe, Stuart Gilmour and Shuhei Nomura. 2021. "Military Coup during COVID-19 Pandemic and Health Crisis in Myanmar." *BMJ Global Health*, 6: e005801.

Suhardiman, D., Rutherford, J. & Saw John Bright. 2017. "Putting Violent Armed Conflict in the Center of the Salween Hydropower Debates." *Critical Asian Studies*, 49(3): 349-36.

Tharaphi Than. 2021. "Why Does Area Studies Need Decolonization?" *Critical Asian Studies*, Commentary Board, November 20. Available at https://doi.org/10.52698/XPTS4931 (accessed 9 December 2021).

The Irrawaddy. 2022. "NUG: We Control over Half of Myanmar's Territory." *The Irrawaddy*, 7 September. Available at https://www.irrawaddy.com/news/burma/nug-we-control-over-half-of-myanmars-territory.html (accessed 8 September 2022).

The Irrawaddy. 2023. "Over 55,000 Civilian Homes Torched by Myanmar Regime Since Coup." *The Irrawaddy*, 15 February. Available at https://www.irrawaddy.com/news/burma/over-55000-civilian-homes-torched-by-myanmar-regime-since-coup.html (accessed 1 March 2023).

Thinzar Sunlei Yi. 2022. "Why Military Defections Still Matter to Myanmar's Revolution." *Frontier Myanmar*, 3 December. Available at https://www.frontiermyanmar.net/en/why-military-defections-still-matter-to-myanmars-revolution/ (accessed 20 February 2023).

UNHCR. 2022. *Myanmar Emergency Update: 5 December*. Bangkok, Thailand: UNHCR Regional Bureau for Asia and the Pacific.

UNOCHA. 2023. *Myanmar Humanitarian Needs Overview 2023 (January 2023)*. Available at https://reliefweb.int/report/myanmar/myanmar-humanitarian-needs-overview-2023-january-2023 (accessed 12 February 2023).

Vigh, Henrik. 2008. "Crisis and Chronicity: Anthropological Perspectives on Continuous Conflict and Decline." *Ethnos* 73(1): 5-24.

Watts, Michael. 1983. *Silent Violence*. Berkeley: University of California Press.

II

On Crisis

2

MYANMAR'S POST-COUP 'CRISIS': REFLECTIONS ON A HISTORY OF FAILED NATION BUILDING

Khin Zaw Win

What Myanmar[1] is currently experiencing is often referred to as a 'post-coup crisis'. Within the country, people call it the 'Spring Revolution', because it began in February, Myanmar's 'Spring'. As significant parts of the country descended under armed conflict, political analysts and pundits began to start speaking of 'civil war' and the concept of a 'failed state'. All these terms are accurate to some extent and reflect a certain kind of reality. And yet, they are inadequate and incomplete. In a world where unspeakable happenings occur almost daily, those who write pieces on Myanmar for the media will find the words 'crisis' and 'tragedy' a common feature of their news articles. In Myanmar we see and encounter such things with numbing regularity. And yet even we, ourselves, have not come up with a common term or phrase to label what we are faced with on a daily basis.

By calling it a 'cataclysm' one comes closer to the mark. Sifting through different descriptive terms of trauma goes together with plumbing the nature of the upheaval. An outsider may not comprehend the magnitude of the trauma and the depth of suffering that is being experienced — or indeed, that has been experienced collectively over the course of our history. That is one reason the remedies prescribed by external actors (like 'dialogue' for instance) fall flat on Myanmar ears. The United Nations and its various representatives have become the butt of jokes for their repeated expressions of 'concern'. Because what is happening is unprecedented in living memory. While one can go back a number of decades to look at comparable circumstances, those cases simply don't do justice to the present. To the fear, uncertainty, exhaustion, sadness, anxiety, confusion and overall deep sense of utter devastation at what has and continues to take place on a daily basis.

One event that comes to mind is the fall of the Kingdom of Burma, etched into the history books by the deposition and exile of the last King, Thibaw, and annexation to the British Empire in 1886. Not many people are aware that the subsequent 'pacification' of the country took ten more years, and the deployment of 60,000 troops from the British Empire to quell various forms of resistance. It's interesting to note that when the royal capital of Mandalay was captured, there was no significant resistance and life for many people went on as before. At this stage of the British occupation, Lower Burma and the port city of Rangoon was already established under British rule and thriving as an agricultural hub for the new colonial power. Nonetheless the fall of the Kingdom of Burma to a foreign imperial power went deep into the Burman psyche.

Over the course of colonial rule, a growing anti-colonial movement led to a number of fierce rebellions against the British, notably the Saya San Rebellion of 1930–31. However, before a fully-fledged independence movement could take place, WWII saw Burma become a major theatre of war, with attendant devastation and death — part of a global catastrophe, effects of which engulfed all of east and southeast Asia. In the turbulent years after WWII, Burma gained independence and shortly after was again plunged into another state of war — a civil conflict born off the legacies of British colonial rule. After a failed nation-state building process, conflict between the central Buddhist Bamar-majority government and various ethnic armed 'insurgents' or 'rebel' groups turned into decades-long civil wars that continue to be fought, more than seventy years on.[2] Over that length of time, it became not only a war between combatants but one that was directed against ordinary ethnic peoples and marked by depredations and impunity.

The imposition of military rule in 1962 further hardened the resolve of ethnic nationality leaders and their desire for autonomy and self-rule. In addition to these civil wars, there were also growing episodes of public dissatisfaction with military rule, breaking out in bursts of protests by students and labour workers in particular, in episodes which the military's security apparatus responded with force. The protests around U Thant's funeral in 1974, for example, drew large numbers of young people, who were subsequently arrested and imprisoned under trumped up charges which drew on colonial-era laws, such as section 144 which prohibits gatherings of more than five people.

The upheaval of 1988 was a major turning-point, as it brought down the one-party system of the Burma Socialist Programme Party (BSPP). The protests began in March, and were centred at the universities and Yangon city centre park. I was at the Yangon University Recreation Centre where students with handkerchiefs tied across their faces were giving ardent speeches. It was like a breath of fresh air after the two and a half decades of stifling dictatorship. The massive protests that followed brought the government to a standstill (Yangon was still the capital at that time). Among the concessions the regime was forced to make was the restoration of a multi-party system and the exit of military personnel from the BSPP. In September the armed forces staged a coup and instituted military rule. The primary institution of the military survived intact, and was freed from the encumbrance of the Party and indeed the ideology of Socialism, as it turned towards opening the economy through "state-mediated capitalism".

The slow process of resuming democracy began, and new political figures (like Aung San Suu Kyi) and parties (like the National League for Democracy (NLD)) made their advent upon the political stage. As was to be expected, there was a backlash from what was now an even more brutal military establishment, and for another two decades the lines were drawn against those who supported the democracy movement, loosely allied with the ethnic nationality cause. But overall, there was a feeling of hope, domestically as well as abroad, that there would be a coming-to-terms and a multi-party system would be restored. There was also the belief or assumption that the armed forces would accede to this national 'scheme' that they had committed to and rebuild themselves after the taint and tarnishing of their image following the bloody suppression in 1988. Under their 2003 "roadmap to a disciplined flourishing democracy" it was deemed to be a rational plan of action that fit within the military's own logic, and almost everything else revolved around this.

Under the guise of the State Peace and Development Council (SPDC), the junta took 13 years to draft a new constitution which was adopted in a flawed referendum vote held in May 2008 (less than one month after the devastating Cyclone Nargis hit lower Myanmar and killed over 138,000 people). Multi-party elections in 2010, flawed as they were by the use of 'advance votes' by the military's establishment, seemed to usher in an age of limited democracy and freedoms, and the first term of office under an ex-general U Thein Sein as President and the Union Solidarity and Development Party (USDP) evoked glimmers of hope. Aung San Suu Kyi was released from house arrest and contested a by-election in 2012, which she won and entered parliament, marking her advent into the arena of state. In the second general elections in 2015, her party rode a wave of popular support and achieved a landslide victory. It dominated both the government and the legislature (Hluttaw)[3] and, despite the ongoing power the military maintained over civilian affairs, people remained cautiously optimistic for what was to come and for the future of their children.

All along, however, the military continued to enjoy the privileges conferred by the 2008 Constitution, including a quarter of parliamentary seats and three powerful cabinet portfolios. Its actual influence, however, extended much further, into many aspects of local governance and economic life. Its formal budget was beyond parliamentary and public scrutiny, and it remained very much a state within a state — with exclusive jurisdiction over defence-related matters. During the NLD's time in power, the military expanded its establishment and acquired new weapons systems for the army, navy and air forces. Brutal conflicts continued to be fought in ethnic states, inflicting tragedy and suffering on ordinary civilians in Kachin, Shan and Karen States. From 2017–2020 conflict also spread to Rakhine, which had been hitherto uninvolved, and following the coup it was wrought upon the Bamar people themselves, and with a vengeance.

Despite these many signs, the general impression from many observers was that Myanmar was doing well in its 'transition to democracy'. Thorny and difficult problems remained, including the ongoing conflict and issues facing the peace negotiations with Ethnic Resistance Organisations, the persistent drugs trade, China's presence — both formal and informal — and ongoing land confiscations. On the surface, relations between the top civilian and military leaders looked cordial and even close from the outside through a succession of smiling photo ops and public defence of the military's actions against the Rohingya at the International Criminal Court. Nonetheless, on 1 February 2021, the military claimed power once again, detaining Aung San Suu Kyi and hundreds of other political leaders and civil society activists in a coup d'etat which very few people saw coming.

So the question that arises is: What went wrong?

On the surface, it looks like tensions between the two vain and ambitious leaders, came to a head after much in-fighting, with both vying for the presidency. That is the story that appears easiest to digest for public consumption, and one could stop at that. The tussle and animosity between civilian and military aspirants for power and high office is rationale enough — especially if we look to Myanmar's history. However, it does not do justice to the scale and savagery of subsequent events that followed. The Bamar military's brutality is legendary, and on the side of the people they just could not tolerate the blatant seizure of power. As the months progressed and the unspeakable atrocities and deaths mounted, the quest for an explanation of why and for a way out has become more insistent. But, one has only to look to Myanmar's unstable history to see that the military was never simply going to give up their control over the country, and its civilian affairs.

The once-vaunted military institution had become twisted and warped over the past half-century. This crisis, if nothing else, assures us that it will never be the same for the military. From its own doing it has tumbled from the apex position it has created for itself. However, existing as it does in a world of nation-states, the international community remains stuck on how to support the people of Myanmar, within the current frameworks they have available.

THE NATION-STATE

The concept of the nation-state and its application to non-European countries and societies, has come under criticism in recent decades. The reasons for its longevity and durability lie partly with the disciplines of social sciences and the humanities. With the great wave of independence movements from the late 1940s to the 1960s, the Westphalian state and the nation-state were taken for granted — often based off the arbitrary lines conceived and gifted by colonial states. Every colony and dominion and protectorate that became independent had the label 'state' stamped upon it, at the UN and elsewhere. It became the cornerstone belief (gospel, even) for a vast set of literature and programmes for state-building, including in the aid and development sector. Things became more complicated when the 'nation-state' was brought in, but the ready answer to that was beefing up 'nation-building' as well. Years ago, I myself wrote that "both state and nation-building have not made much headway in Myanmar".[4] This kind of situation was, of course, not simply limited to Myanmar. However, it is exemplified in the country's ongoing ethno-national conflicts and our overall lack of commitment to building an inclusive national identity.

At independence, many of the majority Burman population viewed the country known then as Burma as the natural successor to King Thibaw's Buddhist kingdom which was centred in Mandalay (and the period of colonial rule as a rude interruption). According to widespread views on the country's identity, ethnic nationalities were accepted as appendages. In other words, Burma was regarded as a Burman nation-state. And among the Burmans, two institutions had enjoyed unbroken continuity and influence — the Buddhist clergy (sangha) and the military. It is part of the country's misfortune that the outlook of both institutions narrowed over the decades. The 26-year introversion under junta and later one-party rule (1962–88) only buttressed this inward-looking trend.

The military came to see itself as the absolute guardian of the state and its sovereignty. In its myopic worldview, ethnic nationality aspirations for autonomy and federalism were only a hair's-breadth away from secession. Non-Buddhist religious groups and their adherents had limitations placed upon them and were actively persecuted in some instances. The period of the democratic 'revival' after 2010 saw paroxysms of ultra-nationalism, intolerance and even a system of apartheid. The wholesale persecution and suffering of the Rohingya over the past seven decades provide the most eloquent testimony of this. In parallel, the military's acceptance of steps towards democracy and federalism were grudging, and more of a façade.

The unwholesome and persistent persecution of ethnic nationality communities did not elicit strong resistance among the Burmans. One of the sorrier aspects of the NLD period in office post-2015 is that Aung San Suu Kyi and other MPs acquiesced to the military's Burman-centered ideology. But the crisis precipitated by the February coup has upended many of the comfortable foundations upon which the military is built. For the first time since independence, the majority of Burman people have actively turned against the military, with many taking up arms, resisting vocally and in writings, and withholding support (such as through the powerful Civil

Disobedience Movement). The nation-wide 'Silent Strike' of 10 December 2021 and again on 1 February 2022 and 2023 show ample evidence of this. It may not be an over-statement to say that the Burman nation-state so dear to the military's thinking and which it professes to 'protect' is in serious trouble. This impact will be felt by the NLD too (and their new set of leaders in the National Unity Government (NUG)) and hopefully give its leaders pause for some serious reflection. Moreover, following decades of conflict and repression of ethnic and religious minorities, things are now reaching a bloody climax in Chin, Kayah (Karenni) and Kayin states, and before that, in Rakhine. Despite some optimism within the NLD-led NUG, hopes for a multi-ethnic nation-state are taking a severe hammering.

We now know that the state-driven process towards federalism was leading nowhere under the former civilian-military arrangement. However, at the time, we had confidence that a much more inclusive path did exist and could even work. After 2018 it became very heavy going for federalism, with both the military and the NLD dragging their feet and backpedaling on various commitments. With the disruptions that befell Myanmar in 2021, an entirely fresh set of assumptions is needed. The fundamentals of envisioning a federal system are the same, but for Myanmar the range of possibilities — intended and unintended — have to be enlarged. Another way of putting it, is that the peace process and the 'old' path to federalism is now over.

LOOKING AT A NEW LANDSCAPE

Instead of repeating the now common line that the multiple sets of crises leave people's futures in Myanmar very uncertain, it would be more accurate and perhaps more productive to say they are in a state of flux. The present turmoil gives rise to one certainty — the country will never go back to the pre-coup state of affairs. A great deal of restructuring and reconfiguration is already in process. Indeed, the present revolutionary struggle turns the page and opens a new chapter. It is premature to talk about peace, but when that peace comes it will be of a different kind. Even federalism may no longer be the common goal. The antiquated party system could also be on the way out as well.

This domestic shape-shifting brings major worries to the region as well as to major powers. Neighbouring countries are keeping strict watch on their borders, and refugees fleeing across them are a headache. But more worrisome still are the changing dynamics of relations with various powers who attempt to exert influence and control. The countries which have a direct stake in Myanmar fall into roughly two camps — those who want to stabilise the situation (that is, for the SAC's benefit and their own economies), and those who call for dialogue and restoring democracy. It has to be said that both approaches are rather unrealistic. There are still others who are hedging their bets.

Another noteworthy aspect of the present crisis is the diminished role of the international community (diminished compared to its role post-1988). There are also the different weightings of each country and bloc. Taking ASEAN for example, some countries have been pro-active in trying to address the crisis — Indonesia and Malaysia, in particular. Mainland South-East Asian countries (many of which are majoritarian Buddhist) tend to be more reticent or have aligned with the SAC (such as Thailand and Cambodia). China, regarded as the country's bugbear for a long time with its massive economic interests in Myanmar, has backed ASEAN's primary role, partly to keep the west away. Three countries with long borders with Myanmar — India, China and Thailand — have immediate concerns with refugee and other illicit borderland flows.

It is not much of a surprise that western countries, foremost being the United States, which had regarded Aung San Su Kyi and the NLD as synonymous with democracy in Myanmar, is now content with a second-line role: saying the right things, but not actually doing much. The major new player that has entered the game is Russia, blatantly behind the junta and writing a fresh playbook on inter-authoritarian cooperation. Taken together, international inputs and influences do not put a bright sheen on Myanmar's prospects.

In light of the altered realities, it is exigent to assess and prepare for an entirely new political landscape — one in which won't be defined by the outside, state-centric world, but by the people of Myanmar themselves.

Notes

1. In this paper, Burma and Myanmar, and Burman and Bamar are used according to the period context.
2. The horror of these conflicts and their impacts on communities have been written about in much detail and will not be repeated here.
3. The judiciary is an executive appendage for all practical purposes, and simply does not count.
4. This paper was presented at the 2009 ANU Myanmar Update in Canberra, Australia.

3

THE 2021 MILITARY COUP: CAUSES AND CONSEQUENCES

Morten B. Pedersen

The 1 February 2021 military coup in Myanmar ended a decade of political liberalisation and triggered a near-countrywide popular uprising, which soon turned into armed resistance and ultimately all-out civil war. Nearly two years later, the *Tatmadaw*[1] is locked in an existential struggle for the soul of the country with an array of resistance forces, while the state and economy are collapsing, and tens of millions of people face a deepening humanitarian emergency.

The coup followed months of escalating tensions between the military and the civilian government over the 7 November 2020 elections, which delivered a landslide victory to the incumbent National League for Democracy (NLD), but were already mired in controversy before the polls. The military challenged the results, alleging widespread fraud, and sought to delay the convening of the new parliament until its concerns could be addressed, calling first for a special sitting of parliament and later for a meeting of the National Defence and Security Council. Its demands, however, were flatly refused by the civilian authorities, and after last-minute negotiations between representatives of the NLD and the military failed to resolve the brewing constitutional crisis, Commander-in-Chief Min Aung Hlaing at 16:00 on Sunday afternoon, 31 of January, issued a fateful order to his troops to stop the convening of parliament by force.[2] In the early morning of the next day, just hours before the new parliament was set to convene, the military thus once again took control of the capital, arrested the country's elected leaders, and declared a state of emergency. The initial takeover was quick and bloodless, but the coup triggered a conflict that has cost thousands of lives and fundamentally changed the face of Myanmar politics.

In the present chapter, I set out to do three things.[3] I start by outlining the main contours of Myanmar's post-coup politics. I then try to answer two key questions that have been the focus of much of the post-coup commentary and analysis: What were the reasons for the coup, and what is the likely outcome of the resultant political crisis? The main thrust of the analysis is pessimistic, but the conclusion entertains a few more hopeful possibilities.

THE NEW POLITICS OF POST-COUP MYANMAR

Nearly two years after the coup, it is clear that the changes wrought by the current crisis will have long-lasting and transformative effects on Myanmar politics. While the initial agenda of the new junta was fairly conservative, the general population's hatred of the *Tatmadaw* has sparked a revolutionary war to remove this once-proud institution from politics. The return of armed struggle to central parts of the country has fundamentally changed the tenor of political contestation, as well as the balance of power among key political groupings. The long-standing, towering influence of Aung San Suu Kyi and the NLD over the democracy movement has been significantly diluted, while the influence of ethnic armed organisations has dramatically increased, and their demands for local autonomy have escalated to the point that it is no longer certain that the state of Myanmar will hold together.

The face of the new junta

The generals insisted from the outset that *the coup* was in fact not a coup but merely a temporary military takeover necessitated by the refusal of the NLD government to deal with the allegations of electoral fraud in good faith and attempt to take power by "fraudulent means". According to the initial statements issued on the morning of the coup, the military intended to hold power for one year only under the emergency provisions of the 2008 Constitution, after which it would hold fresh elections and return power to the elected government. The main focus of the emergency administration in the interim, supposedly, would be to investigate the allegations of electoral fraud, combat the COVID epidemic, and revive the economy. Otherwise, it would be a caretaker government only. Myanmar's economic and foreign policies would remain the same, and work on the peace process would continue. The deadline for the return to civilian government has since been pushed back to August 2023. However, this schedule still formally adheres to the provisions of the Constitution, which allow for up to two years of emergency rule and another six months to organise elections. Unlike previous coup leaders in 1962 and 1988, the 2021 generation do not seem to be set on fundamentally changing the political system.

To lead the country until new elections could be held, the military established a new ruling council, the State Administration Council (SAC), headed by Commander-in-Chief, Senior General Min Aung Hlaing, and replaced most politically appointed leaders and bodies, including the entire cabinet, the Union Election Commission (UEC), and the Governor of the Central Bank. It also established lower-level administration councils at each administrative level — regional, district, and township — led by military officers, and replaced many of the country's nearly 17,000 elected ward/village administrators with people considered loyal to the new administration, typically military veterans or members of its proxy party, the Union Solidarity and Development Party (USDP). Yet, in a further attempt to bolster its claim to mean "business as usual", it included eight civilians on the ruling Council, including prominent representatives of non-NLD and ethnic political parties, and appointed several respected civil servants to key ministerial portfolios.

Leaving aside the unconvincing claim that the coup was constitutional, there is little doubt that the SAC's plan A is to return power to some form of civilianised structure according to the schedule laid out and in line with the 2008 Constitution. The *Tatmadaw* has never claimed a right to rule the country but rather sees itself as guardians of the Union, which step in only in times of crisis. Moreover, given the dramatic loss of legitimacy the military has suffered from the coup and subsequent violence, this would seem to be the only chance for the junta to salvage its traditional self-image as protectors of the people, even if only in their own mind.

There are, however, some important caveats: First, while the coup leaders may not have plans to change the constitution or remove the formal democratic elements contained in that document, they are evidently taking steps to eliminate the competition. The re-constituted UEC has officially annulled the 2020 election result, claiming that more than 11 million ballots had to be discounted due to fraud or other irregularities during the vote. In a series of meetings with political parties, election officials have mooted plans for changing the electoral system from "first-past-the-post", which has greatly favoured the NLD, to "proportional representation", which would spread the vote and likely give the military with its 25 per cent of seats in parliament the role as kingmakers. In a final *coup de grace,* the new administration is undertaking criminal proceedings against Aung San Suu Kyi and other senior NLD leaders, which will make them ineligible for standing in future elections. Military officials have also publicly warned that the NLD as a party might be disbanded due to its involvement in the alleged electoral fraud, although its preference would seem to be to separate moderate members of the party from Aung San Suu Kyi and persuade them to run. Although most of these processes are still underway at the time of writing, it seems clear that the junta is intent on ensuring that the new elections will produce a result more amenable to their interests.

Secondly, the SAC has wasted no time in passing a raft of new, repressive security laws, which have effectively eviscerated the hard-won political space of the past decade. The Orwellian "household registration" system, which requires people to report any overnight guests, has been reintroduced; the police have been given wide-ranging new powers to search and detain suspects; and the penalties for any act of political resistance have been dramatically increased. Moreover, the new junta has formally brought the police under military command and moved the General Affairs Department (GAD) back under the Ministry of Home Affairs, thus ensuring that the Commander-in-Chief is in direct and full control of the country's omnipresent security apparatus. While the veneer of civilian government will be retained, the intention is clearly for the second iteration of Myanmar's so-called "discipline-flourishing democracy" to have more discipline and less democracy.

Thirdly, it remains an open question whether the military will be able to sufficiently consolidate control of the country to actually hold new elections in August 2023 without risking further instability. As political analyst Richard Horsey (2022) has observed, "popular anger at the military is such that hardly anyone would see a new government made up of recently retired generals in civilian garb as any kind of step forward. Nor would most people deign to participate in such a farce." In these circumstances, it is more likely that any future polls under the SAC would become a flashpoint for dissent and unrest than a step towards stability. Recent ruminations by senior SAC officials about the possible need for a new constitution may indicate that the military leadership itself is coming to recognise this point. If so, the alternative could well be yet another drawn-out constitution-making process under continued military rule. One thing is clear, the SAC has met unprecedented popular resistance to its plans and nearly two years in, is still struggling badly to consolidate its power grab on the ground.

The rage of the people

Unlike previous coups, which were received by the Burmese people with a certain stoic fatalism, the latest one hit the country like an earthquake, shattering the hopes of millions of people who, after ten years of nascent democratic reforms and growing civil, political and economic freedoms, had finally come to believe that tomorrow would be better than today. What the coup leaders had seemingly envisioned as a relatively simple "course correction" instead sparked a mass uprising, which has brought the state to the brink of collapse. Indeed, it is the popular response to the coup as much as the coup itself that has so dramatically transformed the political landscape.

Mass protests started within 48 hours in Yangon and other major cities, led by human rights activists, trade unionists, and other grassroots organisers, and quickly spread to almost every corner of the country, including many ethnic areas. Significantly, the traditional street demonstrations were reinforced by a large-scale civil disobedience movement. Several hundred thousand public servants walked out of their jobs, refusing to work for the new military government, while countless others joined consumer boycotts of military businesses or stopped paying their taxes and electricity bills. The collective message to the new rulers was abundantly clear: "We don't accept your authority."

The uprising was relatively peaceful at first. However, subsequent violent military crackdowns have prompted a growing radicalisation of the resistance, which by the end of 2022 is much reduced in numbers but increasingly dominated by armed actors. Starting as early as mid-March 2021, fear and anger over the brutality of the security forces led many protesters to conclude that their only option was to fight violence with violence. Over the following months, thousands, mainly young, men and women went underground to launch an armed struggle. Many made their way to areas controlled by ethnic armed organisations where they received military training before returning to central Myanmar to wage guerrilla warfare. Others simply picked up their hunting rifles or other makeshift weapons and started fighting back. Between March and September, around 200 people's militias (also referred to as "self-defence groups") were established across the country (Arnold 2021), and that number has since grown dramatically (Ye Myo Hein 2022). In the main cities and towns where state security forces are heavily present, new resistance fighters have formed loose underground networks and engaged mainly in hit-and-run attacks on soft targets, often using improvised explosive devices. In more remote rural areas, larger, more formally organised militias — in some cases counting hundreds of fighters — have increasingly been engaging in pitched battles with the military. Some of these larger militias have also been conducting joint operations with existing ethnic armed organisations, which have served as a dramatic force multiplier, adding not only firepower but also hard-earned fighting experience. Although it has been explicitly framed as a defensive war, the armed resistance has gradually taken on more offensive forms as the militias have started attacking police stations, ambushing military columns, and assassinating local government administrators, alleged informers, and other non-combatants perceived to be aiding and abetting the SAC.

While the violence of the security forces has succeeded in forcing most protesters off the streets and appears to be gradually wearing down the civil disobedience movement as well, the armed resistance has built up significant momentum and turned large, previously peaceful areas of Magwe and Sagaing divisions, as well as Chin and Kayah states, into war zones. According to one estimate, the SAC by September 2022 was in control of less than half of Myanmar's territory and facing major challenges even within much of this area (Special Advisory Council Myanmar 2022). The rest was either effectively ungovernable or under the control of various non-state armed actors. Meanwhile, the goals of the resistance have shifted from restoration of the *status quo ante* to more revolutionary demands, including abolishment of the 2008 constitution, banishment of the military from politics, and establishment of a "genuine federal democracy". This radicalisation of the resistance, coupled with the strength of popular support for those on the frontlines, all add up to something quite different from previous uprisings in 1974, 1988 and 2007. In the words of many resistance fighters themselves, this is not just an uprising but a "revolution", and they are willing to sacrifice their lives for the cause.

The displacement of the National League for Democracy

The popular resistance not only caught the coup leaders on the backfoot but has also forced major realignments in the democracy movement, which since 1988 has been led by Aung San Suu Kyi and her National League for Democracy and staunchly committed to non-violence. Elected members of the NLD who escaped arrest, reacted to the coup by establishing the Committee Representing People's Parliament (CRPH) and demanding that the military return power to the lawful government. However, with their iconic leader under house arrest and sensing the public's revolutionary mood, the CRPH has generally followed the evolving strategy of the grassroots resistance forces rather than seeking — or at least being able — to stamp its leadership on them. This is evident, most notably, in its expanding objectives and abandonment of non-violence.

Unlike in 1990, when the NLD was also denied power after winning elections, the CRPH has sought to build a more inclusive leadership of the anti-coup movement and formally embraced the ambitions of the country's ethnic minorities for a federal Union. While the CRPH is essentially an NLD entity, it acted quickly to establish a National Unity Government (NUG), which incorporated several ethnic and non-NLD ministers, as well as a National Unity Consultative Council (NUCC), which, in principle at least, provides a voice for all members of the anti-military resistance in determining the goals and policies of the parallel government. Significantly, the explicit aim of these new structures, as laid out in the *Federal Democracy Charter,* is not simply to restore the NLD government but rather to build a "genuine federal democracy" with real autonomy for ethnic minorities and human rights for all. The NUG has also proposed the establishment of a Federal Army encompassing all the anti-military armed groups, but has been rebuffed by the existing ethnic armed organisations, which remain sceptical of the sincerity of the NLD's outreach and, in any case, do not share its preference for a strong central government (see further below).

Besides its efforts to build a united front, the rump NLD leadership has abandoned the party's long-standing commitment to non-violence. Already on 13 March 2021, the CRPH publicly declared that the people had a right to defend themselves, thus giving its approval to the emerging armed resistance. Two months later, on 5 May, the NUG announced it was establishing its own army, the People's Defence Force, as the forerunner to a Federal Democratic Army that would bring together all the anti-military armed forces. Finally, on 7 September, it declared a "people's defensive war" against the military junta. Since then, the NUG Ministry of Defence has been working to establish a central command structure for the armed resistance, as well as to raise funds and provide arms for the new people's militias.

Importantly, while NLD members continue to play a central role in the NUG (many critics say "overly central"), which has become the face of the resistance to the international community, the party has had much less influence on the dynamics of the struggle inside the country, which has been dominated by armed actors, including the new people's militias and established ethnic armed organisations. Many of the new grassroots leaders see neither Aung San Suu Kyi nor the traditional non-violent strategy of the NLD as relevant to the revolutionary struggle they are now waging. Highly critical of the former's centralised leadership style, which left little space for other voices, they now see an opportunity to throw off the yoke not only of the military, but also the older generation of pro-democracy politicians. The mostly younger leaders of the grassroots resistance are seeking a transformation not only of civil-military relations (genuine democracy) but also centre-periphery relations (genuine federalism) — and they themselves want to be an integral part of any new power configuration, thus adding a generational dimension to the struggle as well.

The resurgence of the ethnic armed organisations

The eruption of civil war among the Bamar majority has dramatically raised the profile also of Myanmar's long-standing ethnic armed organisations (EAOs) at the centre of Burmese politics. Having now personally tasted the violence of the military to which ethnic communities have long been subjected, many Bamar have come to realise that they have common cause with the country's ethnic insurgents, who they saw before as threats to the Union. Indeed, having chosen the path of armed struggle, they have come to depend on the EAOs for training and arms, as well as combat support. Tellingly, while the rise of the new people's militias has attracted the most attention and brought conflict to many previously peaceful areas, the most successful new fronts in Chin and Kayah states and Sagaing division have all benefitted greatly from the support and cooperation of established ethnic armies, notably the Kachin Independence Army (KIA) in Sagaing Division, the Chin National Army (CNA) in Chin State, and the Karenni Army in Kayah State. Gone are the days when the struggle of Myanmar's ethnic minorities for autonomy was largely hidden away along the country's remote borders.

In the mainstream English-language literature, the EAOs are often treated explicitly or implicitly as part of a NUG-led resistance to the military. Yet, any such pan-ethnic unity remains a far-off prospect and runs up against not only deep historical distrust by many ethnic leaders of Bamar dominated groups but also the great diversity of ethnic aspirations, ideologies, and interests (see Ong 2021; Hmung 2021). Courted by both the SAC and the NUG, yet sceptical that either of them is truly willing — or able — to deliver on their promises, most EAOs have taken positions that reflect more immediate local calculations. While a few of the smaller, militarily weaker groups (notably, the Chin National Front, CNF) quickly aligned themselves with the NUG, all of the major EAOs have effectively rejected the leadership of both the SAC and the NUG and are seeking to chart their own course through the shifting political and military landscape. This is most evident for the two largest EAOs, the United Wa State Army (UWSA) and the Arakan Army (AA), which have both explicitly distanced themselves from the broader resistance movement and instead have used the distraction of the chaos at the centre to expand and deepen administrative control in their own areas in the far east and west of the country (see, for example, Davies 2022). However, even the Kachin Independence Organisation (KIO) and the Karen National Union (KNU), which have provided safe havens and training for large numbers of anti-coup activists and, at times, undertaken joint operations with the new people's militias, do not appear to see this as part of a broader military campaign to defeat the SAC and institute a regime change in Naypyitaw but rather as a chance to regain lost ground in their own areas. Tellingly, neither of them has agreed to join the Federal Army proposed by the NUG or accepted the establishment of new, independent militias in their core areas, instead insisting on maintaining a monopoly on armed force in areas under their control.

In sum, while the SAC and the NUG are fighting over administrative control in contested areas in central Myanmar, the majority of EAOs have been making the most of the opportunity to consolidate and expand control of their homelands along the country's borders. This has potentially far-reaching consequences for the future of the Burmese state. Even if the revolution were to succeed, and a new elected government were to be seated in Naypyitaw and committed to fulfilling the NUG's pledge to establish a federal democracy, the growing strength and ambition of the major EAOs all but guarantee that this new system will be more confederal than federal with extensive autonomy for several of the most powerful ethnic groups. Some might even push for independence, although the international context would make that very difficult to achieve.

The collapse of the state and economy

While the ultimate outcome of the ongoing political crisis remains out of sight, the eruption of civil war at the heart of the Myanmar state has set in motion a process of state and economic collapse that has had a devastating impact on the country and its 54 million people (see Htwe Htwe Thein and Gillan, this volume). Indeed, the battle for control of state and economic structures has become part of the wider war.

The popular response to the 2021 coup has further diluted the military's already limited monopoly on the means of violence and dramatically increased physical insecurity and lawlessness across much of the country. Aside from the expansion and intensification of the civil war, crime rates have soared, even in the major cities, as the police have become preoccupied with managing political dissent and poverty has increased (Naw Theresa 2023). The civil disobedience movement, meanwhile, has "gutted" the state, effectively bringing many state functions to a near-standstill. The health and education sectors have been particularly hard-hit. The remaining skeleton of the state has been further weakened by the assassination of local state administrators by resistance forces who view them as collaborators with the military regime and an integral part of its system of repression. Several hundred local officials have been killed, and possibly thousands more have been chased out of the local communities where they, in addition to serving a key role in monitoring the population, were also responsible for organising the delivery of social and other services. The NUG and local resistance groups have sought to replace and improve the displaced state, much as ethnic armed organisations have been doing for decades in areas under their control. Indeed, the struggle over control of state structures has become a second front within the wider civil war. However, with very limited resources and lacking a centralised administrative system on the ground to set and enforce standards and coordinate delivery, to date, most of this has been patchy and highly reliant on the capacity of local groups and the degree of stability, which can vary widely from village to village.

With violence expanding and public services crumbling, the broader economy is in virtual freefall. According to World Bank estimates, Myanmar's Gross Domestic Product fell by 18 per cent in the 2021 Fiscal Year and remains deeply depressed with continuing strong downward risks (World Bank 2022). A near-collapse of the banking sector, coupled with frequent internet shutdowns and general instability, has wreaked havoc for many local businesses, which had modernised during the decade of reform. Faced with greatly impoverished financial prospects, as well as significant reputational risks, many international businesses have also suspended or terminated their activities, especially in manufacturing and services. Meanwhile, reports of major increases in illegal logging, gold mining, drugs trafficking and other illegal activity all point to further criminalisation of the economy (see, for example, Clapp and Towers 2022).

Ominously, the destruction of the state and the economy is not simply collateral damage of an expanding civil war; it is to a large degree intentional. For the anti-military resistance, it is part of a deliberate strategy to make the country ungovernable and deny the junta all sources of legitimacy and funding. Conversely, the military is violently resisting all efforts by the resistance to establish parallel state structures outside of their control. The state and the economy — even schools and hospitals — have thus become sites of violent contestation and seem destined to remain so until one side gains the upper hand, or a political settlement is reached. In fact, there are grounds to worry that this may now have become part of a "new normal" in an increasingly militarised polity.

CAUSES OF THE MILITARY COUP

We will likely never know for sure why the military staged the coup. These decisions are taken by secretive men for reasons they may never admit to. However, several plausible explanations present themselves at both the personal and institutional level.

The official explanation

There is little doubt that the military leaders were genuinely shocked by the November 2020 election results and probably felt that the NLD could not possibly have won by such a large margin by fair means. There was widespread anticipation even among pro-democratic observers that the NLD would struggle to repeat its 2015 results in the face of widespread criticism over their governance record, especially from ethnic leaders and the business community. Moreover, several opposition parties had been complaining about political bias in the election process, including the cancellation of elections in areas outside government/NLD control, censorship of television campaign messages, and alleged misuse of state COVID payments for electoral benefit. Given the low level of trust between the military and the NLD — not to mention parallel developments in the United States, where Donald Trump was similarly alleging widespread election fraud — it is plausible that some in the military camp genuinely suspected foul play. That said, to understand why the military saw the need to overturn a system that it had itself established and risk both domestic unrest and renewed international opprobrium, we will need to consider the deeper reasons why it felt that the election results could not be allowed to stand.

The pending retirement of Min Aung Hlaing

The personal interests of Senior General Min Aung Hlaing provide a useful place to start. The Commander-in-Chief had made no secret of the fact that he had ambitions to become president and often seemed to act more like a politician than a commander. The election results brought that dream crashing down. This would have been a major blow not only to his ego, but also to his personal interests and security. As commander-in-chief, he was facing compulsory retirement in July 2021, which would have left him without any formal power base or reliable means to protect his interests, including the threat of the ongoing investigations at the International Criminal Court (ICC) for his role in the army's mass atrocities against the Rohingya in 2017. His predecessor, Senior General Than Shwe, overcame this perennial dilemma for authoritarian leaders by placing trusted officers in key positions in the military, as well as in the first post-military government. However, Min Aung Hlaing has never been able to consolidate power within the *Tatmadaw* to the same degree,[4] and he may not have felt confident that he could do the same. As such, the coup offered a solution to many of his personal dilemmas. It is unlikely to be a coincidence that one of the first actions of the SAC after the coup was to remove the age limits for the senior general and his deputy.

Growing threats to the Tatmadaw's institutional interests

The motivations of top leaders matter greatly in a political system that is as highly personalised as the Burmese. Still, Min Aung Hlaing would not have been able to carry out the coup without general support among the wider officer corps. In fact, some observers have suggested that he may have been pushed to act by more hard-line officers.[5] Here, it is necessary though, to first clear up some common misconceptions about the decade of liberalisation preceding the coup.

During the ten years of political reform from 2011–2020, the conventional wisdom in the English-language press, as well as much of the scholarly literature, was that the *Tatmadaw* was benefitting from the political transition (for an overview of this literature, see Selth 2017). Some argued that the military effectively remained in power despite the democratic shift. Others criticised Aung San Suu Kyi for failing to challenge the military's prerogatives, or even justifying their abuses. These narratives were always misleading. While civil-military relations went through ups and downs with periods of apparent rapprochement, there were deep underlying tensions, which originated in the very framing of the transition as a system of power sharing between long-standing enemies and had never been resolved.

Many of the post-2011 reforms were not planned and never had the full support of many senior officers. Rather, President Thein Sein and his closest confidants went off-script after they retired from the military in 2010 to lead the first post-military administration from 2011–2015. They were able to pull it off, in part, because they retained authority among the new military leaders who were more than ten years their juniors and, in part, because they were successful in bringing in major, early rewards for the country and the military alike by securing the lifting of Western sanctions, attracting large-scale new foreign investment, and improving the military's reputation after two decades of international opprobrium. However, there was serious disagreement within military circles around the time of the 2015 elections about the wisdom of handing over government power to their long-standing nemesis, opposition leader Aung San Suu Kyi.[6] After the NLD government took office in early 2016, civil-military relations quickly entered a downward spiral. This was evident at the person level between Aung San Suu Kyi and Min Aung Hlaing who, from the outset, were locked in a power struggle for the future presidency and clearly disliked each other, but also at the institutional level where issues of *power, policy,* and *pride* all served to create tensions.

Contrary to popular perceptions, the NLD government had real power and used it. Although the new civilian leaders mostly refrained from openly challenging the military on core issues, such as its constitutional reserve powers and the defence budget, they sought from the outset — and often in quite petty manners — to marginalise it in matters of day-to-day governance. The establishment of an extra-constitutional position for Aung San Suu Kyi as de facto head of government, above the President, challenged if not strictly the letter, then certainly the spirit of the 2008 Constitution, which formed the basis for the military's acceptance of the broader reform process. While the generals, according to Burmese scholar Maung Aung Myo (personal communication), had anticipated this and in some respects were resigned to it, they grew increasingly incensed as the former opposition leader, first, refused to convene the National Defence and Security Council, which was intended as the main mechanism for coordinating national security policy between the civilian and military sides of the government, and later appointed a civilian national security adviser. These steps clearly crossed the lines the military had drawn to protect its long-standing monopoly on security decision-making. The later transfer of the General Affairs Department from the Ministry of Home Affairs to the Ministry of the Union Government Office, which was under civilian control, must also have raised the hackles of the military leadership, although the impact of this was felt more at the local level and did not at the time cause any open military dissent.

The Rohingya crisis became a particular flashpoint for civil-military tensions. While the outside world condemned Aung San Suu Kyi for supposedly protecting the military, this was not how they perceived it (and probably not her intention either). The generals had always seen the NLD as being soft on the "Muslim issue", and they were infuriated, particularly, by the efforts of the government to placate the international community by including foreigners on several key committees established to help resolve the crisis, including the so-called Annan Commission, which was led by former UN Secretary-General Kofi Annan and charged with finding long-term solutions (Maung Aung Myoe 2018). When Aung San Suu Kyi later decided to personally go to The Hague to defend the state of Myanmar against allegations of genocide at the International Court of Justice, they saw this as a political stunt to rally popular support and probably worried that she was secretly working to "throw them under the bus".[7]

The stress of winner-takes-all elections

During the first three years of the NLD government, the two sides managed to keep the worst tensions private, presumably because they both wanted the power-sharing arrangement to last even as they tussled over their respective shares. However, as 2019 ticked around and everyone began positioning themselves for the elections the following year, the underlying tensions became more and more apparent and public. The NLD fired the opening salvo in late January that year, when it went against vocal opposition from the military MPs and established a parliamentary committee to recommend constitutional amendments. The NLD was never going to get any amendments through parliament without the support of the military MPs, but the generals saw it for what it undoubtedly was: a deliberate move to put them and their proxy parties on the spot ahead of the upcoming elections. While they easily blocked the effort, they would also have been greatly concerned that the NLD targeted several of the core clauses in the Constitution, which dictate the military's participation in parliament and give them veto over constitutional amendments. Over the following 18 months, Senior General Min Aung Hlaing became increasingly vocal about his displeasure with the NLD's management of the country, which became a frequent topic of his public engagements, including meetings with foreign leaders, that increasingly took on an air of election speeches. On several occasions, he explicitly encouraged people to vote for nationalist parties who would "protect race and religion", causing an outcry among NLD members and supporters who saw it as unwarranted interference in matters beyond his remit.

Given the fragility of civil–military relations, the elections were always going to be a highly sensitive time and potential breaking point. There is a lot at stake in Myanmar's winner-takes-all election system, and emotions were running high on all sides. In the lead up to the elections, close observers of the country's evolving civil–military relations were warning that it might be necessary for the NLD to take a step back and invite the military to join a "national unity government" or risk upsetting the fragile balance of power and interests undergirding the transition (personal communication). Yet, riding high on their success in the polls, the party ignored all warnings and ploughed ahead, perhaps believing that popular support would protect it.

It is possible that the 2020 election results effectively sealed the fate of Myanmar's embryonic democracy. However, it is also possible that Aung San Suu Kyi and the NLD made one final and fatal mistake in purely dismissing the military's allegations of electoral fraud. Many officers would have been insulted by the flat-out refusal by the NLD and the Union Election Commission (UEC) to take their complaints seriously. For Min Aung Hlaing, this dismissal of his demands would have been not only a personal affront but also a threat to his image of authority, which is critically important to any military commander. But for other officers, too, this would have been galling. Rhetoric aside, the self-image of the military is that of an institution above politics, morally superior to civilian politicians. They would have seen the members of the UEC, in particular, as a "bunch of nobodies" that should know their place. We should never underestimate the pride many Burmese officers take in the institution of the *Tatmadaw* and its, part, historical and part, self-proclaimed role in establishing and guarding the independent Union of Myanmar. It is quite possible that this was the lost drop after what for many military officers had been five years of growing resentment over the loss of authority and respect that they had grown accustomed to.

From an idealist point of view, the NLD was of course only doing what was expected of it as the vanguard party of the democracy movement. In fact, many pro-democracy activists both inside and outside of the country felt that it should have done a lot more to challenge the military and the remaining authoritarian elements of the transitional system. However, from a more practical — or realist — perspective, the NLD went too far, too fast in their efforts to wrest control from the military. To the generals, many of the party's actions in government would have been seen as contrary to the 2008 Constitution and disrespectful of the military's historical role in establishing and protecting the state. They probably also feared that a second NLD government, emboldened by another landslide victory, was going to try to do an end run around the constitution or in other ways challenge more fundamental military interests. Thus, it is likely that Min Aung Hlaing had broad support for the coup, at least among senior military leaders.

FUTURE SCENARIOS

Theoretically, the ongoing civil war may result in one of four ideal type outcomes: (1) the resistance wins; (2) the military wins; (3) no side is able to gain the upper hand, and Myanmar settles into a protracted conflict similar to the situation in the borderlands since the 1960s but affecting larger areas of the country; or (4) there could be some kind of peace settlement that satisfies, if only in part, the core interests of the main protagonists. Each of these military outcomes, in turn, would open up a range of different political futures. A win by the resistance, for example, might pave the way for a more inclusive federal democratic union, or it could degenerate into a new set of violent local conflicts, dominated by those with guns. A military win, on the other hand, might be followed either by a return to de facto dictatorship or a second attempt at establishing some kind of hybrid system. For the purposes of this section though, I will limit my focus to the likely military outcome.

Prospects for a resistance victory

There is no question that the new junta has failed to consolidate its grab for power and today faces greater military challenges than at any time since the immediate post-independence period when the Burma Army suffered massive defections by regiments loyal to anti-government forces and the central government for a brief period had little control beyond the capital. Like all coup-makers, the generals had undoubtedly hoped to quickly normalise the situation and minimise the need for violence. This explains many of the SAC's early actions, including their claim to be acting in line with the constitution, their insistence that they were a caretaker government only, and their efforts to establish a "mixed" civil–military administration. Instead, they have found themselves embroiled in a civil war of their own making, fighting scores of armed resistance groups on multiple fronts across the country, including many areas that had otherwise long been peaceful. The coup has caused a catastrophic loss of legitimacy for the military-led state, and the SAC's efforts to restore control through violence and intimidation have only compounded the problem as long-standing popular rejection of military rule as a system of government has turned into visceral hatred of the new generation of military rulers, as well as the soldiers that are doing their bidding and indeed the *Tatmadaw* as an institution.

Many members of the resistance appear confident that the strain from these developments will cause the military to either give up or splinter; or they believe they can defeat it on the battlefield. Yet, the odds for any of these scenarios delivering a clear-cut transition out of military rule are long (however much we may wish otherwise). First, it is inconceivable that the military leadership would simply "fold" and accept the resistance's demand for an end to the military's role in politics. The *Tatmadaw* has ruled Myanmar directly or indirectly for more than half a century, longer than any other military in the world — and for all this time and longer, it has been fighting a plethora of ideological, ethnic, and economic insurgencies. There has not been a single year since Independence in 1948 without major fighting somewhere in the country. This experience has deeply shaped the self-image of successive generations of military officers who see themselves as "guardians" of the Union and the only defence against centrifugal forces threatening to pull the country apart. There may well be senior officers who disagreed with the coup or have come to regret it after seeing the consequences unfold. However, it can be assumed that they all subscribe to the motto that "only when the *Tatmadaw* is strong can the Union of Myanmar be strong". To many officers, the escalating demands of the resistance, coupled with the shift to armed struggle, would only have reinforced their belief that the Union is under threat from extremists and must be defended at all costs. This ideological belief in the necessity — and, indeed, righteousness — of their actions is undoubtedly reinforced by self-interest. Rulers who oversee mass atrocities tend to stay in office for life. They cling to power, even in the face of massive and mounting cost, for the simple reason that giving it up poses too high a risk. Such concerns are particular acute for Min Aung Hlaing and other top generals who already before the coup were under active investigation by the ICC, as well as the UN-sponsored Independent Investigative Mechanism for Myanmar, for their role in the 2017 mass atrocities against the Rohingya and now face further allegations of crimes against humanity during the post-coup violence. However, similar fears have been expressed even by junior officers and rank-and-file soldiers who are worried about potential popular retribution for their role in the repression (Frontier Myanmar 2022d). As the old maxim says, "they must hang together, or they will hang separately".

Second, although the resistance has gained strong momentum over the past 18 months, the belief that it can win on the battlefield stretches the limits of realistic analysis. Its current troubles notwithstanding, the *Tatmadaw* has major advantages over the resistance forces across most conventional measures of military power, including manpower, firepower, and command structures. By most estimates, the military leadership at the time of the coup had direct command of 300–350,000 soldiers and around 80,000 police (Selth 2022),[8] as well as controlling influence over tens of thousands of local militias forces (Militia Entity in Myanmar 2021). It also had a large reservoir of veterans and auxiliary forces who can be called upon to bolster its ranks. Even if the military's ranks have since been significantly depleted through battlefield losses and desertions, they are still much larger than the combined forces of the new people's militias (50–100,000)[9] and EAOs that are *actively* aligned with the resistance against the military (20–30,000).[10] Adding firepower to the equation, the advantage of the *Tatmadaw* is overwhelming. Since the 1988 uprising, which initially presented similar challenges to today, the *Tatmadaw* has invested billions of dollars in upgrading its weapons and transport systems. What was then a poorly-equipped infantry force is today a well-equipped modern army with numerous artillery battalions, as well as a significant air force and navy, which have increasingly been integrated into its counter-insurgency operations to devastating effect. By contrast, many of the resistance fighters are effectively unarmed. Interviews with members of the new people's militias indicate that less than a quarter of the members of many groups have automatic weapons, and that ammunition is in such short supply that clashes with the military often must be quickly wrapped up before they simply run out bullets (Frontier Myanmar 2022a; also Ye Myo Hein 2022). Although the armed resistance is likely to strengthen further over time, it does not have either the levels of funding or access to arms that would be needed to develop into a fighting force that can match the *Tatmadaw* in major head-on confrontations. Even the established EAOs, which are much better funded than the new people's militias, have few effective countermeasures to remote attacks by air or long-range artillery. Importantly, the *Tatmadaw* is under a single, unified command, and all of its soldiers and arms can, in principle at least, be deployed across the country where they are most needed in support of a national strategy. The NUG, as noted, is working to establish a joint command structure for the various forces aligned against the military. However, the best they can hope for in the absence of a pan-ethnic political settlement, as well as large-scale increases in revenue, is to impart some level of strategic direction for forces that are essentially locally based (and many of which have primarily local objectives). The resistance forces have several more intangible advantages, typical of guerrilla groups, including high morale, the support of local communities, and superior knowledge of the terrain. This has served them well in the early phase of what is essentially a classic guerrilla war, and it is possible — even likely — that some of the new insurgencies will be able to consolidate and deny the SAC control of parts of Chin and Kayah states, as well as Sagaing division. However, taking and holding territory in remote areas is one thing; an offensive across the central valley to take Naypyitaw or any of the major cities is something entirely different. Faced with an enemy that not only has a monopoly on artillery and airpower but also a total disregard for collateral damage, it is hard to see how the resistance forces could achieve an outright military victory and take control of the country.

In the absence of any plausible scenario where a unified military either capitulates or is defeated, much attention has been directed to a third possibility: that large-scale defections could cause the military to collapse from within. The resistance understandably was buoyed in the early months of the uprising when scores of police and soldiers started arriving in liberated areas, expressing their disillusionment with an army that was killing its own people and with some suggesting that up to three-fourths of the security forces would change sides if they could (Kyed and Ah Lynn 2021). However, early predictions that the defections would escalate over time to present a serious threat to the military have not borne out. Even by resistance estimates, the total number of defectors has yet to reach more than 1 per cent of the total forces of the *Tatmadaw*, and the number of new arrivals declined significantly in 2022 (Frontier Myanmar 2022c). Moreover, the large majority of those who have defected are junior ranks from non-combat units. In order for defections to make a decisive difference, they would almost certainly have to involve senior officers leaving with entire battalions and their arms (Selth 2021), or the number of individual rank-and-file would have to reach tens of thousands, including a significant number of combat troops. Neither of these scenarios are plausible in the absence of a major shift in battlefield fortunes favouring the resistance forces. The resistance thus faces a "catch-22": in order to motivate large-scale defections, they will have to create a perception that the military is losing; yet in order to do that, they probably need large-scale defections.

The balance of power could shift both quickly and dramatically if all or even most of the established EAOs were to join the resistance, or sympathetic foreign governments were to start providing large-scale economic and military assistance. However, neither of these potential game changers is likely to eventuate. Shared hatred of the *Tatmadaw* is nothing new, yet at no point in Myanmar's history has the Bamar majority and ethnic minority groups — or even the ethnic armed groups among themselves — been able to effectively unite. There are simply too many divergent ideologies and interests and too much distrust. Meanwhile, no western country has shown any inclination to provide lethal assistance to the resistance, and no regional country would accept it if they tried. Instead, international support has been limited — and is likely to remain limited — to largely symbolic, "feel good" measures in the form of public statements, a few sanctions, and some gestures towards international justice, none of which makes any significant difference to the will or capacity of the military to continue its repressive ways.

Alternative futures

In the absence of an unlikely implosion of the *Tatmadaw*, the short- to medium-term outlook is for continued armed conflict. The revolution has significant momentum; thousands of mainly young, women and men have committed to a fight to the death; and popular support for the struggle remains strong. The *Tatmadaw*, however, maintains control of the capital, as well as most cities and towns, and has the firepower to repel any larger attacks in the Burmese heartland. With limited and mostly depleting resources on all sides, the intensity of the fighting is likely to remain relatively low across most of the contested territory. However, the conflict could well drag on for years and will be extremely difficult to settle.

The possibility of an ultimate *Tatmadaw* victory is unthinkable to many, but perhaps mainly because it is normatively unacceptable. While there is little to indicate that such a turn of events is imminent, the question is whether the resistance can maintain momentum through an extended war of attrition. Should hopes for an outright victory wane, the resistance faces two key challenges. First, the large majority of the new resistance fighters are not soldiers by profession or upbringing, and many have had to leave their homes in the cities of central Myanmar to fight in distant parts of the country where conditions are more favourable to guerrilla warfare. This imposes strains that are more psychological than material in nature, including homesickness and potentially a growing feeling of wasting their lives. While insurgency, in the memorable words of Martin Smith, has become "a way of life" for tens of thousands of ethnic rebels who control their own homelands and are able to stay close to their families in the environs where they grew up, this is less likely to be a sustainable, long-term choice for many of the new insurgents. Secondly, conflict fatigue is likely to set in among the general population. Despite clear evidence of broad-based popular support for the resistance forces, gaps are likely to widen over time between what is probably a small minority who are fully committed to supporting the revolution and the large majority of ordinary people who, ultimately, will prioritise survival. Among the latter, the financial burden of supporting the resistance fighters, coupled with the suffering arising from indiscriminate retaliatory military attacks on local communities, is likely to see growing demands for peace (see Frontier Myanmar 2022b).

The military faces its own long-term challenges of attrition. While reports from resistance sources that the *Tatmadaw* is losing every battle and suffering catastrophic losses should be read with caution, it is clearly bleeding personnel. Every week, scores of soldiers are killed or defect. Meanwhile, reports that the military is struggling to fill the places as its elite Defence Services Academy, exhorting family members of soldiers to undergo military training, and trying to raise new pro-military militias, all suggest that it is facing serious challenges in attracting new recruits to fill the gaps. Still, the *Tatmadaw* has much greater resources than the resistance forces and can count on the continued support of the three strongest regional powers: Russia, China, and India. It might even benefit from the collapse of the domestic economy, which will hurt society much more than it will hurt the rump state and may ultimately compel impoverished youth to again seek a military career, as many have done in the past, simply as a means of survival. If the conflict settles into a more stable pattern, history shows that the *Tatmadaw* is likely to be able to reorganise, rebuild, and divide and rule. In such a situation, the ability of many of the new resistance groups to withstand escalating all-out military assaults will be tested, especially since they do not have the sanctuaries in neighbouring countries to retreat into that have been so important to the survival and sustainability of earlier generations of insurgents. The SAC — or any successor government under military control — will certainly struggle to re-establish any kind of "normal politics", but again, past experience suggests that they will simply "dig in" and try to wait out the resistance.

Most wars end with negotiations – and, theoretically, a window of opportunity should open as the conflict settles into a mutually hurting stalemate. However, the prospects for a negotiated settlement are greatly complicated by the highly decentralised structures and diversity of interests of the resistance movement, which would make it immensely difficult for any negotiator to make credible commitments on its behalf. Moreover, in Myanmar's zero-sum political culture, no side has ever shown much taste for negotiations or compromise, and the international community lacks the unity that would be required to assert sufficient pressure on the domestic parties to have any real hope of breaking this deadlock.

Clearly, any attempt to predict how the conflict will develop beyond the next year or two is hazardous. In the longer term, most of the factors discussed here may shift and possibilities not currently in view could open up. "Black swan" events, like the death of Min Aung Hlaing or release of Aung San Suu Kyi, or perhaps a Chinese cross-border incursion to protects its economic interests, could dramatically change the dynamics of the conflict. However, from the vantage point of late 2022 — and with a view to Myanmar's modern history and its institutional legacies — it is hard to be optimistic about a positive outcome.

SOME CONCLUDING REFLECTIONS

The 2021 military coup ended a decade of significant progress and renewed hope for the future for many people in Myanmar, and the popular response has led to an unfortunate, if perhaps unavoidable, "hardening" of politics. The post-coup political landscape is dominated by armed actors and the use of extreme violence for the purposes of control and, ultimately, defeat of the enemy. Civil society has been largely sidelined; formal policymaking has become almost irrelevant; and social service delivery has become part of the war. The short- to medium-term outlook is for protracted conflict and deepening state and economic collapse, with a significant risk that the military will be able to reassert control over the longer term. I do not, however, want to end on such a pessimistic note. So, at the risk of engaging in the very form of wishful thinking that I have implicitly been warning about, let me finish by offering some more hopeful observations.

While the preceding discussion of material factors provides little scope for optimism, there are some positive elements if we focus instead on changes in underlying ideas and values — possibly on the military side and certainly on the civilian side. It is easy to forget in the midst of the brutality that we have been witnessing from the military on a daily basis since the coup (and that many minority communities have suffered for much longer). However, it was a group of recently retired generals who kick-started the reforms in 2011, and it is quite possible that like-minded officers exist in the military today. Indeed, it is reasonable to expect that the massive popular repudiation of the coup has given pause for thought for at least some officers about the future role of the military in politics. The chances of a decisive break in military unity during a period of active fighting are miniscule, but the possibility of a second run at reform in peace time should not be discounted. Meanwhile, the new, and mostly younger, leaders of the federal democracy movement have put forward a compelling new vision of a more inclusive, tolerant and just society, both rhetorically and in action. The ongoing processes of deliberation and compromise within political platforms like the NUCC are also encouraging for the future, even if their practical impact remain uncertain. While value shifts can take decades to filter through, the rupture created by the events of the past two years may speed up the process. Much, however, depends on the new generation of leaders on all sides. Their elders have failed; Myanmar's future now rests with them.

Notes

1 The official term for the Burmese military, the *Tatmadaw* (meaning "Royal armed forces"), is maintained in this chapter for the sake of familiarity only, not as a sign of respect. Since the coup, many Burmese have started referring to it as the *Sit-tat* instead, which simply means "military".
2 Personal communication, confidential source.
3 The chapter is based on remarks prepared for the Myanmar Update Conference on 17 July 2021 but has been expanded and updated to include developments until the end of 2022.

4   Personal communication, multiple confidential sources.
5   Personal communication, confidential source.
6   Personal communication, confidential source.
7   Personal communication, confidential source.
8   The number of combat troops was always much lower, perhaps no more than a third. But the same presumably applies to the people's militias and ethnic armed organisations.
9   Estimates of the number of people's militia forces vary widely and have shown a sharply upward trend (compare, for example, Ye Myo Hein and Myers 2021 and Ye Myo Hein 2022). However, considering that they are entirely sourced from the resistance itself, the lower estimates are likely to be more accurate. Moreover, many of the new resistance fighters need to work between battles to sustain their families and are therefore effectively part-time soldiers (Frontier Myanmar 2022a).
10 This number includes the KIO, KNU, CNF, and Karenni National Progressive Party (KNPP) and takes account of a significant influx of new members to these organisations since the coup. It does *not* include other EAOs, like the AA or the Myanmar National Democratic Alliance Army (MNDAA), who are fighting the *Tatmadaw* but have no meaningful alignment with the NUG or the anti-coup resistance more broadly.

References

Arnold, Matthew. 2021. "Myanmar's Shifting Military Balance", 9 September 2021. Unpublished briefing paper (in author's possession).

Clapp, Pricilla A. and Jason Towers. 2022. "Myanmar's Criminal Zones: A Growing Threat to Global Security". United States Institute of Peace, 9 November 2022, https://www.usip.org/publications/2022/11/myanmars-criminal-zones-growing-threat-global-security#:~:text=International%20media%20and%20law%20enforcement,labor%20in%20these%20ungoverned%20enclaves.

Davies, Anthony. 2022. "Wa an early winner of Myanmar's post-coup war". *Asia Times*, 22 February 2022, https://asiatimes.com/2022/02/wa-an-early-winner-of-myanmars-post-coup-war/.

Frontier Myanmar. 2022a. "'We are selling everything': Resistance groups struggle to arm fighters", 4 July 2022, https://www.frontiermyanmar.net/en/we-are-selling-everything-resistance-groups-struggle-to-arm-fighters/.

Frontier Myanmar. 2022b. "Can PDFs stay solvent?". *Political Insider*, 19 August 2022 (only available to members).

Frontier Myanmar. 2022c. "Abort mission: Why are fewer soldiers defecting?". *Political Insider*, 27 November 2022 (only available to members).

Frontier Myanmar. 2022d. "Bunker mentality: Where do military families stand?". *Political Insider*, 11 December 2022 (only available to members).

Hmung, Samuel. 2021. "New friends, old enemies: Politics of ethnic armed organisations after the Myanmar coup". SEARBO Policy Briefing, Australian National University, June 2021.

Horsey, Richard. 2022. "One Year on from the Myanmar Coup". International Crisis Group, 25 January 2022, https://www.crisisgroup.org/asia/south-east-asia/myanmar/one-year-myanmar-coup.

Kyed, Helene Maria and Ah Lynn. 2021. "Soldier Defections in Myanmar: Motivations and obstacles following the 2021 military coup". DIIS Report, No. 6/2021, https://www.diis.dk/en/research/defecting-soldiers-are-a-significant-symbolic-blow-to-myanmars-military-rule.

Maung Aung Myo. 2018. "Partnership in Politics: The Tatmadaw and the NLD in Myanmar since 2016". In Justine Chambers, Gerard McCarthy, Nicholas Farrelly, and Chit Win (eds), *Myanmar Transformed: People, Places and Politics* (Singapore: ISEAS), 201-230.

"Militia Entity in Myanmar: Establishment, Resiliency, and Future Prospects", December 2021. Confidential report (in author's possession).

Naw Theresa. 2023. "A Tsunami of Crime Washes Over Post-Coup Myanmar". *The Diplomat*, 11 January 2023, https://thediplomat.com/2023/01/a-tsunami-of-crime-washes-over-post-coup-myanmar/.

Ong, Andrew. 2021. "Ethic Armed Organisations in Post-Coup Myanmar: New Conversations Needed". ISEAS Perspective, 11 June 2021, https://www.iseas.edu.sg/articles-commentaries/iseas-perspective/2021-79-ethnic-armed-organisations-in-post-coup-myanmar-new-conversations-needed-by-andrew-ong/.

Selth, Andrew. 2021. "Could defections threaten the survival of Myanmar's military regime?", AsiaLink, University of Melbourne, 18 October 2021, https://asialink.unimelb.edu.au/insights/could-defections-threaten-the-survival-of-myanmars-military-regime.

Selth, Andrew. 2022. "Myanmar's Military Numbers", *The Interpreter*, 17 February 2022, https://www.lowyinstitute.org/the-interpreter/myanmar-s-military-numbers.

Special Advisory Council Myanmar. 2022. "Effective Control in Myanmar". Briefing paper, 5 September 2022, https://specialadvisorycouncil.org/2022/09/briefing-effective-control-myanmar/.

World Bank. 2022. "Economic Monitor", July 2022, https://www.worldbank.org/en/country/myanmar/publication/myanmar-economic-monitor-july-2022-reforms-reversed.

Ye Myo Hein. 2022. "Understanding the People's Defense Forces in Myanmar". United States Institute of Peace, 3 November 2022, https://www.usip.org/publications/2022/11/understanding-peoples-defense-forces-myanmar.

Ye Myo Hein and Luke Meyers. 2021. "Seizing the State: The Emergence of a Distinct Security Actor in Myanmar". Wilson Centre, November 2021, https://www.wilsoncenter.org/publication/seizing-state-emergence-distinct-security-actor-myanmar.

4

COVID, COUP AND PRISONS: EXPLORING CRISIS AS CONTEXT IN MYANMAR

Tomas Max Martin and U Win[1]

This chapter analyses the compounding effects of the COVID-19 health crisis and the political crisis of the February 2021 military coup in the context of Myanmar prisons. We want to start off this analysis by describing a particular photo. We suppose most fellow researchers and other people, who try to follow and understand both COVID-19 and the coup have been inundated with intense and disturbing photos and accounts of suffering in Myanmar. Unsurprisingly, we did so too in preparation for writing this chapter. One photo stood out for us. It is a photo of a young man by the name of Ko Manzar Myay Mon, an activist from Chang-U township in Sagaing region, who was arrested and detained on 8 June 2021. The photo, which was posted on Twitter, among others by the UN Special Rapporteur on Myanmar,[2] shows Ko Manzar Myay Mon sitting crossed legged with his hands tied behind his back. One sees the boot and the camouflaged arm of a security officer next to him, who seems to pull his head back for the camera. The young man's face is bruised but expressionless, his t-shirt torn. Accounts of the injuries and torture that Ko Manzar Myay Mon was victim of after his arrest caused widespread condemnation[3] and his trial is still pending as we write this chapter. Yet, in direct relation to the issue in focus here something else also stands out as particularly absurd and deeply disturbing. His captors have blindfolded him with a disposable facemask, which is lifted off his mouth to cover his eyes, strings around the ears still attached.

The photo documents as well as symbolizes — in a basic and brute way — how detention and COVID-19 collide in Myanmar today. The facemask over Ko Manzar Myay Mon's eyes shows how the agents of the junta menacingly distort and disregard the need to respond with minimal care and caution to the threat of COVID-19. Most apparently, placing the facemask over Ko Manzar Myay Mon's eyes shows a disregard for basic health safeguards. At a deeper level, this seemingly banal act changes a formally protective health technology into a tool of coercion and connotes the junta's readiness to distort the pandemic response and turn the threat of COVID-19 against the public.

Since the military coup of 1st February 2021, Myanmar has witnessed massive civic protests, bomb blasts in the middle of cities and towns, intensifying armed conflicts between Ethnic Resistance Organisations (EROs) and the military junta in ethnic areas, as well as expanding clashes between the newly emerged People's Defense Forces (PDFs) and the army in central Myanmar. The military-led State Administration Council (SAC) has arrested and detained thousands of people who have participated in anti-junta protests, political and civil society leaders, and civilians, continuing a deep tradition of political imprisonment, torture, and inhumane treatment (AAPP 2016; Gaborit 2020). Even before the coup Myanmar prisons were characterized by deplorable conditions, climates of fear and harsh discipline (Jefferson, Htaik et al. 2019; Martin 2021). The coup has unsurprisingly propelled prison life in Myanmar into further injustices and human rights violations at a time when the country was already under severe pressure to deal with the health and economic implications of a raging COVID-19 pandemic.

Since the pandemic took off in 2020, the prison system in Myanmar has struggled to respond adequately to the COVID-19 virus, with various restrictions, pardons, ad hoc training and piecemeal protection efforts (Oo and Martin 2020). This chapter explores the Myanmar Prison Department's (MPD) responses to COVID-19 and considers how the coup is making already difficult matters worse. Even though the SAC claims to follow COVID-19 precautionary procedures and guidelines from the Myanmar Health Department, our analysis indicates that the mass incarceration of political activists seriously aggravates staff and prisoners' vulnerabilities and undercuts MPD's feeble COVID-19 responses. Contextualized by field research, careful consideration of the MPD's early responses to the pandemic, and accounts of recently released detainees, this chapter describes how the pandemic and the coup is affecting prison life and reflects more generally on the "amplified vulnerabilities" (Jefferson, Caracciolo et al. 2021) of detainees in post-coup Myanmar.

In conclusion, we draw attention to a theoretical point about the analytical approach to the crisis — that is the health crisis of COVID-19 as well as the political crisis of the military coup. Drawing inspiration from the anthropology of crisis (Fassin 2020; Vigh 2008), we suggest that the apparent and unfolding crises in Myanmar prisons are neither unique nor exceptional. Crisis is chronic in Myanmar prisons. The experience of crisis is not aberrational, but rather a condition of everyday life for prisoners and guards. We thereby analyse both the crisis of COVID-19 and the crisis of the coup as part of a perpetual context of volatility and violations in Myanmar prisons. This perspective does not seek to diminish the intensity and acceleration of the serious problems and violations that the virus and the junta represent. Rather, it draws attention to a deeper and enduring carceral crisis of poor governance and neglect that the acute crises of COVID-19 and the coup are folded into.

The primary empirical material for this chapter is drawn from six in-depth interviews (face-to-face and online) with former prisoners from two prisons in central Myanmar, and one in the northern part of the country. Interviews took place in June, July, and August 2021 in the aftermath of the coup. Given the ongoing risks of reprisals and harm to former political prisoners and the enhanced sensitivity of the situation we are unable to be more specific about the methodology. Suffice to say, informant and researcher safety was of primary concern in the data collection process and in writing up this chapter. More generally, the analysis rests on five years of fieldwork-based exploration of everyday prison life, prison reform dynamics, and penal history in Myanmar, where the two authors have worked closely together doing ethnographic interviews with prisoners and staff and observing prison practices inside selected prisons, at headquarter level in Naypyitaw, and among leading international prison reform organisations.

COVID-19 IN MYANMAR PRISONS

At the time of writing the COVID-19 pandemic has infected more than 500 million people and caused more than 6 million deaths worldwide according to the World Health Organization.[4] The first case of COVID-19 in Myanmar was detected on 22 March 2020.[5] Since then, the number of infections has increased alongside uneven responses from the civilian-led National League for Democracy (NLD) government (2015–2020), and more recently from the junta.

First, second and third wave

The first wave of the pandemic from March to August 2020 was (according to official records) quite "mild" in Myanmar, with reports of approximately 360 cases and 6 deaths (Deshpande, Hnin et al. 2020). The government banned large gatherings, and instituted a partial lockdown and travel restrictions — but it was difficult to trace persons who had had contact with other infected people, and generally hard to enforce the new guidelines due to economic constraints and a lack of test kits. As part of the initial responses, the government also suspended visas for foreign nationals, and urged migrant workers to delay their return so that appropriate quarantines measures could be set up. However, due to lockdowns and the loss of job opportunities — notably in Thailand — about 100,000 migrant workers returned home to Myanmar in late March 2020. The country was not equipped to handle such huge flows of returnees (ILO 2020). Despite late and incoherent responses, and the under-resourced healthcare system, some observers — most notably the WHO — applauded Myanmar for managing to keep the recorded cases relatively low, while expressing caution and urging authorities to prepare for the worst (Oo, Tun et al. 2020).

The second wave of COVID-19 coincided with the campaign period for the national general election in late 2020. The opposition parties called for a postponement of the election, but the Union Electoral Commission went ahead, urging candidates to campaign online, banning campaigning in viral hotspots, and continuing the lockdown. Around this time, the government also initiated vaccination programs for health workers, high-ranking government officials, and politicians, set up testing facilities at town entrances, and introduced new travel restrictions to try and stop the spread of the virus. The regulations were introduced as directive orders, but they were incomplete and confusing (with no mention of protective equipment for instance), and very few campaigners followed them in the lead up to the election (Lidauer and Saphy 2021). When the second author of this chapter went to vote, he observed that members of the local COVID-19 Committee had different interpretations of quarantine and testing. The township administrator argued that travellers should not quarantine if their tests were negative, while the responsible doctor from the health authorities said the opposite. Coordination among these different departments was lacking. While the election was implemented, the infection rate rose. By 3 February — just days after the coup — the total number of infections was at an all-time high, with 140,927 positive cases and 3,160 COVID-19 related deaths.[6]

The coup interrupted the COVID-19 measures and updates, but after a four-month gap in which the military tried to regain control of the country, the junta started reporting on COVID-19 infections and deaths at the beginning of June 2021. After months of continued arrests and uprising, the third wave of COVID-19 was building rapidly, with infection rates at about 5,000 a day, gaining considerable momentum due to the political crisis. A massive number of health workers joined the Civil Disobedience Movement (CDM) — where civil servants refused to work for the junta — causing the Myanmar healthcare system to almost collapse, while the vaccination programme initiated by the NLD government came to an abrupt halt (Kyed 2021). With a lack of trust in the public healthcare sector and minimal available medical equipment to respond to the rapid increase in cases, many patients began treating themselves at home through a thriving black-market economy or consulting doctors privately (often online) — tactics that people challenged by poverty could obviously not afford. People were found dead in their beds after several days, testing positive for COVID-19 after autopsies, and bodies began piling up at crematoria in Yangon. In response, the military junta promised Yangon residents that they would build more crematoria so that people did not have to queue for cremation,[7] while international media were flooded with stories of oxygen shortages and claims that the military was deliberately withholding supplies.[8] As people struggled to access life-saving oxygen for infected relatives, the junta warned private producers not to distribute oxygen to individuals. For the first time, people in Myanmar began to conduct online funerals so that family and friends could say goodbye to the many people, who succumbed to the virus. By 11 October 2021, the total number of positive cases in Myanmar had reached 479,848 and 18,162 people had died with COVID-19 according to official reports. Actual numbers are likely much higher.

Prisons and COVID-19 — amplified vulnerabilities

The first reported case of COVID-19 in Myanmar prisons was detected at Tharrawaddy Central Prison in Bago Region on 23 October 2020. On 16 May 2020, the total number of infected prisoners were 157, plus two prison staff and one teacher. Three days later, Maubin Prison in Ayeyarwady Region reported that seven staff and 97 prisoners were COVID-positive, of which three were about to be released.[9] These new clusters were transmitted from the transfer of prisoners and staff from Tharrawaddy. In January 2021, the Myanmar Times reported the first official death of a 22-year-old prisoner who had tested positive.[10] Following the coup, the reports on COVID-19 cases in prisons were interrupted, but on 3 June 2021, Dr Khin Khin Gyi, an SAC health ministry official, said in an interview with VOA that a cluster of COVID-19 cases in Tamu township started with the infection of three prison inmates.[11] This highly negative synergy between COVID-19 and prisons was already forewarned.

Global media, academics, activists and international agencies have drawn attention to the particular vulnerability of prisoners during the COVID-19 pandemic (Novisky, Narvey et al. 2020). Prisoners very often suffer from underlying medical problems that increase their risk of getting infected, which are further aggravated by stigma, sub-standard conditions, overcrowding and the prioritization of security over care. Prisons risk becoming incubators of infectious diseases, which put detainees, staff and their families at direct risk, and may impact negatively on society as a whole (Ross 2013).

Based on her study of COVID-19 responses in United States prisons during the initial months of the pandemic, Marcum (2020) argues that imprisonment by its very nature places prisoners in constant contact in shared facilities, which makes the maintenance of appropriate distance and hygienic precautions almost impossible. Yet, health experts are adamant in warning prison managers against the urge to resort to crude isolation measures. The absence or reduction of meaningful social contact can cause serious mental health problems, increase conflicts, and undermine prisoners' right to contact with the outside world. Therefore, experts propose to pursue strategies that balance protection against the dangers of both viral exposure and social isolation: for instance, through the expansion of contactless social engagement and the application of both indoor and outdoor opportunities for safe contact in prison settings (Stewart, Cossar et al. 2020).

Some scholars, like Franco-Paredes et al., point out that prison institutions, in practice, are unable to adhere to the recommended isolation regimes and quarantine guidelines that will prevent the transmutation of the infection in a safe and humane way (2020). Thus, they argue that the depopulation of prisons is the only feasible way by which authorities in practice may achieve the required social distancing and protection of vulnerable people in the institutional settings.

Pearce, Vaisey et al. (2021), studied about 200 peer-reviewed and grey literature sources from across the globe to identify the guidance given to combat the virus in custodial settings and to rate the most prominent recommendations from jurisdictions as diverse as Brazil, Latvia, the Netherlands, and Pakistan. They found that scholars and expert stakeholders came up with a variety of suggestions as to how prisons might best respond to the pandemic due to the complex nature of COVID-19. This included, inter alia, remote and urgent court hearings, quarantine measures, and replacing of custodial sentencing with fines.

In sum, international experts and organisations generally advise prison administrations to seek to combat the virus by implementing diverse and smart strategies in a transparent manner based on evidence, rights, care, and ongoing monitoring, and as far as possible take the similar measures and respond to the same recommendations that are provided to the general population outside (UN 2020). Otherwise, the prison administrations' responses to the COVID-19 pandemic might turn prisons into epicentres of certain and widespread death — what Sanchez and colleagues (2020) refer to as a form of "necropolitics".

MPD responses — pardons, restrictions, and health

Prohibition of visits, emergency releases and protective health measures have been the most common initiatives taken by prison services across the world to respond to the threat of infection, and Myanmar is no exception

(Rapisarda and Byrne 2020). The foundational penal infrastructure of Myanmar was introduced and set up during British colonial rule. Myanmar prisons have been integral to the systematic persecution and silencing of political opposition and activists during military dictatorships since 1962 (Gaborit 2020). During the period of democratic thaw from 2010 to 2021, tentative openings towards piecemeal prison reforms were noted, while political imprisonment and human rights violations endured (Martin 2021). According to Human Rights Watch (HRW), there were 46 prisons and 50 labour camps across the country in 2021.[12] Soe Tint Naing, a deputy minister of Home Affairs told the Myanmar Times in May 2020 that these institutions had a capacity to confine up to 89,938 inmates, but currently housed 100,324 prisoners. He also estimated that the prison population would increase every month of 2020 with 1,000 to 1,200 prisoners.[13] There is a long tradition in Myanmar of dealing with overcrowding through mass pardoning of prisoners, which was also MPD's most prominent — though not officially acknowledged — response to the pandemic.

Pardons

A little less than 25,000 prisoners, or around a quarter of the prison population in Myanmar, were released on 17 April 2020 by the NLD government. As has been the case in previous mass pardons after the Buddhist New Year celebrations, the criteria for these releases were not publicly announced or explained. This lack of timely and credible information caused massive unrest among Myanmar prisoners in the aftermath of the previous pardon in 2019, as prisoners protested and complained that the pardons were arbitrary and not according to the rule of law (Gaborit and Jefferson 2019). Our own research indicates that prison superintendents may use their power to recommend pardons to reward prisoners who are close to staff.

International agencies including the World Health Organization, the Office of the High Commissioner for Human Rights, the United Nations Office on Drugs and Crime and the Joint United Nations Programme on HIV/AIDS strongly recommend release mechanisms as a key measure to protect prisoners against COVID-19 and reduce the pressures of forced proximity in overcrowded prisons, with a special focus on prioritizing the most vulnerable, the elderly and the sick (UN 2020). Easing the perennial burden of overcrowding in Myanmar prisons is commendable, but the opportunity to implement pardons transparently and with a view to enhance the protection of the most vulnerable prisoners was lost once again.

Raghavan (2021) notes similar paradoxes and ossified security thinking in the response to COVID-19 in Indian prisons. While the Indian Supreme Court strongly pushed state governments to release vulnerable prisoners, the prison authorities, and especially the lower courts, were reticent to release prisoners on health grounds. In practice, emphasis was put on the prisoners' offences rather than their vulnerability, and despite serious health problems and comorbidities prisoners serving time for serious offences were seldom considered eligible for release. As Raghavan concludes on the Indian case of COVID-19 pardons and releases:

> The pandemic provided an opportunity to the policy makers to undergo a paradigm shift with regard to viewing prisoners as human beings with individual needs, but one finds that they continued to be treated as categories that needed to be segmented and watched over, based on their perceived risk to society (Raghavan 2020, 396).

Moreover, to repeatedly address pressing penal problems by expelling prisoners en masse reveals and maintains a criminal justice system that imprisons many unnecessarily. The COVID-19 response is again no exception and draconian measures were quickly taken against people who did not obey the preventive emergency regulations. To control the transmission of disease, the NLD government introduced two new tough laws on the prevention of communicable diseases and disaster management, which in a matter of few months led to the prosecution of over 8000 people.[14] These harsh criminal charges and ensuing imprisonment obviously undermined the short-term benefits of the pardons.

Finally, the release of such a massive number of prisoners did not, in any way, enhance the capacities of the prison to deal with health risks. HRW noted that the number of released prisoners only landed the total population just above the official capacity. The prisons still do not have adequate facilities for social distancing and prisons continue to be ill-equipped to address the pressing needs — illustrated, for instance, by the number of prison doctors and nurses, which amount to approximately 30 doctors and 80 nurses for the entire prison population in Myanmar (HRW 2021).

Restrictions on visits

Many prison services across the world, including in Myanmar, quickly rushed to restrict or reduce family visits to decrease the risk of prisoners and staff being infected with COVID-19. Recent ethnographic research on Myanmar prisoners' contact with the outside world shows the enormous importance of prison visits (Jefferson and Martin 2020). Family visits provide vital foodstuff, medicines, and money that prisoners use in the informal economy to exchange for extra food, obtain lighter labour duties,[15] and better sleeping places, which are crucial for survival (Jefferson, Htaik et al. 2019). The COVID-19-related ban on visits are therefore very likely to have a severe negative impact on prisoners' very basic livelihood needs.

Research on prisoners' contact with the outside world generally shows that family visits are crucial for prisoners' emotional well-being (Duwe and Clark 2013). It is a clear recommendation from international human rights agencies that the protective restrictions on visits should be minimal and that alternative measures for keeping contact to the outside world should be ensured (see for instance CoE 2020; SPT 2020). In Myanmar, the total ban on telephone contact could, for instance, have been lifted, to allow prisoners emergency access to digital or telephone communication, but this opportunity was neglected.

Health

Researchers and activists alike emphasise that the pandemic can turn into a death sentence for prisoners, who are caught up in systems that do not take mitigation measures and protection seriously. As pointed out by Sanchez and colleagues above, prison health, therefore, should not be neglected by state authorities, but match strategically and financially the general national health response to this crisis (2020). Yet the lockdown restrictions, which the government instigated after the first cases of COVID-19 were detected, were not easy to follow in prisons with very limited capacity to respond adequately to health emergencies. U Aung Naing Pe, the head of Myingyan prison, told Frontier media that "the prison has only one doctor, who will decide whether a patient has symptoms similar to COVID-19".[16] Some prisons in remote areas do not even have health staff, resulting in prisoners living in abysmal health conditions. The depth and endurance of poor prison health facilities is vividly illustrated by testimonies of women former prisoners, who have reported about the unavailability of health professionals, insufficient care of reproductive health and HIV/AIDs sufferers, and inadequate responses to health emergencies (Jefferson and MyanmarResearchTeam 2022; MyanmarResearchTeam 2022).

The severe challenges to prison healthcare include absence of preventive measures such as monitoring, medical check-ups, and health education, which are particularly important in the face of a highly contagious viral disease like COVID-19. MPD announced on Facebook on 23 March 2020 that Myanmar prisons have been provided with personal care items and other health supplies, and that inmates had been educated about the virus in cooperation with the Health Department.[17] But released prisoners argued that the authorities did not provide adequate health awareness and that prison staff knew little about the prevention and control of communicable disease.[18]

News media reported on the distribution of ginger tea to prisoners — apparently to boost their immune systems.[19] This kind of information practice – akin to the discourses about Myanmar's natural resistance to COVID-19 due to the traditionally turmeric-rich diet, or the Chief Minister of Tanintharyi's encouragement to eat more onions (Tu-Maung and Venker 2020) — contributed to disinformation and vulnerability among Myanmar prisoners.

On 25 April 2020, MPD announced on its website that 290 washbasins would be put up to improve handwashing for Myanmar's approximately 100,000 prisoners. UN agencies also supported the MPD by raising awareness of the virus, and distributing masks and hand sanitizer. The MPD's Facebook showed prison personnel in protective gear spraying wards, toilets and visiting rooms with disinfectant. It also showed prison officers temperature-testing their colleagues, prisoners, visitors, and police officers coming from court. Procedures were also introduced to place newcomers in quarantine for 21 days in separate wards. Yet our interview material indicates that these precautions — for instance, the wearing of face masks — were unevenly applied from prison to prison.

In sum, the responses to the COVID-19 crisis in Myanmar prisons feature some novel, commendable and immediate actions, but more profoundly, these actions were stunted by a perennial penal crisis of securitization, short-term thinking, and neglect — issues that have only compounded since the military coup.

IMPLICATIONS OF THE COUP

As noted above, the MPD took a number of steps to respond to the virus, but these measures were insufficient and hampered by an authoritarian impulse. The 'war-on-approach' to deal with society's problems – the war on terror, the war on drugs, the war on cash, etc. – unfortunately also latches on to 'the war on corona'. These martial discourses tend to play power even more firmly into the hands of authoritarian actors and short-term tactical rationales of controlling the immediate threat (cf Warburg and Jensen 2018). Yet, the vast and seemingly indiscriminate spread of COVID-19 also held an initial potential to boost solidarity and long-term thinking. The fact that both rich and poor across the globe – and in this case people inside and outside prison walls – faced a common threat could ideally have spurred a shared interests in addressing underlying problems strategically and innovatively. COVID-19 might have motivated authorities to enhance prison transparency, letting go of tendencies to always prioritise security and engaging in constructive dialogues to develop with concerned stakeholders instead of suspicion (Oo and Martin 2020).

A little less than two years after the start of the pandemic, we have learned that this was not the case. On a global scale, COVID-19 seems only to have deepened inequalities and excluded poor and marginalised populations even further. In the case of Myanmar, the coup has turned the 'war on corona' into an unfolding 'war on the people'. A report by UNDP documents the compounding negative shocks of COVID-19 and the coup — especially for the poor — which is setting human development in Myanmar back to 2005-levels, quashing almost 20 years of significant progress in poverty reduction (UNDP 2021). Since the 1 February 2021, the potential to deal sensibly and adequately with the virus in Myanmar prisons has been replaced by disregard and aggravation.

The mass arrests of protesters, politicians, journalists and civil society activists in the wake of the coup have worsened overcrowding dramatically. As we write this chapter, more than 10,000 people have been arrested for opposing the military coup and the arrests are increasing day by day as reported by the Assistance Association for Political Prisoners (AAPP).[20] According to an ex-prisoner who was released in May 2021, the number of incarcerated peoples on criminal charges also continues to grow. He told us:

> The prison is also fully packed. For example, I stayed in ward no.5. and there were 160 prisoners in it. And when I moved to a separate ward,

there were also lots of people there — approximately 160 as well. Because I worked outside [the wards in the common areas], I know there are lots of people coming in every day. I think there are 30 to 40 people coming into prison every day, from Monday to Friday.

When people are arrested, they are taken to either police cells or military camps for interrogation. COVID-19 testing is only done at the gate of the prisons. In some prisons, COVID-19 testing does not exist. One ex-prisoner told us that his hometown used to be one of the strictest in compliance with COVID-19 regulations. But since the coup, prisoners no longer discussed COVID-19. In public consciousness, and among prison actors more specifically, the pandemic was displaced by the coup, though the threat of the virus became no less dangerous or acute.

A recent article on post-coup imprisonment argues that:

[t]hough Myanmar has gone through several lockdowns to prevent major COVID-19 outbreaks, and overcrowded prisons across the country have taken precautions to prevent the disease from entering their premises, none of these precautions were taken when the protesters were detained (Gaborit 2021:54).

A woman prisoner, who was released from Insein prison about a month after the coup, was interviewed by one of our researcher colleagues confirmed this point:

Insein Prison did not have any test kit to detect COVID-19 when we came there. They did not even provide masks and soap. I learnt that there had been so many washbasins in Insein Prison posted by the prison department before the military coup. After the military coup, there was not any basin for hand washing. Instead, the prison staff provided three 20-liter water bottles for each inmate. The label outside the bottle said "Pure Water" for drinking, but inside the bottle, the water was impure, and I saw algae mixed in with water. The algae looked as if it was a green mountain we could climb….

She continued:

Besides, they put so many prisoners in the small room. Some old political activist women did not have masks [but were] sitting and sleeping closely [in the ward]. For these poor conditions, our 'generation-z prisoners' were so worried about COVID-19 infection. When our family members came to the prison, we called for masks and hand sanitizer to [give to] these old women and poor prisoners.

Information about these conditions remains scarce, but one of the few sources that has retained some level of access to Myanmar prisons after the coup are prisoners' defence lawyers. Despite the illegality of the coup and the systematic violation of rule and law and access to justice, the junta maintains a paradoxical attempt to uphold a veneer of legality to its actions. This entails an ensuing need to implement trials through special courts that are set up inside prison compounds. In this adverse judicial environment, defence lawyers are nevertheless able to carve out a space for representing their detained clients and, to some extent, meet them, pass on information to and from families and get an idea of how they are doing. One such lawyer had this to say about the impact of COVID-19 to local media.[21]

> Even on a normal day, the health system is very poor in Insein Prison compared to outside. The condition is so bad. With the current situation, we do not know how many are infected with COVID-19. It is even more worrisome for people in the prison. We might be able to help each other outside, but it is not possible in the prison. The situation is very worrisome for people in the prison. [authors' translation]

In August 2021, at the peak of the third wave of the virus, the media was overflowing with reports of well-known detained political activists dying from COVID-19, while contradictory information about infection rates, causes of death and vaccine-coverage from the authorities dripped out on Facebook and junta-controlled media outlets. MPD claims to have set up a system of testing and quarantining newly admitted prisoners and blames external factors like the court hearings and escorting police officers for the COVID-19 cases in prisons, rather than internal mismanagement.[22] Yet it seems certain that the combination of overcrowding and suppression has caused COVID-19 to "surge" in Myanmar prisons after the coup, as HRW put it in August 2021.[23]

The strikes of civil servants, including health workers and an unknown number of prison staff, have undoubtedly further contributed to the limited capacity of prisons to respond to COVID-19. A source close to prison authorities told 74 Media[24] on 4 August 2021 that:

> The COVID-19 situation is getting serious in the prison. All the prisoners seem to have lost their sense of smell. All of them. And the treatment of prisoners is out of question. They cannot treat even the staff. Staff are asked to rest for half a day, and they are then forced to work again. Even though the staff are sick, they cannot get leave. Not only prisoners, but also the staff do not get their rights fully respected" [authors' translation].

The frustration of staff is reported to have played a part in the prison protests of July and August 2021. According to Myanmar Now[25] a group of inmates at Insein Prison staged a protest on 23 July, chanting anti-junta slogans for one hour. The chants, which were heard by a resident who lives close to the prison, started at 7 AM: "The fall of the military dictatorship, our cause! Our cause! Boycott, Boycott! The revolution must succeed! Return power to the public!". AAPP stated that they had heard from one of the detainees that the protesters demanded access to healthcare since many people inside the prison were getting sick from COVID-19. According to a lawyer who spoke to Myanmar Now, staff also joined the protest to express their grievances over the COVID restrictions that prohibited them to leave the prison compound (though this could not be verified).

Later that week, state media claimed that nearly 4,300 prisoners had been released to curb COVID-19[26] following the announcement of plans to drop charges for petty crimes (like theft and prostitution) that were handed down before the coup. There is reason to believe that this release had something to do with the junta trying to improve its image concerning prison conditions following the protests in Insein Prison. On state television, viewers were treated to images of junta home affairs minister Lieutenant General Soe Htut touring Naypyitaw prison in the capital, with images of prisoners exercising and standing on parade.[27] Social media users were quick to point out that none of them were wearing masks or practicing social distancing, and that weak responses to the COVID-19 threat in prisons – evidently displayed during the minister's propaganda visit – sparked the Insein protest.

As noted above, the impulse to release prisoners to momentarily solve perennial problems of prison overcrowding has a long tradition in Myanmar. Unsurprisingly, the SAC also released 23,184 prisoners from prisons during the 2021 New Year pardons, trying, we presume, to display sovereign might and mercy. In addition to the inherent and persisting paradoxes of this practice, this round of pardoning was met with deep public suspicion. On the one hand, the junta's pardoning exercise was seen to clear carceral space for political activists and protesters. On the other hand, the public also feared that the junta used the pardons to coax, coerce and arm groups of newly released prisoners to create chaos in the streets and attack protesters. This was apparently the case in earlier uprisings, though we could not confirm this information.

The deep lack of trust in the junta's pardoning practices and objectives was pointed out by the Executive Director of AAPP, U Aung Myo Kyaw, in an interview with RFA/Burmese.[28] He urged the released prisoners to support the public good by participating in the opposition to the military and said:

> The release is nothing more than a showcase in the face of the international community that prisoners are free, or it can be [a military tactic] to scare the public. It is like they are engaging in psychic warfare to scare the public not to go out, I think. I would like to request the released prisoners to participate as the people desire and contribute to the people's struggle in every possible way [authors' translation]

Our interlocutors also note how COVID-19 after the coup affects not only the grand penal politics of pardoning, but also mundane everyday prison life in many peculiar and inconsistent ways. One ex-prisoner for instance told us:

> If prisoners are seen not wearing the masks, they will be beaten and tortured. That is the problem. So, prisoners have to look for used masks which other fellow prisoners have thrown away. For them, this is gold. Some prisoners will wash the masks again and again.

However, the burden of not having soap can be avoided, because it cannot be regulated. He continued:

> Soap is not the problem. Whether or not the prisoners have washed their hands, it is not important in the prison. Because the staff cannot check their hands. Even if the prisoners don't wash their hands, they can just lie.

And the imposition of rules and regulations can be quite different from one prison to the other. One ex-prisoner from a small, rural town, said that prisoners and staff including army officers never wear masks. During the interrogation army officers and he would simply sit opposite each other by the table without wearing masks.

But some rules are as per tradition diligently observed in disregard for the health risks. One ex-prisoner for instance told us how all prisoners must recite the prison rules every day. "Whenever we recite the rules", he said, "we are not allowed to wear the masks. We must take them off. If our voices crack or are not fully audible, we will be trouble."

CONCLUSION: CRISIS IS CONTEXT

In this chapter, we have illustrated the compounding negative effects that the COVID-19 health crisis and the political crisis of the military coup have had on Myanmar prisons. By way of conclusion, we want to consider a theoretical perspective on the analysis of prison life in such situations of seemingly unique, acute, and intense crises. This perspective is developed by anthropologist Henrik Vigh, who argues that scholars, who seek to understand the lives of structurally violated, socially marginalised, and poor people, should approach the issue as 'crisis as context' (Vigh 2008).

Based on long-term fieldwork among marginalised urban youth in Guinea Bissau, Vigh argues that crisis situations, which his interlocutors are caught up in, do not represent a distinct rupture from otherwise 'normal' situations of balance, peace, and prosperity. Crisis is not episodic. It is rather endemic. Volatility and violations dominate the everyday life of the vulnerable people who Vigh encountered. Crisis is not something that they live through, but something that they live in. In that sense, crisis is a chronic condition that can be seen as the very context of social life, as the normal state of affairs. The fact that crisis is ever present does not mean that people passively accept uncertainty and insecurity. When crisis is context, people still reflect on their lives, adapt, and adjust to make the best out of things. Yet, people typically do so in pragmatic and provisional ways and with a view to generate some momentary semblance of order, within or alongside the perpetual situation of disorder that pervade their environment. Crisis as context, Vigh argues, "allows us to see how people struggle to find their bearings, gain a sense of control and balance, and navigate their life through difficult environments...revealing both the brutality of social forces and resilience of [social] agents" (ibid, 20).

We suggest that the prison in Myanmar is a context of enduring and perpetual crisis. It is both a principled crisis of legitimacy and dignity and a practical crisis of overcrowding and institutional failure. Scarcity, volatility, exclusion, and violence are part of everyday prison life in Myanmar, before, during and after COVID-19 and the military coup. Drawing on Vigh's "crisis as context" perspective offers a sobering and important dimension to understanding how both COVID-19 and the coup affect prison life in Myanmar. The immediate viral and political effects of both crises are folded into the context of a deeper, underlying carceral crisis in Myanmar which routinely puts prison actors at risk and in harm's way. Crisis is, to a great extent, business as usual. Disorder is the order of the day, which prompts prisoners, relatives, staff, lawyers, and other prison actors to appropriate the challenges of COVID-19 and coup in pragmatic and provisional ways, which resonate with their already volatile and violative everyday life. Indeed, the actual and practical responses of authorities to both COVID-19 and the coup are built on already established practices of governance and survival in Myanmar prison settings. How this pans out will need to be explored through further empirical research, but based on our previous research experience, we suggest that some key features may be quite prominent. We mention four below.

Firstly, COVID-19 and the coup are likely to latch on to underlying problems and processes of governance and reinforce systems of economic privilege around prisoner leadership structures. These structures are known as the *tanzee* system, whereby staff outsource authority to powerful prisoners, who distribute resources, manage access to basic services (including health) and discipline fellow prisoners (MyanmarResearchTeam 2022; Martin and Jefferson under review). Secondly, both COVID-19 and the coup are also likely to worsen the routinised depreciation of equality — including gender and minority concerns — which is integral to the carceral crisis in Myanmar (MyanmarResearchTeam 2022). Thirdly, the tenuous boundary-making between the prison institutions and the outside world and the ensuing policing of information, resources, and people going in and out, is also a core feature of carceral volatility that is accelerated by COVID-19 and the coup. Fourthly, the two compounding crises are likely to activate some of the enduring fault-lines between Myanmar prison actors. The tensions between criminal and political prisoners, and between prison staff and military officers will re-emerge as these groups seek to grapple with the challenges of COVID-19 and the coup.

Credible observers, like the AAPP, state that torture and violations after the coup not only display a continuity of the military's history of atrocity but appear even more brutal than before.[29] To argue that the crises of COVID-19 and the coup become dimensions of a grander carceral crisis is not an attempt to disregard the impact of these emergencies and their effects on both prisoners and the wider civilian population. It is rather an effort to register, as Didier Fassin points out in his analysis of COVID-19 in French detention centres, that "the health crisis did not provoke the crisis in detention centres, but instead uncovered their appalling ordinary reality" (2020: 614). Thus, the analytical perspective of crisis as context unearths the ordinary reality of imprisonment that the current crises are folded into and emphasises that the chronic crisis of imprisonment is likely to endure, unless genuine reforms are put on future agendas. The carceral crisis will persist after COVID-19 and after the coup and the knowledge, solidarity and concern gendered by the present loudness of ongoing atrocities and deprivations should be retained and directed towards changing the context of people deprived of their liberty in Myanmar.

Notes

1. U Win is a pseudonym. The identity of the second author is known to the first author.
2. See: https://twitter.com/rapporteurun/status/1403071954287050753 (accessed 3 May 2022).
3. See for instance: https://www.fidh.org/en/issues/human-rights-defenders/myanmar-armed-attacked-and-detention-of-man-zar-myay-mon (accessed 3 May 2022).
4. See: https://covid19.who.int/ (accessed 19 May 2022)
5. See: https://www.myanmar-now.org/en/news/myanmar-announces-first-coronavirus-cases (accessed 3 May 2022).
6. See: https://www.facebook.com/MinistryOfHealthMyanmar/photos/pcb.4184852494877357/4184733614889245/ (accessed 3 May 2022).
7. See: https://www.irrawaddy.com/news/burma/myanmar-junta-to-build-new-crematoriums-as-COVID-19-death-toll-soars.html (accessed 3 May 2022).
8. See: https://www.nytimes.com/2021/07/15/world/asia/myanmar-covid-oxygen.html (accessed 3 May 2022).
9. See: https://burma.irrawaddy.com/news/2020/10/28/232444.html?__cf_chl_jschl_tk__=pmd_7XOcQxBPvE1cFQvXK.ia3CRbcu8ogfciz3JxUtTOek4-1635920272-0-gqNtZGzNAiWjcnBszQl9 (accessed 3 May 2022).
10. See: https://www.mmtimes.com/news/55-more-inmates-get-covid-19-bago.html (accessed 3 May 2022).
11. See: https://burmese.voanews.com/a/myanmar-COVID-dr-khin-khin-gyi/5909684.html?fbclid=IwAR01fRG-SR1TZoyLwjLyjzT8Kt2Vfax8xUFkhgh1yXuMR5AQ6JJAr85gsC8.html (accessed 3 May 2022).
12. See: https://www.hrw.org/news/2020/04/03/myanmar-reduce-prison-populations-limit-covid-19 (accessed 3 May 2022).
13. See: https://www.mmtimes.com/news/myanmar-prison-population-grows-1200-month.html
14. See: https://www.irrawaddy.com/news/burma/8000-citizens-prosecuted-myanmar-covid-19-breaches.html (accessed 3 May 2022).
15. For a broader discussion and analysis of prison labour in Myanmar see the analyses of women prisoners' labour practices (MyanmarResearchTeam 2022), prisoner self-governance of labour distribution (Martin and Jefferson under review) and the colonial legacies of Myanmar labour camp system (Jefferson and Martin under review).

16 See: https://www.frontiermyanmar.net/en/overcrowded-prisons-battle-COVID-19-with-ginger-water-handbasins-as-authorities-consider-early-release-plan/ (accessed 3 May 2022).
17 See: https://www.facebook.com/myanmarprisonsdepartment (accessed 3 May 2022).
18 See: https://www.irrawaddy.com/news/burma/myanmar-prisons-educate-inmates-coronavirus-work-prevention.html (accessed 3 May 2022).
19 See: https://www.frontiermyanmar.net/en/overcrowded-prisons-battle-COVID-19-with-ginger-water-handbasins-as-authorities-consider-early-release-plan/ (accessed 3 May 2022).
20 See: the daily updates of deaths and detentions at AAPP I Assistance Association for Political Prisoners (aappb.org)
21 See: https://www.myanmar-now.org/mm/news/7825 (accessed 3 May 2022).
22 See: https://www.rfa.org/burmese/news/insein-prison-COVID-19-07162021040517.html
23 See: https://www.hrw.org/news/2021/08/16/covid-19-surge-myanmars-prisons (accessed 20 May 2022).
24 See: https://www.the74media.com/?p=16206 (accessed 3 May 2022).
25 See: https://www.myanmar-now.org/en/news/prisoners-stage-anti-dictatorship-protest-inside-insein-prison (accessed 20 May 2022).
26 See: https://www.myanmar-now.org/en/news/more-than-4000-released-as-COVID-19-cases-surge-in-myanmars-prisons (accessed 3 May 2022).
27 See: https://www.myanmar-now.org/mm/news/7597 (accessed 3 May 2022).
28 See: https://www.rfa.org/burmese/news/nationwide-prisoners-released-02122021050910.html (accessed 3 May 2022).
29 See: https://apnews.com/article/myanmar-torture-military-prisons-insein-abuse-390fe5b49337be82ce91639e93e0192f (accessed 3 May 2022).

References

AAPP (2016). *Prison conditions in Burma and the potential for prison reform.* Mae Sot, Assistance Association for Political Prisoners (Burma).

CoE (2020). *COVID-19 Related Statement by the Members of the Council for Penological Co-operation Working Group* (PC-CP WG). Council of Europe, Council of Europe.

Deshpande, A., K. T. Hnin and T. Traill (2020). "Myanmar's response to the COVID-19 pandemic".

Duwe, G. and V. Clark (2013). "Blessed Be the Social Tie That Binds: The Effects of Prison Visitation on Offender Recidivism". *Criminal Justice Policy Review* 24(3): 271-296.

Fassin, D. (2020). "Hazardous confinement during the COVID-19 pandemic: The fate of migrants detained yet nondeportable". *Journal of Human Rights* 19(5): 613-623.

Franco-Paredes, C., K. Jankousky, J. Schultz, J. Bernfeld, K. Cullen and N. e. a. Quan (2020). "COVID-19 in jails and prisons: A neglected infection in a marginalized population". *PLoS Negl Trop Dis* 14 (6).

Gaborit, L. and A. M. Jefferson (2019). "Rioting for Rule of Law – Prison Amnesties and Riots in Myanmar". *Tea Circle - A Forum for New Perspectives on Burma/Myanmar*.

Gaborit, L. S. (2020). *We are Like Water in Their Hands: Experiences of Imprisonment in Myanmar*. PhD, Roskilde University.

Gaborit, L. S. (2021). "Dancing with the Junta Again: Mistreatment of Women Activists by the Tatmadaw Following the Military Coup in Myanmar." *Anthropology in Action* 28(2): 51-56.

HRW. 2021. "Myanmar: Reduce Prison Populations to Limit COVID-19." *Human Rights Watch*. Available at https://www.hrw.org/news/2020/04/03/myanmar-reduce-prison-populations-limit-covid-19 (accessed 10 December 2022).

ILO (2020). *COVID-19: Impact on migrant workers and country response in Thailand*. Bangkok, International Labour Organization Country Office for Thailand, Cambodia and Lao PDR.

Jefferson, A. M., G. Caracciolo, J. Kørner and N. Nordberg (2021). "Amplified Vulnerabilities and Reconfigured Relations: COVID-19, Torture Prevention and Human Rights in the Global South". *State Crime Journal* 10(1): 147-169.

Jefferson, A. M., U. T. Htaik, N. N. Aung, E. Cakal, K. L. Naing, A. L. Oo and T. M. Martin (2019). *Prisoners' contact with the outside world in Myanmar*. Copenhagen, Justice for All and DIGNITY.

Jefferson, A. M. and T. M. Martin (2020). "Connecting and Disconnecting: Exploring Prisoners' Relations with the Outside World in Myanmar". *The Cambridge Journal of Anthropology* 38(1): 105-122.

Jefferson, A. M. and T. M. Martin (under review). "Imperial Carcerality and Legacies of Penal Duress in Myanmar". *Theoretical Criminology*.

Jefferson, A. M. and MyanmarResearchTeam (2022). "Gender and Imprisonment in Contemporary Myanmar". *Gender, Criminalisation, Imprisonment and Human Rights in Southeast Asia*, edited by A. M. Jefferson and S. Jeffries. Bingley, Emerald Publishing.

Kyed, H. M. (2021) "The military junta in Myanmar weaponizes COVID-19 against its opponents".

Lidauer, M. and G. Saphy (2021). *Running Elections under Stringent Covid-19 Measures in Myanmar*. Stockholm, International Institute for Democracy and Electoral Assistance.

Marcum, C. D. (2020). "American Corrections System Response to COVID-19: an Examination of the Procedures and Policies Used in Spring 2020." *American Journal of Criminal Justice*, 1-10.

Martin, T. M. (2021). "The politics of prison air: Breath, smell, and wind in Myanmar prisons." *Punishment & Society* 23(4): 478-496.

Martin, T. M. and A. M. Jefferson (under review). "When prisoners are staff: On proxy governance and the distribution of penal power in (post)colonial prisons." *Prison Officers: International Perspectives on Prison Work*. H. Arnold, M. Maycock and R. Ricciardelli. Camden, Palgrave MacMillan.

Myanmar Research Team (2022). "Catching Flies: How Women are Exploited through Prison Work in Myanmar." *Gender, Criminalisation, Imprisonment and Human Rights in Southeast Asia*, edited by A. M. Jefferson and S. Jeffries. Bingley, Emerald Publishing.

Novisky, M. A., C. S. Narvey and D. C. Semenza (2020). "Institutional Responses to the COVID-19 Pandemic in American Prisons." *Victims & Offenders* 15(7-8): 1244-1261.

Oo, A. L. and T. M. Martin (2020) "The COVID-19 Situation in Myanmar Prisons: Many Grave Risks and a New Opportunity?" *Tea Circle - A Forum for New Perspectives on Burma/Myanmar*.

Oo, M. M., N. A. Tun, X. Lin and D. E. L.-P. III (2020). "COVID-19 in Myanmar: Spread, actions and opportunities for peace and stability." *Journal of Global Health* 10(2).

Pearce, L. A., A. Vaisey, C. Keen, L. Calais-Ferreira, J. A. Foulds, J. T. Young, L. Southalan, R. Borschmann, R. Gray, S. Stürup-Toft and S. A. Kinner (2021). "A rapid review of early guidance to prevent and control COVID-19 in custodial settings." *Health & Justice* 9(1): 27.

Raghavan, V. (2021). "Prisons and the pandemic: the panopticon plays out." *Journal of Social and Economic Development* 23(2): 388-397.

Rapisarda, S. S. and J. M. Byrne (2020). "An Examination of COVID-19 Outbreaks in Prisons and Jails Throughout Asia." *Victims & Offenders* 15(7-8): 948-958.

Ross, M. (2013). *Health and Health Promotion in Prisons*. London, Routledge.

Sánchez, A., L. Simas, V. Diuana and B. Larouze (2020). "COVID-19 in prisons: an impossible challenge for public health?" *Cad Saude Publica* 36(5).

SPT, U. (2020). "Advice of the Subcommittee on Prevention of Torture to States Parties and National Preventive Mechanisms relating to the Coronavirus Pandemic (adopted on 25th March 2020)." Available at https://www.ohchr.org/Documents/HRBodies/OPCAT/AdviceStatePartiesCoronavirusPandemic2020.pdf (accessed 15 March 2022).

Stewart, A., R. Cossar and M. Stoové (2020). "The response to COVID-19 in prisons must consider the broader mental health impacts for people in prison." *Australian & New Zealand Journal of Psychiatry* 54(12): 1227-1228.

Tu-Maung, N. and M. Venker (2020) "Wavering at the Turning Point: Myanmar's response to COVID-19 in March 2020." *Tea Circle - A Forum for New Perspectives on Burma/Myanmar.*

UN. (2020). "UNODC, WHO, UNAIDS and OHCHR joint statement on COVID-19 in prisons and other closed settings (13 May)." Available at https://www.who.int/news/item/13-05-2020-unodc-who-unaids-and-ohchr-joint-statement-on-covid-19-in-prisons-and-other-closed-settings (accessed 15 March 2022).

UNDP (2021). COVID-19, *Coup d'Etat and Poverty: Compounding Negative Shocks and Their Impact on Human Development in Myanmar.*

Vigh, H. (2008). "Crisis and Chronicity: Anthropological Perspectives on Continuous Conflict and Decline." *Ethnos* 73(1): 5-24.

Warburg, A. B. and S. Jensen (2018). "Policing the war on drugs and the transformation of urban space in Manila." *Environment and Planning D: Society and Space* 38(3): 399-416.

III

A State in Crisis

5

MYANMAR UNDER CONTESTED MILITARY RULE

Nicola S. Williams

Since the February 2021 coup, the Myanmar junta, known as the State Administrative Council (SAC), has tried to embed its government and exert control over the population through administration, organised violence, and warfare (Callahan 2004). In response, a revolutionary movement has emerged contesting the military's legitimacy at national levels and resisting their authority at sub-national levels using violent and non-violent tactics.

This paper provides a contemporary snapshot of contested military rule in Myanmar more than a year after the coup d'etat, using evidence up to August 2022. First, it charts Myanmar's reordered political context. Second, it analyses overlapping realms of national contest over who has the legitimacy to govern between the junta and parallel National Unity Government (NUG), and the historically contested structure of the Myanmar state with new movements for democratic federalism. Third, it analyses the mix of new and old conflict dynamics, including waves of guerrilla warfare across once-peaceful areas in the Bamar heartland. Fourth, it introduces new evidence to examine changes to subnational contests for authority, including new practices of local governance by resistance forces, the post-coup expansion of territory for ethnic resistance organisations (EROs), and contested administration by the junta.

In this disrupted era, resistance to military rule and coercion has a new cast of characters and multi-ethnic alliances. While the military has consolidated and restructured control over the central state apparatus, this paper argues that subnational and local authority has become more complex and contested than ever before, including in the Bamar heartland. The post-coup political landscape is one of altered power struggles, revolutionary contests, civil disobedience, and increased conflict intensity which shows no signs of abating.

METHODOLOGY

The new realities of Myanmar's post-coup environment provide unique security challenges for international and local researchers. This paper draws on new qualitative research conducted in Yangon Region, Sagaing Region, Rakhine State, Mon State, and Northern Shan State by Myanmar researchers between November 2021 and February 2022. A template of case study questions was prepared and shared with researchers who conducted semi-structured key informant interviews in Myanmar language with known contacts in different sites. Much of the research was done through safe electronic practices to avoid meeting in public places. For their safety, the researchers are anonymous. The author wishes to acknowledge their essential contribution to this work. This paper presents selected case studies on sub-national contests and additional data from key informant interviews throughout the chapter. Other evidence and analysis are drawn from secondary sources, including political science literature, area studies journals, news articles, reports on Myanmar by research institutes, and online media to offer a rich empirical narrative on Myanmar under contested military rule. Direct observations from the author's experience working on peace and reform agendas between 2015–2020 are included in the analysis.

CONTEXT

Until 2011, for almost five decades, Myanmar was run by a series of military regimes that earned the country a 'pariah' status and made it synonymous with anti-democratic clampdowns and wilfully inept economic management (Farrelly and Win 2016, 38; Turnell 2010, 21). There are many narratives about what drove the military's retreat from its dominant political role towards a hybrid military-civilian system of government with multi-party electoral democracy. Whether it was to hedge the influence of China, deal with the country's economic woes, part of an effort to recover from Cyclone Nargis, or incorporate rather than annihilate some of the resistance elements, no-one knows which pull factor had the most strength. Scholars have long argued that past sanctions from the international community had little effect (Taylor 2013). What is clear is that this former political and economic transition was a long-term plan by the junta involving the design of the military's 2008 Constitution.

The first installation of a new form of government under the 2008 Constitution framework involved green-uniformed military men de-robing and donning *longyis* as civilian politicians in the military-backed United Solidarity and Development Party (USDP). They went on to implement an impressive slew of reforms,[1] many of which have been reversed since the 2021 coup. The second phase followed 'free and fair' elections in 2015, which ushered in the National League for Democracy (NLD) as the governing partner of the military. Celebrated as a historic step 'forward' in the transition from military dictatorship, many outside observers and political analysts, spellbound by the moment, imagined the next phase would be one of continuous linear change in the same direction, albeit complex. The governing period, however, was marred by toxic civil-military power-sharing, some security policy alignment between the civilian and military power centres (including aspects of the violent crackdown against Rohingya communities), a sluggish pursuit of reforms available to the NLD (there were, of course, limits), and bullish rejection by the military of many proposals for structural change by the NLD or the country's numerous ethnic groups (see Chambers et al. 2020).

Much of the analysis diagnosing the coup suggests an elite spat between General Min Aung Hlaing and Aung San Suu Kyi surrounding the 2020 election results, which the military deemed to be fraudulent. Given the fragile and often fraught power-sharing relationship between military and civilian leaders, it is possible this dynamic contributed to the crescendo toward the coup. However, in this chapter, I will resist speculating about 'what happened' or attempt to read the institutionalised mindset of military men, and focus instead on what is observable. While the transition from military dictatorship to a civil-military system took over a decade of preparation, the return to military rule appears to be merely a few months of planning at the elite level. Indeed, many USDP politicians and military leaders believed the party was set to successfully contest the November 2020 election, which led to a huge defeat for the military-backed party and a supermajority for the NLD (Nitta and Htway 2020).[2] The military was also woefully unprepared for the scale of resistance that followed their takeover.

Following the February 1 coup and months of unrest, in August 2021 Myanmar's junta institutionalised its rule as a "caretaker government" with General Min Aung Hlaing at its head backed by a hard-line military faction. The approach to military rule by the Commander-in-Chief cherry-picks from the dictatorship transitions of 1962 to 1988 and the Thai government's approach to transitioning from coup to governance. While the 2021 coup is arguably not ideologically driven, it resonates with the previous junta's post-1988 positioning of the military as the ideology when it replaced the socialist system.[3] Yet this coup-maker and former General Than Shwe have many differences as leaders. General Than Shwe was respected by his peers for having foresight and a vision that soldiers and senior military figures could get behind. Whereas General Min Aung Hlaing is known to be a reactionary figure and widely unpopular among those around him.[4]

In the face of mounting coup and conflict costs — mass protests, violent resistance, wars on multiple fronts, the death of civilians and its soldiers, a crumbling economy, and new sanctions — the new junta's zero-sum game speaks to its raison d'etre to rule at all costs to maintain national unity.[5] A veneer of constitutional and legal limits continues to shape the junta and General Min Aung Hlaing's public performance, much of which is posturing to the military itself. The SAC Chairman's plan outlines that elections will be held in 2023, which would see a return of the military-designed unitary system of civil-military power-sharing but with the NLD wiped off the political map and the electoral system likely changed from first-past-the-post to proportional representation, which is now seen to favour the NLD with its thumping victories. The current debate around proportional representation is not new, and as Robert Taylor (2013) highlights, goes back to the 2008 Constitution convention process.

The SAC has consolidated and reshaped central control over the state apparatus, but its control over subnational governance remains contested and varied, an argument I will make throughout this paper.

The Civil Disobedience Movement (CDM) of striking civil servants has gutted the state apparatus and many of its services. What remains of the state is focused nearly entirely on regime survival with the police, courts, municipal services, and the historically coercive tool for population control, the General Administration Department (GAD). The junta's caretaker government has also attempted to replace the elected national and subnational parliaments and government roles right down to the local ward and village tract levels, inserting military appointments into all administrative layers. Not all such appointments have been possible, and scores of positions across wards and village tracts remain vacant across the country due to resistance and new security challenges (Arnold 2021a).[6]

In opposition to military rule, the Committee Representing the Pyidaungsu Hluttaw (CRPH), the elected Myanmar parliament, and a parallel National Unity Government (NUG) formed. While the NUG is campaigning for bilateral recognition, no country has formally recognised the NUG as the government of Myanmar. On the one hand, most countries cited policies on recognising states, not governments or regime changes (Joint Standing Committee on Foreign Affairs, Defence and Trade 2021). On the other hand, western countries are walking a diplomatic tightrope attempting to reframe from legitimising the junta while maintaining an in-country diplomatic presence. Several western countries have also recently placed new Ambassador positions on hold, downgrading the diplomatic status of the highest representative in-country (RAF 2022).

The NUG's goal is to remove the military from politics and install a 'genuine' federal democracy. To dislodge the junta, disrupt its ability to govern, and build alternative services, tactics include the civil disobedience movement (CDM) involving striking civil servants — of which there are estimated to be 400,000 — boycotts of taxes and revenue payments to the state, creating local governance committees, and armed resistance through People's Defence Forces (PDFs) (The Irrawaddy 2021a). The NUG is also supporting dialogue and drafting a federal charter via the National Unity Consultative Council (NUCC), a body including exiled MPs, members of the NUG, Ethnic Resistance Organisations (EROs), General Strike Committees, civil society, youth organisations, and other anti-regime groups. Despite ongoing divisions, the council aims to allow for consensus-building around decision-making on federalism (Tun and Thuzar 2022).

EROs are central actors in Myanmar's complex conflict landscape, with some fighting for more than seventy years for autonomy and federalism.[7] Among EROs, the support given to the NUG is not homogenous. Some EROs are aligned with the NUG's resistance movement, including the Karen National Union (KNU) and the Kachin Independence Organisation (KIO). Others remain reluctant to join what they see as a Bamar-dominated initiative given the inclusion of many NLD officials, such as the Arakan Army (AA), and the Ta'ang National Liberation Army (TNLA). Other groups such as the United Wa State Army (UWSA) continue to pursue their goals unilaterally or via other armed group coalitions. How, and if, the NUG can bring together a broader coalition of EROs is critical for building a revolutionary movement with stronger military capacity behind goals of democratic federalism.

Beyond the known armed groups and politicians, a new cast of characters play a critical role in the revolutionary movement. This includes youth, labour unions, neighbourhood strike committees, and the CDM collectives within government agencies of education, health, and the Central Bank. Like Myanmar's '88 Generation, youth are integral to all phases of the revolutionary movement, from leading protests across the country to developing people's defence forces and local armed groups. Indeed, many young people have taken up the use of violence to fight for a different political vision to military dictatorship. Some new youth-initiated armed groups have since been integrated into the NUG's armed resistance, while others remain separate. Prominent among the many resistance groups are women leaders who have been at the forefront of protests, armed responses, and underground social services.

Since the coup, media and policy debates have focused on whether Myanmar is, or is becoming, a 'failed state'. Given the fuzziness around this concept, critical conceptual distinctions are needed between *functional* failure and *institutional* collapse, with entire state collapse being a rare event (Milliken and Krause 2002). Considering scenarios against a Weberian standard of how the state *should* function – for instance, to maintain a monopoly of the use of force, exercise control over sovereign territory, maintain a functioning market, or provide social welfare — Myanmar can be characterised as having persistent state functional failure and experiences of institutional collapse for decades while evading total state collapse on different occasions.[8] On the one hand, it can be argued the military stronghold at the centre has helped to circumvent full collapse and hold 'the union' together (Taylor 2013). On the other hand, decades of military rule show how the Myanmar military is the dominant source of state fragility caused by extremes of incapacity and illegitimacy. Coups (1958, 1962, 1988 and 2021), uprisings (1988, 2007, and 2021), over 70 years of internal armed conflicts, and many governance and economic failures highlight such extremes.

Governance failures and existing weaknesses from past governments are currently exacerbated by new resistance from within and outside of state institutions since the 2021 takeover. After the coup, the health and education systems collapsed due to the civil disobedience movement, with the health system currently operating below 30 per cent capacity and the education system crippled by capacity shortages.[9] Both non-government services and informal coping mechanisms have become even more critical at local community levels. Indeed, many practices of self-reliance drawn on by Myanmar communities have been developed throughout decades of governance failures during military rule. Undoubtedly, there will be significant effects on people's lives as state institutions continue to 'fail' or exist on life support as the protracted crisis evolves.

The term 'contested' is used throughout this paper. It aims to cover different realms of violent conflict and non-violent contests before and during the current revolution. This includes armed conflict and national struggles over the structure of the state and who has the legitimacy to govern. It also covers subnational levels of contests over the authority to govern and efforts to disrupt and replace local administration by resistance forces and ethnic armed groups. 'Contested military rule', as used in the title, further suggests the relationship between the junta and the population it seeks to coercively control is not settled. It remains in flux, with the regime actively resisted by both Bamar and ethnic communities. This syncing of perceptions and resistance across ethnic lines with new alliances is historic and central to the revolution playing out.

NATIONAL CONTEST: THE STATE, LEGITIMACY, AND NEW POWER-STRUGGLES

Who yields power over the Myanmar state and people, and how power is shared among Myanmar's ethnic jigsaw are kernel issues driving protracted conflicts, contested state-society relations, and resistance movements. In the post-coup environment, realms of national contest and power struggles have new actors, deepening fault lines, and revolutionary dynamics, including the contest between the National Unity Government (NUG) and the military. As the junta slides backwards to more authoritarian and coercive practices, the resistance movement has expanded methods and tactics and denounced any accommodation of the military's role in politics in the future.

For decades, post-colonial state-society relations in Myanmar have been shaped by the military's centrality and practices of coercion and warfare. In her account of Burmese authoritarianism, Mary Callahan describes "the unusually coercion-intensive history of post-war Burmese politics" in which the military-dominated national power, edging out other players, and the chasm that emerged between their self-appointed paternalist role and viewing its citizens as potential enemies (2004, 7). In 1962, the military's coup was justified by its early phase of state formation, ethnic and communist insurgencies, and foreign threats due to cold war dynamics at home that risked swallowing up the barely formed nation (Callahan 2004, 6–7). Economic structures of the colonial era were aggressively deposed of by General Ne Win's *Burmese Way to Socialism*,[10] while the colonial security apparatus was remodelled and deployed (Brown 2013, 204–5; Callahan 2004, 17). From a reading of documents in 1990s, Robert Taylor argues that "the army leadership knew exactly who their political opponents were, and they were not some generalized 'citizenry'" (Taylor 2013a, 601). The military's concept of enemies has undoubtedly shifted in the post-coup environment. The jailing of striking medical professionals and social workers for supporting COVID-19 patients outside of the state's response, demonstrates a far larger net has been cast over potential 'enemies'. The military has also reworked aspects of the colonial-era penal code and weakened laws from the Thein Sein government's era to target enemies of the state, including a return to using the death penalty.[11]

While the goal for a federal democratic state is not new, the movement behind it has transformed in the post-coup period with some converging of once separate agendas for democracy, among the Bamar, and federalism, among ethnic groups. Resistance to the military's national rule has a new rancour, violent and non-violent actors, new methods, and a pan-ethnic support base. This includes the exiled National Unity Government, civil society organisations operating within and outside the country, youth and women's groups, local community groups, some ethnic armed groups and people's defence forces, the civil disobedience movement, and general strike committees. Diverse resistance actors involved in the National Unity Consultative Council (NUCC), including members of the National Unity Government (NUG), are currently debating a proposed system for a federal democratic union.

The structure of the Myanmar state has been a source of national contest and conflict since the nation's independence. Minority ethnic groups have long demanded federalism to overcome discrimination and exclusion perpetuated through the unitary system under authoritarian military rule and the more recent hybrid military-civilian arrangement (Breen 2018). In each system, Bamar-Buddhist dominance over minority groups was maintained and the central state continued to expand its reach into ethnic areas through state-building, including security and administrative arrangements, and via policies on languages, development, and education. These coercive central-peripheral practices and protracted armed conflicts across decades shape state-society relations within ethnic communities.

The promise of federalism — to promote diversity and unity through its features of shared and self-rule (Riker 1964) — takes on an almost mythical status in Myanmar and is often touted as a panacea to its internal conflicts and ethnic grievances. The early federalism story in Myanmar derives from the 1947 Panglong conference and agreement, and "myths" around this historic event are important for understanding ethnicity in Burma and prospects for ethnic unity (Walton 2008, 890). Narratives by ethnic leaders on why civil conflict continues in Myanmar since independence uphold the significance of the Panglong moment of 'ethnic unity' — although the conference was not inclusive of all ethnic groups — and how failure to implement the agreement changed the country's political trajectory.[12] While many ethnic groups and forums continued to debate ethnic-based systems for federalism, some in exile and others underground, these types of processes have mostly been informal.

Myanmar's most recent government-led peace process to debate the state's structure started under the Thein Sein government in 2011. Under the Union Solidarity and Development Party (USDP), the government focused heavily on bilateral and multilateral ceasefire negotiations. In 2015 the (so-called) Nationwide Ceasefire Agreement (NCA) was signed committing parties — the government, the military, and some EROs — to a range of ceasefire provisions and political dialogue on a system of 'democratic federalism', a term itself which is hotly contested as ethnic groups have long preferred to use 'federal democracy', and more recently a 'federal democratic union'. Given the military's long-held view that federalism was an existential threat to the union due to risks of succession, this commitment appeared to demonstrate a significant shift in sentiment. Yet this commitment, and subsequent support for state-level constitutions, were envisaged by the military to exist within the framework of the 2008 Constitution, at least for the next few decades.[13] Their scepticism remained strong and in conversations with military leaders involved in former peace negotiations it was often stated: "We don't want Myanmar becoming Yugoslavia due to federalism."[14]

The NLD and ethnic groups have long opposed the military's 2008 Constitution. According to Robert Taylor (2013, 398), the 2008 Constitution aimed to change public political and economic institutions while preserving the existing order and maintaining of security. It was never intended to solve all of Myanmar's ills, but attempted to offer some concessions with quasi-federal features of two orders of government, and ethnic-demarcated subnational territories of states and special administrative zones (Farrelly 2014, 252). During the 2008 Constitution convention, the military prohibited any discussion on federalism. In the peace process, the military stonewalled federalism proposals by EROs, stating that many of the federal features already existed in the 2008 Constitution: "We have already given you 'federalism' and what you are asking for," one leader stated.[15] In response, narratives among ethnic groups converged on the concept of "fake federalism" — essentially federalism in name or authoritarian forms without power-sharing.[16] Progress on the political dialogue of the peace process was consistently thwarted by the military, with leaders proving incapable of genuine negotiations for power-sharing while simultaneously pursuing armed conflict in ethnic areas (Williams 2022).

Under Aung Sun Suu Kyi's leadership and during the NLD's time in power, the party focused on the parliamentary process for constitutional reforms, leaving the peace process on life support. After four years in power, when the NLD submitted reforms to the 2008 Constitution via a parliamentary process, the party essentially proposed more democracy, without federalism (Kyaw 2019). According to political figures close to the NLD leaders, the strategy of avoiding constitutional change negotiations with EROs and ethnic leaders fits with Aung Sun Suu Kyi's opinion of the many armed groups; she believed her path to democratic leadership and use of non-violent strategies against the military were superior to that of violent conflict pursued by the ethnic armed groups.[17] She ring-fenced the political space captured by the predominantly-Bamar NLD through elections and excluded groups — including ethnic political parties struggling to contest the NLD at elections – without the majoritarian electoral 'legitimacy' she believed was bestowed upon her party and leadership. Areas where Aung San Suu Kyi's NLD found policy coherence with the military were essentially security issues in ethnic areas and competing yet similar approaches to Bamar domination (Medail 2018).[18] Very little, if any, political capital was invested in reconciling majority-minority relations.

After more than a decade of democratisation and elite-level peacebuilding experiments in Myanmar, little common ground has been made on how the Myanmar state should be structured and what it means to be 'Myanmar' for all its nationalities. Efforts to build a nation by successive military governments and the NLD government failed to make grounds to accommodate minorities and address social and political cleavages or move beyond inane ethnic tokenism practices. As David I. Steinberg (2021) wrote on nationhood in the coup's aftermath, "There is effectively no overarching inclusive emotional reaction that places all the peoples together in a primary self-defined nation... A sense of "we-ness" is lacking despite considerable coercive but ineffective efforts by a variety of governments, both military and civilian, to instil such concepts." As ongoing processes for dialogue, such as the NUCC, continue to deliberate a system of federalism, how to reconcile decades of failed state- and nation-building remains critical. Given the history of conflict and efforts to divide ethnic groups by the military, and the many 'ethno-nationalisms' this has created, there are risks that proposals for ethnic-based federalism could deepen and entrench some of the identities and relational dynamics shaped during military rule. Moderating extremes from all sides, ethnic groups and the Bamar majority, will be needed to enable dialogue without fragmentation of the process. Discussing the 'we-ness' question may be needed before debating prickly topics, such as ethnic territorial demarcation.

Common among different parts of the resistance movement and the military is the animated use of the legitimacy and illegitimacy paradigm around who has the right to govern. There is clear agreement among coalescing voices and resistance movements around the military's 'illegitimacy' since it effectively axed its former legitimate political cover via the 2021 coup — the elected civilian branch. The National Unity Government, deemed 'illegal' and a 'terrorist' organisation by the military, and civil society groups are regular producers and users of the concept of legitimacy and illegitimacy in advocacy to Myanmar citizens, the diplomatic and international community, and businesses, with efforts to drive behaviours in the direction of the 'legitimate' government. The junta, in turn, has been attempting to gain diplomatic recognition via countries to increase its own legitimacy as the government of Myanmar since it takeover. To members of the public, the resistance has called for boycotts on taxes and fees to the junta and donations for local governing committees set up by the NUG, local people's defence forces (PDFs), and civil disobedience members and their families. Resistance movements have also been calling for behavioural changes from government and businesses, attacking leaders for bestowing political 'legitimacy' on the junta via high-level meetings, or working with the junta and state-owned companies that could benefit the 'illegitimate' regime economically. Both outside countries and businesses have fallen into realms of national contest facing vitriol from the military, for meeting with the NUG, or parts of the resistance for perceived 'legitimacy' endowments on the junta (see also Coppel, this volume).

There is widespread support, albeit not homogenous among all ethnic communities and armed groups, for the National Unity Government as a 'legitimate' government or at least a movement representing a preferred system of government instead of military rule. This form of legitimacy is mostly derived from the 2020 electoral process, and likely heightened by representation of different ethnic nationalities within the current body. Yet this source of electoral legitimacy also comes with its own winners and losers. Many minority and ethnic political parties who have contested seats at the 2015 and 2020 elections have found the first-past-the-post system favours major political parties and the NLD unwilling to form alliances with minority ethnic groups. For some ethnic groups feeling disenfranchised by the NLD's electoral pathway to 'legitimacy' (an issue raised in several key informant interviews), or for ERO leaders side-lined for not having 'electoral legitimacy' in the past (while having decades of governance experience), legitimacy sources are in many respects sources of contest too.

Whether former NLD leaders involved in the National Unity Government (NUG) can truly unite and work with a diverse and factious movement under the democratic federalism goal is yet to be seen, but is critical for both political and military strategies of the resistance. In the current state of national contest, the NLD's relevance has tumbled with more revolutionary goals taking hold than restoring the elected parliament of 2020. For Bamar leaders, any process of dialogue on building a nation and structuring the state will need to involve stepping back from tightly-held constructs of their 'legitimate' rule, conceived through majoritarian politics, and appreciating how fraught and varied the concept of legitimacy is among Myanmar's diverse people, with vastly different experiences of state-society relations (Steinberg 2007). As early tensions emerge in the NUCC process around proposed pathways to a new system of government, NLD leaders will need to adjust, rather than cling to, their constructs of legitimacy to encourage broad engagement in a revolution that is truly revolutionary.

Many parts of the resistance movement, including the NUG, are unwilling to go back to the military's system of governance as designed by the 2008 constitution. The window for rolling back the coup and returning to the 2008 constitutional framework, as called for by many international leaders, arguably closed a few months after the coup following the killings and jailing of thousands of peaceful protestors, elected officials, political opponents, and citizens revolting against dictatorship. New resistance actors have since organised around various violent and non-violent campaigns against military rule. More than one year since the coup, the resistance shows little signs of abating in the face of coercion, brutality, and counterinsurgency. I subsequently explore the armed resistance and conflict dynamics.

Armed conflict and revolution from the heartland

Distinct to the last few decades of multiple subnational armed conflicts, many new and old groups are now fighting for revolutionary goals, including the overthrow of the military government and creation of a federal democratic system without them. Resistance to the junta's rule has proliferated across the country, spreading armed violence to the once peaceful Bamar heartland — including Yangon, Mandalay, Sagaing, and Magway — and intensifying existing armed conflicts in ethnic areas. New waves of guerrilla warfare in the country's interior, including urban and peri-urban areas, now map onto decades-old insurgencies mostly fought in rural and frontier areas. Townships affected by armed conflict have dramatically risen from one-third to more than two-thirds of the country since the coup (Burke et al. 2017; Arnold 2021).

In 2022 a complex array of non-state armed groups is battling the Myanmar military across multiple fronts and frontless conflicts (see also Jolliffe, this volume). A failed peace process has reengaged the military in live conflict with several former ceasefire groups. In addition to more than twenty Ethnic Resistance Organisations (EROs) and thousands of militias, new groups have emerged in opposition to the junta's rule known as People's Defence Forces (PDFs). This movement to arms has been encouraged by the NUG which declared a national uprising in September 2021. It is estimated that there are hundreds of new groups, including PDFs who are aligned with the NUG and other unaligned small local armed groups defending their communities at the township level (Arnold 2021). Several leading EROs are providing training and support for PDFs, such as the Kachin Independence Army (KIA) and the Karen National Union (KNU), while increasing coordination among EROs and PDFs is expanding the collective reach of non-state armed groups into new territory. New armed resistance tactics include guerrilla warfare, such as ambushes, sabotage, hit-and-run attacks on government buildings, and targeted assassinations. IED attacks are increasingly being used in urban to rural areas by new armed groups who have limited access to more sophisticated weaponry.[19]

With the new revolutionary threat from the heartland, the military is now stretched more than it has been in decades, mobilising troops across large swaths of the country's expansive interior and frontier regions and drawing on different elements of the police. It continues to unleash its signature waves of counterinsurgency savagery in response — burning and pillaging villages, displacing entire communities, torturing suspected informants and collaborators to death, and using civilians as human shields — while imprisoning suspected or known collaborators with the resistance. To handle stretched resources and reduce the number of threats the military faces simultaneously in the post-coup environment, there have been attempts to divide EROs through ceasefire negotiations. These old tricks should be viewed by outsiders as nothing more than a strategy to gain tactical advantage, rather than an opportunity for a 'breakthrough'. Notably, PDFs and new resistance forces are excluded from talks led by the military. Some EROs, formerly engaged in peace negotiations, now also refuse to meet with the military.

The long survival of EROs against the Myanmar military is bolstered by factors including mountainous terrain, local support and intel networks, strong mobilisation and recruitment strategies, legitimacy in the eyes of local populations, and bases inside and outside of the country (Fearon and Laitin 2004, 2011; Cunningham, Gleditsch, and Salehyan 2009; Brenner 2019). Once EROs embed in territory with governance systems, they prove difficult to uproot, growing their services over time, often in mixed-control arrangements with government. In many areas with strong ERO presence and rebel governance, these groups are often the highest political authority in areas of quasi-sovereignty, roles they have consolidated in local administration vacuums since the coup.

While anti-junta armed forces have shown considerable resilience surviving the first fight year, they face strategic and tactical level challenges. The Myanmar military significantly outweighs PDFs and many ERO opponents' capacity (numbers of soldiers) and capability (ground, air, and naval) (Selth 2002). Based on comparable military strength alone, the military should have defeated insurgent groups within one battle year. But decades of conflict in Myanmar also demonstrates that the military can win tactical battles yet lose wars strategically, never defeating rebel contenders entirely who continue to regroup, mobilise personnel and resources, and embed themselves in communities. In fact, Myanmar is the leading country for having conflicts which end in 'non-decisive' outcomes, meaning they are never solved through political solutions or effective end through clear military victories.[20] Given that new armed groups have survived the first fight year, they are now in a more likely position to endure across the coming years.[21]

PDFs aligned with the National Unity Government (NUG) are calling for weaponry support as they fend off an increasingly aggressive military through gritty guerrilla tactics and the use of limited small arms and home-made IEDs (Davis 2022). While the NUG aims to operate as a central command structure, groups are often left to create their own resources and operate in self-directed and decentralised ways with limited coordination among different branches (Davis 2022). To improve its military strategy the NUG will not only need to attract a far broader base of EROs, but it will also need to improve central command structures, coordination between different cells and units, and build supply chains for weapons and ammunition to advance the revolution it seeks.

SUBNATIONAL CONTEST: AUTHORITY, RESISTANCE, AND DISRUPTED ADMINISTRATION

A key battleground in Myanmar's conflicts is the ability to maintain or gain control over territory, resources, and populations (Burke et al. 2017). Local administration has long been part of the military's efforts to coerce and control people, used in concert with organised violence and warfare (Callahan 2004). During decades of dictatorship, the military oversaw the executive branch while managing administration through the General Administration Department (GAD), which served as a vital tool for surveillance and people movement while carrying out basic services (Arnold and Jolliffe 2021).[22] Key informants for this research highlighted that when raids are conducted, the police, military, and special branch work closely with GAD administrators who lead teams of citizens for arrest. Where there is an absence of GAD local officials in the post-coup environment, this constrains the junta's ability to monitor people's movement and places further pressure on police and military personnel, many of whom do not know the local populations.

In the wake of the coup, the military has replaced or attempted to replace thousands of NLD-appointed local administrators with former military representatives and Union Solidarity and Development Party (USDP) loyalists across the country. In turn, local officials working for the junta have increasingly become targets of the resistance. Factors contributing to mass vacancies across the country include civil disobedience resignations among civil servants, the National Unity Government calling for officials to resign as they launched an armed resistance, and hundreds of targeted attacks and killings by resistance forces (Arnold and Jolliffe 2021).[23] As of January 2022, scores of local leadership positions remain vacant in wards of Yangon and Mandalay, to villages across Sagaing, Magway, Chin, Karen, Karenni, and Kachin.[24] In many wards or townships, local administration by the government is non-existent and carried out in nearby locations where new security arrangements can be maintained by the military and police. Across townships of the business capital, Yangon, life for many is punctured by new forms of urban armed violence, coercive state control, and disruptions to local administration. The below case study delineates these post-coup dynamics.

Case Study 1: Disrupted and coercive administration in Yangon Region

Sanchaung and Hlaing townships host many young people. These areas are historically breeding grounds for student uprisings.[25] *As of December 2021 and January 2022, both townships are highly militarised, with armed trucks of police and soldiers patrolling the areas day and night. There are night raids by security forces, and curfews are imposed from 10 pm to 4 am. Cordon and search operations block certain roads.*

Yangon's Hlaing township experiences frequent IED-related explosions (The Irrawaddy 2021c). In the first week of January 2022, daily blasts took place.[26] *Other tactics used by armed resistance groups include hit-and-run shootings and targeted killings of persons involved in local administration and USDP supporters. Several ward administrators' offices are not operating, with their tasks managed at the township level where the offices are barricaded with cement walls and sandbags. After the killing of one of the ward administrators, others went into hiding to avoid being targeted by underground cells.*

Young people around the country are known to come and study in Yangon while staying at hostels in Hledan. These hostels hosted many students who led anti-coup protests in February and March 2021. Since the security forces' mass arrests and night raids, many young people fled from here to Ethnic Armed Organisation (ERO) areas for safety and to seek basic combat training. Some returned to Yangon to attack junta forces and pro-junta individuals.[27]

Many apartments and houses were raided in recent months resulting in the arrest of young people and seizure of weapons. People are arrested for returning from ERO territory, supporting the civil disobedience movement (CDM), and promoting social punishment against junta collaborators online. Arrests occur in other hotspots of Yangon for minor offences, such as not reporting overnight guests, overstaying the curfew hours, taking videos of soldiers raiding houses, and participating in the non-violent campaign against the junta by banging on pots and pans.[28]

In nearby Sanchaung, the Township Administrator U Kyaw Kyaw, appointed during the NLD government, has continued to work for the junta. He has become an infamous figure responsible for the crackdowns in Sanchaung, leading to the arrests and deaths of scores of young protesters and CDM workers. Chills were felt throughout the community when four young people were publicly tortured and shot dead on the road next to a flyover in September 2021. Among the dead were a doctor and nurse volunteering to support patients affected by COVID-19

(The Irrawaddy 2021b).

Several months since the coup, resistance activities against local government officials and junta-affiliates mainly come from the Yangon Urban Guerrillas (YUG). Several attacks have killed or injured junta soldiers in the township, and IED attacks have been committed by both pro-and anti-junta movements in Sanchaung and surrounding townships (The Irrawaddy 2021a; Eleven Media 2021). Creative non-violent resistance also continues; for instance, flash protests with citizens coming together in snap processions and then scattering to avoid arrest (Nikkei Asia 2021).

Outside of Yangon, across the Bamar heartland, new governance practices by opposition movements are emerging in hotly-contested areas. The National Unity Government (NUG) and Committee Representing the Pyidaungsu Hluttaw (CRPH) have sought to establish local governance bodies to further their legitimacy and disrupt the junta's ability to govern. This started in late February 2021 following the coup with calls for people to form local committees, known as *Pyithu Aochoteye a Pweh* (PAPs), across townships engaging former civil servants, CDM supporters, and elected officials, MPs, civil society, youth leaders, and teachers (Arnold and Jolliffe 2021). According to Arnold and Jolliffe (2021), there are PAPs across hundreds of townships, all taking different forms. These types of committees were reported in Sagaing Region during research conducted for this paper. The below case study from Monywa Township highlights new governance developments and support for PDF governance.

Case Study 2: People's Defence Forces and governance in Sagaing Region

In the previously peaceful Bamar heartland, Sagaing Region now hosts some of the strongest People's Defence Forces (PDFs) that have emerged since the coup. In Monywa Township, the capital of Sagaing, and broader areas, observers are witnesses of many violent incidences by the junta's forces, including the burning of homes and razing of villages, as well as attacks on the junta by PDFs.

Observers highlighted the effects of the military's brutal attacks on civilians which is turning them more towards PDFs. When returning to town, communities welcome the PDF leaders with standing ovations lining the streets and throwing flowers. One observer characterised the encounters with emotion, describing it as "like a reunion of father and son after years of separation".[29] Given new security risks for the junta, the military and police focus on youth and PDF suspects in their patrolling. *This involves interrogating young people and doing spot checks of mobile phones. Many of the arrests in the area made by junta forces involve checking phones and discovering images of the National Unity Government (NUG) or NLD and social media posts supporting the resistance.*

While there is a high presence of junta security personnel in some towns of Sagaing Region, the junta's administrative system has collapsed in many rural areas with junta-appointed administrators absent at the village tract level, and offices closed.[30] With the local administration crumbling, new governance structures include committees by local PDFs with guidance from the National Unity Government. The guidance includes engaging local MPs, ex-political prisoners, youth group representatives, civil society representatives, NLD political party members, and teachers.[31]

According to people interviewed for this research, the practices of PDFs and the new committees are like that of EROs who run their services in the country's "liberated areas".[32] With schools closed, some of these groups are helping to provide education services via volunteer teachers and CDM staff. This nascent phase of providing civic services is happening underground.

Given the limited military capability of PDFs compared to the junta's forces, competition over who has the legitimacy to govern will remain a critical area of local contest for the NUG in the coming years of resistance (Arnold and Jolliffe 2021). While current conflict dynamics are fluid and constantly changing, PDFs in Sagaing Region have shown they can effectively consolidate support from local populations and engage local leaders in service provision.[33] As observers highlighted, these practices mimic the activities of more established EROs which have long contested the state's local authorities, providing governance and services for local populations in ethnic areas (Jolliffe 2014, 2015).[34]

In recent years, ERO governance has featured in areas of mixed control arrangements with government presence in towns and stronger ERO presence in rural areas. Informal practices between EROs and the state government or local administration developed over many years and existed under ceasefire arrangements (Jolliffe 2014, 2015; Burke et al. 2016). In the post-coup environment, many informal boundaries, local power-sharing arrangements, and ceasefire relationships have been dramatically reordered, shaping how local governance is contested. Changes in how territory is controlled by EROs also took place during waves of COVID-19 as several groups worked to manage shutdowns, including restrictions on people's movement, and administer vaccinations to communities.

In the aftermath of the coup, several EROs have expanded or consolidated their control of territory. ERO territorial expansion by the Arakan Army (AA) in Rakhine State and by the Myanmar National Democratic Alliance Army (MNDAA) in Northern Shan State has been reported (Arnold and Jolliffe 2021). In some mixed control areas, such as Karen state, where the Karen National Union (KNU) and the state have both existed, new appointments by the military have not been permitted by armed groups. In other instances, where local administrators of the junta have been permitted, they report to both the ERO and the junta, sometimes leaning towards the former in loyalty, as has been reported in Rakhine State. The below case study highlights changes in local governance in Rakhine State and local contests after the coup.[35]

Case Study 3: Local contest and the AA's expansion in Rakhine State

While Rakhine people and civil society groups joined the national protest movement and issued statements after the coup, there have been significantly fewer resistance activities, violent and non-violent, compared to other parts of the country.[36] Limited support for the NLD's cause was not surprising given the history of conflict between the minority ethnic Rakhine and the majority-Bamar political establishment.[37] Observers in Rakhine highlighted that after the coup there were initially troop deployments and military vehicles roaming the capital Sittwe and other northern townships, creating alarm among local communities. The military presence soon reduced, with resources presumably needed in other parts of the country where there were stronger resistance movements than those witnessed in Sittwe.[38]

Crippling effects of the bloody civil war in Rakhine before the coup are widely felt across communities. Impacts of fighting on local administration include restrictions on government officials' movements and reduced government presence in rural areas leaving vacuums for the AA to fill.[39] Government administrative roles were for a long time carried out in Sittwe, Mrauk U, and Kyauk Phyu towns with a loss of presence in villages during high-intensity conflict periods.

Building on several years of efforts to advance its administration and services, the Arakan Army (AA) has expanded its territorial reach and de-facto authority in the post-coup period.[40] While the junta provides some municipal and judiciary services from the main cities, scores of rural areas have become mixed-control governance arrangements with strong AA presence. In some areas, junta-appointed local administrators or village leaders are recognised by both the junta and AA, with some community members observing that local leaders take their orders primarily from the AA.[41]

The AA's embedding in communities includes the expansion of judicial and policing services and greater engagement in local development projects. Since the coup, local communities, including some Rohingya communities and other Muslim minority groups, are reportedly starting to seek judicial dispute resolutions from AA, believing that they provide improved and fairer services than the junta which has less authority locally. Key informants reported incidents of the AA's system being used to solve disputes concerning land, commercial activities, theft, and other forms of criminal acts at the village level.[42]

Given the long history of dictatorship and situations of failed subnational governance across Myanmar, there are many approaches to self-reliance among local communities (Thawnghmung 2019).[43] Observers interviewed for this study highlighted social and medical services provided by community-based groups, neighbourhood networks, religious organisations, and civil society. They also highlighted donations and support from communities to the civil disobedience movement personnel and their families.[44] To deal with COVID-19, economic hardship, cash shortages, and other aspects of the post-coup fallout, various local self-reliance practices have re-emerged. Yet in the coup's aftermath many community networks and social workers have been forced to operate secretly due to being seen as 'CDM affiliated' and becoming targets of the junta. As a volunteer providing oxygen and running funeral services commented, "We are treated like drug dealers."[45] With the junta seeking to punish and thwart non-violent resistance, the perceived enemies of the state are boundless.

LOOKING AHEAD

There is rolling speculation about what is ahead for Myanmar's post-coup crisis; are political solutions feasible? Can the resistance dislodge the military? Will the junta embed its administration and defeat the resistance? Currently, there are numerous bargaining problems and commitment challenges within Myanmar's crisis for political solutions (Williams 2022; Shelling 1960; Walters 2009). For instance, there is no bargaining space between the military and the NUG with both sides seeking to defeat the other militarily and decisively, and there is no common ground concerning perceived outcomes to the crisis and the future of the Myanmar state. There are, however, important forums for dialogue involving the NUG which address the unsolved puzzle of how to share power through a federal democracy for Myanmar's diverse ethnic jigsaw.

The junta is highly unlikely to achieve a decisive victory over the NUG and EROs. Throughout its long history of war-making and internal armed conflicts, the Myanmar military rarely achieves decisive outcomes, be that through an outright military victory or a political settlement. Internal armed conflicts most frequently reach non-decisive outcomes in Myanmar, more so than any other country affected by conflict since the end of WWII.[46] While the military is capable of winning tactical-level battles, they have often failed to defeat insurgencies, which are left to fester and transform without the political roots of the conflict addressed.

In one year since taking up arms against the junta, resistance forces and the NUG reshaped the country's conflict landscape through violent and political tactics. They are likely to continue consolidating territory and creating new governance arrangements contesting the political authority of the junta. EROs are similarly likely to expand and deepen their control over territory as conflict thrives. Whether the NUG can broaden a coalition of ethnic groups and EROs behind an inclusive vision of federalism is critical to its success against the military.

In the foreseeable future, devastating armed conflict will likely continue as a nationwide phenomenon, including contests over territory and governance. After several years of battles without a decisive outcome, there are risks that the revolutionary movement could transform into a protracted, low-intensity conflict alongside other ethnic conflicts in Myanmar. In this scenario, a military and political stalemate could lead both the NUG and the military to retreat without a strategic outcome.

CONCLUSION

This chapter analyses political changes in Myanmar, including new revolutionary dynamics and the transformation of old power struggles in the post-2021 coup environment. Resistance to military rule and coercion in this era has a new cast of actors and multi-ethnic alliances, using both violent and non-violent tactics from guerrilla warfare to civil disobedience. At the national level, political contests centre around who has the legitimacy to govern and the structure of the state. Both opposition groups and the military increasingly use concepts of legitimacy and illegitimacy to influence the behaviours of diplomatic and business communities by encouraging constraints in conferring 'legitimacy' upon the other's right to rule. To build support for its rule, the NUG is working to have dialogue without the military and develop a new constitution for a federal democratic union. As this paper highlights, separate movements for democracy, by the Bamar, and federalism, by ethnic groups, are at an early stage of converging in the post-coup environment.

In exploring subnational contests, this paper introduces new case studies from Rakhine State, Yangon Region, and Sagaing Region. This evidence delineates a patchwork of recent attempts to build local governance by resistance forces in the Bamar heartland and expand ERO authority and territory in ethnic areas. It also highlights coercive practices by the junta and failing attempts to administer control over populations in the country's business capital. The data is by no means comprehensive, yet it tells an important story emerging from Myanmar's reordered political environment; while the military has consolidated control over the central state apparatus, subnational and local authority has become more complex and contested than ever before, including in the Bamar heartland. Resistance to military rule and coercion in this era has new violent and non-violent actors with a multi-ethnic support base. Whether the resistance can broaden its coalition and dovetail its political and military strategies will determine the outcomes ahead. Myanmar, for now, remains under contested military rule.

Notes

1   As Taylor (2012) highlights, early reforms included: reducing press constraints and censorship, parliaments at national and state/regional levels, law for the establishment of independent trade unions and the right to demonstrate under conditions, putting the national budget in the public domain, increasing spending on health and education and decreasing military spending proportionally, releasing political prisoners, establishing a National Human Rights Commission, holding elections and bi-elections, and suspending construction on the Myitsone dam. President U Thein Sein also went on to advance decentralisation and many other reforms.
2   Observations about USDP's possible victory in the 2020 election were made by military officials and USDP members in December 2019.

3   The State Law and Order Restoration Council (SLORC) was established after the 1988 uprising and pro-democracy demonstrations. Its mission was initially to eliminate internal rebellion. The SLORC was later reorganised and renamed the State Peace and Development Council (SPDC), the official name used by the Myanmar junta from 1997–2010.
4   Observations by former USDP-aligned politicians, October 2021.
5   The military's three national pledges include (1) non-disintegration of the union; (2) non-disintegration of national solidarity; and (3) perpetuation of sovereignty.
6   This was demonstrated by new research across states/regions in Myanmar in November-December 2021.
7   For an overview of the term Ethnic Resistance Organisations (EROs), see Kim Jolliffe, this volume.
8   For more on the role of legitimacy and capacity and state fragility, see Organisation for Economic Cooperation and Development, "The State's Legitimacy in Fragile Situations: Unpacking Complexity," *Conflict and Fragility Series* (Paris: OECD Publishing, 2010).
9   Observations from key informants, November–December 2021.
10 This includes the nationalisation of foreign interests, the Burmanisation of the labour force, and state-led industrialisation.
11 The junta has rolled back changes to laws from the Thein Sein government era on telecommunications and surveillance, village tract and administration, press and speech freedoms, and civic spaces. Legal changes also include the British Code of Criminal Procedure (1898) to create new and revised offenses without bail and allow for warrantless arrests, and the Penal Code (1861) to expand offences and target criticism of the military and coup, including support to the civil disobedience movement (CDM). The junta has also suspended parts of the Law Protecting the Privacy and Security of Citizens (2017), removing the right to be free from arbitrary detention, warrantless surveillance, as well as search and seizure protections.
12 Including the Mon, Arakanese, Wa, and Naga, to name a few.
13 Observations by the author through engagement in peace and reform processes in Myanmar.
14 Observations by the author through engagement in peace and reform processes in Myanmar.
15 Observations by an ethnic leader to the author engaged in the peace process in Myanmar, Yangon, 2017.
16 Observations by the author through engagement in peace and reform processes in Myanmar.
17 Observations from Myanmar political leaders, Yangon, 2016.

18 As Progressive Voice stated soon after the 2020 election; "The liberal democracy-lite NLD-government of 2015–2020, despite its limitations in exercising its power due to the military-drafted 2008 Constitution, has continued to embody the Burmanization agenda. Building statues of Bamar heroes in ethnic minority towns and cities at the expense of local figures and martyrs, or naming a major new bridge in Mon State after Burman independence hero, General Aung San rather than a local ethnic Mon figure, as would have been more appropriate and in the spirit of building a federal democratic union." To read the full statement see: Karen Human Rights Group Website https://khrg.org/2020/11/newly-elected-nld-led-government-must-work-end-burmanization.
19 Verified through multiple conflict monitoring reports accessed by the author.
20 Based on analysis using the Uppsala Conflict Data Program (UCDP) Conflict Termination Data, the majority of rebel defeats happen within the first fight year, while the likelihood of rebel group survival increasing significantly after sustaining the first fight year. For more information and access to the dataset see: Kreutz (2010: 243–250).
21 Based on analysis using the Uppsala Conflict Data Program (UCDP) conflict termination data, the majority of rebel defeats happen within the first fight year, while the likelihood of rebel group survival increasing significantly after sustaining the first fight year. For more information and access to the dataset see Kreut (2010: 243–250).
22 For more on the General Administrative Department (GAD) see Kyi Pyar Chit Saw and Arnold (2014).
23 Observations from key informants, November 2021–January 2022.
24 Observations from key informants, November 2021–January 2022.
25 Observations from key informants, November 2021–January 2022.
26 Observations from key informants, November 2021–January 2022.
27 Observations from key informants, November 2021–January 2022.
28 Observations from key informants, November 2021–January 2022.
29 Observations from key informants, November–December 2021.
30 It was highlighted that the collapse of the local administration is having numerous effects on people's daily lives, from not being able to sell or register property, register new births or deaths, or gain recommendation letters to travel during COVID-19.
31 Observations from key informants, November–December 2021.
32 Observations from key informants, November–December 2021.
33 Observations from key informants, November–December 2021.

34 A series of research papers by The Asia Foundation study EAO administration: Bill Davis and Kim Jolliffe, *Achieving Health Equity in Contested Areas of Southeast Myanmar*. (San Francisco: The Asia Foundation, 2016); Kim Jolliffe, *Ethnic Conflict and Social Services in Myanmar's Contested Regions* (San Francisco: The Asia Foundation, 2014); Kim Jolliffe, *Ethnic Armed Conflict and Territorial Administration in Myanmar* (San Francisco: The Asia Foundation, 2015); Kim Jolliffe and Emily Speers Mears, *Strength in Diversity: Towards Universal Education in Myanmar's Ethnic Areas* (San Francisco: The Asia Foundation, 2016).
35 Observations from key informants, November–December 2021.
36 This includes statements against the Arakan National Party (ANP) taking a seat in the junta's government.
37 Many link the military and the NLD together as 'Bamar occupiers', according to research carried out for this study. In the eyes of many Rakhine people, the NLD delivered centralised governance by giving opportunities for Rakhine leadership to Bamar leaders. Observers also highlighted restrictions on their access to the internet during the conflict, and liberties with the cancelling of 2020 elections in their region without clear public communication.
38 Observations from key informants, November 2021–January 2022.
39 Observations from key informants, November–December 2021.
40 Observations from key informants, November–December 2021. Similar observations are made by Kyaw Hsan Hlaing (2021).
41 Observations from key informants, November–December 2021.
42 Observations from key informants, November–December 2021.
43 For more on community-reliance post-coup, see Green (2021).
44 Observations from key informants, November 2021–January 2022.
45 Observations from key informants, November 2021–January 2022.
46 Based on analysis using the Uppsala Conflict Data Program (UCDP) Conflict Termination Dataset, 1946¬–2020. For more information and access to the dataset, see Kreutz (2010).

References

Al Jazeera Economy. 2022. "Oil giants Total, Chevron to leave Myanmar citing human rights". *Al Jazeera*, 21 January. Available at www.aljazeera.com/economy/2022/1/21/oil-giants-total-chevron-exit-myanmar-due-to-human-rights-abuses#:~:text=Energy%20giants%20TotalEnergies%20and%20Chevron,in%20a%20coup%20last%20year (accessed 16 October 2022).

Asia Development Bank (ADB). 2015. *Asian Development Outlook 2015: Financing Asia's Future Growth*. Manila: ADB.

Arnold, Matthew B. 2021. "Myanmar at War: D-Day and Its Repercussions". *Brief 3*, 8 October.

Arnold, Matthew B and Kim Jolliffe. 2021. "Myanmar's Shadow War: The Role of Local Administrators in the SAC Military Regime". *Brief 4*, 12 November.

Burke, Adam, Nicola Williams, Patrick Barron, Kim Jolliffe and Thomas Carr. 2017. *The Contested Areas of Myanmar Subnational Conflict, Aid and Development*. San Francisco: The Asia Foundation. Available at https://asiafoundation.org/publication/contested-areas-myanmar-subnational-conflict-aid-development/ (accessed 16 October 2022).

Breen, Michael G. 2018. *The Road to Federalism in Nepal, Myanmar and Sri Lanka: Finding the Middle Ground*. Politics in Asia series. Abingdon, Oxon and New York: Routledge.

Brenner, David. 2019. *Rebel Politics: A Political Sociology of Armed Struggle in Myanmar's Borderlands*. New York: Cornell University Press.

Brown, Ian. 2013. *Burma's Economy in the Twentieth Century*. Cambridge, UK: Cambridge University Press.

Callahan, Mary Patricia. 2004. *Making Enemies: War and State Building in Burma*. Singapore: Singapore University Press.

Chambers, Justine, Charlotte Galloway, and Jonathan Liljeblad (eds.). 2020. *Living with Myanmar*. Singapore: ISEAS-Yusof-Ishak Institute.

Cunningham, David E., Kristian Skrede Gleditsch and Idean Salehyan. 2009. "It Takes Two: A Dyadic Analysis of Civil War Duration and Outcome". *Journal of Conflict Resolution* 53 (4): 570–597.

Davis, Anthony. 2022. "Is Myanmar's military starting to lose the war?" *Asia Times*, 30 May. Available at https://asiatimes.com/2022/05/is-myanmars-military-starting-to-lose-the-war/ (accessed 16 October 2022).

Eleven Media Editorial. 2021. "Explosion occurs in Sanchaung on Sept 9, causing casualties". *Eleven Media Group*. 10 September 2021. Available at https://elevenmyanmar.com/news/explosion-occurs-in-sanchaung-on-sept-9-causing-casualties (accessed 16 October 2022).

Farrelly, Nicholas and Chit Win. 2016. "Inside Myanmar's Turbulent Transformation". *Asia & the Pacific Policy Studies* 3 (1): 38–47.

Farrelly, Nicholas. 2014. "Cooperation, Contestation, Conflict: Ethnic Political Interests in Myanmar Today". *South East Asia Research* 22 (2): 251–266.

Fearon, James D. 2010. "Governance and Civil War Onset". *World Development Report 2011 Background Paper*. Washington: The World Bank. http://web.worldbank.org/archive/website01306/web/pdf/wdr%20background%20paper_fearon_0.pdf (accessed 16 October 2022).

Fearon James D. and David D. Laitin. 2011. "Sons of the Soil, Migrants, and Civil War". *World Development* 39 (2): 199–211.

Fearon, James D., and David D. Laitin. 2004. "Ethnicity, Insurgency, and Civil War". *The American Political Science Review* 97 (1): 75–90.

Green, Duncan. 2021. "How can Outsiders support Civil Society in coup-torn Myanmar?" FP2P Oxfam, 14 September. Available at https://oxfamapps.org/fp2p/how-can-outsiders-support-civil-society-in-coup-torn-myanmar/ (accessed 16 October 2022).

Hill, Jack Jenkins and Miles Kenny-Lazar. 2021. "Dispossession, deforestation and deceit in Myanmar". *New Mandala*, 3 November. Available at https://www.newmandala.org/dispossession-deforestation-and-deceit-in-myanmar/ (accessed 16 October 2022).

The Irrawaddy. 2022. "Myanmar Junta's New Cyber Law to Jail Anyone Using VPN". *The Irrawaddy News*, 24 January. Available at https://www.irrawaddy.com/news/burma/myanmar-juntas-new-cyber-law-to-jail-anyone-using-vpn.html (accessed 16 October 2022).

The Irrawaddy. 2021. "Over 400,000 Myanmar Civil Servants Still on Strike Against Military Regime". *The Irrawaddy News*, 25 August. Available at https://www.irrawaddy.com/news/burma/over-400000-myanmar-civil-servants-still-on-strike-against-military-regime.html (accessed 16 October 2022).

The Irrawaddy. 2021b. "Myanmar Regime Arrests Wife of Doctor Reportedly Killed by Troops". *The Irrawaddy News*, 28 September. Available at https://www.irrawaddy.com/news/burma/myanmar-regime-arrests-wife-of-doctor-reportedly-killed-by-troops.html (accessed 16 October 2022).

The Irrawaddy. 2021c. "Myanmar's Commercial Capital Yangon and Mandalay Rocked by Bomb Blasts". *The Irrawaddy News*, 30 August. Available at https://www.irrawaddy.com/news/burma/myanmars-commercial-capital-yangon-and-mandalay-rocked-by-bomb-blasts.html (accessed 16 October 2022).

Joint Standing Committee on Foreign Affairs, Defence and Trade. 2021. "Australia's response to the coup in Myanmar: Interim report for the inquiry into certain aspects of the Department of Foreign Affairs and Trade Annual Report 2019-20". *Parliament of the Commonwealth of Australia*, June.

Jolliffe, Kim. 2014. *Ethnic Conflict and Social Services in Myanmar's Contested Regions*. San Francisco: The Asia Foundation.

Jolliffe, Kim. 2015. *Ethnic Armed Conflict and Territorial Administration in Myanmar*. San Francisco: The Asia Foundation.

Kreutz, Joakim. 2010. "How and When Armed Conflicts End: Introducing the UCDP Conflict Termination Dataset". *Journal of Peace Research* 47 (2): 243–250.

Kyaw Hsan Hlaing, 2021. "After Myanmar's Military Coup, Arakan Army Accelerates Implementation of the 'Way of Rakhita". *The Diplomat*, 14 April. Available at https://thediplomat.com/2021/04/after-myanmars-military-coup-arakan-army-accelerates-implementation-of-the-way-of-rakhita/ (accessed 16 October 2022).

Kyi Pyar Chit Saw and Arnold, Matthew. 2014. *Administering the State in Myanmar: An Overview of the General Administration Department*. San Francisco: The Asia Foundation.

Medail, Cecile. 2022. "Forming an Inclusive National Identity in Myanmar: Voices of Mon People". *In Myanmar Transformed? People, Places and Politics*, edited by Justine Chambers, Gerard McCarthy, Nicholas Farrelly and Chin Win. Singapore: ISEAS-Yusof-Ishak Institute.

Milliken, Jennifer and Keith Krause. 2002. "State Failure, State Collapse, and State Reconstruction: Concepts, Lessons and Strategies". *Development and Change* 33 (5): 753–754.

Nikkei Staff Writers. 2021. "Myanmar protesters stage 'flash mobs' to avoid bullets". *Nikkei Asia*, 4 May. Available at https://asia.nikkei.com/Spotlight/Myanmar-Crisis/Myanmar-protesters-stage-flash-mobs-to-avoid-bullets (accessed 16 October 2022)

Nitta, Yuichi and Thurein Hla Htway. 2020. "Myanmar election latest: Opposition suffers huge defeat". *Nikkei Asia*, 8 November. https://asia.nikkei.com/Politics/Myanmar-election/Myanmar-election-latest-Opposition-suffers-huge-defeat (accessed 10 November 2022).

RAF Myanmar Service. 2022. *Myanmar junta gets effective diplomatic downgrade as a result of military coup*. Radio News Asia, 19 May. Available at https://www.rfa.org/english/news/myanmar/junta-ambassadors-05192022173518.html (accessed 16 October 2022).

Schelling, Thomas C. 1960. *The Strategy of Conflict*. Cambridge, Massachusetts: Harvard University Press.

Selth, Andrew. 2002. *Burma's Armed Forces: Power Without Glory*. Norwalk, CT: EastBridge.

Steinberg, David I. 2021. "Myanmar: Failed State or failed nation?" *Frontier Myanmar*, 11 August. Available at https://www.frontiermyanmar.net/en/myanmar-failed-state-or-failed-nation/ (accessed 16 October 2022).

Steinberg, David I. 2007. "Legitimacy" in Burma/Myanmar: Concepts and Implications". *In Myanmar: State, Society and Ethnicity*, edited by N. Ganesan and Kyaw Yin Hlaing. Singapore: ISEAS Publishing.

Taylor, Robert H. 2013. "Myanmar's 'Pivot' Toward the Shibboleth Of 'Democracy'". *Asian Affairs* 44 (3): 392–400.

Taylor, Robert H. 2013a. "Strong Soldiers, Failed Revolution: The State and Military in Burma, 1962-88". *Southeast Asian Studies* 2 (3): 599–602.

Taylor, Robert H. 2012. "Myanmar: From Army Rule to Constitutional Rule?" *Asian Affairs* 43 (2): 221–236.

Thawnghmung, Ardeth Maung. 2019. *Everyday Economic Survival in Myanmar: New Perspectives in Southeast Asian Studies*. Wisconsin: University of Wisconsin Press.

Tun, Htet Myet Min and Moe Thuzar. 2022. "Myanmar's National Unity Consultative Council: A Vision of Myanmar's Federal Future". *FULCRUM*, 5 January. Available at https://fulcrum.sg/myanmars-national-unity-consultative-council-a-vision-of-myanmars-federal-future/ (accessed 16 October 2022).

Turnell, Sean. 2010. "Finding dollars and sense: Burma's economy in 2010". In *Finding Dollars, Sense, and Legitimacy in Burma*, edited by Susan L. Levenstein. Washington, DC: Woodrow Wilson International Center for Scholars.

Walters, Barbara F. 2009. "Bargaining Failures and Civil War". *Annual Review of Political Science* 12 (June): 243–261.

Walton, Matthew J. 2008. "Ethnicity, Conflict, and History in Burma: The Myths of Panglong". *Asian Survey* 48 (6): 889–910.

Williams, Nicola. 2022. "Achieving the Best Outcome in Myanmar's Civil War". *War on the Rocks*, 19 October. Available at https://warontherocks.com/2022/10/achieving-the-best-outcome-in-myanmars-civil-war/ (accessed 1 November 2022).

World Bank. 2022. *Myanmar Economic Monitor: Contending with Constraints*. Washington, D.C.: World Bank Group. Available at https://thedocs.worldbank.org/en/doc/c3299fac4f879379513b05eaf0e2b084-0070012022/original/World-Bank-Myanmar-Economic-Monitor-Jan-22.pdf (accessed 16 October 2022).

6

CONTESTED POLITICAL AUTHORITY IN POST-COUP MYANMAR

Kim Jolliffe

The attempted coup of February 2021 by the State Administration Council (SAC) has catalysed dramatic shifts in Myanmar's political and security landscapes. As the SAC has failed to assert its political authority, new governance systems have emerged under the National Unity Government (NUG) and a range of local level revolutionary coalitions. Meanwhile, ethnic resistance organisations (EROs) both aligned and non-aligned to the NUG, have been able to expand their areas of control.[1]

This chapter examines the ways that political authority is established by competing actors in the context of Myanmar's post-2021 civil war and explores the implications of emerging governance dynamics for the country's future. I draw on a range of concepts from the international literature to highlight the importance of political authority and governance for the resistance movement's immediate struggle to take down the military junta and for its long-term agenda of establishing a lasting, peaceful, federal democratic union of Myanmar.

The governance systems of Myanmar's many resistance organisations have not gained significant academic attention until recent years, despite large areas of the country having been governed by them for many decades. The political authority and governance systems of resistance organisations are only mentioned in passing in the most influential studies on armed conflict and ethnic politics in Myanmar (Yawnghwhe 1987; Gravers 1999; Lintner 1999; Smith 1999; Thawnghmung 2007; Callahan 2007; South 2008; Sakhong 2010; Woods 2011; Sadan 2013). But recent years have seen increased interest in these themes, with Brenner (2017; 2019) exploring the politics and governance of so-called "rebels", South (2017) discussing "hybrid governance" and Kyed et al. (2020) providing a seminal contribution on informal justice systems in both ERO and government-controlled areas (see also Decobert 2016; Paul 2018; Loong 2019; Ong 2020; and Kim 2021, among others). These recent works have demonstrated how large populations of the country have been subject to overlapping forms of localised authority completely independent from the central state. They have also demonstrated how the governance systems of EROs often demonstrate considerable legitimacy, especially in relation to the violent and invasive Myanmar Armed Forces, due to bottom-up collaboration between EROs and community-based actors.

In this chapter, I will examine three main groups of governance actors that are filling the void left by the steady collapse of the SAC's public administration system. The first are around fifteen EROs, which have governed their own territories and "mix-controlled areas" since before the coup and in many cases since the 40s, 50s or 60s (Jolliffe 2015). The second are the NUG and the various bodies operating underneath them at the township level, such as people's defence forces (PDFs) and people's administration bodies — *pyithu aochoteye a'pweh* (Pa-Ah-Pa). The third set of actors are new local level coalitions in Karenni and Chin States, including state-level bodies called the Interim Chin National Consultative Council (ICNCC) and the Karenni State Consultative Council (KSCC), as well as township-level bodies.[2]

This chapter provides a descriptive overview of these governance systems and draws on a range of theoretical approaches to explore the implications they could have both for the ongoing struggle to topple the military junta and for the prospects of forming a lasting and peaceful federal union in the future. I draw on literature about insurgency and counterinsurgency, including works by revolutionary writers themselves, to emphasise the practical importance of public administration to strengthening and sustaining armed revolutionary movements. I also look at South's (2022) notion of "emergent federalism" and the concept of infrastructural power (Mann 1984; 1986; Ziblatt 2004; Breen 2018) to look at the potential for resistance governance systems to provide a foundation for federated states in the future.

Most of the information in this article is based on my personal observations and experiences volunteering with and advising a wide range of political, social and humanitarian organisations in Myanmar since 2021. It is supplemented by knowledge gained through earlier research projects on the governance systems of resistance organisations in Myanmar (Jolliffe 2011, 2014, 2015, 2017a, 2017b, 2018).

The next section provides contextual background to the current situation, including an overview of the main political and governance actors. I then go on to introduce a range of key terms theoretical concepts, highlighting the importance of resistance governance systems to the goal of taking down a target regime and for long-term goal of forming federal democratic union. The section after is mostly descriptive, providing an overview of the various forms of resistance governance that are taking hold in the wake of the attempted coup. The conclusion section focuses on the implications that these systems of political authority could have for the ongoing revolution and the potential for building a lasting federal union.

BACKGROUND

In this section, I will introduce the major political actors and key events that have shaped the dramatic expansion of resistance political authority since the attempted coup. The most advanced public administration systems among resistance organisations in Myanmar are the decades-old structures of some EROs. There are around 15–20 EROs holding territory in Myanmar, depending on how they are classified and categorised. Many have held and governed territories for decades, in some cases since independence. These territories are mostly in areas that were under varied levels of indirect rule under British rule, and which have never been under centralised authority (Smith 1999).

The most well-known revolutionary actor in post-2021 Myanmar is the NUG, which was formed in April 2022 by elected politicians of the NLD and a wide range of political allies, including a number of EROs. The NUG provides political and legal representation for the country's federal democratic forces but is just one of many actors in a much wider coalition taking part in what is referred to as the "Spring Revolution".

This coalition is represented by the National Unity Consultative Council (NUCC), that was formed in March 2021 and appointed the cabinet of the NUG. The NUCC membership includes elected members of parliament, an estimated seven EROs, multiple ethnic and pro-democracy political parties, strike committees and civil society organisations. The four best known EROs in the NUCC are the Chin National Front (CNF), the Kachin Independence Organisation (KIO), the Karenni National Progressive Party (KNPP) and the Karen National Union (KNU).

The NUCC has drafted a Federal Democracy Charter (FDC) that provides a political roadmap and vision for the movement, committing to the complete removal of the military from national politics and the formation of a federal constitution that provides ethnic states with significant local autonomy. The FDC also establishes a wide range of protections of human rights, women's rights and indigenous rights in line with the demands of the NUCC's diverse membership. The FDC was first released in April 2021, but it has been through numerous re-negotiations and edits since.

Since the attempted coup, a range of transformational changes on the ground have greatly weakened the junta's governance capacity and created space for resistance organisations to establish their authority across much of the country. The most immediate shift came as a result of the civil-disobedience movement (CDM), which saw hundreds of thousands of civil servants join protests nationwide, including a few thousand police and military personnel. The CDM movement, alongside mass boycotts of taxes or utility bills, soon led to a year-on-year loss in state revenues amounting to around 35 per cent, without accounting for extensive inflation (World Bank 2022, 11). The CDM movement effectively denied the junta control of state infrastructure and decimated its hopes of stabilising control. Village Tract and Ward Administrators (VTWAs) were among the most significant CDM participants, as they made it difficult for the junta to assert control in areas without a strong direct security presence.

Violent crackdowns soon followed, leading the UN to declare that the "illegal military junta has waged a relentless war against the people of Myanmar and their fundamental rights" (UNOHCHR 2022). The junta's violence had two major impacts that propelled the anti-coup movement to a next level, catalysing the launch of full-fledged revolutionary movement. The first impact was that thousands of politicians and democracy activists fled to areas controlled by EROs who housed them in displaced persons camps. This shift greatly improved the popularity of EROs among democracy activists and the wider public. At the same time, many people who had never experienced human rights abuses first-hand, began to empathise with ethnic nationality communities who had faced such abuse for decades, greatly increasing inter-ethnic solidarity among the general public (Crisis Group 2022).

The second impact of junta brutality was that it led large numbers of defiant citizens to the conclusion that armed resistance was the only route to democracy, catalysing the formation of hundreds of armed 'defence forces'. While politicised youth provided much of the energy and determination driving this turn to armed resistance, the new forces gained recruits and funding from people of all ages and backgrounds, and were seen by many rural communities as necessary for self-defence against an increasingly unhinged military (Ye Myo Hein 2022).

The armed conflict escalated dramatically after the NUG's September declaration of 'defensive war' against the SAC. Between September 2021 and at least March 2022, the number of armed conflict incidents increased month-on-month to levels that had not been seen for many decades (SAC-M 2022; Ye Myo Hein 2022). By this time, there were hundreds of defence forces across the country, including 'People's Defence Forces' (PDFs) officially associated with the NUG, as well as local defence forces (LDFs) that acted more autonomously or under the authority of EROs.

In September 2022, a report launched by a panel of former UN diplomats called the Special Advisory Council for Myanmar (SAC-M 2022), claimed that the junta had stable control over just 72 of the country's townships (23%), while resistance organisations held increasingly secure territories in 127 townships (38%), spread across the majority of states and regions. It is in these latter areas, that resistance organisations have been strengthening their political authority and systems of governance.

Part Two of the FDC is intended to provide a legal framework for governance during the revolutionary (or 'interim') period. At the time of writing, some of the stakeholders in the NUCC are still not satisfied with the text and consider it a working draft, meaning that it has not been fully employed in practice. This document or another text developed for the same purpose 'could prove to be very important for resistance organisations to gain external legal recognition of their authority, potentially allowing them to be recognised as the bearer of duties and obligations of the Myanmar state.

CONCEPTS AND THEORY

In this section, I will define some key terms and introduce some theoretical concepts that help to understand the significance of resistance political authority and governance. It is separated into four sub-sections. The first sub-section defines political authority, public administration and governance and explains their relevance to this discussion. The second sub-section defines civil wars as spaces of contested political authority. The third sub-section looks at the importance that insurgent and counter-insurgent theorists have owed to public administration, emphasising its functional importance to winning asymmetrical civil wars in particular. The fourth sub-section draws on the concepts of 'emergent federalism' and 'infrastructural capacity' to provide a framework for speculating on the ways that revolutionary governance systems could provide a foundation for a future federal system of government.

Governance, political authority, and public administration

In the past decade, there have been a number of influential studies on the governance systems of so-called 'rebels' (Weinstein 2007; Mampilly 2011; Arjona et al. 2015; Arjona 2017) or 'violent non-state actors' (Risse 2011; Börzel and Risse 2021). Brenner (2019) has looked at "rebel politics" in Myanmar and usefully departs from the rationalist models used in those other works. He views "rebellion" as a figuration, or a collection of social relations, that shape the behaviours of those who take part. Specifically, he explores how rebel elites and non-elites are bound together in a kind of social contract that satisfies their social expectations.

I do not use the term 'rebel' and opt instead for resistance and revolutionary, in tune with the Burmese term တော်လှန်ရေး, which is typically translated as 'revolution' but sometimes as 'resistance'.[3] This is how the main organisations and movements discussed in this article define themselves, as the Burmese for 'rebel' (သူပုန်) is used as pejorative slander by the Myanmar Armed Forces and state media, along with 'terrorist' (အကြမ်းဖက်). While the term 'rebel' emphasises pushback against an existing order, 'resistance' implies the protection of an existing, desired order against a malevolent intrusion. Revolution indicates the complete removal of a problematic system of power and is essentially constructive as well as destructive. These are both apt in the context of Myanmar's

EROs and NUG.

Furthermore, I use the concepts of political authority and public administration as they are more specific than governance per se and speak more closely to the particular relationships that armed resistance organisations have with the communities in areas they control. Börzel and Risse (2021, 3) define governance as "the provision of collective goods and services, such as security, human rights, and the rule of law, democracy, health, education, food security, and others", opening up the concept to a vast range of actors other than those explicitly considered governments, including corporations and non-profit organisations. I still regularly use the term 'governance' in this way, but use additional terms to make the nature of this form of governance more specific.

'Political authority' relates to the capacity of a political entity to make and enforce rules for society. More specifically, it requires that the political entity also claims a right to do so, and is recognised as having that right by a meaningful portion of society (Kletzer & Renzo 2020, 195–196; Christiano 2020). As Mampilly (2011, 1529) notes in his landmark study on 'rebel rulers', "Authority requires a degree of consent even if this is partially derived from the coercive capacity of the political regime". In my usage of political authority, I see both of these elements as crucial. There must be both coercive capacity on behalf of the authority and a degree of consent among the society that is governed. What matters is that the people subject to authority are not responding to pure coercion in the way that they would to a gang of criminals issuing threats. Rather, where political authority exists, it suggests that social norms have arisen where a certain actor has a widely recognised role in making and enforcing rules for society.

Political authority, therefore, highlights how governance by resistance organisations is much more analogous to that of modern-day states than it is to governmental organisations and private companies. This is not to say that resistance organisations are embryonic states or on some kind of linear path to statehood — rather, they exist in direct relation to modern states and compete in the same field (Mampilly 2011, 936). Like states, resistance organisations in Myanmar regularly engage in public administration, which further separates them from kinds of non-state governance actors. Rumki Basu (2019, 2) lists a range of activities that all public administrators carry out regardless of regime type or ideology: tax collection, maintenance of law and order, and provision of public goods and utilities. These activities all require a degree of political authority and generally rely on a system of laws as well as a claim to the legitimate use of force.

In Myanmar, administration (အုပ်ချုပ်ရေး) is the main term for political decision-making and for governance of civilians within the Myanmar state system and in most armed organisation governance systems. The same word is used for the 'executive' branch of government, and it literally translates to both executive decisions and to control of a particular area or system. Under successive regimes the most powerful civilian-facing department of the government has been the General Administration Department (GAD) (Chit Saw and Arnold 2014). Rather than citizens each having independent relationships with each ministry or relevant office, much of their interaction with the state is funnelled through their ward or village-tract administrators. At township and district levels, the central administrators coordinate all other departments. At the local level, every village, village tract and ward has a central administrator who is seen as the community's political leader and representative of the state (Chit Saw & Arnold 2014).

ERO governance systems are typically based explicitly on features from political party structures or military command structures. But, in practice, they also often use a similar graded hierarchical administration system, with central administrators or chairpersons at each level being the fulcrum of all civilian activities and village or village-tract leaders being the central interface between the public and their key departments (Jolliffe 2015). As we will see, these modes of "administration" are central to the way that new resistance governance systems are taking shape.

Contested political authority and the nature of Myanmar's civil war

Civil wars represent contexts where two or more parties that were previously under a common political authority are engaged in armed combat (Kalyvas 2006, 17). For both Trotsky and Lenin, a defining feature of revolutionary wars is the existence of "dual sovereignty" (Tilly 1978, 190–191) or "dual power" (Lenin 1975), whereby multiple blocs compete for political authority. Tilly (1978, 192) builds on this, emphasising that a revolution can be identified by the existence of a contestant to an existing authority, to whom members of the public begin paying taxes, providing military recruits, honouring symbols and so on, "despite the prohibitions of a still- existing government they formerly obeyed". As such, contest over political authority and governance should be understood as a central feature of civil and revolutionary wars, not a by-product or idiosyncrasy.

Myanmar's current civil war largely fits the definitions above, but there remain large areas controlled by EROs that have never been under a common authority and where incursions from Naypyitaw are experienced as something akin to foreign invasion. This makes the nature of contestation similar to processes of early state formation, that have been studied in Southeast Asia (Tambiah 1976; Wolters 1982; Young 2007; Scott 2009), in Western Europe (Tilly 1976; Tilly 1990), Central Asia (Tapper 1990), and elsewhere. These processes all involved combinations of sustained war (see Giustuzzi 2011, 6-12) and diplomacy (see Wolters 1982), leading larger central political authorities to secure dominion over smaller or less powerful political entities. Scott (2009) has shown how, for much of history, consolidation of political authority in Southeast Asia's mountainous areas has not been on a linear scale of progress, with states incrementally asserting increased authority over smaller orders. In many ways, Myanmar still remains in the throes of this cycle.

Political authority and governance as means to win revolutionary wars

Governance has long been considered a crucial element of armed resistance, by insurgent and counterinsurgent theorists alike. Writing in the 1930s, Mao (1989) famously noted that guerrilla warfare requires you to operate behind enemy lines, meaning that armed revolutionaries have to mix in with the population like fish in water. Ernesto 'Che' Guevara (2006, Chapter 3) emphasised how winning and sustaining support from the people requires guerrillas to defend "their interests and punishing anyone who attempts to take advantage of the instability in which they live". For this reason, he wrote, a judicial system, laws for penal and civil cases as well as agrarian reform projects are "vital to help the peasant to normalize and institutionalize his life within the rebel zone".

Eqbal Ahmad (1982, 241–242) from the National Liberation Front in Algeria wrote how victory depends "on out-administering, *not* on outfighting the enemy" in order to "morally isolate" the regime. He argued that revolution is "a constructive and not simply a destructive undertaking", meaning that the building of new institutions was not something that comes after the old ones have been destroyed (Ahmad

1982, 246). This, he explained, requires "an administrative structure to collect taxes, to provide some education and social welfare, and to maintain a modicum of economic activity," without which the guerrilla "would degenerate into banditry" (Ahmad 1982, 249). Similarly, Kwame Nkrumah's revolutionary strategy in Ghana focused on winning popular support through economic change. This strategy targeted peasants because they were "the overwhelming majority" and "because the revolutionary units live in their midst and depend on their assistance to survive" (Nkrumah 1969, 76). He emphasised how armed revolutionaries must establish "civilian organisations" responsible for taxation, supply, propaganda, and the formulation of laws (Nkrumah 1969, 121).

Counterinsurgent theorists going back to the 1960s — such as Fall (1965), Galula (1964), Trinquier (1964), Kilcullen (2010) and others — all made similar observations and emphasised to military commanders how important winning the battle for civilian administration was to outlasting guerrilla movements. More recently, the modern US counterinsurgency manual, authored by retired army general and former Central Intelligence Agency director David Petraeus (2006, 1), was based largely on the goal of winning popular support through governance, justice provision and social support. It claims that "political power is the central issue in insurgencies and counterinsurgencies; each side aims to get the people to accept its governance or authority as legitimate" (Ibid.).

This means that claiming and defending territory is not merely a military task, which then lays the foundation for governance to come later. Particularly for armed actors that are much weaker militarily than their opponents, establishing political leadership and governance systems is a necessary part of the bid to claim and hold territory from the beginning. Ibrahim et al. (2022) propose a new model for understanding armed group control based on three spheres: economic, political and social. Control is claimed in each of these spheres using a range of practices, of which 'violence' is only one among others including "dispute resolution", "taxation", and so on. In addition to "coercive capacities", armed organisations are required to maintain organisational and financial capacities in order to hold territory.

Given the clear utility of governance systems to armed organisations, the majority of works on the topic are notably rationalist, viewing "rebels" or "violent non-state actors" as cohesive organisations with well-defined interests, which then purposefully develop governance systems as a means to achieve those interests (Olson 1993; Weinstein 2007; Mampilly 2011, 5598–5530; Chojnacki and Branovic 2011; Kasfir 2015, 1; Arjona 2017, 9; Arjona et al. 2015, 2; Staniland 2014, 2; and Börzel and Risse 2021, 134). In these works, rebels and civilians are seen as separate categories of actors that bargain with each other to achieve their interests. Brenner (2019, 170) rightly cautions us against excessively functionalist interpretations of this dynamic, arguing that "rebel" soldiers and taxpayers alike are socialised into their roles and perform them out of "preflexive, routinised, practice flowing from the rebel habitus rather than as the result of conscious deliberations over material payoffs".

Nonetheless, it remains evident that success in revolutionary war hinges on a capacity to establish political authority and publicly administer the population. The public administration systems of resistance organisations in Myanmar are, therefore, of crucial importance to their bid for control of the country and the defeat of the military junta. Despite gains by PDFs, NUG and other revolutionary organisations, the Myanmar Armed Forces is likely to maintain superior firepower across the country for some time. The goal for NUG and its allies will be to gain effective leadership over civilians so that their policies can be implemented, their social services can be delivered, their rules are followed, and their taxes are paid.

Bottom-up (emergent) federalism?

A federal solution that provides Myanmar's ethnic states with much greater autonomy has long been seen as the most appropriate mechanism for peacefully managing the country's ethnic divides, not least by ethnic politicians and revolutionary leaders (Silverstein 1959; Yawnghwe 1987; Smith 1999; Yawnghwe and Sakhong 2003; South 2008; Sai Aung Tun 2009; Sakhong 2010; Yawnghwe 2013). This goal was explicitly denied by the military, which tended toward a relentless centralisation of power, but in the process fuelled the decades-old resistance movements that have kept large areas outside of centralised control and outside of the official constitutional order (Smith 1999; Jolliffe 2015).

Reflecting on this decades-old discourse, Ashley South (2022: 451) notes that federalism in Myanmar has long been "discussed in terms of constitutions, roadmaps and other 'top-down' aspects". He argues, instead, that the focus (the analytical focus for scholars and the practical focus for EROs themselves) should be on the de facto federated arrangement emerging from "the many federal-like structures and practices of local autonomy already present in the country" (South 2022, 451). This approach encourages us to look past the specific legal arrangements that exist on paper and focus more on how political authority and governmental capacity is actually distributed.

This is of particular importance in Myanmar's post-2021 environment, where an illegal junta has effectively overridden the already questionable 2008 Constitution (Crouch 2021) and where resistance organisations and their plural governance and legal systems have far greater legitimacy than the military-controlled 'state' centred in Naypyitaw. For the duration of this civil war, Myanmar will remain in a state of constitutional ambiguity, meaning that the actual systems of authority on the ground will be of far more significance to the country's population than anything on paper.

These de facto arrangements will then take on further salience if the junta is defeated. While the federal democracy charter lays out a roadmap for a negotiated transition through multiple constitutional documents to a new permanent order — and even South (2022, 453) concedes that "Myanmar no doubt needs a blueprint for a federal political settlement at the elite level" — the realities on the ground will undoubtedly influence what emerges out of that process.

For now, the age-old challenge of uniting "the various indigenous ethnic groups so that each could enjoy a reasonable degree of cultural and political autonomy, retain its ethnic identity and at the same time share a common allegiance and national feeling with the other groups in the new state" (Silverstein 1959, 97) falls largely on the practical statebuilding activities underway and the actual power dynamics in play.

Specifically, the chances of a federal arrangement emerging and being successful could hinge on the level of "infrastructural power" that is present in each of those devolved states (Ziblatt 2004; Breen 2018). Infrastructural power is distinguished from despotic power as it relates to the existence of more consistent and impersonalised rules and procedures that enhance the capacity of the state to become routinised in everyday life and practices (Mann 1984, 189; Mann 1986). Ziblatt (2004) argues that such capacity — and the way it shapes "vertical state-society relations within the subunits of a potential federation" — is ultimately more important than the horizontal relations between the subunits themselves. In other words, local capacity for governance *within each sub-state* will be a major determinant of a federal political system's success.

Importantly, we should not assume that infrastructural capacity is only inherent in western-style formalised governance structures and systems. Indigenous, traditional or other customary governance practices are widespread in Myanmar and are often far more resilient and deeply embedded in local ways of life, compared to the more top-down and contrived systems of the central state. Resistance governance systems typically exhibit a wide range of cultural influences and backgrounds (Jolliffe 2016; Paul 2018; South 2022). Infrastructural power may indeed be strongest where stable systems of authority are built on the foundations of existing norms and customary practices.

Systems of political authority in the Myanmar resistance

This section provides a descriptive overview of the main systems of political authority and governance taking shape in territories controlled by Myanmar's resistance in 2022. It is separated into three sections, focused on EROs, the NUG and then local level coalitions in Chin and Karenni States, respectively. The information in this chapter is based on my observations while working with political and social organisations in Myanmar, and is supplemented by past research on governance systems in ethnic armed conflict areas.

It should be noted that all governance systems in Myanmar are heavily undergirded by a uniquely high degree of community-level organisation and self-governance. None of the systems discussed in this section were developed centrally by their respective organisations and then introduced and implemented across the territories. They all rely heavily on the existing political authority established at the village, village tract or ward level and depend on high levels of social capital in those local communities.

In both state and non-state areas, before and after the coup, most people have interacted with governance authorities through their village or ward leaders rather than directly with each government department. The majority of justice cases are handled at this level (Kyed 2020) and most people depend on local administrators for claiming property rights and for handling local disputes, amongst other essential actions (Chit Saw and Arnold 2014). Furthermore, large portions of funding and labour for schools, local roads and other key services are organised at the local level by public volunteer committees or by local *parahita* and other welfare organisations (Speers-Mears and Jolliffe 2016; Griffith 2019).

Therefore, resistance organisations (and the Myanmar government or junta) govern by establishing superstructures that are recognised by village, village-tract and ward leaders as well as by elders, local businesspeople, and other influential figures in those communities. All governance projects, rules and orders depend on strong coordination with recognised leaders at this local level. The challenge for aspirant political authorities is, arguably, to establish institutional superstructures that connect these units under a common overarching framework. These superstructures involve rules (sometimes officiated as laws) for society, and rules about rules (i.e. powers and limitations for administrators, soldiers and others within their system of authority).

Throughout its history, the Myanmar military has been extremely weak in establishing popular support or harnessing local networks and knowledge. As such, the superstructures it has sought to create in rural areas where it is competing with local customary authorities or EROs have been focused on cutting off recruits, intelligence and resources to its enemies. Even where civilian and service-oriented agencies of the state have reached these areas — as they did increasingly during the 2010s, owing to partial democratisation of the government and increased investments in social welfare — they have often been top-down in nature, failing to integrate local languages and cultures, thus often being experienced as an intruder (South 2010; South 2017; Paul 2018; Kim 2018; Kyed 2020).

Most visibly, the military-dominated state has typically sought to establish its authority in areas where resistance is strong by using extreme violence against all civilians it believes to be supportive of resistance forces. This is evident across the country today, where the military has responded to the presence of resistance actors by burning villages, livestock, rice stores and even people to sow fear and clear out entire populations. This emphasis on civilian governance as a means to control the public is also why the state's primary administrative body, the GAD, has been long kept under military command and is used to enforce curfews and other security measures (Kyit Saw and Arnold 2014; Crouch 2016).

When reading the following descriptions, therefore, it should be noted that practices of governance in Myanmar remain highly localised and that the governance systems of resistance organisations are at best an overarching superstructure atop much more deeply embedded customary practices (see also Decobert 2016; Jolliffe and Speers-Mears 2016; Kyed 2020).

Ethnic resistance organisations

ERO territories have grown enormously since the attempted coup of 2021, having been slowly eroded and degraded over successive decades since the late 1980s. In 2020, most EROs had been pushed further and further into remote mountainous areas and away from major roads that connect Myanmar's commercial and administrative hubs to border crossings and international borders. This was achieved through successive barbaric offensives aimed at physically removing people from ERO territories (Smith 1999, 259; Maung Aung Myoe 1999, 135-136; KHRG 2020), ceasefire capitalism initiatives that persuaded EROs to focus on extractive private projects (Woods 2011; Brenner 2015), and the expansion of the state into ceasefire areas via social services and international aid initiatives (Smith 1994; Jolliffe 2016; Kim 2019; Paul 2018). However, EROs are now increasingly able to operate in territories they had control of in previous decades due to the relative collapse of the SAC's public administration system and the swell of popular support for revolution, both locally and from communities in other parts of the country.

All EROs have some form of public administration system[4] but these vary greatly in their form, their institutional influences, their capacity and their overall effectiveness. Most have both civilian and military wings, with the former adopting a political party-like structure, holding congresses at regular intervals and electing committees to lead in the interim periods. These committees then oversee line departments for specific sectors, such as finance, natural resource management, justice, health and education.

Most EROs have written constitutions that stipulate rules for elections and the organisation of their departments and some also have written laws. The KNU's laws, for example, are based on the English Common Law system, adopted from the colonial government in addition to Karen customary concepts. Meanwhile, the United Wa State Party and some others adopted their constitutional structure from the Communist Party of Burma and have laws influenced by the those of the Chinese Communist Party. Many EROs have their own mapping systems that layout the boundaries of administrative units like village tracts, townships and districts. In some cases, these correlate to the operational areas of their military units; in others, they are based on traditional or colonial-era maps.

Many of the EROs have designated administration departments, similar to the General Administration Department of the Myanmar state, that oversee central administrators at various levels (e.g., village, township, district, or other local equivalents). These central figures act as executive decision-makers for their designated area and have to coordinate with all other departments. In some cases, they have ultimate control over the budget and ration distribution to all personnel in their areas. Some EROs — notably the KNU, KNPP and New Mon State Party — hold elections at each administrative level to select these central administrators, who stand as party chairpersons for their village tract, township or district. In these organisations, the civilian leaders are more senior to their military counterparts at each level. For example, in the KNU, district chairpersons are direct superiors to corresponding brigade commanders, and the Central Chairperson (sometimes called President) is superior to the Chief of Staff of the army. However, senior commanders at each administrative level enjoy automatic representation.

Most other EROs have closed election systems, participated in by existing members of the organisation, so communities do not elect them directly. Some are notably autocratic, with charismatic individual leaders or dynastic wealthy families at the helm. Others cooperate closely with local civil society, religious actors and political parties and have to generate support bases and consensus throughout the general public. Arguably, the KNU is the most legalistic in nature, displaying a strong reliance on well-established laws, rules and norms, while the Restoration Council of Shan State stands out as one of the most reliant on the charismatic aura of their principal leader, Yawd Serk.

EROs and other affiliated local organisations provide crucial social services to millions of people, in areas under their direct control and even in contested areas where the Myanmar state has a strong presence (Jolliffe 2014; Davis and Jolliffe 2016; Jolliffe and Speers-Mears 2016). EROs along the Thailand–Myanmar border have particularly advanced social assistance programmes, benefiting from vibrant networks of community-based organisations and indirect funding from foreign donors and NGOs. EROs in the north of the country have received private and state support from China. EROs along both borders have, for example, delivered hundreds of thousands of COVID-19 vaccines in recent years and were pivotal to maintaining safe border migration and quarantine regimes during the height of the pandemic.

For decades, the Myanmar military has used ceasefires and economic concessions for EROs as a strategy to distract them from their political goals and tie them into an extractive centralised economy (Woods 2011; Brenner 2015). This has added considerably to inequality, land confiscation and environmental degradation (Woods 2011; Paul 2018). In the north of the country, multiple EROs have benefited from proximity to China's booming economy and have developed their areas economically, bringing in considerable organisational revenue (in addition to significant profits for leaders). In the southeast of the country, "ceasefire capitalism" has only benefited a handful of individual leaders, splinter groups and factions (Brenner 2017; Jolliffe 2016; Kim 2018; KHRG 2020). Meanwhile, community-based indigenous and environmental organisations have collaborated with EROs in some areas to actively protect forests and establish locally-owned conservation areas. The most notable of these is the Salween Peace Park in northern Karen State, which is a community-led initiative managed by indigenous Karen communities in collaboration with the KNU (Jolliffe 2016; Paul 2018).

Since the attempted coup, the administration systems of the KNU, KIO and KNPP among others have been pivotal in the protection and shelter of persecuted politicians, civil servants and democracy activists. Collectively they received thousands of people, sheltering them in their territories or assisting them to reach other countries for their safety. These operations required comprehensive processes of COVID-19 screening and quarantine, as well as the provision of shelter, washing facilities, mosquito nets, food and other basic necessities. They and other EROs have also seen rapid increases in demand for social services, with school enrolment rates soaring and caseloads at clinics up considerably due to the collapse of the Myanmar state. In some cases, they have also been able to improve the quality of services by recruiting CDM health workers, teachers and other professionals.

EROs are also regularly called upon to adjudicate or enforce punishments in justice cases by local people. Justice is regularly one of the most rudimentary areas of governmental responsibility assumed by non-state armed organisations (Kilcullen 2010; Mampilly 2011; Arjona 2017). Some EROs have law books, formalised justice procedures and even independent judiciaries, while others form more *ad hoc* dispute resolution committees or act as guarantors for decisions made by local leaders or customary authorities (McCartan & Jolliffe 2016). In all areas, ERO justice systems draw heavily on traditional and customary systems and tend to be much more integrated with village and village tract-level justice practices than the Myanmar state system is (Kyed 2020).

Since the attempted coup, ERO justice systems have experienced much higher caseloads, and some have been investing considerably in hiring more judges or preparing their existing networks. EROs have also had to take greatly increased numbers of live enemy combatants during this period and detain them in accordance with international law. This has required significant institutional capacity and commitment and many of these systems are facing resource constraints.

The National Unity Government

In the months following its declaration of a "People's Defensive War" in September 2022, the NUG began coordinating its ministries and local networks to establish a public administration system for the growing territories coming under PDF control. An inter-ministerial committee was established at the central level and the Ministry of Home Affairs was tasked with overseeing and organising township level Pa-Ah-Pa units. Hundreds of Pa-Ah-Pa had been formed in March 2021, following an initial announcement by Committee Representing the People's Hluttaw, led by elected NLD members. The Pa-Ah-Pa sit alongside Pyithu Kakwe a'Pweh (Pa Ka Pa) units for defence, which report to the Ministry of Defence and are tasked with coordinating the multitudinous PDF and LDF forces under each township.

A decision was made early in 2022 to not establish NUG-affiliated public administration structures in any ERO areas or areas where local coalition councils claimed this responsibility. As a result, the NUG has focused primarily on establishing its administration system in central predominantly Bamar areas of Sagaing and Magway regions and to a lesser extent, Bago and Mandalay. The NUG has delivered nationwide and region-specific trainings and distributed funds to the priority townships and districts and has conducted pilot projects in key townships. PDFs and LDFs in these regions have steadily increased their hold on territories, taking over large rural areas in 2022, despite constant violent backlash from the SAC (SAC-M 2022).

In these rural areas, the Pa-Ah-Pa have been primarily occupied with the facilitation of humanitarian assistance. As zones of control have become more stable, NUG-affiliated bodies have been able to reopen schools and resume other fixed-point services, such as clinics and childcare centres. All of these services rely heavily on bottom-up efforts from the communities where they operate, while the NUG bodies generally play a coordination, facilitation or policy guidance role, in addition to the sporadic distribution of funds. The NUG Education and Healthcare Ministries have both been highly active in collaboration with existing community-based and ethnic social service networks to bring in external funding, provide training guidelines, assessment frameworks and other education and health systems infrastructures. This has included support for service delivery on-the-ground and online.

But Pa-Ah-Pa are also active in areas with limited territorial control, such as major cities, where they mobilise the public to boycott SAC taxes and utility bills, to join the CDM movement and to take part in rallies and strikes. They also facilitate legal aid and cash or food assistance to political prisoners and their families. Some Pa-Ah-Pa have been active in organising recruits and collecting donations for the PDFs. Over time, we may see the Pa-Ah-Pa take on a more explicit township-level leadership role by coordinating the activities and budgets of other departments or taking on other local level executive functions. It is also possible that more executive responsibility will be handed to district or regional level bodies that oversee Pa-Ah-Pa in the future.

The NUG Ministry of Home Affairs and Immigration and Ministry of Justice have also been developing a justice system, which includes remote and online elements and on-the-ground bodies for territories coming under their control. These include township-level justice committees formed by Ministry of Justice as well as union-level and more localised police forces tasked with local law enforcement and war crimes investigations. The justice system includes independent judges and committees, state prosecutors and detention facilities. This builds in some cases on local justice efforts initiated much earlier by community leaders, LDFs or other actors. The NUG justice system is very much still a work in progress and remains constrained by the security situation as well as capacity and resources constraints.

Local coalitions in Chin and Karenni States

In Chin and Karenni[5] States, dynamic coalitions of diverse revolutionary actors have emerged and are undertaking public administration activities. These include politicians elected to local constituencies, EROs, local political parties, student activists, and CDM workers from varied sectors and civil society organisations. Both states have long-standing EROs that struggled to hold large territories before the attempted coup but have grown in stature since 2021, through intensive collaboration with their new coalitions. The KSCC and ICNCC were both established in the week prior to the formation of the union-level NUG, announcing that they would take the lead in political and governance affairs for their states. This effectively marked the formation of two autonomous states within an interim federal union that could co-exist with the NUG under a common framework.

In Karenni State, there has been significant coalition building at the state level through the KSCC, which includes multiple local parties, NLD politicians, multiple EROs, youth leaders, women's organisations and CDM representatives, among others. The most prominent ERO, which currently chairs the KSCC, is the KNPP. The KNPP formed a Karenni Government in the 1950s, which remains in place and operates in coordination with the KSCC.

The KSCC was established on 9 April 2021 (one week before NUG), with an announcement stating ambitions to form a "genuine federal state" and to practice self-determination. The statement also emphasised the goal of achieving national unity within the state, highlighting the KSCC's efforts to bring together a diverse set of political and armed factions, from the Kayah, Kayan and other local ethnic groups. Remarkably, the coalition includes numerous border guard forces and militia groups that had splintered away from resistance forces in earlier decades to support the Myanmar military.

On 18 April 2021, the KSCC welcomed the formation of the NUG and vowed to work together with the NUCC and NUG from the interim period until a federal democratic state could be achieved. Importantly however, the KSCC stated that it would lead the administration, legislative affairs, judiciary affairs for Karenni State during the interim period in partnership with NUCC and NUG. This set an important precedent for an ethnic state claiming local rights to political autonomy during the revolutionary period, under a legal framework compatible with that of the NUG.

At the time of writing, the KSCC is developing a framework for a Karenni State interim governing authority that will assume the state's responsibilities for the period while the war against the junta is ongoing. This has taken some time due to the multiplicity of actors and existing territorial arrangements in place. In the meantime, the council has been able to undertake a wide range of governance activities through a range of sub-committees.

Through its security and defence committee, the KSCC oversees the Karenni Nationalities Defence Force, a coalition of LDFs with 21 battalions under a single command. In February 2022, the KNDF announced that together with the KNPP, they control 90 per cent of Karenni State, having limited the junta troops to precarious garrison positions in the towns, dependent on airlifted supplies.

The security and defence committee also oversees the Karenni State Police, a newly formed service with around 300 personnel. Most members are former Myanmar police force officers, who joined the CDM. The KSP's founding documents and mission were developed in consultation with local civil society human rights organisations and it is envisaged as a service rather than a force. It has been receiving cases since mid-2021 and implemented a mechanism for processing and questioning all suspected informants apprehended by defence forces, to reduce arbitrary violence and killings. The KSP has also played an active role in investigating war crimes, identifying victims and facilitating the return of bodies among other important tasks.[6]

The KSCC also oversees state-level committees for education, healthcare, humanitarian assistance, defence and security, and alliance affairs. It has helped communities to reopen hundreds of schools across the state in addition to facilitating emergency assistance and other support. The Karenni Mobile Healthcare Committee has been active for many years as a coalition of ERO health wings from various organisations in the state. They have been able to deliver thousands of COVID-19 vaccines and, since the coup, provide critical primary healthcare services to IDPs and rural communities.

In Chin State, the most active coalitions focused on public administration are People's Administration bodies formed at the township level. These are essentially Pa-Ah-Pa but have been organised under local authority rather than the NUG, citing the 1948 Chin Act, which provides official recognition to customary Chin law and has never been repealed. Nonetheless, they have coordinated and cooperated closely with the NUG and some have received funding from the NUG budget.

The most active of these bodies have been in Mindat, Thantlang, Kanpetlet, among others. There are also strong Chin community initiatives in Kalay Township of Magway Region. They have re-opened thousands of schools across the township and have established police forces, agricultural departments and units for other key sectors. They tend to work in parallel with corresponding township level Chinland Defence Forces (CDFs) or other defence units.

At the state level, the ICNCC was formed on 13 April 2021 by elected MPs (all from the NLD), Chin political parties, the Chin National Front and civil society organisations (including youth and student activists). Each of these four blocs provides eighteen representatives and two co-chairs. In its founding statement, the ICNCC announced that it would establish an Interim Chin State Government to take care of administrative (executive), legislative and judicial affairs for the interim period. At the time of writing, this process is still ongoing as the ICNCC has received various proposals and is balancing the needs and perspectives of many groups, tribes and geographical differences within the state. In the meantime, the township administrations have begun increasingly coordinating and some state level boards and departments have been formed for certain areas of governance.

In October 2021, the Chinland Joint Defence Committee (CJDC) was formed to coordinate the defence forces in the region, including the Chin National Front's armed wing, the CDFs and the Chinland National Defence Force. The CJDF's headquarters is in the territory of the CNF and that group plays a leadership role. These forces collectively control the majority of territory in Chin State with certain townships around 80–90 per cent under the control of the resistance and the junta restricted to remote use of air strikes, artillery and the occasional dispatch of well defended armoured convoys.

IMPLICATIONS FOR THE OUTCOME OF THE CIVIL WAR

In these final two sections, I will examine the implications of resistance political authority and governance for the objectives of the federal democracy movement. In line with the theoretical concepts introduced earlier, I will firstly discuss the importance of these governance systems for the ongoing struggle to defeat the military junta. In the following section, I will then discuss their potential to provide a foundation for a lasting federal democratic union that addresses the root causes of Myanmar's protracted conflicts and human rights crises.

So far, the NUG and LDFs have relied heavily on widespread popular support and huge sacrifices made by ordinary people and communities that refuse to go under military rule. This popular support will likely continue to be their primary strength. But, as observed by insurgent theorists such as Mao, Che, Nkrumah and Ahmad, as well as counterinsurgent theorists such as Fall, Petraeus and Kilcullen, long-term success will likely depend on this popular support being institutionalised in governance structures that cement a kind of two-way relationship between the revolutionaries and the general public. As Brenner (2019) notes, it is simplistic to view 'rebels' and 'civilians' as distinct rational actors in a kind of negotiation for mutual benefits. Nonetheless, governance systems and political authority clearly have huge practical value for armed resistance efforts, as proven by Myanmar's largely undefeatable EROs.

According to the FDC, this stage of the movement is the "interim" phase, with a focus on collaborating to defeat the junta. This will be followed by the implementation of a transitional constitution, while the final version of a permanent federal democratic constitution is negotiated. Interim governance arrangements are covered in the FDC, which establishes a basis for the NUG in addition to state governments and 'federal units', as well as autonomous state-level courts. The document also recognises customary law in ethnic areas and the existing justice and governance systems of EROs. However, the text is vague and most of these provisions are open to interpretation. In practice, numerous NUCC stakeholders remain unsure about the text and consider it to be a working document.

In the meantime, the NUG has de facto authority to lead local governance in Sagaing, Magway and other areas considered majority Bamar, while ERO areas remain autonomous and the Chin and Karenni States are under the authority of their consultative councils. This has created a de facto arrangement that is similar to the 1947 constitution, whereby 'Myanmar proper' is governed by the central government (in this case, the NUG) while certain areas are official devolved to local governments. This coincidentally resembles the division of powers that exists in the United Kingdom, but is not really a federal structure. During the interim period, this may remain the most practical option for ensuring all resistance territories are under a common constitutional framework while allowing certain territories and communities to exercise self-determination.

Governance during the interim phase could be very important simply because this phase could be very long. Despite the focus on ending dictatorship, there are urgent humanitarian, social and other crises that require a governance response and cannot wait. The primary task of these governance institutions will be to increase humanitarian aid to the hundreds of thousands of internally displaced people, in partnership with local humanitarian organisations. Over time, it is likely that provision of justice, local taxation and regulation of natural resources will also emerge as core functions of these actors, as has been the case for EROs for decades.

Each of these sectors provides opportunities for service-oriented approaches that will sustain the popularity of the resistance. But they also present risks that resistance organisations will abuse their power and get distracted by parochial or private interests at the expense of the public. These governance institutions will be shaped as much by the local communities and spontaneous organisations that have driven the revolution so far than the top-down leadership of the NUG or locally led coalitions. Sustained investment from the many revolutionary actors, from the general public and from the community of international Myanmar networks will be needed to ensure that governance institutions emerge that are beholden to the public interest.

The security situation will also have a major impact on the success of resistance governance systems. Without local administrators in place and lacking any trust or goodwill from the public, the junta has resorted to forcibly displacing entire populations from areas where the resistance is strong. This is extremely resource- and time-consuming for the SAC and is only possible in a few specific locations at a time, meaning that flexible and mobile local governance initiatives have huge space to provide services. However, the most immediate challenge for new resistance administration systems is the non-stop violent campaigns being meted out by the Myanmar military against women, men and children wherever the defence forces gain an upper hand. The SAC cannot re-establish control of these territories so it simply uses brute force to send them into disarray.

Another tool the junta will try to use to its advantage is the political economy. Its primary collaborators in conflict-affected regions across the country have long been those who can make money, whether that be through legitimate businesses that require stability or illegal entities that pay bribes for protection, like drug producers and traffickers or local gambling dens. It also includes legitimate business owners who depend on junta permissions for things like travelling across the country through checkpoints. Businesses and employees who rely on this kind of infrastructure appear to be among the few who do not outright reject SAC authority and provide it with taxes, fees and information. But their calculations are likely starting to change as PDFs exert increase control over roads and riverways.

The goal for resistance organisations will be to establish sufficient security so that people can return to their farms or jobs and schools can reopen. This will depend in large part on how much control the resistance can gain over major arteries, such as rivers like the Ayeryawaddy, Chindwin, Salween (Thanlwin) and Kaladan as well as strategic roadways like Kale-Gangaw-Taze, Loikaw-Taunggyi-Taungoo Hpapun-Hpa-an- Bilin and Monhyin-Myitkyina. Territorial control and security will likely not be a zero-sum outcome for a long time, with communities sporadically being displaced for days at a time and, in some cases, young and elderly relocating to more stable areas (deeper in resistance areas, into government-controlled towns) or across borders, while others stay to retain access to land and livelihoods. Eventually, we may see urban areas falling under the control of the resistance, opening up a whole new set of challenges and possibilities for these emerging governance systems.

Another important factor will be the evolution of civilian-military relations at various levels of the resistance movement. Stronger and more capable civilian governance bodies will be in a much better position ensure checks, balances and oversight to the PDFs. As seen in Karenni State and some EROs, military wings are likely more willing to come under unified command and civilian leadership in areas where there are capable and active civilian leaders providing a wide range of auxiliary functions for the benefit of local people and for the revolution writ large. Similarly, successful governance will require security bodies in the resistance to maintain distance from affairs that are not their direct responsibility.

International action or inaction will also be highly influential. CDM staff and other first responders at the local level are calling repeatedly for increase assistance that bypasses SAC and gets straight to the people who actually work with and lead in their communities. EROs and the NUG have also made proposals for an internationally mandated aid forum that can deliver aid via their institutions and pressure the SAC to allow humanitarian access. On the other hand, the SAC will likely become increasingly dependent on foreign military and development assistance in order to survive.

CAN RESISTANCE GOVERNANCE PROVIDE A FOUNDATION FOR FEDERAL DEMOCRACY?

What potential is there for resistance governance systems to support the creation of a lasting federal democratic union that balances power effectively between the various territories and national communities that inhabit it? It could be argued that Myanmar's endemic struggles with military rule, ingrained kleptocracy, and systematic human rights violations all stem from a central cleavage between the central state and the indigenous societies that surround it and maintain alternative national visions. The Myanmar military has long justified its dominant role in politics by framing itself as a guardian, without whom the country would break apart and descend into chaos (Egreteau 2016). Specifically, it has repeatedly argued that comprehensive constitutional reform can only take place when EROs have disbanded (Min Zin 2018). EROs, meanwhile have insisted that they will not even consider integration or disbandment without constitutional reform towards federalism that provides their people with self-determination.

This has created a vicious cycle of mutually-reinforcing trends. On the one hand is the state's tendency towards militarisation and centralisation. On the other, is the tendency of non-Bamar communities to invest in their own self-determination and their own governance and security institutions, outside of state control. These two trends reinforce each other in perpetuity. Federalism is regularly – and understandably – put forward as the solution to this problem, by ensuring a compromise between the desire for unity and the local demand for autonomy (Yawnghwe 1987; Sai Aung Tun 2009; Yawnghwe and Sakhong 2003; Sakhong 2010).

The NUCC and NUG have thus far focused their political vision on the promise of federal democracy as a means to solve this central problem and finally push the military out of politics at the same time. This will require an immense transformation to undo the legacy of colonialism and decades of military rule, which have constructed a state that is focused on centralised coercion and extraction, and which treats service and inclusion as afterthoughts.

Despite hopes embedded in the FDC that the revolution will come to a neat end and give way to an inclusive process of dialogue, it is also quite possible that this 'interim' phase will drag on and that the most significant institutional developments will be those that emerge from the existing power dynamics on the ground (see South 2022). Myanmar may never have a single watershed moment when a blueprint constitutional document can be agreed by consensus, and the dilemma of unity versus self-determination can finally be solved so that harmony can finally reign. As has been the case in many ethnic areas since independence, it is quite possible that politics and governance in Myanmar will continue to be defined by contestation for many years. Peace and democracy will likely come, if at all, from the slow and painstaking process of building new institutions that can incrementally replace those of oppression and warfare.

Nonetheless, it could be argued that Myanmar sits at a critical juncture, as so many pre-coup institutions and embedded practices have broken down (see Collier and Collier 1991). It is therefore likely that new institutions and practices that take hold during this period will have lasting impacts on the politics of coming decades. Governance structures that emerge in the throes of revolution, however rudimentary, will be of crucial significance to the way that the country emerges from this period of turmoil (South 2022). For a sustainable federal system of government to emerge, it will be necessary for the constituent states to have significant infrastructural power relative to the centre (Ziblatt 2004; Breen 2018). If a core of proto-states emerge from this revolution with significant governance capacity and authority, and if they manage to develop a legal framework that connects them and maintains unity, the country will be on a firm footing for the negotiation of a permanent federal democratic system of government.

In summary, if the SAC continues to collapse, even if it does not conclusively lose for some time, the strength and nature of civilian interim administration will be a core determinant of the political future of the country. All later negotiations for constitutional reform will be shaped by the realities on the ground. In key parts of the country, the work has already begun of constructing new governments that are entirely separate from the coercive and extractive institutions which evolved through centuries of colonial and military rule. These could be the seeds of Myanmar's peaceful and democratic future.

Notes

1. EROs refers to all ethnic-based armed resistance movements that are politically opposed to the military regime centred in Naypyitaw, regardless of whether they have ceasefires in place or whether or not they are explicitly aligned with the NUG. Ethnic Armed Organisations (EAOs) was the most common English language term for these groups between 2013–2021, after it was agreed in the negotiations leading up the Nationwide Ceasefire Agreement. However, even during those negotiations, the ERO delegation stated a preference for including the term တော်လှန်ရေး, (which is usually translated as revolution, or sometimes resistance). This marker separates them from purely armed militant groups and from militia that are aligned with the Myanmar Armed Forces. Since 2021, EROs has become the term agreed among the various revolutionary forces and appears in the Federal Democracy Charter and other core documents. It also appears in position papers of the Federal Political Negotiation and Consultative Committee that represents seven EROs, led by the United Wa State Party. Objectively, EROs is a more apt term than EAOs for armed organisations that engage in multi-dimensional resistance, including politics, governance, international diplomacy, mass mobilisation, and so on.
2. Some of the analysis in this chapter draws on earlier work by the author, which appeared in two unpublished papers, called "Brief 5: Gaining Ground: Local Administration by Resistance Actors in Myanmar", co-authored by Matthew Arnold and Kim Jolliffe in January 2022, and "Self-determination under an interim constitutional framework: Local administration in ethnic areas of Myanmar", co-authored by Naw Show Ei Ei Tun and Kim Jolliffe in June 2022. The author would like to thank Naw Show Ei Ei Tun and Matthew Arnold for the opportunity to collaborate on those earlier papers and for knowledge co-creation that contributed to this chapter.
3. 'Revolution' is a more common translation but the FDC uses 'resistance'. I use both interchangeably.
4. This section provides a cursory overview of ERO administration systems. See existing research by this author and others: Jolliffe 2015; Davis and Jolliffe 2016; Jolliffe and McCartan 2016; Jolliffe 2017; South 2017; Saferworld 2019; Brenner 2019; Kyed 2020; Ong 2020; South 2022.
5. Karenni State refers to the territory of the independent Karenni kingdom that existed until Myanmar's independence under a treaty to the United Kingdom. It corresponds to all of Kayah State, plus some adjacent parts of Shan State. It is still recognised by the KNPP and KSCC and forms the basis for their administration systems.

6   For example, the KSP played a central role in identifying victims and assisting body return and funeral arrangements following the Moso Christmas Eve Massacre of 2021. The KSP is investigating and collecting evidence on the case for future trial. See https://www.mizzima.com/article/karenni-police-confirm-details-christmas-eve-massacre (accessed 10 February 2023).

References

Ahmad, Eqbal (1982). "Revolutionary Warfare and Counterinsurgency." In *Guerrilla Strategies: An Historical Anthology from the Long March to Afghanistan*, edited by Gérard Chaliand. Berkeley and Los Angeles: University of California Press, 241–62.

Arjona, Ana (2017). *Rebelocracy, Social Order in the Colombian Civil War*. New York: Cambridge University Press.

Arjona, Ana, Nelson Kasfir, and Zachariah Mampilly (2015). "Introduction." In *Rebel Governance in Civil War*, edited by Ana Anjona, Nelson Kasfir and Zachariah Mampilly. Cambridge: Cambridge University Press, 1–20.

Bahiss, Ibraheem, Ashley Jackson, Leigh Mayhew and Florian Weigand (2022). "Rethinking Armed Group Control: Towards a New Conceptual Framework." *Centre for the Study of Armed Groups Working Paper*. Overseas Development Institute: London.

Basu, Rumki (2019). *Public Administration in the 21st Century: A Global South Perspective*. London and New York: Routledge.

Börzel, Tanja and Thomas Risse (2021). *Effective Governance Under Anarchy: Institutions, Legitimacy, and Social Trust in Areas of Limited Statehood*. Cambridge: Cambridge University Press.

Breen, Michael (2018). "The Origins of Holding-Together Federalism: Nepal, Myanmar, and Sri Lanka." *Publius: The Journal of Federalism* 48 (1):26–50.

Brenner, David (2017). "Authority in Rebel Groups: Identity, Recognition and the Struggle over Legitimacy." *Contemporary Politics* 23 (4): 408–426.

----- (2019). *Rebel Politics: A Political Sociology of Armed Struggle in Myanmar's Borderlands*. Ithaca and London: Cornell University Press.

Callahan, M. (2007). *Political Authority in Burma's Ethnic Minority States: Devolution, Occupation and Coexistence*. Washington DC: East West Center.

Chit Saw and Arnold (2014). "Administering the State in Myanmar: An Overview of the General Administration Department." *The Asia Foundation and Myanmar Development Resource Institute Discussion Paper No. 6*. Available at https://asiafoundation.org/resources/pdfs/GADEnglish.pdf (accessed 10 February 2023).

Christiano, Tom (2020). "Authority." *The Stanford Encyclopedia of Philosophy* (Summer 2020 Edition), edited by Edward N. Zalta. Available at: <https://plato.stanford.edu/archives/sum2020/entries/authority/>.

Chojnacki, S. and Z. Branovic(2011). "New Modes of Security: The Violent Making and Unmaking of Governance in War-Torn Areas of Limited Statehood." In *Governance Without a State? Policies and Politics in Areas of Limited Statehood*, edited by T. Risse. New York: Columbia University Press.

Collier, D. and Collier, R. B. (1991). *Shaping the Political Arena: Critical Junctures, the Labor Movement and Regime Dynamics in Latin America*. Princeton: Princeton University Press.

Crisis Group (2022). "Myanmar's Coup Shakes Up Its Ethnic Conflicts," *International Crisis Group*. Available at https://www.crisisgroup.org/asia/south-east-asia/myanmar/319-myanmars-coup-shakes-its-ethnic-conflicts (accessed 10 February 2023).

Crouch, Melissa (2016). "The Everyday Emergency: Between the Constitution and the Code of Criminal Procedure in Myanmar." In *Constitutional Change and Legal Reform in Myanmar*, edited by A. Harding. Oxford: Hart Publishing.

----- (2021). "The Illegality of the Myanmar Coup." Melissa Crouch's website. Available at: https://melissacrouch.com/2021/02/07/the-illegality-of-myanmars-coup/

Davis, Bill, and Kim Jolliffe. 2016. *Achieving Health Equity in Contested Areas of Southeast Myanmar*. The Asia Foundation. Available at: http://asiafoundation.org/publication/achieving-health-equity-contested-areas-southeast-myanmar/ (accessed 10 February 2023).

Decobert, A. (2016). *The Politics of Aid to Burma: A Humanitarian Struggle on the Thai-Burmese Border*. Oxon: Routledge.

Egreteau, R. (2016). *Caretaking Democratization: The Military and Political Change in Myanmar*. London: Hurst.

Fall, Bernard B (1965). *The Theory and Practice of Insurgency and Counterinsurgency*. Naval War College Review, U.S. Naval War College: Newport Rhode Island.

Galula, David (1964). *Counterinsurgency Warfare; Theory and Practice*. New York: Praeger Security International.

Giustuzzi, Antonio (2011). *The Art of Coercion: The Primitive Accumulation and Management of Coercive Power*. New York: Columbia University Press.

Gravers, Mikael (1999 [1993]). *Nationalism as Political Propaganda in Burma*. Surrey: Curzon.

Griffiths, Michale P. (2019). *Community Welfare Organisations in Rural Myanmar: Precarity and Parahita*. New York: Routledge.

Guevara, Ernesto (2006 [1961]). *Guerrilla Warfare*. London: Harper Millenial.

Jolliffe, Kim (2011). "Dilemmas of Burma in Transition.", *Forced Migration Review* 37.

--- (2014), "Ethnic Conflict and Social Services in Myanmar's Contested Regions." *The Asia Foundation*.
--- (2015) "Ethnic Armed Conflict and Territorial Administration in Myanmar." *The Asia Foundation*.
--- (2017a). "Ceasefires, Governance and Development: The Karen National Union in Times of Change." *The Asia Foundation*.
--- (2017b). "Security Integration in Myanmar: Past Experiences and Future Visions." *Saferworld*.
--- (2018). "Peace and Reconciliation." *Routledge Handbook of Contemporary Myanmar*, edited by Adam Simpson, Nicholas Farrelly and Ian Holliday. Oxon: Routledge.
Jolliffe, Kim, and Emily Speers-Mears (2016). "Strength in Diversity: Towards Universal Education in Myanmar's Ethnic Areas." *The Asia Foundation*.
Kalyvas, Stathis N. (2006). *The Logic of Violence in Civil War*. Cambridge: Cambridge University Press.
Karen Human Rights Group (KHRG) (2020). *Foundation of Fear: 25 years of Villagers' Voices from Southeast Myanmar*. Available at https://khrg.org/2017/12/foundation-fear-25-years-villagers-voices-southeast-myanmar (accessed 20 April 2022).
Kasfir, N. (2015) "Rebel Governance – Constructing a Field of Inquiry: Definitions, Scope, Patterns, Order, Causes." In *Rebel Governance in Civil War*, edited by A. Arjona, N. Kasfir and Z. Mampilly. Cambridge: Cambridge University Press.
Kilcullen, David (2010). Counterinsurgency. New York: Oxford University Press.
Kim, Kyungmee (2021). *"Civil Resistance in the Shadow of War: Explaining Popular Mobilization against Dams in Myanmar."* PhD Dissertation. Uppsala University.
Kletzer, C., and Renzo, M. (2020). "Authority and Legitimacy". In *The Cambridge Companion to the Philosophy of Law*, edited by J. Tasioulas, . Cambridge: Cambridge University Press, 191–207.
Kyed, Helene Maria (Ed.) (2020). *Everyday Justice in Myanmar: Informal Resolutions and State Evasion in a Time of Contested Transition*. Copenhagen: Nordic Institute of Asian Studies.
Landemore H. (2011). "Political Authority." In: Chatterjee D.K. (eds) *Encyclopedia of Global Justice*, edited by D. K. Chatterjee. Springer, Dordrecht. Available at https://doi.org/10.1007/978-1-4020-9160-5_349 (accessed 10 February 2023).
Lenin, Vladimir (1975). "The Dual Power." *The Lenin Anthology*. London: Norton,301–304.
Lintner (1999 [1994]). *Burma in Revolt: Opium and Insurgency since 1948*. Chiang Mai: Silkworm Books.
Loong, Shona (2019). 'Notes from the Salween Peace Park.' *New Mandala*. Available at https://www.newmandala.org/notes-from-the-salween-peace-park/ (accessed 10 February 2023).
Mampilly, Zachariah Cherian (2011). *Rebel Rulers: Insurgent Governance and Civilian Life During War*. Kindle Version: Columbia University Press.

Mao Zedong (1989). *On Guerrilla Warfare*. US Marine Corps
Mann, Michael (1984). "The Autonomous Power of the State: Its Origins, Mechanisms and Results." *European Journal of Sociology* 25 2, 185–213.
Mann, Michael (1986). *The Sources of Social Power*. Cambridge: Cambridge University Press.
Maung Aung Myoe (1999). "The Counterinsurgency In Myanmar: The Government's Response To The Burma Communist Party." PhD Thesis. Australia National University, Canberra.
Maung Aung Myoe (2009). *Building the Tatmadaw: Tatmadaw Since 1948*. Singapore: Institute of Southeast Asian Studies.
McCartan, Brian and Jolliffe, Kim. (2016). "Ethnic Armed Actors and Justice Provision in Myanmar." *The Asia Foundation*. Available at: http://asiafoundation.org/publication/ethnic-armed- actors-justice-provision-myanmar/.
Min Zin (2018). "Evolving Preference and Strategy of Myanmar Armed Forces Regarding Peace Process in Myanmar." *The Institute for Strategy and Policy*. Available at: https://issuu.com/themyanmarquarterly/docs/evolving_preference_and_strategy_of (accessed 10 February 2023).
Nkrumah, K. (1969). *Handbook of Revolutionary Warfare: A Guide to the Armed Phase of the African Revolution*. New York: International Publishers.
Nikkei Asian Review. "Myanmar coup sparks unprecedented unity of ethnic groups." Available at https://asia.nikkei.com/Spotlight/Myanmar-Crisis/Myanmar-coup-sparks-unprecedented-unity-of-ethnic-groups (accessed 10 February 2023).
Olson, M. (1993). "Dictatorship, Democracy, and Development" *American Political Science Review*, 87 (3): 567–576.
Ong, Andrew (2020). "Tactical Dissonance: Insurgent Autonomy on the Myanmar–China border" *American Ethnologist* 47 (4): 369–386.
Paul, Andrew (2018). *'With the Salween Peace Park, We Can Survive as a Nation': Karen Environmental Relations and the Politics of an Indigenous Conservation Initiative*. M.A. thesis. York University, Toronto.
Petraeus, David (2006). *Counterinsurgency*. US Army Field Manual.
Risse, T. (2011). "Introduction and Overview."' *In Governance Without a State? Policies and Politics in Areas of Limited Statehood*, edited by T. Risse. New York: Columbia University Press.
Sadan, Mandy (2013). *Being and Becoming Kachin: Histories Beyond the State in the Borderworlds of Burma*. Oxford: Oxford University Press.
Saferworld (2019). "Security, Justice and Governance in Karen Ceasefire Areas: A Knowledge, Attitudes and Practices Survey." *Saferworld*.
Sai Aung Tun (2009). *History of the Shan State: From Its Origins to 1962*. Chiang Mai: Silkworm Books.
Sakhong, Lian (2010), *In Defence of Identity*. Chiang Mai: Silkworm.

Silverstein, Josef (1959). "The Federal Dilemma in Burma" *Far Eastern Survey* 28 (7): 97–105.

Scott, James (2009). *The Art of Not Being Governed: An Anarchist History of Upland Southeast Asia.* New Haven: Yale University Press.

Smith, M. (1994). *Ethnic Groups in Burma: Development, Democracy and Human Rights.* Anti-Slavery International: London.

Smith (1999 [1991]). *Burma: Insurgency and the Politics of Ethnicity.* London: Zed Books.

South, Ashley (2008). *Ethnic Politics in Burma: States in conflict.* New York: Routledge.

--- (2010). *Conflict and Survival: Self-protection in South-East Burma."* Chatham House, Programme Paper. Available at http://www.ashleysouth.co.uk/files/17342_0910pp_burma.pdf (accessed 10 February 2023).

--- (2017): "'Hybrid Governance" and the Politics of Legitimacy in the Myanmar Peace Process" *Journal of Contemporary Asia* 48 (1): 50–66.

--- (2022). "Towards 'Emergent Federalism' in Post-Coup Myanmar" *Journal of Contemporary Southeast Asia* 43 (3): 439–460.

Staniland, P. (2014). *Networks of Rebellion: Explaining Insurgent Cohesion and Collapse.* Ithaca: Cornell University Press.

Tambiah, Stanley Jeremiah (1976). *World Conqueror and World Renouncer: A Study of Buddhism and Polity in Thailand against a Historical Background.* Cambridge: Cambridge University Press.

Special Advisory Council for Myanmar (SAC-M) (2022). *Briefing Paper: Effective Control in Myanmar.* Available at https://specialadvisorycouncil.org/2022/09/statement-briefing-effective-control-myanmar/ (accessed 10 February 2023).

Tapper, Richard (1990). "Tribe and state in Iran and Afghanistan: An Update" *Études rurales* 184 [online].

Tilly, Charles (1976). *The Formation of National States in Western Europe.* Princeton: Princeton University Press.

--- (1978). *From Mobilization to Revolution.* New York: Random House.

--- (1990). *Coercion, Capital, and European States, AD 990-1990.* Cambridge: Basil Blackwell.

Trinquier, Roger (1964). *Modern Warfare: A French View of Counterinsurgency.* New York: Praeger.

United Nations Office of the High Commissioner for Human Rights – (UNOHCHR) (2022). *Report of the Special Rapporteur on the situation of human rights in Myanmar, Thomas H. Andrews (A/HRC/49/76).* Available at https://www.ohchr.org/en/documents/country-reports/ahrc4976-report-special-rapporteur-situation-human-rights-myanmar-thomas, accessed 20 April 2022.

Weinstein, J.M. (2007). *Inside Rebellion: The Politics of Insurgent Violence.* Cambridge: Cambridge University Press.

Wolters, O. W. (1982). *History, Culture, and Region in Southeast Asian Perspectives.* Singapore: Institute of Southeast Asian Studies.

Woods, K. (2011). "Ceasefire capitalism: military–private partnerships, resource concessions and military–state building in the Burma–China borderlands." *The Journal of Peasant Studies*, 38 (4): 747–770.

World Bank (2022). "Myanmar Economic Monitor: Reforms Reversed." *World Bank*, July 2022. Available at https://pubdocs.worldbank.org/en/597471658359366101/July-MEM-2022-Final.pdf (accessed 10 February 2023).

Yawnghwe and Sakhong (2003). "Federalism, State Constitutions and Self-Determination in Burma." *Peaceful Co-Existence: Towards Federal Union of Burma [Series No. 5]*. Available at http://www.burmalibrary.org/docs09/Series05-unld.pdf

Yawnghwe, Chao Tzang (1987). *The Shan of Burma: Memoirs of a Shan in Exile*. Singapore: Institute of South East Asia Publishing.

Yawnghwe, S. (2013). *Maintaining the Union of Burma 1946–1962: The Role of the Ethnic Nationalities in a Shan Perspective*. Bangkok: Institute of Asian Studies, Chulalongkorn University.

Ye Myo Hein (2022). "One Year On: The Momentum of Myanmar's Armed Rebellion." *The Wilson Centre*. Available at https://www.wilsoncenter.org/sites/default/files/media/uploads/documents/ASIA_220519_1YearOn-BRIEF_V1r2.pdf (accessed 10 February 2023).

Young, Ken (2007). "State Formation in Southeast Asia." *Thesis Eleven* 50: 71.

Ziblatt, Daniel (2004). "Rethinking the Origins of Federalism: Puzzle, Theory, and Evidence from Nineteenth-Century Europe." *World Politics* 57 (October): 70–98.

7

THE CDM AND ITS ALLIES: MYANMAR'S HETEROGENEOUS ANTICOLONIAL PUBLIC(S)

Michael R. Dunford

On the 1st of February, the Sit Tat[1] staged a coup that overthrew the democratically elected government. After a brief period of stunned silence, the country erupted with anger and dismay. From eight o'clock that evening, Yangon and Mandalay were overtaken with the sound of mass pot-and-pan banging: long a traditional symbol of casting out demons, the pot-banging was repurposed as a symbol of mass protest, couched within the plausible deniability of the traditional act of exorcism. Within a few days, such nebulous and inchoate acts gave way to a mass social movement, started by nurses and doctors. Health sector workers exhorted their fellow public servants to refuse to work for the junta; knowing that this was in violation of civil service laws (Pyidaungsu Hluttaw 2013), they knew they would likely be arrested, and — citing Gandhi — released a statement on Facebook referring to their actions as "civil disobedience". Myanmar's Civil Disobedience Movement (CDM) was born. Teachers and other education sector staff were quick to follow health workers, joining demonstrations and releasing public statements; in a little over a week, the CDM had snowballed into a general anti-coup uprising. "CDMers," or striking civil servants, were joined by labour unions, political activist networks, and a huge assortment of other groups and associations, forming the largest street demonstrations the country has witnessed since the mass demonstrations of 1988.

In the months that followed, "CDM" became a kind of shorthand for one's political allegiances. Striking government staff became known as "CDMers;" government staff who remained in their posts began to be called "non-CDM". If someone is spoken about as "non-CDM," the implication is that they are pro-junta. "Non-CDM" workers (and even their families) were identified online and recommended for a tactic that came to be known as "Social Punishment" (SP): the public (or online) harassment and ostracism of those non-CDM workers, particularly soldiers, and often their families as well, with particular focus on shutting down or boycotting military-aligned businesses. As long-time Myanmar observer and anthropologist Courtney Wittekind puts it, "neutrality is no longer possible" (2021) in post-coup Myanmar. A side must be chosen.

In this chapter I critique the binary framing of post-coup politics in Myanmar. However, this chapter is not a call for neutrality, or a liberal "third position". Instead, it is an exploration of the heterogeneity of the Civil Disobedience Movement itself, and the wide array of political actors who support it and have a stake in it. I argue that using the CDM to divide or to bifurcate — as a code for those who are against the military and those who are with it — obfuscates the more inclusive and more political public that is already latent in Myanmar, and which the military coup has (perhaps ironically) made more concrete and visible.

The CDM and its allies are heterogeneous because they have a wide array of political goals, which are sometimes internally contradictory. They are also anticolonial: civil disobedience is itself a decolonial political practice, employed specifically to non-violently counteract imperialist or colonial violence (Pineda 2021). The CDM and its allies are anticolonial furthermore because the Sit Tat is a hostile occupying force within their own country, a postcolonial political formation that uses the logic of colonisation as a governance strategy. Because this movement is heterogeneous, its politics and its organisation strategies cannot be easily co-opted. By calling it anticolonial (rather than, say, anti-authoritarian), I also draw attention to the dictatorship's reliance on an atavistic politics of domination pulled from the playbook of colonial governance.

This chapter is based on conversations with friends and acquaintances who were still inside Myanmar when the coup happened, many of whom are politically active and some of whom have now left. It is also based on publicly-available news articles and Facebook posts, along with notes that I took about what was happening across Myanmar during the immediate aftermath of the coup. In a few instances, I have included some of my friends' and acquaintances' stories, with their permission — I gave them pseudonyms in every instance of this. Still, the majority of the data represented here concerns publicly-observable phenomena, rather than the privately-held opinions of individuals. This follows the spirit of Warner's classic formulation of "a public:" a particular group of people "witnessing itself in visible space" (Warner 2002, 50), as in a theatre audience, with the additional meaning of a group of people "who comes into being only in relation to texts and their circulation" (ibid.). These two forms of public are not mutually exclusive and often bleed into one another, as they do in the case of the CDM and the anti-junta movement more broadly. Street demonstrations are a classic example of the former type of public, in which protestors — in addition to protesting — witness themselves doing so. The latter form of public, the public who forms around texts, is the public that forms in relation to the huge efflorescence of (mostly online) texts that have flooded the internet since the coup: statements, images, memes, copy-pasted text, and so on. In this case, the public I address is the CDM and its diverse supporters, as they witness themselves protesting in the streets and posting their actions and convictions on the internet. My focus is thus mainly on nonviolent resistance to the Sit Tat, rather than the armed resistance actions of the People's Defence Forces and Ethnic Resistance Organisations,[2] whose actions would require a different analysis to the one I present here.

In this chapter, I will begin by briefly situating Myanmar's interpretation of "civil disobedience" as a concept. From there, I will provide a summary of the heterogeneous political landscape of the CDM, its supporters, and its sympathisers. This summary will focus primarily on the first six months after the coup, when public demonstrations were at their largest and the heterogeneity of the revolution was at its most visible. To interpret how this heterogeneous public stands in relation to the junta, in the following section I will draw on the concept of "the politics of domination" (Chakrabarty 2007; Foucault and Ewald 2003), which stands in contrast to the "politics of sovereignty". Following Chakrabarty and Foucault, the politics of domination theorises what it means for people in a society to be willing to die for the sake of regime change; the politics of sovereignty, by contrast, theorises what it takes for people to be willing to live with a regime — even a repressive one.

The politics of domination is the predominant political dynamic in colonial regimes: as I argue below, Myanmar's military should be understood as a form of colonial regime. The junta's strategy of governance operates according to the logic of territorial colonisation, carried out through a politics of violent domination, as it has done so since the 1950s, if not earlier (see Callahan 2003). The CDM and its allies are thus engaged in an anticolonial political project, which I will argue has pried open a space between acquiescence to power, on one hand — what Chakrabarty (2007) and Foucault (2007 [1992]) call the politics of sovereignty — and on the other hand, fighting the regime with the expectation of death (the politics of domination). By refusing to die for their cause, but also refusing to live with the post-coup status quo, the CDM movement has thus helped solidify an anticolonial public politics of resistance in Myanmar. The paper will conclude with an analysis of how the CDM has changed over time, and what its implications are for Myanmar's political future.

CDM IN GENERAL AND IN MYANMAR

By and large, in Myanmar, the Civil Disobedience Movement refers to public servants who have left government jobs in protest of the coup, including health workers, teachers, railway workers, and other government employees. This framing is idiosyncratic to Myanmar. In academic political theory and in the world of activist tactics, "civil disobedience" is a much more capacious concept. From Erin Pineda, a theorist of civil disobedience, the most basic "hallmark" of civil disobedience is the active defiance of particular laws (Pineda 2021, 6). However, other liberal scholars — most famously John Rawls — emphasise the notion of "civility" within the notion of civil disobedience (Pineda 2021, 34). In the liberal view, activists should behave civilly and accept their punishments willingly, in the spirit of respecting the law as a social institution (even as activists break particular laws). For Pineda, this liberal definition of civil disobedience ought to be contrasted with the way activists themselves understand civil disobedience and nonviolent direct action more broadly: as a form of *"decolonizing praxis"*

(Pineda 2021, 52) (emphasis in original), a means to "self-emancipation" (ibid.) from imperial formations of political domination. From the Indian anti-colonial movement to the American civil rights movement, the most "classic" mass civil disobedience actions have always served to highlight the egregiousness of colonial domination by opposing it with nonviolent resistance. Civil disobedience thus need not be limited to the direct breaking of a single rule and willingly accepting punishment for it; civil disobedience can include a whole suite of nonviolent actions. It may be useful for activists in Myanmar to return to the concept of civil disobedience itself and explore how the boundaries of "the CDM" might be widened to include other kinds of action — and even the actions of "watermelons"[3] and "returnees," who are currently working for the junta but could play a key role in destabilising it.

In the early days of the CDM, conscious rule-breaking did play a significant role in activists' rhetoric. The law in question was the Civil Services Personnel Law (Pyidaunghsu Hluttaw 2013), which forbids civil servants from participation in "party politics". Although the law is not particularly clear on what "party politics" entails, civil servants who participate in the CDM — hereafter "CDMers" — were well aware that public political demonstrations in the wake of the coup could cost them their jobs and likely land them in jail (or worse) (Anonymous 2021). The practice of conscious law-breaking (and accepting the punishment for it — particularly jail time) played a major role in early online conversations about the CDM, when doctors and teachers called on other civil servants to join their strike and accept arrests in solidarity with their colleagues who had been arrested overnight on 1 February 2021. What is curious is that despite the decolonial history of civil disobedience — and the enormous array of nonviolent tactics that could fit into it — in Myanmar, "CDM" almost always refers relatively narrowly to the strike movement. This does not mean that tactics within the protest movement have been limited to striking; there have been a wide variety of creative tactics that fit the political and personal heterogeneity of the resistance movement overall. The "htamein campaign,"[4] for example, made creative use of traditional beliefs about the polluting power of women's garments (see Marlar, Chambers & Elena 2023). By hanging skirts over roads and building entrances, activists simultaneously poked fun at soldiers' superstitious attachment to traditional norms of masculinity while also providing would-be strikers with another reason to stay at home and participate in the CDM with some degree of plausible deniability: a man who wanted to strike could say, plausibly (if cheekily), "I'm not leaving the house as long as there are those htamein everywhere — what kind of a man would I be, then?"[5]

Crucially, the htamein campaign opened an opportunity for sympathetic members of the police and military to disobey orders: soldiers reluctant to conduct raids or round up protestors would be able to make this semi-plausible excuse ("it will damage my hpon!") to avoid entering a street or neighbourhood — or at least stall for time by taking down the htameins rather than engaging in the violence that has typified their actions since early 2021. Plausible deniability tactics subvert the us/them binary by opening a space for both soldiers and protestors to participate in the same action. I will return to this particular affordance of plausible deniability tactics in the next section; for now, the important takeaway is that tactics like the htamein campaign exemplify the CDM at its best, and are indicative of the openness and heterogeneity of the political public that is the subject of this chapter. Tactical creativity is one of the hallmarks of civil disobedience in the more expansive sense of the word, which includes all forms of nonviolent action that contravene the accepted laws of a given place. The htamein campaign is especially creative in that it subverts a gendered social norm, rather than a law: perhaps this type of tactic is particularly effective in Myanmar, where the legal code is messy and often self-contradictory.

The type of tactical creativity exemplified by the htamein campaign appeared again and again during the early days following the coup. Another striking example: protestors repeatedly plastered streets with images of the Sit Tat's Commander-in-Chief Min Aung Hlaing, especially streets where military or police personal were likely to walk. In Myanmar culture, stepping on an image of something or someone is an act of extreme disrespect. By placing images of Min Aung Hlaing on the street and forcing soldiers to walk over them, protestors were effectively forcing them to disrespect and insult their leader. Again, this is a tactic that works on both sides of Myanmar's socio-political binary: protestors can stomp on the images, using them to insult and degrade Min Aung Hlaing. Soldiers, too, could use the images as an excuse to delay their more violent and coercive tasks, either by refusing to walk over the signs or by wasting time cleaning them up. This portrait campaign, along with the htamein campaign and other similar actions, are evidence that there is a strong political will in Myanmar for actions that fit the wide "activist" (Pineda 2021) vision of civil disobedience (rather than the narrow "liberal" vision, which focuses on laws and legality). By making use of the physics of plausible deniability, CDM and protest actions have been able to serve two purposes at once: by one reading, they are direct political actions in their own right, taking nonviolent aim at the Sit Tat and the cultural institutions that support it (e.g., Bamar masculine authority). At the same time, they also work to build the broadest possible support base. More than direct actions against an adversary that have no alternate reading or meaning, actions that allow for plausibly deniable participation are an invitation to join a maximally diverse protest movement.

A HETEROGENEOUS PUBLIC

The diversity of tactics deployed by protestors in the early days of the coup is an indication of the diversity of people involved in the resistance: these diverse tactics come from diverse identities. CDMers and their allies have joined the protest movement for different reasons at different times, and represent a wide variety of political leanings. The massive participation of the education sector in CDM — and especially teachers' participation — is somewhat surprising, particularly given teachers' reputation for conservatism (Saito 2021; Maber et al. 2022). Although the teachers who joined the CDM are mostly relatively young (i.e., part of "Generation Z"), teacher participation in the CDM has been colossal, with over 200,000 joining the movement (and over 130,000 formally suspended by the junta) (RFA Burmese 2022). Some of these teachers certainly have a hard-line anti-military stance, and have only been pushed into a stronger political positionality by the junta's abuses since the coup began (Saw Yan Naing 2022). Some of my own acquaintances left their teaching posts to join People's Defence Forces (PDFs) and Ethnic Resistance Organisations (EROs) and have fully committed to living as revolutionaries for the foreseeable future.

At the same time, CDM participation does not directly correlate with political convictions. Some former teachers who I spoke with in Thailand remarked that they joined CDM at least partially out of peer pressure: although they agreed with the political objectives to some degree, the reason they chose to participate was less related to a strong ideological position than to a desire to join a movement and not be left on the wrong side of history. After months of displacement and hardship, in which many were forced to live constantly on the run or in makeshift camps (Maung Oak Aww 2022; Saw Yan Naing 2022), some CDMers have quietly expressed regret about their decision. Some teachers and other civil servants have even returned to their posts, and restarted work for the government — a phenomenon that I will discuss in a later section. The point is that CDMers themselves are a diverse political entity, and not a bloc with a uniform identity and uniform goals.

The CDM has been so successful in attracting participants and maintaining its strong anti-junta politics specifically because it has been supported by a wide range of actors with equally diverse political inclinations. The most well-known of these is the National Unity Government (NUG), which runs in parallel to the junta-led government. The NUG consists largely of lawmakers elected to the legislature in 2020, who were deposed by the coup: the NUG began as the Committee Representing the Pyidaungsu Hluttaw (CRPH), a group of mostly National League for Democracy (NLD) legislators, who then combined with representatives of various ethnic parties and other opposition groups to form the NUG. The NUG appear to be positioning themselves as the primary support organisation for CDMers: they have a CDM Success Committee to help identify alternative livelihoods for CDMers and to provide them with mental health resources (Chanayuth 2021); they have also committed to paying CDMers' lost salaries, although budget problems have thus far prevented this plan from materialising (Myanmar NOW 2021b). Still, many of the NUG representatives have at least five years of experience in Myanmar's government and would be well-positioned to turn CDMers back into a viable public resource in the wake of the revolution. That said, the NUG also represents a desire to return to (or at least start from) the politics of the transition period. It is dominated by the NLD and the NLD's allies, who took power in 2015 and won the 2020 election as well: the NUG is largely composed of people who were already in Myanmar's political vanguard before the coup and is the definitive "elite" opposition group to the coup.

At the street level, the NUG is just one of many opposition groups, some of which have much more radical political positionalities. The General Strike Committee (GSC) and General Strike Committee of Nationalities (GSC-N) played an important organising role in the opposition and were a crucial support to the CDM, especially in the first half of 2021. The GSC is a decentralised network of political activists who organised street demonstrations in major cities and large towns; many GSC members had some background as political activists or political organisers, and some had connections to Myanmar's organised labour networks (especially in Yangon). The GSC-N was a group that split from the GSC and emphasised the importance of ethnic diversity: GSC-N demonstrators tended to wear non-Bamar "national costume" from Myanmar's various ethnic groups, and carry flags and signboards written in a range of languages beyond Burmese and English. The GSC-N also emphasised that for many of Myanmar's ethnic groups, the coup was not a new condition at all, but a larger-scale version of the same repression that those groups had experienced since independence (Naw Esther Wah 2021). In some areas of the country, public demonstration was more aligned with General Strike groups than with liberal centrist groups like the NUG: Dawei had a famously prominent GSC group, which managed to shut down the city for weeks. Military crackdowns in Dawei were some of the most aggressive uses of force in urban areas outside of Yangon and Mandalay.

Perhaps one of the reasons that the military seems to be particularly threatened by the General Strike groups is the fact that they are acephalous, without obvious leadership that can be eradicated. New groups seem to constantly appear. Recently, another prominent splinter group has emerged: the General Strike Coordination Body (GSCB), which became prominent in late 2021 or early 2022, and has been more active in disseminating online information about the resistance than either the GSC or GSC-N. Most small cities in the Dry Zone have one or more General Strike groups; they are constantly appearing and disappearing. The number of variations of these groups and the lack of obvious leadership personalities is indicative of the far-left political leanings of these groups. Both the GSC and the GSC-N expressed more radical visions about the possibility of post-revolutionary Myanmar than those proposed by the CRPH/NUG; they also tend to be relatively anonymous groups and to avoid vanguardism (although some protest leaders inevitably became prominent either for their organising activities or as "martyrs" for the cause). Still, I do not mean to imply that the GSC and the NUG are entirely at odds; GSC organisers have been imprisoned for treason due their contacts with the CRPH and NUG (Myanmar NOW 2021a). However, by and large, the demands of the GSC, GSC-N, and GSCB have tended to be more radical than those made by the NUG itself. While the CRPH and NUG largely represent a call for continuity—the continuation of Myanmar's liberal "transition" — the

General Strike groups have called for a revolutionary restructuring of Myanmar's politics and have above all been the primary coordinators of much direct action throughout the country.

I want to highlight the role of the General Strike groups as organisers of mass social action — and, especially, to return to the intertwined themes of heterogeneity and plausible deniability. Often, the General Strike groups enabled CDM participation by establishing scenarios that would give strikers plausible deniability to participate in the CDM while claiming that they were simply avoiding public spaces for the sake of convenience. According to Maung Pan, an acquaintance who was very active in organising one of Yangon's General Strike groups, a core strategy was to coordinate with workers who wanted to join CDM but were unable to do so — for example, a group of people working at a particular bank in Yangon. The bank in question was under heavy military surveillance by the end of Feburary 2021, and although staff wanted to join the CDM, they knew they could not participate; soldiers or police would show up at the houses of any bank employees who did not show up to work and did not have a sufficient excuse (e.g., testing positive for COVID-19). Maung Pan and the General Strike body in that township agreed to organise an enormous rally in a key intersection near that bank, which would inevitably draw out police battalions and bring traffic to a halt; with the neighbourhood in a state of chaos, the workers in that bank would then have a reasonable excuse not to attend their office. The GS group made space for their less radical allies to participate in the CDM.

These different forms of creativity were visible in many different forms in the early months after the coup. Two weeks after the coup, I began seeing calls on Facebook for participation in a "taxi CDM" — a mass public action also known as "why you break down, car?" On the scheduled day, 15 February, photos started emerging of enormous traffic gridlocks, especially on Yangon's many bridges and flyover roads. Chaos ensued: nobody who was still working could get to their office, huge parts of the city were effectively shut down, and even the police themselves were largely unable to carry out their duties. The taxi protests produced one of the most striking (and hilarious) images from the early days of the anti-coup movement, and an image that represents the core of this paper's argument:

The CDM and Its Allies: Myanmar's Heterogeneous Anticolonial Public(s)

Figure 7.1: A police officer gives engine repair advice to a Yangon motorist participating in "Taxi CDM," also known as the "why you break down, car?" protest. In this protest action, motorists stopped their vehicles in crucial intersections and pretended to have broken engines. Source: Facebook.

The photo was circulated widely across Facebook and other social media platforms. In this image, a taxi driver is engaged in heated conversation with a police officer. The driver has lifted the hood of his car, and the officer is pretending to help the driver "diagnose" the problem with his vehicle. The taxi driver's "engine problem" has created a window of opportunity for the police officer — a direct agent of the Sit Tat — to join the CDM, while maintaining plausible deniability that he is simply going along with his job: "I'm not participating in the protest," the cop could say to his boss, "I'm trying to figure out the problem with this car! I want to get the traffic moving again!" In this case, the "taxi CDMer" can enable the emergence of a (tacit, but actual) "police CDMer," someone who would ostensibly be on the "other side" of the current political environment, but — through the affordance opened by the taxi CDMer — can (at least momentarily) join the revolution. At its best, the CDM allows actors from disparate political positionalities to unite under the common cause of damaging the dictatorship at any cost. When resistance tactics emerge that allow participants to plausibly deny their participation in political action, a possibility for action opens for people who are hesitant to protest to join the movement. Actions that enable plausible deniability are different from covert protest/resistance actions, or "internal sabotage" — both of which will be discussed later — in that plausible deniability tactics allow people who have not necessarily left their government posts to *publicly participate* in protest actions — like the police officer pictured above.

Despite the prevalence of plausible deniability tactics, many would-be dissidents are unwilling or unable to join the CDM or the wider resistance movement and are still working for the junta in spite of a strong desire to quit. This group of "sympathetic non-CDMers" has come to be known as "watermelons" (in Burmese, *hpayethi*), i.e., green on the outside and red on the inside. This is a reference to the fact that green is the colour of military uniforms (and of the military-aligned Union Solidarity and Development Party (USDP)) and red is the colour of the pro-democracy National League for Democracy (NLD) Party. The implication is that a "watermelon" may publicly present as a soldier or a loyal employee of the SAC, but secretly or covertly sympathise with the resistance and the pro-democracy movement. Tactics like social punishment, which target anyone with a prominent military affiliation who has not actively renounced such ties (McMichael 2021), seem to miss the potential of watermelons to actively contribute to the goals of the revolution. The junta itself certainly sees watermelons as a threat and has been conducting a prominent campaign to identify them and remove them from their positions, or worse (Frontier 2022). By focusing on the heterogeneity of the resistance rather than a simplistic binary formation that pits the military against the people, I aim to identify the space in which watermelons can operate and can contribute to the resistance.

Watermelons have already played important roles in leaking information and providing the resistance with counter-intelligence; furthermore, watermelons' very existence has enabled the spread of rumours about their potential power. In November 2022, a Sit Tat helicopter gunned down dozens of its own soldiers in Sagaing region (Irrawaddy 2022), and rumours began almost immediately that a watermelon had been behind the shooting. The category of "watermelons" thus has a potential to destabilise and divide the Sit Tat. This is a powerful potential that gets lost when CDM is defined narrowly, and when participation in the revolution is limited to those who participate by publicly declaring their renunciation of ties to the Sit Tat or military-led government. The existence of watermelons (and possible defectors) is a key point of paranoia for Sit Tat leadership, thus making open CDM participation dangerous: soldiers who attempt defection (or who are thought to be defection risks) receive harsh punishments, and their families are often punished as well (Kyed and Ah Lynn 2021, 63). These risks are increased for watermelon soldiers, who still live and work amongst obedient Sit Tat soldiers who are unsympathetic to the democratic cause. Still, watermelons could play a crucial role in damaging the Sit Tat from the inside.

In addition to watermelons, there is another group whose position is somewhat ambiguous in Myanmar's polarised political climate: former CDMers who have returned to their jobs, or "returnees". Returnees defy the Manichean "with us or against us" ethos espoused by many in the wake of the revolution. They joined the CDM and are thus clearly willing to take some serious risks on behalf of their political convictions; however, for one reason or another, they have returned to their post. For most returnees, something has happened in their personal lives to cause them to return to their post. In some cases, the military or police harassed or assaulted CDMers' family members to coerce them to return; in other cases, CDMers themselves were detained, then forced to return to work. Some returnees ran out of money or found that they were unable to cope with the isolation and fear that CDMers fear on a daily basis. The few returnees who I know personally did not take this decision lightly. The decision to return has weighed heavily on them: they should not be treated flippantly or dismissed as traitors. Indeed, returnees could play a crucial role in the longer-term trajectory of the Spring Revolution: they can help active CDMers sabotage departments from the inside, help arrange leaks, or pass various forms of intelligence to dissident groups. Like watermelons, returnees present one way that CDM actions could continue to expand even if the movement itself does not accumulate new members. However, many returnees face significant levels of insecurity, due to ongoing monitoring by the SAC and local *dalan*, pro-military spies, who closely monitor their movements, alliances and activities.

My analysis up to this point has not considered the role of armed resistance groups — an extensive discussion of armed revolutionary activity is outside the scope of this paper. For a detailed analysis, see Kim Jolliffe's

(2023) chapter in this volume. Jolliffe provides comprehensive coverage of the administrative and governmental role of non-Sit Tat armed actors in post-coup Myanmar; here, I will focus primarily on the People's Defence Forces, which have a more explicit link to the CDM than Myanmar's various Ethnic Resistance Organisations, most of which existed long before the coup. In the wake of the coup, new armed actors — mostly known as People's Defence Forces (PDFs) — have emerged across the country. PDFs are especially active in Sagaing Region, Magway Region, and Chin State. They are grassroots militias who sometimes engage in guerrilla tactics such as targeted bombings, and sometimes engage in direct assaults on Sit Tat installations. In cities, and especially in Yangon, covert and largely anonymous PDF-type actors have begun to carry out targeted assassinations on high-ranking military officials and their families (Myanmar NOW 2022). A leader from one of Yangon's General Strike groups explained to me that activists considered PDFs one part of a three-part path to toppling the junta: street protests would overwhelm the cities and help enable strike actions; CDMers and private sector strikers would bring the economy and the functioning of government to a halt; and PDFs would make the military feel like they are no longer able to secure the interior of the country. I highlight this three-part strategy to emphasise that even the most radical activists (the General Strike groups) acknowledge the importance of nonviolent public political action. Although the PDFs have gradually garnered more media attention than the ongoing nonviolent resistance, the PDFs cannot overthrow the junta without the CDMers.

Postcolonial Colonisers: The Sit Tat's Politics of Domination

The street protests that exploded in the wake of the coup are a new manifestation of an immanent political public in Myanmar, a public that is often overshadowed in media coverage (and especially foreign media coverage) of sectarian anti-Muslim violence (on one hand) and the macro-level liberalisation of the 2010s (on the other). Beyond these two political forms — the anti-Muslim violence that has plagued Myanmar for the last decade, and the liberal political-economic reforms of the 2010 and 2015 governments — Myanmar has an engaged and critical public with a long and continuous history of protest and political action, which is fundamentally located at the grassroots. This public has tended to remain inchoate for long stretches, simmering below the surface of every day public discourse —

largely the result of oppressive censorship laws and penalties for publicly speaking about politics (Prasse-Freeman 2012). This political public has been most visible when its political actions are spectacular in scale, such as during the mass protests of 1962, 1988, 2007, and now 2021; however, this political public does not simply stop existing when it is not engaged in massive demonstrations.

During the Thein Sein era (2010–2015), there were frequent small but intense demonstrations in major cities, held on behalf of a wide array of political movements and actors (Prasse-Freeman 2015). These demonstrations were public manifestations of an even earlier current of public political participation in Myanmar. According to Jennifer Leehey, public opposition to the Sit Tat was so widespread by the 1990s that they had largely given up on trying to convince the people of their legitimacy through ideological means and relied instead on governance by coercion (Leehey 2010, 45). To put it differently: without anything like "legitimacy" on their side, the Sit Tat has always relied on a different tactic — territorial occupation in the colonial style, made possible by a politics of violent domination.

I am certainly not the first to point out that the Sit Tat relies on a colonial mode of governance. Although the Sit Tat was restructured several times throughout its early history, one of Mary Callahan's (2003) most compelling points about the current socio-political role of the Sit Tat comes from her analysis of its behaviour in the early 1950s, when they placed most of Shan State under martial law. Martial law was ostensibly deployed to offset the destabilising effects of the Kuomintang, which had retreated into Shan State from China. Ultimately, the Sit Tat went much further than this. They uprooted the *sawbwas*, the traditional hereditary rulers of Shan State, and redrew the administrative boundaries of the area in such a way that former sawbwa territories were literally erased from the map; operating in the mode of territorial colonisation, they behaved as an "occupying force" rather than a protective one (Callahan 2003, 158). Although the Sit Tat under Ne Win had largely been purged of loyalists to the British, the notion of "military as state-builder" — an ideology that continues to drive Sit Tat action in the present — was built on a history of colonial-style governance.

Following Kuan-Hsing Chen, I take colonial politics to be first and foremost a politics of *violent domination* (Chen 2010, 72). As long as a state relates to its constituents through a politics of violent domination, that state has not been decolonised. To show how violent domination can perpetuate a colonial politics even inside an apparently postcolonial state, I will borrow terminology from Dipesh Chakrabarty, who is in turn drawing on Foucault. For Chakrabarty and Foucault, the politics of domination should be understood in contrast to what they term the "politics of sovereignty". In both cases, "politics" is constituted by the behaviour of the public in question — more specifically, the willingness (or unwillingness) of the public to die on behalf of political change. This is roughly their formulation: a "politics of domination" is a politics in which the public is willing to risk death to overthrow the ruling regime. A "politics of sovereignty," by contrast, is a politics in which the public is willing to live with a regime — even a repressive one. As Chakrabarty argues for India, the politics of domination was the political mode established during the British colonial years: the mass demonstrations and hunger strikes, which continued even in the face of certain death, formed the basis of public political action in colonial India; the echoes of this historical process are still felt in Indian public life. When the Indian state engages in violent repression against strikes or demonstrations, which then continue despite this violence, the Indian state is re-enacting the colonial politics of domination. In Chakrabarty's formulation, no colonial state can ever achieve a politics of sovereignty: the (usually racialised) hierarchy built into colonial governance ensures that the relationship between state and public is always one of domination (Chakrabarty 2007).

At first glance, the "politics of domination" as formulated by Chakrabarty appear to apply directly to the present political situation in Myanmar. In the several months immediately following the military coup (approximately February through May 2021), enormous public street protests continued across Myanmar despite the junta's open willingness to deploy deadly force against the people of Myanmar. Although public resistance to the coup has significantly decreased since the heady days of 2021, when hundreds of thousands of protestors took to the streets in Myanmar, resistance is still ongoing; protests are still being held across the country (albeit at a smaller scale than in the past). Perhaps troublingly, new (and possibly more violent) dynamics are emerging, with People's Defence Forces (PDFs) playing an increasingly large role in the anti-junta resistance. PDF members are certainly willing to put their lives on the line for the sake of regime change, as are Myanmar's many EROs, some of whom have been resisting the Myanmar for multiple generations. All of this is evidence pointing to the veracity of Chakrabarty's formulation for the present dynamic between the Sit Tat — as internal colonisers — and the heterogeneous publics who have risen up against them.

The problem with Chakrabarty's formulation is that the "politics of sovereignty," in his model, implies a kind of acquiescence. His two-part formulation of "domination" and "sovereignty" implies that a public must either be willing to die, or willing to give up the fight. However, what the CDM so clearly demonstrates is that the space *between* domination and sovereignty — where a public refuses to accept violent domination, but also refuses to fight to the death — is exactly the space where nonviolent resistance occurs. This is necessarily a messy and heterogeneous space. The main thing that unites the anti-junta public exemplified by the CDM is their stance towards the Sit Tat in general and the act of the coup in particular. Apart from this goal, the CDM and their allies are diverse. Hard-line and militant groups like PDFs and some EROs will view the anti-junta struggle as one that necessarily entails deadly force. Groups like the CDM, by contrast, have access to an enormous repertoire of nonviolent resistance tactics, and an equally vast pool of reasons for engaging in them.

The political public I describe here — the CDM and its allies, from the more liberal (e.g. the NUG) to the more radical (e.g. the General Strike groups) — are possibly in a better position to continue their nonviolent resistance campaigns than any previous generation. They are building on a strong tradition of nonviolent action: political activists in Myanmar have been building theories and developing tactics for nonviolent action for decades (La Ring et al. 2020; Thawnghmung 2011). In the early 1990s, activists translated Gene Sharp's (1973) classic compendium of nonviolent resistance strategies into Burmese, and wrote their own takes on his strategies. The book circulated widely in resistance circles in Myanmar throughout the 1990s. Since then, Sharp's handbook of strategies has been expanded and updated to include resistance strategies that make use of 21st century technological affordances, and resist 21st-century surveillance techniques and mis-/dis-information tactics (Beer 2021). The generation who led the protests against the coup came of age under a liberalising regime, with access to vastly more information and technology than previous generations. The space between domination and sovereignty is mostly occupied by this generation, who were born after 1990. This generation is refusing to acquiesce to the military's attempts to claim sovereignty; they are also (by and large) refusing to die.

AS TIME GOES ON

The purpose of this chapter has been to explore the heterogeneity of Myanmar's Civil Disobedience Movement, and to account for why Myanmar's political public has chosen a specifically decolonial set of political tactics. This exploration is intended to challenge the binary formulation of Myanmar politics so prevalent on social media and in popular discourse about the anti-junta resistance. This binary formulation has had harmful consequences for the revolution, leading to tactics like social punishment (McMichael 2021) and overlooking the revolutionary potential of "watermelons" and "returnees" — a potential that the junta sees and is frightened by (Frontier 2022). The heterogeneity of the resistance is an indicator of what postrevolutionary Myanmar could look like: not a perfectly harmonious political public, but one that is able to operate without the constant threat of violent domination in the colonial mode. The heterogeneous political public that stands in opposition to the junta is not newly-formed, but has a long history. For as long as the Sit Tat has operated according to colonial logics of governance, a political public has existed to resist them. The resistance may not be able to overthrow the junta instantaneously, but it has already survived for decades.

The total political "physics" of the situation thus far gone something like this: widespread popular critique and dissatisfaction with the military coup (February 2021) led to widespread peaceful protests — and, most significantly, at the heart of the CDM, a widespread public sector strike, accompanied by an enormous range of protest actions. These strikes and other political actions were met with a violent backlash, an eruption of the politics of domination. The politics of domination does not simply entail a politics of violence, which is more widespread, but a politics in which the public who is *subject* to that domination is willing to face it, and indeed, willing to die for it. Death, in the politics of domination, does semiotic work: every act of public protest is a defiance of death, a refusal to die; when protestors do die during public action, they become martyrs. The fact that public protests have continued at all in the wake of 2021's bloody crackdowns is an indication of the power of this semiotics of death-defiance: the politics of domination established between the Sit Tat and Myanmar's political public have (perhaps ironically) only served to strengthen the potency of any nonviolent public action. Even small gatherings of protestors index the ongoing public refusal to accept the military coup, despite the clear threat of death. Momentary demonstrations become public assertions of the refusal to die, and the refusal to capitulate.

Still, political organising has been pushed deep underground. The media focus has largely shifted to the People's Defence Forces (PDFs). As nonviolent civilian organising has become more difficult, anti-coup political action now seems to rest primarily in the hands of people who are willing to take up arms for the cause. I hope that this is not the case, and that the incredible nonviolent resistance actions that coalesced during the early days after the coup can regain some traction, either by recruiting watermelons and returnees or by drawing on new resistance tactics, and finding new opportunities to reduce the junta's ability to govern and to reproduce itself politically and economically. While I acknowledge the political heterogeneity of PDFs and Ethnic Resistance Organisations (EROs), their choice to use deadly force against the Sit Tat puts them in a markedly different category of political action than the Civil Disobedience Movement.

Depending on how much faith one puts in the junta's surveillance systems, life inside Myanmar appears to be increasingly dangerous for activists. This seems to be especially true in major cities, and when entering or exiting the country. According to friends inside the country, the SAC maintains a list of the National Registration Card (NRC) numbers of all employees who participated in the CDM public sector strike (this is unlikely to be true, since NRC numbers are not recorded on a centralised database, but it is concerning nonetheless). Anyone seen to be conducting public political organising activities now runs the risk of a treason charge, which — after new rules imposed by the SAC — could incur the death penalty. The stakes have never been higher for dissidents in Myanmar, and yet the protests and other forms of civil disobedience are ongoing.

This conclusion should not be mistaken as a call to naïve pacifism. I am sceptical that any nonviolent solution to Myanmar's current political crisis is even possible. The Sit Tat itself is Myanmar's political crisis. They are attacking Myanmar itself, the country they are supposed to protect; the PDFs and many of the EROs are, in turn, responding to the real need to destabilise the Sit Tat and eliminate the SAC. Removing the SAC and the Sit Tat are among the first conditions for any political progress towards a democratic future — however that may look in the wake of the revolution. The Sit Tat represents the enduring cancer of the politics of violent domination. The political technique of violent domination is, of course, a kind of political hangover from the colonial years, a hangover that in the case of Myanmar is attached to a fascistic political element. I have no qualms about calling the SAC (and its popular support base, including the *pyu saw hti* thugs and post-MaBaTha Buddhist nationalists) what they are: fascists of the most basic blood-and-soil type, a political form that the world simply does not need. As the Civil Disobedience Movement demonstrated, the Sit Tat is very far from the only voice in Myanmar politics; the same can be said of the NLD. By recruiting heterogeneous actors to put constant nonviolent pressure on the Sit Tat, the CDM could be capable of dismantling the Sit Tat forever and installing a new, more equitable and more authentically democratic government in Myanmar.

ACKNOWLEDGEMENTS

I am grateful to Nick Cheesman and Elliott Prasse-Freeman for their extensive comments and advice on this piece. This chapter would never have made it into this volume without co-editor Justine Chambers' support and guidance. I would also like to thank Maung Pan for allowing me to share his stories, Maung Oak Aww for his extensive insights into Yangon's street movements, and all of the unnamed friends in and out of Myanmar who tolerated my questions about their experiences. The CDM as a whole continues to humble me every day, and I am in awe of them for putting their lives and livelihoods on the line.

Notes

1. The military organisation who staged the coup on 01 February 2021 goes by many names. For a detailed discussion, see Aung Kaung Myat (2022). "Tatmadaw" is the term most frequently used in scholarly and journalistic work, contains a respectful linguistic particle ("daw," "royal" or "venerable" depending on context) and is thus seen as unsuitable by many in the wake of the coup and the atrocities that followed it. Although Aung Kaung Myat prefers the neutral "Myanmar military," the widespread alternative term used in Myanmar itself is "Sit Tat" (Desmond 2022). "Sit Tat" does just mean "army," but when used without qualification (e.g., a qualification like "Kachin Sit Tat" to refer to the Kachin Independence Army), it is understood (within Myanmar) to refer to the organisation headed by Min Aung Hlaing, who staged the 2021 coup. The military considers "Sit Tat" disrespectful; by using it, I am joining Desmond and others in waging a "metapragmatic attack" (Jacquemet 1994), a linguistic act aimed at damaging a dominant group.
2. The more prevalent term is Ethnic Armed Organisation (EAO), but I am intentionally using ERO in line with recent research conducted in Burmese (Saw Chit Thet Tun 2022). According to Saw Chit Thet Tun, calling groups like the KNLA or KIA "EROs" emphasizes their opposition to the Myanmar Sit Tat. The Sit Tat itself is an armed ethno-nationalist organisation (in short, an EAO); it just happens to claim representation of the Bamar ethnic majority. The Sit Tat is simply the largest EAO. Calling groups like the KNLA or KIA "EAOs" performs two kinds of erasure: it erases the fact that the Sit Tat is also an EAO; and it erases the political positionality of groups like the KNLA or KIA, whose political aims are very different from groups who have willingly signed ceasefire agreements (like the RCSS, whose leadership is collaborating directly with the Myanmar military) or groups who have been converted into Border Guard Forces (BGFs) or other paramilitary allies of the Sit Tat. The phrase "Ethnic Resistance Organisation" is an attempt to clarify these erasures. For detailed recent analysis of armed groups in Myanmar, see Kim Jolliffe's (2022) chapter in this volume.
3. Watermelons, or *hpayethi*, are soldiers and civil servants who pretend to be obedient employees of the military but secretly support democratic or radical political causes. The next section of this chapter will discuss them in more detail.
4. A *htamein* is a traditional sarong worn by women.
5. *Hpon* is a form of merit, highest in men, which can be damaged by the polluting force of women's clothing.

References

Aung Kaung Myat. 2022. "Sit-Tat or Tatmadaw? Debates on What to Call the Most Powerful Institution in Burma". *Tea Circle*, 3 October. Available at https://teacircleoxford.com/politics/sit-tat-or-tatmadaw-debates-on-what-to-call-the-most-powerful-institution-in-burma/ (accessed 10 December 2022).

Beer, Michael. 2021. *Civil Resistance in the 21st Century*. ICNC Monograph Series. Washington, DC: International Center on Nonviolent Conflict.

Callahan, Mary P. 2003. *Making Enemies: War and State Building in Burma*. Ithaca, N.Y.: Cornell University Press.

Chakrabarty, Dipesh. 2007. "'In the Name of Politics': Democracy and the Power of the Multitude in India". *Public Culture* 19 (1): 35–57.

Chanayuth. 2021. "Myanmar's National Unity Government Promises to Support Striking Civil Servants". *The Irrawaddy*, 6 May. Available at https://www.irrawaddy.com/news/burma/myanmars-national-unity-government-promises-support-striking-civil-servants.html (accessed 10 December 2022).

Desmond. 2022. "Guest Column | Please Don't Call Myanmar Military Tatmadaw". *The Irrawaddy*, 25 May. Available at https://www.irrawaddy.com/opinion/guest-column/please-dont-call-myanmar-military-tatmadaw.html (accessed 10 December 2022).

Foucault, Michel, and François Ewald. 2003. *"Society Must Be Defended": Lectures at the Collège de France, 1975-1976*. Allen Lane.

Frontier. 2022. "'Watermelon Suppression': Doxing Campaign Targets pro-Democracy Soldiers and Police". *Frontier Myanmar* (blog), 14 March. Available at https://www.frontiermyanmar.net/en/watermelon-suppression-doxing-campaign-targets-pro-democracy-soldiers-and-police/ (accessed 10 December 2022).

Irrawaddy, The. 2022. "Myanmar Regime Helicopter Kills At Least 60 Junta Troops in Sagaing Region: Resistance". *The Irrawaddy*, 14 November. Available at https://www.irrawaddy.com/news/burma/myanmar-regime-helicopter-kills-at-least-60-junta-troops-in-sagaing-region-resistance.html (accessed 10 December 2022).

Jacquemet, Marco. 1994. "T-Offenses and Metapragmatic Attacks: Strategies of Interactional Dominance". *Discourse & Society* 5 (3): 297–319. https://doi.org/10.1177/0957926594005003003.

Kyed, Helena Maria, and Ah Lynn. 2021. *Soldier Defections in Myanmar*. DIIS Report 2021:06. Copenhagen: Danish Institute for International Studies. Available at https://www.diis.dk/en/research/defecting-soldiers-are-a-significant-symbolic-blow-to-myanmars-military-rule (accessed 10 December 2022).

La Ring, Khin Sandar Nyunt, Nist Pianchupat, and Shaazka Beyerle. 2020. "Nonviolent Action in Myanmar: Challenges and Lessons for Civil Society and Donors". Special Report 483. United States Institute of Peace.

Leehey, Jennifer. 2010. "Open Secrets, Hidden Meanings: Censorship, Esoteric Power, and Contested Authority in Urban Burma in the 1990s". PhD Thesis. Seattle, W.A.: University of Washington.

Maber, Elizabeth J. T., Khin Mar Aung, Hla Win May Oo, and May May Win. 2022. "The Precarious Politics of Teacher Education in Myanmar". In *Handbook of Research on Teacher Education: Innovations and Practices in Asia,* edited by Myint Swe Khine and Yang Liu, 847–63. Singapore: Springer Nature.

Marlar, Chambers, J. & Elena. 2023. "Our Htamein, Our Flag, Our Victory: The Role of Young Women in Myanmar's Spring Revolution". *Journal of Burma Studies* 27 (1): 1-35.

Maung Oak Aww. 2022. "Effective Third-Sector Actors in Aid on the Thailand-Myanmar Border". *New Mandala* (blog), 29 April. Available at https://www.newmandala.org/effective-third-sector-actors-in-aid-on-the-thailand-myanmar-border/ (accessed 10 December 2022).

McMichael, Clara. 2021. "Myanmar's Social Punishment". *Slate,* 23 April. Available at https://slate.com/technology/2021/04/myanmar-coup-social-punishment.html (accessed 10 December 2022).

Myanmar NOW. 2021a. "Junta Accuses Wai Moe Naing of Treason as Charges Pile Up". *Myanmar NOW,* 21 April. Available at https://www.myanmar-now.org/en/news/junta-accuses-wai-moe-naing-of-treason-as-charges-pile-up (accessed 10 December 2022).

― ― ―. 2021b. "NUG Says It Will Pay Salaries of Striking Civil Servants". *Myanmar NOW,* 27 April. Available at https://myanmar-now.org/en/news/nug-says-it-will-pay-salaries-of-striking-civil-servants (accessed 10 December 2022).

― ― ―. 2022. "Multiple Junta Affiliates Targeted in Assassination Attempts across Yangon". *Myanmar NOW,* 3 August. Available at https://myanmar-now.org/en/news/multiple-junta-affiliates-targeted-in-assassination-attempts-across-yangon (accessed 10 December 2022).

Naw Esther Wah. 2021. "For Some the Nightmare Has Returned, but for Ethnic People the Nightmare Never Stopped". *Myanmar NOW,* 13 March. Available at https://www.myanmar-now.org/en/news/for-some-the-nightmare-has-returned-but-for-ethnic-people-the-nightmare-never-stopped (accessed 10 December 2022).

Pineda, Erin R. 2021. *Seeing Like an Activist: Civil Disobedience and the Civil Rights Movement.* Oxford: Oxford University Press.

Prasse-Freeman, Elliott. 2012. "Power, Civil Society, and an Inchoate Politics of the Daily in Burma/Myanmar". *The Journal of Asian Studies* 71 (2): 371–97.

― ― ―. 2015. "Grassroots Protest Movements and Mutating Conceptions of 'the Political' in an Evolving Burma". In *Metamorphosis: Studies in Social and Political Change in Myanmar,* edited by Renaud Egreteau and François Robinne, 69–100. Singapore: NUS Press.

RFA Burmese. 2022. "Teachers in Myanmar Caught in Crossfire as Conflict Rages". *Radio Free Asia*, 25 June. Available at https://www.rfa.org/english/news/myanmar/teachers-crossfire-06242022173224.html (accessed 10 December 2022).

Saito, Eisuke. 2021. "Ethical Challenges for Teacher Educators in Myanmar Due to the February 2021 Coup". *Power and Education* 13 (3): 205–12.

Saw Chit Thet Tun. 2022. "People's Defence Forces: Federal Army or NLD Army?" *ANU Myanmar Research Centre Working Papers Series*. Available at https://myanmar.anu.edu.au/sites/default/files/uploads/2022-08/saw_chit_thet_tun_2022_federal_army_or_nld_army.pdf (accessed 10 December 2022).

Saw Yan Naing. 2022. "The Life of Resistance: School Teachers and the Civil Disobedience Movement in Karen State, Myanmar". MA thesis. Bangkok, Mahidol University.

Sharp, Gene. 1973. *The Politics of Nonviolent Action*. P. Sargent Publisher.

Thawnghmung, Ardeth Maung. 2011. "Beyond Armed Resistance: Ethnonational Politics in Burma (Myanmar)". Available at http://hdl.handle.net/10125/22293 (accessed 10 December 2022).

Wittekind, Courtney T. 2021. "Learning from 'Social Punishment:' Neutrality in Myanmar Is No Longer Tenable". *FULCRUM*, 16 April. Available at https://fulcrum.sg/learning-from-social-punishment-neutrality-in-myanmar-is-no-longer-tenable/ (accessed 10 Dec 2022).

IV

An Economic Crisis

8

THE MYANMAR ECONOMY, COVID-19 AND THE MILITARY COUP: ISSUES AND PROSPECTS FOR RECOVERY

Linda Calabrese, Maximiliano Mendez-Parra and Laetitia Pettinotti

COVID-19 triggered an economic shock in Myanmar and the world over. The pandemic disrupted the economy of many countries, affecting not only their domestic environment, but also their connections with other countries through trade, foreign investment and aid, migration, and remittances. Travel bans and border controls, supply chain disruptions, and economic slowdown in many outward investing countries has blocked trade and production, causing economic turmoil. This matters for livelihoods in the short- and long-term: not only does international trade, investment and aid support job creation and income generation, but earning foreign exchange is also crucial to managing debt and stimulating economic recovery. As such, countries' connection to the global economy can shape their prospects for recovery. This can take different forms: it can bring the country back to its pre-pandemic path, for a 'business as usual' approach; or it can aim to build the foundations of a more resilient, climate-compatible, gender-sensitive and transformative growth.

Consider the case of Myanmar. While the official number of recorded cases of COVID-19 was small compared to surrounding nations,[1] the country experienced great economic damage due to the disruption to its international linkages, in particular through the impact on trade, investment and development finance (Turnell 2020). Moreover, on 1 February 2021, the military overthrew the country's elected government. The junta remains in power at the time of writing, generating political and economic instability and substantially undermining any prospects for recovery.

This study examines the impact of COVID-19 and the coup on the Myanmar economy through the country's international economic linkages, while also assessing its prospects for recovery. Rather than assessing the overall impact of the pandemic, it focuses on international trade, investment, aid and migration as transmission channels for the impact of COVID-19 and the coup. Therefore, this study does not aim to be a comprehensive assessment of the impact of these challenges, but rather to highlight some key areas that the international community can contribute to.

The study relies on analysis based on secondary data provided by national and international sources and on grey literature. The authors worked on the Myanmar economy, in particular on economic transformation, foreign direct investment and manufacturing, prior to the military coup. The authors also have extensive experience researching the impact of COVID-19 and of shocks in general, having conducted similar analyses in other countries in Asia, Africa and Latin America. We first outline the pre-pandemic economic context, with a focus on Myanmar's international linkages. We then consider the impact of COVID-19 and the plans for recovery made by the National League for Democracy (NLD) government. We provide some assessment of the impact of the military coup on the economy — an attempt made difficult by the paucity of data. We conclude with some consideration of the challenges faced by the Myanmar economy going ahead, and the resilience of its economic model.

MYANMAR'S ECONOMY: AN OVERVIEW

This section presents an overview of Myanmar's economy, identifying its most important sectors and understanding their trends pre-pandemic. This provides a baseline to assess the impact of COVID-19 and the military coup.

Formal trade

Prior to the onset of COVID-19 and the coup, over the course of Myanmar's liberalisation period its exports grew considerably, from US$13.7 billion exported in 2013, to US$20.2 billion (a 47% increase) in 2018. Services exports grew particularly fast, from US$2.8 billion in 2013 to US$4.7 billion in 2018. At the same time, the export basket diversified considerably. In 2013 services exports were dominated by information and communication technology (ICT), while in 2018 travel and tourism were the top services export. Albeit small compared to other South-East Asian countries, in the lead up to the 2015 national elections and a period of monumental change, Myanmar's travel and tourism sector saw the fastest growth rate in the region (World Bank 2016). China was an important partner in this sector: in 2019, of over 4.3 million tourist arrivals, almost 1.5 million were Chinese (World Tourism Organization 2021).[2]

Oil, gas, minerals and agricultural products dominated Myanmar exports until a few years ago. In 2018, however, textile and garment exports grew considerably to become the main export, while agricultural products and gems and precious stones shrunk. Diversification took place in terms of export destinations, too. Until 2015, almost all of Myanmar's exports were directed to Asia but, by 2018, Europe and North America took 26% of the total (authors' calculations based on UN COMTRADE data). This was due to the removal of sanctions by the United States and European Union in the 2010s (World Bank 2016), and also to preferential market access: Myanmar had duty-free and quota access to the European Union for all its products through the Everything But Arms (EBA) scheme. Another notable change was the emergence of China as the main destination for Myanmar's exports. This is the outcome of closer China–Myanmar commercial relations due to intensive investment by China (Gelb, Calabrese and Tang 2017), and of preferential market access given by China to some of Myanmar's exports.

But Myanmar's export potential remained unfulfilled. Gas exports continued to be concentrated in a few destinations (mainly Thailand). Beans and pulses, among the main agricultural exports, remained largely unprocessed, and their export to India (one of the main markets) constrained by India's import quotas but also by Myanmar's own challenges such as export restrictions, land control measures and unavailability of quality inputs (World Bank 2016; Government of Myanmar 2017).

Myanmar's imports also diversified prior the impacts of COVID-19 and the coup. There was some changes in the composition, with imports of services increasing from US$2.2 billion in 2013 to US$3.5 billion in 2018. Imports of agricultural goods (in particular food products) and textiles (as inputs to the garment sector) increased, surpassing imports of vehicles and machinery. Sources of imports remained stable, with China as the main import market (though the European Union gained ground as a large importer).

Illicit trade

In addition to formal trade flows, Myanmar has extensive unrecorded trade concerning products extracted or harvested illegally (such as timber or jade), and illegal products (such as wildlife or drugs) often traded across the land borders of conflict-affected areas. These trade flows form a big part of Myanmar's economy, but due to their illicit nature, information relies on estimates rather than on official figures.

Drugs: Myanmar is part of the opium-producing Golden Triangle, and one of the largest producers of opiates globally. Land dedicated to opium production was shrinking due to crop replacement programmes aimed at substituting opium with rubber, but this stabilised in 2020 (Woods 2018; UNODC 2021). In 2016, the opium-based drug economy in Myanmar was estimated at US$2 billion (Routray 2018), or around 10% of total exports.

Jade is widely sought after in China. Most of Myanmar's jade is extracted in Kachin State, and the trade amounted to at least US$31 billion in 2014, equivalent to roughly 48% of Myanmar's official GDP (Global Witness 2015).

Rare earth minerals are found throughout the country. Myanmar is considered to be among the world's top three largest producers, with an estimated production of 22 tons in 2019 (Barrera 2020). One of the main destinations for Myanmar's exports of rare earth minerals is China, itself the largest producer of rare earth minerals globally, but also a large consumer for industrial purposes (Yu and Mitchell 2020). Trade in rare earths between China and Myanmar has been bumpy, with both countries prohibiting border exchanges at various points in time. In 2019, Myanmar stopped exports several times, in an attempt to curb smuggling (Reuters 2019) and reduce environmental degradation (Liang and Backerberg 2019). However, there is evidence to suggest that this has increased since the coup (Maran 2022; Khin Maung Nyane and Whong 2022).

Gambling: Since the passing of the Gaming Law in 2019, gambling is legal in Myanmar for foreigners only (Rajah and Tann Asia 2019). The government is yet to grant licences to casinos, but many establishments already operate in border areas outside the full control of authorities (Chan Mya Htwe 2019). Some gambling operations were stopped prior to the pandemic due to suspected irregularities, but appear to have resumed after the military coup (The Irrawaddy 2021c).

Timber: Myanmar's timber, particularly teak, is widely sought after. Officially, all of Myanmar's teak is owned by the state, which regulates logging and trade. However, government forestry operations have prioritised revenues over conservation. Illegally logged teak is sold to China, India and Thailand, but also Europe and North America (EIA 2019). Myanmar also exports rosewood to China, with exports having reached an estimated US$350 million (EIA 2015).

Wildlife: Myanmar's biodiversity and limited state control over border areas enables wildlife trade. Many species are hunted and sold in markets, often exported to China and in a smaller measure Thailand (McEvoy et al. 2019). Studies raise concern over the potential for pathogens, but also contend that eliminating hunting may not be feasible in Myanmar because of its symbolic, economic and subsistence value (Smiley Evans et al. 2020).

Investment

Regarding foreign investment, data from the Government's Directorate of Investment and Company Administration indicate oil and gas is the sector that received the most investment, since 1988, followed by telecommunications and manufacturing. The sectoral pattern of investment has undergone diversification over the past decade, with manufacturing, transport, livestock and fishery increasingly becoming important sectors for investment.

The largest foreign investors are mainly east and southeast Asian countries, with Singapore and China (including Hong Kong) topping the list (although investment from Singapore may also be originally from other countries, through 'round-tripping'; Gelb et al. 2017).

Migration and remittances

The World Bank estimates that in 2017 there were almost 3 million migrants from Myanmar across the globe, from a population of over 50 million. 62% of these migrants were in Thailand, and the rest in Malaysia (10%), Bangladesh (8%) and Saudi Arabia (8%) (World Bank 2017a). Over 40% of these migrants are women (UNDESA 2015). Migrants contribute massively to the Myanmar economy: in 2019, inward remittances amounted to US$2.8 billion, equivalent to 4.3% of GDP, up from US$1.6 billion in 2013 (World Bank 2017b).

Development assistance and development finance

Prior to the coup, Myanmar received a considerable amount of aid: donors provided US$1.5 billion in official development assistance (ODA) in 2018. From OECD countries alone, in 2013, Myanmar ranked third among the largest recipient of aid globally. It went down to the seventh position in 2015, but it remained one of the main aid recipients in the world. In terms of ODA per capita, it was in line with the average of its South-East Asian neighbours (Carr 2018).[3] The largest providers of ODA are Japan, the European Union institutions, the United States and the United Kingdom. No data is available on the assistance Myanmar receives from China, but it is likely to be a non-negligible amount (Carr 2018).

In addition to receiving aid, the government of Myanmar has also borrowed from various lenders. World Bank data on outstanding debt and debt service for 2020 and 2021 shows that in terms of official lending, Myanmar owes most of its debt to China and Japan.

THE IMPACT OF COVID-19

Myanmar reported its first confirmed case of COVID-19 on 23 March 2020. In addition to the health and social impacts, the pandemic affected the country's economy: GDP growth was estimated to decline from 6.8% in FY2018/19 to 0.5% in FY2019/20 (World Bank 2020a). This section reviews the main impacts of COVID-19 on the Myanmar economy.

Formal trade

The pandemic triggered price volatility, supply chain disruptions and changes in demand in importing countries that affected both domestic production and global value chains. China, the first country affected by the pandemic, is Myanmar's main import and export partner. Below we examine trends in some of the main areas affecting Myanmar's trade patterns, both in terms of formal and illicit trade.

Agricultural products

Myanmar is a large exporter of agricultural products. As a staple food, rice exports were controlled by the government, to guarantee domestic consumption and build up a 'rice buffer stock' (ITC 2020). Export reductions across Asia have caused rice prices and demand, in particular from China, the main importer of Myanmar's rice, to surge, which benefitted Myanmar's rice exporters (ITC 2020). As non-perishables, beans, pulses and oilseeds have been less affected by the COVID-19 outbreak, and global demand has remained largely stable. Myanmar's exporters have experienced limited disruption (ITC 2020), notwithstanding border closures, in particular with India, as well as logistical restrictions on trucking and shipping. Sales of fish and seafood saw a drop in demand, both domestically (due to the closure of restaurants and hotels) and internationally, in particular to the main export markets of China and Japan. Moreover, limited supply of inputs, transport and logistic constraints have caused a reduction in exports (ITC 2020). Finally, Myanmar's forestry sector was affected by containment measures that disrupted the supply chain, especially for trade with China (ITC 2020). The sector also experienced drops in demand from foreign partners.

In the longer term, it is difficult to anticipate the evolution of agricultural exports. Rice and sugar prices have been more stable than others throughout the pandemic, but global food prices remain sensitive to global supply, demand and stock situations. Given the low elasticity of demand for agricultural products, the variation in income in importing countries is expected to have a limited impact on Myanmar's exports. Together with a potential fall in exports of garments, discussed below, the rise in the exports of agricultural products anticipates increased reliance on primary products of Myanmar's trade.

Extractives

Prices of extractives (e.g., natural gas) have been particularly volatile during the pandemic and it is difficult to forecast how they will impact Myanmar's outbound trade in the coming years. Exports of natural gas and copper follow changes in the demand from the importing countries, primarily China and Thailand. China is recovering quickly, suggesting that demand is likely to return to pre-crisis levels soon. Demand from Thailand may take slightly longer to recover, however. It is therefore expected that extractives will become a larger share of Myanmar exports in the coming years.

Manufacturing

Supply chain disruptions in China, one of the main input suppliers, and then the collapse in demand in Myanmar's main markets (Japan, Europe and the United States) created significant challenges for the garment sector. As garments are non-essential, the industry is vulnerable to downturns and shocks in demand. Survey data confirms this for Myanmar, finding that the majority of garment firms had their orders reduced or cancelled, and were strongly affected by the pandemic (ITC 2020).

In the longer term, income and exports for garments and footwear to Europe are expected to take longer to return to their 2019 value, and based on IMF and OECD data, a full recovery is not expected until 2023. European consumers' income and job security have been significantly hit, which will result in lower demand for these products for both the levels of 2019 and the expected levels for 2021 and 2022.

Increase in regional exports

Myanmar can expect an increase in regional (Asian) exports. The recovery in China and Myanmar's neighbouring countries is expected to be faster than in Europe and the United States (IMF 2022). In addition, exports to these countries tend to be primarily in commodities, which have seen a recovery in price in the early months of 2022. Although it is unclear what would be the level of prices for these products in the coming years, it is reasonable to assume that these will remain at the current levels as the global economy recovers.

A possible shortening of value chains may reinforce their regional ties. Retailers worldwide are looking to make their supply chains more robust to sudden changes in demand. This implies a search for closer partners, especially for the provision of critical production inputs and essential products. This, in turn, entails a possible disengagement from geographically distant (i.e., European) suppliers and a re-engagement in the region.

Regional trade could be further bolstered by the recently negotiated and announced Regional Comprehensive Economic Partnership (RCEP), which creates a Free Trade Area (FTA) where members agree to reduce and eliminate barriers to trade. Its signatories include the ten members of the Association of Southeast Asian Nations (ASEAN) economic community (Brunei Darussalam, Cambodia, Indonesia, Laos, Malaysia, Myanmar, the Philippines, Singapore, Thailand, and Vietnam) and five countries with existing FTAs with the group (Australia, China, Japan, South Korea, and New Zealand). The impact of RCEP on Myanmar exports is expected to be limited, at least in the short run. On the one hand, the implementation of the agreement is likely to fall beyond the economic recovery horizon. On the other, Myanmar already has duty-free access to most of the partners through ASEAN and agreements between ASEAN and other partners (e.g. ASEAN–China, ASEAN–Australia, ASEAN–Japan). The main winners of the agreement are expected to be China, Japan and South Korea, rather than smaller economies like Myanmar (Petri and Plummer 2020). Moreover, the agreement is shallow, as it offers relatively weak protection of intellectual property rights and allows for carve-outs and concessions in tariff negotiations (Tanjangco et al. 2021). RCEP is likely to play a larger role in the long run, by strengthening economic links among the participating countries beyond the removal of trade barriers.

Services sector

Service exports have been strongly affected by the pandemic. Given the travel restrictions, the tourism sector has been strongly hit. The lockdowns and travel restrictions (including the closure of Yangon airport) have meant a drop in tourist services, which represents nearly 40% of Myanmar's total exported services. The Asian Development Bank estimated a decline in tourist revenue of US$100-320 million between March and September 2020 (Abiad et al. 2020).

The recovery in this sector will be slow. Even after domestic lockdowns eased, travel restrictions remained well into 2022. Even after these have lifted, people may still be afraid of travelling due to the unstable political situation in Myanmar. The recovery of travel and tourism activities will take several years and will depend heavily on the country's political trajectory.

Border Trade and Illicit Trade

While Myanmar's overall international trade performance remains solid, in 2020 its land border trade with China and Thailand declined by 3% and 5% respectively, whereas border trade with Bangladesh significantly increased, from US$21 million in 2019 to US$727 million. The increase was attributable to exports and imports at the Sittwe border post, in Rakhine (World Bank 2020c). The Bangladesh–Myanmar land border is one of the main corridors for illicit trade, and disruptions at the border do not seem to have stopped these flows. Drug production and other forms of trade have thrived in the pandemic, as authorities have shifted their attention away from border trade, having other pressing concerns to address (Beech and Nang 2020). In May 2020, the police seized the largest-ever haul of methamphetamines in the northeast Shan state (BBC 2020). Similarly, the gambling business, and in particular the construction of new casinos, does not seem to have been deterred by the pandemic (Tower and Clapp 2020).

Other illicit trade flows have been disrupted more severely. Wildlife trade in particular, given its close connection with the COVID-19 pandemic, has been affected by the disruption of trade with China and the implementation of strict cross-border regulatory mechanisms. This may be beneficial for wildlife, and stop the spread of related diseases, but it may also affect the livelihoods of those involved in the trade, some of whom may be part of more marginalised groups.

Investment

The global economic crisis has generated significant excess capacity across production sectors and, consequently, has slowed down new investment and expansion plans. Low oil and gas prices are threatening profits for the sector, with potentially adverse effects on government revenues and new investment (ITC 2020). However, the recovery of demand in China and Thailand in 2021 suggests that investment in these sectors may recover faster. The textile and garment sector is experiencing uncertainty in global demand and challenges with supply chain operations, which endanger profits and thus the survival of the industry in countries operating at the low-margin end of the value chain, like Myanmar. This threatens the jobs of the 350,000 workers involved in the industry (ITC 2020). There is a significant excess capacity in the sector generated by the crisis, implying that no further investments are expected. The food and agribusiness sectors have experienced stable demand and increasing prices, making these good sectors for investment (ITC 2020). However, supply chain and logistics issues may make new investments complicated, especially since the implementation of new laws regulating investment by the military State Administration Council (SAC).

Infrastructure Construction

Due to the impacts of COVID-19, infrastructure investment and construction are at risk of long delays and cancellations. Of particular relevance is the China–Myanmar Economic Corridor (CMEC), a series of infrastructure projects to connect the South-western Chinese province of Yunnan to the Bay of Bengal through Myanmar. The CMEC includes oil and gas pipelines, road and railway networks, ports and industrial parks, financed and built through public and private arrangements. Research points to a complex array of winners and losers in large infrastructure projects in Myanmar, with local communities usually seeing limited benefits from the infrastructure they host (Mark, Overland and Vakulchuk 2020).

Chinese stakeholders are among the main players in infrastructure development, financing and building large projects. Globally, Chinese-financed infrastructure has often been linked to debt sustainability issues. However, prior to the coup, the GoM was showing a careful approach to managing its finances (Calabrese and Cao 2021).

The risk of delays in rolling out the CMEC was particularly acute in the first months of the pandemic when workers (in particular Chinese) failed to return to work after the Chinese New Year (Zhai and Tostevin 2020). However, the appetite for work in some infrastructure areas has not stopped. In 2020, the government of Myanmar put up for tender 29 solar plant projects, 28 of which were won by Chinese companies (Liu 2020). In the longer term, infrastructure projects may face increasing challenges due to economic recession, decreased appetite for lenders and borrowers for infrastructure, and resources being diverted toward more pressing priorities. As we will see, the former Government of Myanmar's COVID-19 Economic Recovery Plan (CERP) prioritised private and publicly-funded high-impact infrastructure as an instrument for recovery.

Remittances

The global pandemic and economic crisis affecting countries hosting migrant workers from Myanmar reduced the flow of remittances from March 2020. Thailand, Malaysia, Bangladesh and Saudi Arabia, the main destinations for Myanmar migrants, are, however, estimated to have recovered in 2021 or 2022 (IMF, 2022). Therefore, remittances from these countries are likely to return to their previous levels. However, migrants may now experience new challenges due to the political situation in Myanmar, including challenges in sending money home through some of the usual channels, such as through travelling friends or acquaintances due to the banking restrictions now in place.

Development Assistance and Development Finance

The former GoM requested support to deal with the pandemic (GoM 2020a; 2020b), and the international community responded. In July 2020, the European Union and six of its member governments announced a moratorium on debt repayments due from Myanmar, worth almost US$100 million, or 20% of Myanmar's current debt payments schedule. Under the Debt Service Suspension Initiative (DSSI) supported by the G20 and Paris Club of creditor nations, Myanmar was provided with a debt service suspension worth around US$1.2 billion (Turnell 2020). The International Monetary Fund (IMF), the Asian Development Bank (ADB), the European Union and the Japanese International Cooperation Agency (JICA) and the Export-Import Bank of Korea also provided financial support to address urgent fiscal needs and social assistance to the poor and micro, small and medium-sized enterprises (ADB 2020; Chan Mya Htwe and Aung Loon 2020; IMF 2020b). Moreover, garment brands such as H&M, Inditex, Next, C&A, Bestseller and Tchibo signed an agreement to protect garment factories and workers in 2020 (ITC 2020).

In addition to sanctions by the United States and European Union, and suspension of trade engagement with Myanmar by the United States, other donors have reacted to the coup by revising their financial support to Myanmar. The European Union, the World Bank, the United States, Australia, Japan and the United Kingdom have suspended their support, halted new aid commitments or redirected away from the government, towards humanitarian assistance and support to civil society. Others, in particular China, have continued providing financial support to the junta.

PROSPECTS FOR BUILDING BACK BETTER

Countries have responded to the COVID-19 economic crisis in many ways, ranging from a 'business as usual' approach to bring economies back on their previous growth paths, to 'Building Back Better' (BBB) approaches, which take into account not only economic growth, but also gender and environmental issues.

In April 2020, the GoM issued a COVID-19 Economic Recovery Plan (CERP). The CERP aimed to mitigate the pandemic's impact on the economy at the micro and macro level, supporting the private sector and easing the impact on workers and households (GoM 2020a). The CERP sets out goals, strategies, and actions and was accompanied by an implementation matrix to monitor progress and also linked to other domestic plans (such as the GoM's Health Sector Contingency Plan) and international commitments, such as the Sustainable Development Goals (SDGs) (GoM 2020b).

While addressing economic and social challenges, the CERP lacked an explicit green and gender-sensitive approach, indicating a 'business as usual' path to recovery. This may be due, at least in part, to a scarcity of resources: Myanmar's stimulus package, at 2.9% of GDP, was estimated to be low compared to the resources deployed by other ASEAN countries (Lim 2020). Even so, the CERP entailed considerable financial support, and therefore had a chance to set the country on a better track in terms of its gender and environmental dimensions, if the coup did not take place.

The CERP comprehensively addressed economic issues. The plan aimed to respond quickly to the crisis when it first unfolded, and minimise the negative consequences of the pandemic, but also kickstarting the recovery. Crisis response measures aimed to: reduce the strain on the banking sector; support the workforce, in particular through extending social protection and creating job opportunities through infrastructure projects; strengthen the healthcare system; and reallocate financial resources to respond to COVID-19. Recovery measures aimed at providing a monetary stimulus, injecting liquidity into the economy; providing easier access to capital for firms, and deferring or waiving fees and taxes; promotion of private investment and fast-tracking public ones; facilitation of import and export processes; promoting e-commerce and mobile payments, and additional development finance to respond to the pandemic.

However, under the plan, social and environmental aspects were not devoted enough attention. The CERP recovery plan was also gender-blind and made no specific provisions for women. Moreover, its interventions had the potential to aggravate already existing gender inequality in Myanmar and work against the objectives of the country's National Strategic Plan for the Advancement of Women 2013–2022. These non-gender sensitive recovery packages come in a context of years of underspending on gender equality related matters (Z. Oo et al. 2015).

Moreover, the CERP did not directly earmark a budget line for climate. Worse, some actions such as the ones related to "implement labour-intensive community infrastructure projects", "expedite investment approval process" could potentially lock Myanmar in a carbon-intensive development pathway (risking saddling itself with stranded assets) and indirectly impact Myanmar's emissions and/or further widen its adaptation gap.

THE ECONOMIC IMPACT OF THE MILITARY COUP

Amid the COVID-19 pandemic and the arduous recovery process, a military coup took place in February 2021. Contesting the results of the general elections held in November 2020, the army arrested many of the incoming Members of Parliament (MPs) and seized power. At the time of writing, the military junta remains in power. There is yet to be an agreement among scholars on the drivers of the coup. Some attribute it to increasing tensions between the elected civilian government and the military, or to personal tensions between State Counsellor Aung San Suu Kyi and military leader Min Aung Hlaing; others point to internal conflict between different factions in the military (Moeller 2022).

This study focuses on economic implications; it is beyond our scope to discuss the political and social impact of the military coup. Attempting an estimation of the economic consequences of the coup is hampered by a lack of data. However, as outlined by Htwe Htwe Thein and Michael

Gillian (this volume) the military takeover has had significant impacts on different aspects of the economy, especially international investment, and the potential for recovery after the COVID-19 pandemic is now severely limited.

Economic Disruption in the Aftermath of the Coup

Following the coup, a powerful civil disobedience movement drew in millions of state government workers who refused to work under the military State Administration Council (SAC). The protests were effective in shutting down many sectors of the domestic economy (education, transport, internet, financial services). As outlined in the introduction, the military responded harshly, killing more than 2900 people.

In the immediate aftermath of the coup, the protests and repression disrupted economic activity around the country. A survey of 400 foreign companies found that firms around Myanmar introduced a hiring freeze, terminated contracts or reduced salaries, and around 10% of them terminated operations (Wallace and Robinson 2021). The hardest-hit companies were Asian ones (in particular Myanmar), and those operating in agriculture, infrastructure and tourism (FCCM 2021). In addition, many companies have divested or have halted plans for investment in Myanmar. These include China's financial Ant Group, Norway's telecom Telenor, Hong Kong-listed energy company VPower, German wholesaler Metro, Kempinsky Hotel and British American Tobacco (Liu and Frontier 2021; D. Oo and Liu 2021). In the garment sector, many factories stopped operations and brands suspended orders from Myanmar (Ringstrom 2021). It is estimated that COVID-19 and the military coup jointly erased more than two-thirds of the 600,000 jobs in the garment sector by April 2021 (Myanmar Now 2021a; Brehm and Magnusson 2021). The World Bank (2021) also notes that physical currency is in short supply, and access to banking and payment services is limited. The *kyat* has depreciated rapidly, leading to an increase in the price of imported goods, including fuel. In April 2022, the Central Bank of Myanmar fixed the exchange rate to MMK 1,850 to the dollar (compared to the MMK 1,300 to the dollar pre-coup), but was later forced to revise it to MMK 2,100 to the dollar, an amount which still does not reflect the value of the currency in unofficial markets (Greene 2022; The Irrawaddy 2022).

Border trade has also been disrupted, creating issues for Myanmar's agricultural exports (Frontier 2021). Not all sectors, however, have suffered. The illicit trade conducted at the border seems to continue with little interruption. Cross-border trade in rare earths minerals, but also timber and so on, seem to have continued, allowed by the military government to proceed (The Irrawaddy 2021a). Similarly, infrastructure planning and construction seem to have resumed. For instance, in 2021 the Myanmar Investment Commission approved 15 new investment projects, including a US$2.5 billion power plant that will run on liquefied natural gas (Myanmar Now 2021b). Moreover, the military government had reorganised members of the CMEC Joint Committee, and the central committee for the implementation of the Myanmar–China Cross-Border Economic Cooperation Zone, and it is likely to push for a continuation of these projects (The Irrawaddy 2021b).

The international community has responded to the coup (see Coppel, *this volume*). The European Union, United States, and United Kingdom have imposed targeted sanctions aimed at individual members of the military elite, and suspended arms sales. New Zealand and the Philippines rejected Myanmar's inclusion in the RCEP because of the country's political situation.

Medium-term impact

The most recent data at the time of writing indicates a negative outturn for the Myanmar economy (World Bank 2022). The negative impact of the military coup is estimated to be much larger than that of the COVID-19 pandemic — and both, combined, have severely impacted the economy. The World Bank and the International Monetary Fund estimated a contraction of the economy of 18% in the fiscal year 2020/21, and a total contraction of 30% since the beginning of the pandemic (World Bank 2021; IMF 2022).

Private investment has fallen, and weak demand has made previously viable projects unviable; the *kyat* has depreciated against foreign currencies, and the cost of imports has risen, affecting not only consumer goods but also fuel and other inputs to production. Firms are increasingly affected by electricity outages and internet disruptions, and continue to suffer from disruptions to input supplies and access to financial services, as well as weak consumer demand, reporting reductions in sales and profits (World Bank 2022). There are some signs of recovery: manufacturing and agricultural exports and activity have recovered, albeit at low levels; some border crossings have re-opened and FDI commitments and company registrations have increased modestly. But overall, the economic challenges are felt in terms of public finances, having caused a steep decline in government revenues, which in turn reduces the room for further stimulus. This will have dramatic consequences for poverty and vulnerability. Employment is estimated to have fallen by around 1 million since the military coup, with many people expected to have been forced to move to jobs with poorer working conditions and lower pay. The share of Myanmar's population living in poverty is expected to have more than doubled compared to pre-COVID-19 levels (World Bank 2022).

ECONOMIC RECOVERY AND INTERNATIONAL RESPONSE UNDER THE MILITARY JUNTA

Economic recovery under the military coup

The impact of the military coup on the country leaves little hope for economic recovery, at least in the short run. Before the coup, the elected government was working on the Myanmar Economic Resilience and Reform Plan (MERRP), a successor to the CERP aimed at economic recovery while at the same time reforming some structural weaknesses of the Myanmar economy. Compared to the NLD plan, the junta's MERP drops the 'R' for 'reform', and with it some of the main structural and governance changes that the NLD government had in the pipeline. In particular, the junta's MERP does not include reforms of State Economic Enterprises and banks, e-commerce regulations, transparency and land reform, and reforms to meet international financial standards that were present in the NLD's MERRP. Rather, the MERP includes measures to support tourism, taxation, and reform of laws, bylaws and procedures. In short, it aims at improving the economic situation through streamlining and facilitating business operations, which are necessary for the military government, but has dropped plans for structural reforms (Liu and Frontier 2021). This suggests that economic recovery is unlikely to be transformative or create a more inclusive economy.

In the longer term, what will happen to trade and investment in Myanmar? This is difficult to predict, but we can make some hypothesis on the future of forex-earning sectors. Tourism, for example, is unlikely to return to pre-pandemic level while the military government is in place. The number of international tourist arrivals in the country has remained low, never reaching a million international tourists a year before the beginning of the political transition in 2011. Since 2012, the number started growing, reaching almost 5 million international arrivals in 2019, but dropped again in 2020 (World Tourism Organization 2021), following the international reputational damage caused by the country's treatment of the Rohingya. While data is not available for the year since the coup, up until July 2022 the borders remained closed to international tourists, with heavy restrictions in place for other foreign visitors. Similarly, for the garment production sector, the situation looks bleak. While the *kyat* has depreciated, making Myanmar more competitive in global markets, access to inputs has become more costly, making Myanmar lose some of its advantage in manufacturing.

Meanwhile, the need for foreign exchange has prompted increased exploitation of sectors such as logging and mining of jade, gold, and rare earth minerals, which exacerbate environmental risks. Moreover, the junta is veering towards more inward-looking policies, with import restrictions, in particular for consumer goods, accompanied by measures such as support to import-substituting manufacturing based on value addition to domestic raw materials (World Bank, 2022). While these measures may support certain sectors and may well prompt some economic activity, they also restrict Myanmar's access to the world economy in ways that can have negative impacts.

Social aspects and gender

The social impact of COVID-19 and the coup has been dramatic. The World Bank estimates that a decade of poverty reduction has been reversed as a result of these two challenges, and poverty levels in 2022 were double compared to those of March 2020 (World Bank 2022). Moreover, the cash and food assistance that had been offered by the government in response to the pandemic has declined sharply, and almost no household was found to receive assistance in mid-2022. Rising food prices have also placed many households in a situation of food insecurity (World Bank 2022).

The crisis caused by COVID-19 and the coup has further entrenched existing gender inequities in the household (World Bank 2020b). Preliminary evidence seems to indicate that a similar share of working men and women employed in 'COVID-19-sensitive' sectors were made redundant in the first year of the pandemic (Diao et al. 2020). The services, manufacturing, construction sectors, and finally agriculture were among the first hit by the crisis. Moreover, women are more likely than men to work in the informal sector, and thus have been more vulnerable (Lambrecht et al. 2020). Distress due to the COVID-19 related economic downturn and the restrictive measures on mobility, increased food insecurity and reduced incomes are likely to have aggravated existing intra-household tensions (Lambrecht et al. 2020). Before COVID-19, Myanmar already had high rates of domestic violence. Since the start of the COVID-19 crisis, hotlines have also reported an increase in domestic violence (Swe Lei Mon 2020).

While we have little information on the impact of the coup on women, we can argue that the current political situation has compounded existing challenges. Women are traditionally in charge of care and reproductive work within the household. The economic challenges and lack of social services brough about by the coup are likely to have had a stronger impact on women as primary caretakers.

Climate change issues

Myanmar's economic development and recovery efforts are set to be undermined by climate change. The country is expected to experience increased frequency and intensity of extreme climate events (e.g. floods, cyclones, droughts, heatwaves) and gradual changes in climate patterns (e.g. reduced and delayed monsoon season, increase in average temperatures; IPCC 2007; 2018). Consequently, climate-sensitive sectors, such as the agricultural sector, which contributes to about 30% of the country's GDP, and assets most exposed such as those located in low lying areas prone to sea-level rise, floods and storm surges, are to be severely affected. The country is among the most vulnerable to climate change and one of the least ready to adapt to it (ND GAIN 2018). Given this situation mainstreaming climate mitigation and adaptation actions in economic recovery programming is critical for the future.

The existing National Environmental Policy (2019), the Myanmar Climate Change Policy (2019) and the Myanmar Sustainable Development Plan for 2018-2030, are all committed to the mainstreaming of climate action in the annual planning and budgeting of ministries. To not be in breach of its own policies, Myanmar would need to ensure green budgeting or at minimum assess the compatibility between recovery packages and its own climate goals as set in its Nationally Determined Contribution under the United Nations Framework Convention on Climate Change (OECD 2020a). Whether the military government is working towards these goals is unclear, but seems unlikely.

One of Myanmar's main exports is natural gas and oil, which contribute to greenhouse gases emissions. The low prices for these two commodities for most of 2020 indicated a risk of unsustainable borrowing and reduced fiscal space for the country given decreased government revenue from this sector (OECD 2020b). Such unsustainable borrowing risk could have potentially provided an entry point to advocacy for reduced fossil fuel dependency. Fossil fuel prices rose again in 2021 and 2022, however and such prospects seems even more distant.

CONCLUSIONS

Starting in 2020, the economy of Myanmar has been hit by two challenges: COVID-19 and the military coup. COVID-19 has affected the Myanmar economy disrupting supply chains and border trade. The military coup which took place in February 2021 threw the country into chaos, disrupting and halting many economic activities. The imposition of military rule has caused turmoil which, together with the sanctions and withdrawal of investment, has exacerbated the COVID-19 crisis. In addition, the junta does not seem to have an innovative long-term plan for the economy and, while continuing some of the stimulus provided by the NLD government, they are not pushing for further reform.

This study has attempted to document the impact of COVID-19 on the economy through its international linkages. At the onset of the COVID-19 pandemic, the NLD government had devised a plan which was more focused on economic performance, but did not take into account social and environmental aspects of the recovery. The government was preparing a longer-term plan but was stopped in its tracks by the military coup in February 2021. Since then, the chaos generated by the coup has endangered the country's prospects for recovery. The economy has been hit hard by the coup, and the recovery plan proposed by the military does not seem to go far enough to repair the damage.

As the situation evolves, it is difficult to draw conclusions. At the time of writing, a few things seem clear. First, the COVID-19 pandemic has prompted a stronger reliance on primary products, in particular agricultural products and oil and gas. Services and industry have taken a hit, and are unlikely to recover anytime soon. This hinders and possibly reverts economic transformation in Myanmar, making the economy less resilient to future shocks. Secondly, the country appears more isolated from the international community, not only politically, but also economically. In addition to the damages imposed by the pandemic, sanctions, aid cuts and divestment in response to the coup constrain Myanmar's international linkages. In this light, the junta's inward-looking approach is not only a policy choice but also a necessity. Finally, the recovery plan currently in place does not seem to serve the country in the longer term. Not only are social and environmental issues unlikely to be adequately addressed; even the economic challenges are not met by the structural reforms needed to promote more inclusive growth. Moreover, the country is currently continuing to deplete its natural resources to gain foreign exchange, in a manner that only makes it further vulnerable to climate change.

In summary, COVID-19 and the military coup have inflicted a hard blow to the Myanmar economy, leading to a considerable increase in poverty and loss of livelihoods. The current economic model does not seem fit to reverse this course of action, and to lead the economy towards more resilience and inclusivity.

ACKNOWLEDGEMENTS

We wish to thank Justine Chambers (ANU Myanmar Research Centre) for her inputs and support, the participants to the ANU's "Myanmar Update conference 2021: Living with the Pandemic", and two anonymous reviewers whose feedback helped us improve our early draft of this chapter.

Notes

1. As of May 2022, despite upsurges in cases in 2021 and 2022, Myanmar has officially recorded a total number of cases (over 600, 000) far lower than other Southeast Asian nations such as Vietnam (over 10 million) and Thailand (over 4 million), even when accounting for differences in population size (John Hopkins University 2022). However, these figures may be an underestimation, considering that the military government installed after the coup may not be keen to share the real figures, and the collapse of the state and health system that followed the coup may mean that there is no capacity to collect and report accurate figures.
2. These numbers do not only refer to leisure tourism, but also to business tourism. In fact, many Chinese tourists enter Myanmar for business purposes (Gelb, Calabrese, and Tang 2017).
3. Myanmar receives lower levels of aid per capita than either Laos or Cambodia, but this is expected as both Laos and Cambodia have smaller populations (Carr 2018).

References

Abiad, Abdul, Mia Arao, Suzette Dagli, Benno Ferrarini, Ilan Noy, Patrick Osewe, Jesson Pagaduan, Donghyun Park, and Reizle Platitas. (2020). The Economic Impact of the COVID-19 Outbreak on Developing Asia'. ADB Briefs. Manila, Philippines: Asian Development Bank.

Barrera, Priscila. (2020). '10 Top Countries for Rare Earth Metal Production'. *Rare Earth Investing News* (blog), 26 May 2020. Available at https://investingnews.com/daily/resource-investing/critical-metals-investing/rare-earth-investing/rare-earth-producing-countries/.

BBC. (2020). 'Myanmar Police Seize Largest Haul of Synthetic Drugs'. *BBC News*, 19 May. Available at https://www.bbc.co.uk/news/world-asia-52712014.

Beech, Hannah, and Saw Nang. (2020). 'Raids Reveal Massive Fentanyl Production in Myanmar'. *The New York Times*, 19 May. Available at https://www.nytimes.com/2020/05/19/world/asia/myanmar-drug-raid-fentanyl.html.

Brehm, Stefan, and Helena Magnusson. (2021). 'Garment Workers in Myanmar: The COVID-19 Crisis and beyond: A Social Media Analysis of Workers' Grievances Using Social@risk™'. Lund, Sweden: Globalworks.

Calabrese, Linda, and Yue Cao. (2021). 'Managing the Belt and Road: Agency and Development in Cambodia and Myanmar'. *World Development* 141, 105297: 1-17. https://doi.org/10.1016/j.worlddev.2020.105297.

Carr, Thomas. (2018). 'Supporting the Transition: Understanding Aid to Myanmar Since 2011'. The Asia Foundation.

Chan Mya Htwe. (2019). 'Casino Operations to Be Legalised under New Gambling Law'. *The Myanmar Times*, 31 March. Available at https://www.mmtimes.com/news/casino-operations-be-legalised-under-new-gambling-law.html.

Diao, Xinshen, Nilar Aung, Wuit Yi Lwin, Phoo Pye Zone, Khin Maung Nyunt, and James Thurlow. (2020). 'Assessing the Impacts of COVID-19 on Myanmar's Economy: A Social Accounting Matrix (SAM) Multiplier Approach'. Myanmar SSP Policy Note 5. Washington, DC: International Food Policy Research Institute (IFPRI).

EIA. (2015). 'Organised Chaos: The Illicit Overland Timber Trade between Myanmar and China'. London: Environmental Investigation Agency.

— — —. (2019). 'State of Corruption: The Top-Level Conspiracy behind the Global Trade in Myanmar's Stolen Teak'. London: Environmental Investigation Agency.

Foreign Chambers of Commerce in Myanmar (FCCM). (2021). 'Joint Survey on the Impact on Business Operating in Myanmar: Report and Summary of Findings'. Foreign Chambers of Commerce in Myanmar. Available at https://eurocham-myanmar.org/2021/05/11/results-of-the-joint-chamber-survey-published/.

Frontier. (2021). '"Prices Are Dropping Exponentially": Border Trade Hit Hard as China Shuts the Gates'. Frontier Myanmar, 2 August. https://www.frontiermyanmar.net/en/prices-are-dropping-exponentially-border-trade-hit-hard-as-china-shuts-the-gates/.

Gelb, Stephen, Linda Calabrese, and Xiaoyang Tang. (2017). 'Foreign Direct Investment and Economic Transformation in Myanmar'. London: Overseas Development Institute.

Global Witness. (2015). 'Jade: Myanmar's "Big State Secret"'. London: Global Witness.

Government of Myanmar. (2017). 'Myanmar Pulses Sector Development Strategy'. NayPyiDaw: Department of Agricultural Research, Ministry of Agriculture, Livestock and Irrigation. Available at http://extwprlegs1.fao.org/docs/pdf/mya190978.pdf.

— — —. (2020a). 'Overcoming as One: COVID-19 Economic Relief Plan'. Naypyidaw: Government of the Republic of the Union of Myanmar. https://www.ccifrance-myanmar.org/sites/ccifrance-myanmar.org/files/resources-documents/covid-19_economic_relief_plan_by_ministry_of_planning_finance_and_industry27.04.2020.pdf.

— — —. (2020b). 'Statement by Ambassador Hau Do Suan, Permanent Representative of the Republic of the Union of Myanmar to the United Nations, at the General Debate of the High-Level Political Forum on Sustainable Development', 17 July. Available at https://sustainabledevelopment.un.org/content/documents/26839Myanmar_General_Debate.pdf.

Greene, Charlie. (2022). 'Myanmar, CBM, Government, Currency, Foreign Countries, 2022'. *Myanmar Insider* (blog), 13 May. Available at https://www.myanmarinsider.com/a-fixed-exchange-rate-system-perhaps/.

IMF. (2020). 'IMF Executive Board Approves a US$356.5 Million Disbursement to Myanmar to Address the COVID-19 Pandemic'. *International Monetary Fund*, 26 June. Available at https://www.imf.org/en/News/Articles/2020/06/26/pr20247-myanmar-imf-executive-board-approves-a-us-356-5m-disbursement-address-covid19.

IMF. (2022). *World Economic Outlook: Countering the cost-of-living crisis*. Washigton, DC: International Monetary Fund.

IPCC. (2007). 'Regional Climate Projections'. In *Climate Change 2007: The Physical Science Basis - A Contribution of Working Group I to the Fourth Assessment Report of the Intergovernmental Panel on Climate Change*.

———. (2018). 'Framing and Context'. In *Global Warming of 1.5°C - An IPCC Special Report on the Impacts of Global Warming of 1.5°C above Pre-Industrial Levels and Related Global Greenhouse Gas Emission Pathways, in the Context of Strengthening the Global Response to the Threat of Climate Change, Sustainable Development, and Efforts to Eradicate Poverty*.

ITC. (2020). 'The Impact of COVID-19 on Myanmar Export Sectors: Supporting the Comprehensive Economic Relief Plan (CERP) Action 2.4.3. – «Facilitate Exportation Processes»'. Geneva: International Trade Center.

Khin Maung Nyane, and Eugene Whong. (2022). 'Illegal Rare Earth Mining Harms Environment in Myanmar's Kachin State'. *Radio Free Asia* (blog), 10 March. Available at https://www.rfa.org/english/news/myanmar/mining-03102022184456.html.

Lambrecht, Isabel, Kristi Mahrt, Catherine Ragasa, Michael Wang, Hnin Ei Win, and Khin Zin Win. (2020). 'A Gender-Transformative Response to COVID-19 in Myanmar'. Myanmar SSP Policy Note 4. Washington, DC: International Food Policy Research Institute (IFPRI). Available at https://ebrary.ifpri.org/digital/collection/p15738coll2/id/133743.

Liang, Lesley, and Niels Backerberg. (2019). 'Rare Earths: Myanmar's Border to China Recloses'. *Roskill*, 23 December. Available at https://roskill.com/news/rare-earths-myanmars-border-to-china-recloses/.

Lim, Al. (2020). 'Myanmar Needs to Redefine Its COVID-19 Stimulus Package'. *Tea Circle* (blog), 25 June. Available at https://teacircleoxford.com/policy-briefs-research-reports/myanmar-needs-to-redefine-its-covid-19-stimulus-package/.

Liu, John. (2020). 'Chinese Developers Sweep up 1GW Solar Bids in Myanmar'. *The Myanmar Times*, 9 September 2020. Available at https://www.mmtimes.com/news/chinese-developers-sweep-1gw-solar-bids-myanmar.html.

Liu, John, and Frontier. (2021). 'Regime Seeks Economic Recovery, but Drops NLD Reform Agenda'. *Frontier Myanmar*, 17 September. Available at https://www.frontiermyanmar.net/en/regime-seeks-economic-recovery-but-drops-nld-reform-agenda/.

Maran. (2022). 'Myanmar's Environment Hit by Rare Earth Mining Boom'. Mekong Eye (blog), 23 May. Available at https://www.mekongeye.com/2022/05/23/myanmars-environment-hit-by-rare-earth-mining-boom/.

Mark, SiuSue, Indra Overland, and Roman Vakulchuk. (2020). 'Sharing the Spoils: Winners and Losers in the Belt and Road Initiative in Myanmar'. *Journal of Current Southeast Asian Affairs* 39 (3): 381–404.

McEvoy, J. F., G. Connette, Q. Huang, Paing Soe, Khin Htet Htet Pyone, M. Valitutto, Yan Lin Htun, et al. (2019). 'Two Sides of the Same Coin – Wildmeat Consumption and Illegal Wildlife Trade at the Crossroads of Asia'. *Biological Conservation* 238 (October): 108197.

Moeller, Anders Kirstein. (2022). 'Peering under the Hood: Coup Narratives and Tatmadaw Factionalism'. *Tea Circle*, 10 January. Available at https://teacircleoxford.com/politics/peering-under-the-hood-coup-narratives-and-tatmadaw-factionalism/.

Myanmar Now. (2021a). 'Nearly a Third of Garment Industry Jobs Wiped out by Coup'. Myanmar NOW, 20 April. Available at https://www.myanmar-now.org/en/news/nearly-a-third-of-garment-industry-jobs-wiped-out-by-coup.

———. (2021b). 'Junta Approves $2.5bn Power Plant Project Backed by Chinese Companies'. Myanmar NOW, 14 May. Available at https://www.myanmar-now.org/en/news/junta-approves-25bn-power-plant-project-backed-by-chinese-companies.

ND GAIN. (2018). 'Rankings'. Notre Dame Global Adaptation Initiative.. Available at https://gain.nd.edu/our-work/country-index/rankings/.

OECD. (2020a). 'Green Budgeting and Tax Policy Tools to Support a Green Recovery'. Tackling Coronavirus (Covid-19): Contributing to a Global Effort. Paris: OECD. Available at https://read.oecd-ilibrary.org/view/?ref=137_137215-2knww1hckd&title=Green-budgeting-and-tax-policy-tools-to-support-a-green-recovery&_ga=2.79062547.666072812.1629393164-2115102471.1625393714.

———. (2020b). 'The Impact of Coronavirus (COVID-19) and the Global Oil Price Shock on the Fiscal Position of Oil-Exporting Developing Countries'. Paris: OECD. Available at https://www.oecd.org/coronavirus/policy-responses/the-impact-of-coronavirus-covid-19-and-the-global-oil-price-shock-on-the-fiscal-position-of-oil-exporting-developing-countries-8bafbd95/.

Oo, Dominic, and John Liu. (2021). 'Investors Spooked by Myanmar Crisis as Economy Braces for Free Fall'. *The Diplomat*, 20 October. Available at https://thediplomat.com/2021/10/investors-spooked-by-myanmar-crisis-as-economy-braces-for-free-fall/.

Oo, Zaw, Cindy Joelene, Paul Minoletti, Phoo Pwint Phyu, Kyi Pyar Chit Saw, Ngu Wah Win, Ian Porter, Mari Oye, and Andrea Smurra. (2015). 'Fiscal Management in Myanmar'. Working Paper 434. ADB Economics. Manila: Asian Development Bank. Available at http://www.ssrn.com/abstract=2702379.

Petri, Peter A., and Michael G. Plummer. (2020). 'East Asia Decouples from the United States: Trade War, COVID-19, and East Asia's New Trade Blocs'. Washington, DC: Peterson Institute for International Economics. Available at https://www.ssrn.com/abstract=3630294.

Rajah & Tann Asia. (2019). 'Myanmar Passes Gambling Law 2019 to Update Its Gambling Regulatory Regime, but Many Questions Remain'. Client Update: Singapore. Singapore: Rajah & Tann Singapore LLP.

Ringstrom, Anna. (2021). 'Fashion Giant H&M Pauses Placing New Orders in Myanmar'. *Reuters*, 8 March 2021. Available at https://www.reuters.com/article/us-myanmar-politics-h-m-suppliers-idUSKBN2B0124.

Routray, Bibhu Prasad. (2018). 'Narco Economy in Myanmar: From Opiates to ATS'. 552. ISPSW Strategy Series: Focus on Defense and International Security. Berlin: Institut für Strategie- Politik- Sicherheits- und Wirtschaftsberatung (ISPSW).

Smiley Evans, Tierra, Theingi Win Myat, Pyaephyo Aung, Zaw Min Oo, Min Thein Maw, Aung Than Toe, Tin Htun Aung, et al. (2020). 'Bushmeat Hunting and Trade in Myanmar's Central Teak Forests: Threats to Biodiversity and Human Livelihoods'. *Global Ecology and Conservation* 22 (June): e00889.

Swe Lei Mon. (2020). 'Domestic Violence Rises in Myanmar during Community Lockdown'. *Myanmar Times*, 1 April. Available at https://www.mmtimes.com/news/domestic-violence-rises-myanmar-during-community-lockdown.html.

Tanjangco, Beatrice, Yue Cao, Rebecca Nadin, Olena Borodyna, Linda Calabrese, and Yunnan Chen. (2021). 'Pulse 2: China Navigates Its Covid-19 Recovery – Outward Investment Appetite and Implications for Developing Countries'. ODI Economic Pulse Series - China's Outward Investment and Covid-19: Emerging Trends for Developing Countries. London: ODI.

The Irrawaddy. (2021a). 'Illegal Rare Earth Mines on China Border Multiply Since Myanmar's Coup'. *The Irrawaddy*, 26 April. Available at https://www.irrawaddy.com/news/burma/illegal-rare-earth-mines-china-border-multiply-since-myanmars-coup.html.

———. (2021b). 'Myanmar Regime Reorganizes Committees to Press Ahead with BRI Projects'. *The Irrawaddy*, 18 May. Available at https://www.irrawaddy.com/news/burma/myanmar-regime-reorganizes-committees-to-press-ahead-with-bri-projects.html.

———. (2021c). 'Chinese Casino City in Myanmar Recruiting Despite COVID-19 Crisis'. *The Irrawaddy*, 19 July. Available at https://www.irrawaddy.com/news/burma/chinese-casino-city-in-myanmar-recruiting-despite-covid-19-crisis.html.

— — —. (2022). 'Myanmar Central Bank's New Leadership, Policies Unlikely to Improve Battered Financial Sector'. *The Irrawaddy*, 1 September. Available at https://www.irrawaddy.com/news/burma/myanmar-central-banks-new-leadership-policies-unlikely-to-improve-battered-financial-sector.html.

Reuters. (2019). 'Inside Metals: Top News'. Newsletter. Thomson Reuters.

Tower, Jason, and Priscilla Clapp. (2020). 'Myanmar's Casino Cities: The Role of China and Transnational Criminal Networks'. Special Report 471. United States Institute of Peace.

Turnell, Sean. (2020). 'Debt Relief Boosts Myanmar's COVID-19 Recovery'. *East Asia Forum*, 21 July. https://www.eastasiaforum.org/2020/07/21/debt-relief-boosts-myanmars-covid-19-recovery/.

UNDESA. (2015). 'Trends in International Migrant Stock: Migrants by Destination and Origin (United Nations Database, POP/DB/MIG/Stock/Rev.2015)'. United Nations.

UNODC. (2021). 'Myanmar Opium Survey 2021: Cultivation, Production, and Implications'. UNODC Regional Office for Southeast Asia and the Pacific. Available at https://www.unodc.org/documents/crop-monitoring/Myanmar/Myanmar_Opium_survey_2021.pdf.

Wallace, Rory, and Gwen Robinson. (2021). 'Telenor Quits Myanmar as Regime Pressures Telco Operators'. *Nikkei Asia*, 8 July. Available at https://asia.nikkei.com/Spotlight/Myanmar-Crisis/Telenor-quits-Myanmar-as-regime-pressures-telco-operators.

Woods, Kevin. (2018). 'Opium, Rubber and a Land Grab on Myanmar's Border with China'. *East-West Wire*, 8 August.

World Bank. (2016). 'Myanmar Diagnostic Trade Integration Study (DTIS): Opening for Business'. Diagnostic Trade Integration Study. Washington, DC: World Bank Group.

— — —. (2017a). 'Bilateral Migration Matrix'. World Bank Group. Available at https://www.knomad.org/data/migration/emigration.

— — —. (2017b). 'Remittances Data'. World Bank Group. Available at https://www.knomad.org/data/remittances.

— — —. 2020a. 'Myanmar Economic Monitor: Myanmar in the Time of COVID-19'. Washington, DC: World Bank Group. Available at http://documents.worldbank.org/curated/en/806001593183687694/Myanmar-Economic-Monitor-Myanmar-in-the-Time-of-COVID-19.

— — —. (2020b). 'Women Endure COVID-19 Unequally to Men'. 2020. Myanmar COVID-19 Monitoring. Washington, DC: World Bank.

— — —. (2020c). 'Myanmar Trade and Mobility Update'. Flash Note 13. Washington, DC: World Bank Group.

— — —. (2021). 'Myanmar Economic Monitor: Progress Threatened; Resilience Tested'. Myanmar Economic Monitor. Washington, DC: World Bank.

———. (2022). 'Myanmar Economic Monitor: Reforms Reversed'. Washington, DC: World Bank Group. https://pubdocs.worldbank.org/en/597471658359366101/July-MEM-2022-Final.pdf.

World Tourism Organization. (2021). 'Yearbook of Tourism Statistics Dataset [Electronic]'. Madrid: World Trade Organization.

Yu, Sun, and Tom Mitchell. (2020). 'State Interference Threatens China's Control of Rare Earth Production'. *Financial Times*, 29 October. Available at https://www.ft.com/content/b13a3c4e-e80b-4a5c-aa6f-0c6cc87df638.

Zhai, Matthew, and Keith Tostevin. (2020). 'Coronavirus Slows China's Belt and Road Push'. *Reuters*, 18 February. Available at https://uk.reuters.com/article/us-china-health-silkroad-idUKKBN20C0RF.

9

COVID-19 AS CRISIS: PANDEMIC CHALLENGES OF FISHING COMMUNITIES IN KYAUK MYAUNG, ON THE IRRAWADDY RIVER

Mie Mie Kyaw

In March 2020, the world was transformed in a matter of weeks as the COVID-19 pandemic spread across borders, forcing governments to implement restrictive measures to try and contain the spread of the highly contagious virus. During this time, people in Myanmar faced significant challenges as they were forced to adapt to new restrictions on movement, with many losing their primary source of income. In Kyauk Myaung, a fishing community of seven villages, the nationwide restrictions put in place significantly impacted livelihoods. Alongside various lockdown orders, fishing communities in Myanmar experienced prohibitions on fishing, stay-at-home restrictions, as well as a of series of other restrictions and new household expenditures concerning health, including masks, face shields, antiseptic handgel and additional personal protective equipment (PPE) (in some cases). In addition to these restrictions, markets and small businesses were closed, meaning fishermen had nowhere to sell their wares. While these measures were put in place to try and curb the spread of the virus, they had a significant impact on people's livelihoods. During 2020–2021, people in Kyauk Myaung who depend on fishing faced many difficulties as a result of stay-at-home orders and severe restrictions on fishing. Their main source of income was lost overnight and many households faced new challenges for their everyday survival.

This chapter examines the impacts of the restrictive measures put in place in Myanmar to try and combat the virus in Kyauk Myaung. This is a response to recent calls to provide detailed analysis about the impacts of COVID-19 on fishing communities across the globe. N.J. Bennett et al. (2020) and C.J. Knight et al. (2020) state that the impacts of COVID-19 on the social, economic and environmental sectors are yet to be quantified globally, although some efforts have already been made at the regional level. Research from Myanmar, highlights the devastating impacts of the pandemic on fishing communities and their livelihoods. This chapter is focused on Kyauk Myaung in Shwebo district, Sagaing region, which is famous for relying on freshwater fisheries. When I began research for this study in 2020, I found that there was an overwhelming crisis in the fisheries sector due to the restrictions put in place to combat the spread of the virus. Furthermore, I found that due the increasing challenges local fishermen faced, there was an increasing use of electric shock fishing — a process which has significant impacts on the ecosystem of the river and the health of its fish supplies.

To help understand this crisis, I will employ the concept of 'vulnerability'. According to Thein et al. (2019), vulnerability can be defined as the extent to which an activity or a group of persons is exposed to a hazard, and also the extent to which they are able to respond or adapt. When assessing the vulnerability of a person or a community, one must also include socio-economic characteristics (e.g. poverty and employment rates, age of the population, and local power dynamics). The issue of access to and over-exploitation of natural resources threatens to deepen vulnerability and undermine the prospects of sustainable development. Furthermore, the study shows that women were more severly impacted than men, with female-headed households particularly vulnerable. The uneven impacts of COVID-19 restrictions on men and women also speaks to findings in India, where pandemic-related economic impacts on fishing communities were significantly gendered (Sekhar et al. 2020). Our own findings on this matter will be discussed further in the final section of the paper.

This research was conducted over the course of 2020–21, as Myanmar and the world, experienced different COVID-19 waves, infection rates and impacts on the economy (see Calabrese et al, this volume). The location chosen for the study was the Kyauk Myaung segment of the Irrawaddy River, on the border of Sagaing and Mandalay Regions in Myanmar. Most people in the study area (and many people beyond it) rely directly on the Irrawaddy River, for their lives and livelihoods. The river is not only a source of income for fishermen, but also a significant cultural, social, and ecological resource for the whole country. It runs 2,107 kms north to south of Myanmar, and has a large variety of fish species, saltwater crocodiles and the endangered Irrawaddy dolphin. Some of the major problems which threaten the important water source are sand dredging, people's increasing reliance on pesticides and other chemical fertilisers for farming along the river and the use of Illegal, Unreported, and Unregulated (IUU) fishing methods, such as electric shock fishing, which causes significant harm to the fragile ecosystem, including its fish supplies. In this chapter, I discuss how the restrictions placed on fishing communities during the pandemic saw an increasing reliance on IUU fishing methods, as a way to circumvent the restrictions put in place.

In this chapter, I analyse the impacts of restrictive measures put in place to combat COVID-19 on the incomes of fisherman in Kyauk Maung and its resultant effects on their livelihoods. I argue that the socioeconomic challenges of fishing communities originate not only from the COVID-19 pandemic but also from IUU fishing, which precedes the pandemic but became much more severe during 2020–21 due to pressures on household incomes. I show how these impacts were compounded by the increasing use of IUU fishing during 2020–21, as fishermen were forced to seek informal (and illegal) sources of income to support their families.

To help situate the study, the first section of this paper will present a summary of research which explores the impacts of the COVID-19 pandemic on the fisheries sector from a comparative perspective. Although the pandemic has impacted different local contexts in diverging ways, a comprehensive review of the challenges posed to fisheries will enable the development of solutions that are adaptable to a variety of locations. I will then present the empirical data from this research, including the details of the problem, research site, and data collection methods. I will then discuss the results of this research and present a conclusion with some recommendations in line with the United Nation's Sustainable

Development Goals (SDGs).

It is my hope that that this paper will contribute to a better understanding of the impacts of COVID-19 on vulnerable communities in Myanmar, such as fishermen, whose lives and livelihoods were significantly disrupted by the pandemic. While the research for this chapter was conducted before the February 2021 military takeover, the lessons from this research are only more urgent in the unfolding political context. As described by Htwe Htwe Thein and Michael Gillan in this volume, Myanmar is facing a deepening economic crisis which is putting further pressure on low socio-economic communities, like those described in this chapter. Fishing communities continue to face significant challenges to their livelihoods, especially as the cost of living continues to rise, with many people taking on more debt and other socially and environmentally pernicious activities as they look for other strategies to survive.

COVID-19 AND THE FISHERIES SECTOR: KYAUK MYAUNG IN A GLOBAL CONTEXT

The research for this chapter must be understood within the global context of COVID-19 and its impact on fisheries, which are particularly vulnerable to a range of shocks and hazards. Across the globe, the pandemic exacerbated existing vulnerabilities and amplified the challenges that fishing communities already face. Vulnerability amongst fishing communities is not unique to Myanmar, and neither are the disturbances felt by the COVID-19 pandemic. Quantitative research on the impacts of COVID-19 show that fisheries have been some of the hardest-hit sectors due to the economic losses experienced by base-level food producers (see for example: European Commission 2020; Giannakis et al. 2020). Smith et al.'s (2020) research shows that commercial fisheries and the communities which rely on them globally experienced "numerous and significant perturbations during the early months of the COVID-19 pandemic, affecting the livelihoods of millions of fishers worldwide." Even prior to COVID-19, fishing communities (and food producers in general) are some of the most vulnerable populations, whose livelihoods are directly exposed to the impacts of climate change and other environmental hazards such as water pollution and the development of unsustainable riverine infrastructure systems. These combined environmental and social vulnerabilities can be usefully brought together under what Manlosa et al. (2021) refer to as "coastal [and riverine] social-ecological systems (SESs)". The delicate balance of these ecological systems has been further affected by COVID-19 and the various infection prevention measures surrounding it.

The impacts of COVID-19 have revealed the extreme vulnerability of people who depend on food system economies, and especially on fisheries, for their livelihoods. In their analysis of fisheries in Mexico, Ines Lopez-Ercilla et al. (2021) describe these vulnerabilities as a kind of "flux" or unpredictability. There are two sides to this unpredictability: while Lopez-Ercilla show how fishers are exposed to sudden and dramatic market changes, Smith (2020) shows how that same collapse of formal markets has allowed fishers new opportunities to sell their fish through informal channels. Although most analysts do not share Smith's optimism about the outlook for fishers themselves, some studies — notably Bennett et al. (2020) — argue that the sudden simultaneous drop in demand for fish and decline in fishing activity may allow stocks to recover in over-fished areas. Whether these sudden changes have any long-term positive ecological impact remains to be seen; however, some research indicates that there is a clear precedent for fishing ecologies to respond to social and economic change (and vice-versa). For example, Folke et al. (2005) and IPCC (2007) mention that fisheries are social-ecological systems, which can demonstrate 1) adaptation, or the ability of the system to change its own structure according to ecological or socio-economic disruption, and 2) resilience, or the ability of the system to absorb disturbances while maintaining the same structure. However, in Myanmar, the delicate ecological balance of the country's riverways are also under threat by Illegal, Unreported, and Unregulated (IUU) fishing.

A worrying side effect of the pandemic — both in Myanmar and elsewhere — has been the increase in Illegal, Unreported, and Unregulated (IUU) fishing. IUU fishing is a "dark side" of the informal markets not mentioned by Smith (2020): as formal channels for fishing and fish selling shut, fishermen across the globe turn toward illegal channels, which can have disastrous ecological impacts. Perhaps more than any other food production system, riverine fisheries are a common resource: as Thein et al. (2019) usefully point out, in many rural areas, these common resources (rivers, lakes, and other water sources) provide the only available livelihood basis as farming becomes increasingly mechanised and new employment opportunities become concentrated in urban areas, away from fishers' (or farmers') homes. This drives fishermen (and especially landless fishermen) away from farming and toward long-term or permanent relocation in urban areas (Ibid.). Growing urbanisation also tends to diminish government and other regulatory attention to communities which depend on fisheries and is a likely driver of IUU fishing. The only way to solve this problem is to increase the profile of fisheries in the eyes of government, policy-makers and other administrative stakeholders.

Bennett et al.'s (2020) analysis suggests that the COVID-19 pandemic presents major challenges for the Small-Scale Fisheries (SSF) sector globally. While there are some positive initiatives to mitigate these challenges, these are likely far outweighed by the negative consequences, especially for groups that are most vulnerable to pandemic-driven socioeconomic changes. An FAO (2020) report states that even though fishing and aquaculture (and the distribution of their products) are considered essential activities in most countries, the measures adopted to contain the spread of COVID-19 have caused serious problems for this sector, thus harming the suppliers of a crucial food source across the world. Inland fisheries are especially important in Southeast Asia, which is one of the world's largest sources of freshwater fish (Kaewnuratchadasorn, et al. 2020). Lynch et al.'s (2016) research shows the importance of fisheries for food security and livelihood sustainability. Because of this heavy reliance on freshwater fish, and the compounding effects of the pandemic, food security should be understood as a kind of "crisis within a crisis" in food insecure countries (UN News 2020). Kyauk Myaung (the study area) is similarly affected by trends that have occurred amongst fishery communities elsewhere in the world. However, the impacts on communities in Kyauk Myaung are amplified compared to those in fishing communities elsewhere, due to the lack of government state support. Across the world, there has not been a clear strategy to mitigate the impacts of COVID-19 on fishing communities. However, research by Bennet et al. (2020) highlights the importance of transforming fisheries governance and supply chains.

The Food and Agriculture Organization (FAO) has also published a range of useful strategies for mitigating the impacts of the pandemic as it relates to fisheries, many of which could immediately be implemented in Myanmar (FAO 2020). These strategies include designating fishermen as essential workers, the establishment of straightforward and transparent lottery/quota systems, and setting mandatory (but locally appropriate) price floors for food fishes, so that nutritionally important species are both affordable for the populace and a reliable source of income for fishers (Ibid.). However, as this paper shows, these processes can be transformed by improved stakeholder mapping and prioritising the perspectives of fishermen themselves. As Lopez-Ercilla et al. (2021) argue, the tactics used to support fisheries must focus on the most vulnerable populations of fishing communities — for example, women, Indigenous peoples, and the elderly. Lopez-Ercilla et al. also argue that fishermen themselves should adopt new strategies: in order to solve the food crisis and mitigate the economic impacts of the market crash, it would be useful for fishermen to spend less time targeting high-value export fish and focus on catching fish that play an important nutritional role in local food supply chains. Keeping with Lopez-Ercilla's focus on flux and unpredictability, they argue that this is a practice that could help fishing communities to adapt to other shocks in the future. Sultana et al. (2021) found that fishing communities in Bangladesh were badly hurt by that country's 65-day total fishing ban, and they would have benefitted from forming fishermen's unions or associations, which could put collective pressure on regulatory authorities. Fishermen were reluctant to attempt coordination of this type in Bangladesh (Ibid.), but it could be a useful strategy in Myanmar, particularly for the prevention of IUU fishing.

This study attempts to identify the unique challenges faced by local fishing communities in Myanmar, and to offer suggestions for their mitigation. This section has identified the challenges facing fishing communities around the globe and the lack of systematic attempts to support their loss in livelihoods. COVID-19 has created a heavy burden on local fishing communities even beyond the destructive impacts of IUU fishing alone, which is present at all times (even when there is not a pandemic). By the third wave of COVID-19 in Myanmar (mid-2021), 90 per cent of fishermen in the study area reported facing serious or devastating financial hardship. The next section examines how the restrictions impacted fishing households in Kyauk Myaung and the impacts it had on their livelihoods.

KYAUK MYAUNG AND COVID-19

The fishing community of Kyauk Myaung suffered a spate of COVID-19 infections right at the beginning of the pandemic in March of 2020. However, the heaviest problems that fishers faced were mainly related to COVID-19 controls: lockdowns, stay-at-home orders, and strict prohibitions against going outside (including for fishing). There were virtually no opportunities for fishing apart from a few exceptional cases. Furthermore, public markets were closed, not only in fishing areas but all across Myanmar, and transportation was prohibited, including on the river. These two factors — markets shutting and the transportation ban — effectively cut off the incomes of local fishermen overnight and led to food shortages for many fishing households.

Due to the COVID-19 control measures, IUU fishing — such as battery shock fishing, also known as electric fishing, and unseasonal fishing (e.g., targeting fish during times that they would ordinarily be spawning, thereby reducing overall fish stocks) — significantly increased. Many fisherman were forced to break the rules and used IUU fishing as a coping strategy. IUU fishing has a significant impact on the environment. In battery shock fishing, for example, fishermen use a large battery to attract and stun fish, which come to the surface near the electrodes attached to the battery. Before the pandemic, there were also opportunities for IUU fishing, but during the pandemic illegal fishing on the river increased, especially at night.[1]

During the pandemic, there was also weak stakeholder mapping to support the implementation of rules, regulations or methods for conservation of fisheries resources and also improvement of socio-economic situations of local fishing communities in the study area. Before the pandemic, there was some efforts to support the conservation of the fisheries sector, including working towards maintaining a sustainable riverine ecosystem, food security, and more effective governance models (Yin Nyein et al. 2020). However, these were weakened during the pandemic because all stakeholders, scientists, researchers, policy makers and fishery-related community groups and NGOs, were also restricted by various stay-at-home orders.

RESEARCH DESIGN AND METHODOLOGY

The purpose of this research work is to identify (and find ways to mitigate) the socioeconomic challenges caused by COVID-19 and their impacts on the livelihood and wellbeing of local fishing communities by providing a knowledge-based evaluation of the situation in order to inform policy recommendations. All primary source data for this paper was collected through open-ended interviews, interview-based surveys, and focus group discussions. Interviews were conducted with fishers and other stakeholders, including ecosystem governance officials and policymakers, to understand the socioeconomic challenges faced by fishermen during the pandemic. I held these interviews under the authority of the local township officer. Using Cernea's (2021) Impoverishment Risks and Reconstruction (IRR) model, I conducted interview-based surveys about fishing incomes in order to understand the economic impact of COVID-19. I also used quantitative surveys to assess the structure of the supply and demand chains of fish in the study area.[2] In addition, I conducted stakeholder mapping to understand the relationship between fishers and others with a stake in Kyauk Myaung's fishing sector. This was designed to enhance communication between local community scientists, researchers, decision makers (e.g. informal authorities and regulatory authorities), policymakers, as well as the local fishing community. In designing the research, I was also inspired by the Sustainable Development Goals (SDGs) which provided a vision for the potential long-term outcomes of the research. For example, during the stakeholder mapping and interviews, I used the SDGs as guideposts to focus the goals and explanation of the intended outcomes of this research. In particular, SDG14, which prioritises the importance of life below the water and on sustainable harvests of water-dwelling animals, as well as SDG 1 and 2, which focus respectively on zero poverty and zero hunger.

This study thus employs empirical data collection techniques to assess (1) the impacts of the COVID-19 pandemic and its effect on fishermen's incomes and livelihoods, (2) comparison of the impacts in the first, second, and third waves of COVID-19, respectively, and (3) collecting and assessing empirical data about the socioeconomic impacts on local fishing communities for policy-making purposes. To implement these findings, the first task of the survey was to identify the impacts of the COVID-19 outbreak on fishing livelihoods from the perspective of fishermen themselves. Second, we conducted an empirical assessment on the impacts of COVID-19 to fishers' socioeconomic situation by examining fishing incomes and the linkages to supply and demand chains and disruptions. The finalised assessment integrated the impact of the pandemic on the fisheries sector and relevant consequences for fishing communities. In this study, surveys and discussions were undertaken in 2020 to describe local fishermen's perceptions and views about the COVID-19 impacts on their livelihoods and socioeconomic activities.

In addition to our focus on livelihood-related topics, the research team carried out several COVID-19 related tasks both as a general public service and for research purposes. This included: (1) raising public awareness about the symptoms of COVID-19 and advice to the study area community on how to avoid COVID-19; (2) how to care for and recover from infection; and (3) conducting interdisciplinary stakeholder mapping of the essential tasks required by different stakeholders in the upper Irrawaddy fisheries in order to mitigate COVID-19 transmission. Stakeholder mapping was therefore used to assess the impact of COVID-19 on fishery economies but also to improve fishing communities' ability to prevent infection and plan for the future.

RESULTS AND DISCUSSION

In this study, we held meetings and focus-group discussions about the challenges faced by fishers in seven villages in the study area and recorded the percentages of those who were facing COVID-19 related challenges. We made three trips to the study area: one in each season (the rainy season, the cold season, and the hot season, respectively), in order to keep track of changes in the community over time. The results of that research are as follows: in the first wave (May–July 2020), 50–70 per cent of the population in the 14 villages of the study area faced socio-economic challenges due to the impacts of COVID--19 to their livelihoods.[3] In the second wave (September–November 2020), we found that this increased to 70–80 per cent in the same study area. In the third wave (June–August 2021), during which time the "Delta" variant of COVID-19 was spreading across Myanmar, the percentage of the village population who faced pandemic-related challenges increased to about 90 per cent in the study area (see Figure 9.1). As is clear from our discussions with these fishing communities, the degree to which the pandemic adversely impacted fishing communities in Kyauk Myaung significantly increased over time. The most common reason given for these increasing difficulties was the barriers against fishing due to COVID-19 containment strategies over the whole study period.

Figure 9.1: Percentage of households facing challenges.

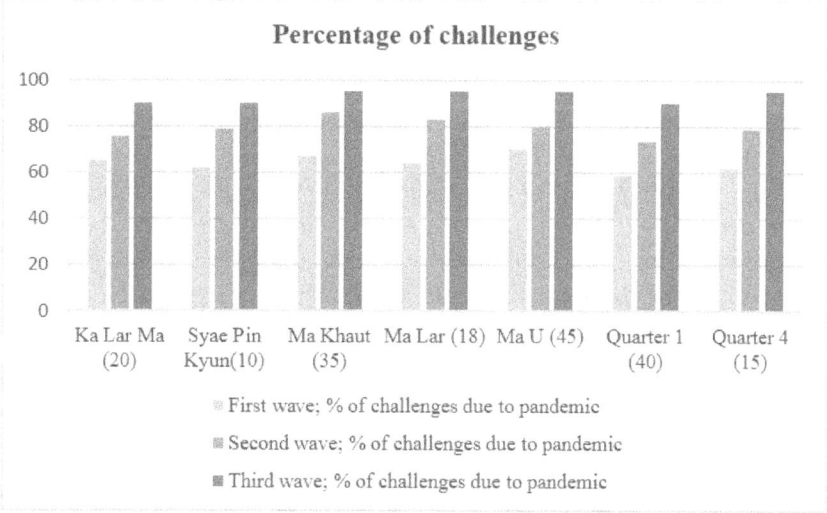

As mentioned in the introduction, one of the overarching objectives of this research was to assess the vulnerability of fishing communities in Kyauk Myaung. Our study observed various causes of vulnerability due to the pandemic, namely: an economic crisis, health challenges, and physical and mental stress. Vulnerability caused by socioeconomic factors was counted as one of the causes of fishers' stresses. Overexploitation of natural resources due to IUU fishing during the pandemic was revealed to be a major challenge for sustainable development on fisheries resources and on livelihoods of fishing communities. In particular, women were more significantly impacted than men.

The knowledge gap between fishing communities and the global consensus about best practices to prevent infection turned out to be one of the main challenges for all fishing communities in the study area.[4] In Myanmar, most people were enthusiastic to respect the measures put in place to prevent the spread of COVID-19, including through the use of personal protective equipment (PPE) and respect for various stay-at-home orders to reduce COVID-19 infection. During the pandemic, most members in the community area used masks, but very rarely used face shields. The concept of ethanol sprays, although common in other areas of Myanmar and some parts of the world, was very new to participants in this research, and they felt that it was an unnecessary measure. However, the most difficult task for local fishermen was to follow social distancing regulations to stay at least 6 feet, which many admitted they often forgot. In the peak of the first, second and third waves, fishing communities, did however, largely remain locked down in their homes, with few exceptional cases. There were also quarantine centres in the local area and many people volunteered their time to help infected persons. At first, the fishermen interviewed for this research did not believe that the impacts of COVID-19 could cause much trouble, nor take people's lives. However, this perception changed over time as the impacts of COVID-19 became more severe, especially during June–August 2021 as the highly infectious Delta variant spread throughout the country.

During the weeks following the first wave of COVID-19 (March–April 2020), the number of infections in the study area gradually increased, including some deaths. However, the most difficult time of the pandemic was during the third wave (June–August 2021), where thousands of people across the country were infected and many died. Delta variant symptoms were more severe than previous variants, and it was essential for many households to get oxygen tubes for each infected patient, which were expensive and in short supply, as a result of the collapsing public health system. At that time, people in Kyauk Myaung and other areas of the country were unable to continue fishing beyond providing meals for their households because of the strict lockdowns impacting much of the country, the extreme risk of infection, and the lack of adequate supplies to care for infected patients (such as oxygen tubes or ventilators). The growing health crisis at the time saw a high number of deaths and the lockdowns that were put in place to stop infection had an increasingly heavy toll on household incomes. During this time, fishermen were forbidden to catch any fish in excess of their immediate family's food requirements. Penalties were put in place, which effectively removed fishermen's ability to generate income. In addition to the ban on commercial fishing, markets were closed due to the possibility of COVID-19 transmission. Consequently, communities which rely on fishing for their livelihoods had very little income.

As part of our survey examining fishermen's livelihoods, we also investigated their households and living conditions. According to our survey, housing in local fishing communities is mostly made with bamboo and wood, including some timber planks that they have purchased and some self-harvested forest products. Only a few houses in the study area used bricks and cement. The furniture in most households was very simple and mostly made from wood and bamboo. This reflects the fact that the fishing community largely sustains itself with goods that are available locally and that households in the study area do not have much surplus income to spend on improving their homes. For hosting visitors, fishermen usually have one big table with two long benches enough for four or five persons per side. It should be noted that fishers' houses generally have good ventilation, which is useful for preventing the spread of COVID-19. Electricity in the village is intermittent: during the flooding season, the electricity is shut down to avoid electric shocks. In terms of road access, there is one main concrete street with small branch dirt roads.

Families in the study area rely completely on the Irrawaddy River for their water supply. Each household pumps water directly from the river into a private storage tank, where it is left until river sediment sinks to the bottom. Water from the top of the tank is then clean enough to drink. River water is also used in accordance with the traditional sanitation system of rural Myanmar, and can be applied to every household need (including bathing, washing, and cooking). Most of the fishermen store drinking water in locally-made clay pots, which are produced using clay from the banks of the river itself.[5] Some people will get drinking water from a small water purification plant, but most of the fishermen drink river water. They boil it, and as it cools from boiling they usually drink the hot water with dried green tea leaves. Some of the participants in this research also drink water directly from the Irrawaddy river.

According to discussions with local fishermen, the majority of households in the Kyauk Myaung area rely heavily on the quality and availability of fishery resources and available fish stocks in the river. Some fishermen can also earn money as boat drivers in the river, ferrying people upstream and downstream. Those fishermen who are comfortable with high-risk work also perform the treacherous task of catching and saving floating trees that move downstream with high momentum during (and immediately after) the rainy season. This forms of livelihood is very dangerous due to the risks involved with catching and manipulating large, heavy trees in the fast-flowing river, and working in the unpredictable weather conditions of the rainy season. Problems associated with low fish stocks or limited riverine resources are more severe for women than for men. Fishermen are often the primary income-earners in their households;

women who do not fish and who do not have financial independence from other sources (e.g., market selling or working in retail) are highly vulnerable to problems in the fishing industry.

The high level of vulnerability experienced by women in the study area is clearest in female-headed households. In these cases, women are expected to be the economic providers for their family — in the study area, this is usually mostly the responsibility of the fishermen — and also expected to manage their household finances, children's education, their family's social relationships, and community matters such as problems in particular households and wider social problems such as IUU fishing. Even in households that are jointly headed by a man and a woman, both play an economic role, with the woman typically selling fish caught by her husband. In female-headed households, the burden of catching fish or finding other means of income is shouldered solely by the woman, in addition to her long list of social responsibilities. Because of the important role that women play in the community affairs of the study area, they are particularly strong advocates for the eradication of IUU fishing, which hinders the entire community's ability to survive by reducing fish stocks from year to year. Women's larger social responsibilities and key role in the marketing of fish meant that women were especially likely to be exposed to COVID-19 infection, and were at greater risk of severe impact from COVID-related crises.

Women were thus some of the most vocal community members in Kyauk Myaung criticising IUU fishing, although household heads and community members of all genders recognised the severity of the threat posed by IUU fishing. Fish stocks provide the most important food source for most households in Kyauk Myaung and their primary source of income. Since households are so reliant on the river as a common resource, both fishermen and women play a major role in protecting it from people who misuse it. During the pandemic, IUU fishing increased significantly along the Irrawaddy River, including in Kyauk Myaung, because of lockdowns in the study area. With far fewer fishermen out on the river, there was no one around to guard it from unsustainable and destructive fishing techniques. As the first wave (early to mid-2020) and third wave (mid-2021) lockdowns also applied to government fishing authorities, those using IUU fishing techniques went unchecked as there was no one — either formal or informal — to prevent their illegal or hazardous fishing strategies. This situation poses a significant threat to the overall health of the fisheries sector and the ecosystem of the Irrawaddy river and its fish supplies.

According to our analysis of livelihood opportunities available in the study area, while most households rely heavily on fisheries for their livelihoods, some people some also rely on farmland in order to cultivate rice and sugarcane. Due to the impacts on the fisheries sector during the pandemic, some people also looked to diversify their incomes between 2020–21. Other respondents moved into other jobs, including carpentry, market vending, farming, various cottage industries, and working in retail. The majority of these jobs are wage labour and sometimes entail migrating to remote areas of the country in accordance with their links and networks.

Livelihood safeguards in Kyauk Myaung are highly unstable and full of challenges that are not only due to COVID-19, but also due to the growing scarcity of fish due to increasing IUU fishing. IUU fishing was already a serious problem before the pandemic began. As noted above, the pandemic exacerbated the pattern of IUU fishing, since there were fewer authorities on the river to monitor and prevent harmful fishing practices and because most fishermen — who act as informal guardians of the common resource of the river — were prevented from spending much time on the water. In this sense, the livelihood safeguards of local fishing communities were also effected by restrictions put in place to curb the the pandemic, further impacting their ability to survive. In interviews and stakeholder mapping, we learned that fishermen rely on complicated informal support networks in their community, especially those related to religion. The relocation systems for the flooding season in the study area mostly relocate fishermen to monasteries where monks help house and feed their families (as well as other members of the public). This is part of the traditional volunteering process overseen by monks and other religious organisations in upper Myanmar.

Over the course of the study, we discovered that environmental conservation standards were getting worse in the study area. The standard of riverine ecosystem management was especially degraded because of IUU fishing. In focus groups with fishermen and other community members, Kyauk Myaung residents explained that fish stocks will only be sustainable for the next generations if there is no IUU fishing. Fishermen reported that some species are becoming so rare that they only encounter it every three or four years; furthermore, fish of all kinds have decreased in comparison with previous years' catches. Fishers' memories are catalogues of fish that they no longer see, and past catches that are much larger than present catches. As they witness this ecological collapse, they also see their incomes decreasing over time. Therefore, some fishers are changing their livelihoods to others such as carpentry, wage labour, retail selling, and odd jobs in very remote areas for new bosses. Despite these challenges, there are two main groups of fishers who still continue their work the river: (A) fishers who are engaged in IUU fishing and (B) fishers who have never engaged in IUU fishing and who want to stop it. The fishermen consulted in this study are mainly in the second group, who want to eradicate IUU fishing. They described experiencing stress and vulnerability because their livelihoods are unstable. These fishermen urged us to take drastic action by giving us the names and addresses of IUU fishermen. This is a demonstration of how seriously some local fishers take the IUU problem, and the extent to which they are willing to risk disharmony in the community to eradicate the problem.

Although IUU fishing has been exacerbated by the onset of COVID-19, it is not the only problem that the pandemic has caused. Like others around the world, fishers in the study area were required to make many changes to their lifestyle and daily behaviours, which also impacted their livelihoods. Following the government-mandated COVID-19 prevention measures was a source of financial hardship for fishermen. Going out in public without a mask was forbidden across most of the country, and the study area was no exception. The PPE requirement meant that masks and face shields were sold out across most of the country, and where they were available, vendors charged six or seven times the true price of items such as masks and sanitation gel.

While all households faced socio-economic challenges, female-headed households appeared to be more vulnerable. Interviews with women from female-headed households showed how disproportionately affected they were and, how, in the absence of income-generating activities, they struggled to feed their families. These narratives contrasted with interviews with women with fishermen husbands, who were still able to catch fish for their everyday consumption needs.

Despite these differences, everyone interviewed was eager to eradicate IUU fishing, especially electric fishing, to stop the decline in fish populations. People interviewed for this study spoke about their fears for their livelihoods — that if IUU fishing continues, fisheries resources will gradually decrease until one day when the fish are finally extinct in the Irrawaddy. Many people described their desire to force a ban on

IUU fishing to preserve the fragile aquatic ecosystem. Indeed, from the perspective of local communities, the restrictions put in place to curb the spread of COVID-19 had far-reaching consequences on fishing communities including, access to markets, supply and demand, but also people's relationship with the environment.

CONCLUSION

The introduction of lockdown measures and stay-at-home orders in response to COVID-19 in March 2020 had significant impacts on people throughout Myanmar. In this chapter, I have described these impacts from the perspective of a small community of fishers in Kyauk Myaung, whose primary source of livelihoods was removed overnight. Not only were fishermen heavily restricted from going out onto the river and engaging in market-based activities, but the price of fish also significantly declined and issues concerning fishery sustainability also became more serious. These sustainability issues seem counterintuitive at first: fishermen were not allowed to go out and harvest fish as much as they were in the past, apart form exceptional cases where they were allowed to collect fish for their own household meals. However, the lower number of people on the river meant that there were more chances for some illegal groups covertly conducting IUU fishing. The impacts of IUU fishing are wide-ranging, and not limited to the decline in fish stocks from overfishing (although this is a major issue): electric fishing also reduces fish stocks' ability to replenish. Fish who are shocked by electricity often become infertile. Electric fishing also disproportionately impacts the smallest fish (known as fingerlings) and breeding cycles, in addition to larger fish which would be traditionally caught.

Like the creators of the SDGs, who link the importance of food security and income security with the health of various ecosystems, fishermen understand their livelihoods as dependent on the health of the Irrawaddy river itself and its fish stocks. In the study, we mostly spoke with 'legal' fisherman, who do not engage in IUU fishing. However, some of these fishermen still occasionally use electric fishing. Fishermen resort to IUU fishing to save time, and collect as many fishes at once. Many of the people who engage in these practices also have poor knowledge of sustainable use of fishery resources and weak ecological conservation ethics. Much of the community would be happy to see strong penalties used against those who engage in illegal and unsustainable fishing practices to try and dissuade them from doing do. Stronger penalties for fishermen who unsustainable fishing techniques might help to bring some fishermen who engage in both pratices over to the fully-legal and fully-sustainable side; stronger penalties and better enforcement would also give fishermen more confidence to report instances of IUU fishing that they see during their days on the river. These fishermen are also aware that these rules will not be impactful to overall fishing supplies if they only apply to Kyauk Myaung segment, but must be applied both upstream and downstream as well.

Fisheries were seriously impacted by COVID-19 in Kyauk Myaung and around the world. COVID-19 has caused a breakdown of the social aspect of fishing life on the Irrawaddy: various stakeholders in the fishery supply chain were unable to connect to one another because both markets were closed and fishermen were prevented from finding fish. This situation ultimately caused the decline in fish prices, and it also meant that there was no communication across different fishery stakeholders about correct fishing techniques and ecological awareness. IUU fish at very low prices flooded the market, both domestically and internationally, but it was totally unregulated. The ecosystems and the fishermen both suffered as a result.

These impacts were also gendered. Female-headed households in Kyauk Myaung were particularly vulnerable to the impacts of the COVID-19 pandemic, just as they were in other parts of the world. It will be difficult to mitigate the gendered impacts of the pandemic on fishing communities unless all stakeholders in Myanmar's freshwater fishing industry work together to find solutions for the lack of income and decreasing fish stocks. They also need to plan for the future: as the climate changes and the impacts of upstream dams continue to be felt, fishing on the Irrawaddy will only become more complicated. It is of vital importance for stakeholders (including fishermen themselves) to hold public forums such as workshops, roundtable discussions, and planning meetings where the future of the Irrawaddy's fisheries can be discussed. As this study shows, it is particularly important for women's voices to be emphasised in these meetings, as they are much more vulnerable than their male counterparts, and therefor more exposed to all kinds of risk.

In this situation, it is important to monitor socioeconomic challenges of local fishing communities, and to identify and observe the sources of challenges and who is most vulnerable. To get the best outcome for communities, it is important to work closely with local fishering communities, as well as other stakeholders including researchers and policy makers, for the sake of preserving fishing livelihoods and the Irrawaddy's fragile riverine ecosystem. In the longer term, stakeholder mapping across the fishery supply chain and across the various authorities responsible for caring for ecosystems should become a regular part of local governance in Myanmar, so that the needs of each community can be clarified and communicated, and policies that more effectively allocate resources can be created. For the fishermen of the upper Irrawaddy, ecological issues are also essentially economic and social. The river is their livelihood, and it is also the centre of their social lives. These actions and next steps are necessary not only for Kyauk Myaung, and not only during the COVID-19 pandemic, but for every community who relies on a riverine or coastal commons for their survival.

ACKNOWLEDGEMENTS

I would like to thank the local fishing communities, village leaders, the township officer of the study area, relevant policy makers, as well as researchers from Myanmar, all persons who were participating in the field trip and research work, and all stakeholders related with these research tasks. We would also like to acknowledge all of the people who arranged the Myanmar Update conference 2021 at the Australian National University, Canberra, Australia. The above research tasks were successfully accomplished with an interdisciplinary approach to stakeholder mapping for the sake of all fishing communities.

Notes

1. It should be noted that even during the pandemic, these communities did not fish during the breeding season (May, June, July) as community norms dictate that fishing during this time is unacceptable.
2. Cernea's (2021) Impoverishment Risks and Reconstruction (IRR) Model was originally designed for analysing displaced populations, but it helped to inform our approach to working with vulnerable fishing communities.
3. Those villages are Kan Gyi Taw, Ohn Pauk, Tae Pin, Shwe Gon, Gway Pin Gone, Ka Lar Ma, Syae Pin Kyun, Ma Khaut, Ma Lar, Ma U, Quarter 1, Quarter 2, Quarter 3, and Quarter 4.
4. This knowledge gap was less severe amongst health workers in the study area: the staff from clinics and hospitals almost always wore masks and even face shields when possible.
5. There is a very famous water pot production zone situated beside the study area, called Nwe-Nyein village. The clay products of this village are of the highest quality and the most popular items sent all over the country, where they are recognisable as a symbol of Myanmar in general and of the upper Irrawaddy river more specifically.

References

Bennett, N. J., Elena M. Finkbeiner, Natalie C. Ban, Dyhia Belhabib, Stacy D. Jupiter, John N. Kittinger, Sangeeta Mangubhai, Joeri Scholtens, David Gill, and Patrick Christie. 2020. "The COVID-19 Pandemic, Small-Scale Fisheries and Coastal Fishing Communities." *Coastal Management* 48 (4): 336–347.

Bennett, N. J. E.M. Finkbeiner, N.C. Ban, D. Belhabib, S.D. Jupiter, J.N. Kittinger, S. Mangubhai, J. Scholtens, D. Gill, P. Christie. 2020. "The COVID-19 pandemic, small-scale fisheries and coastal fishing communities". *Coastal Management* 48 (4): 336–347.

Cernea, Michael M. 2021. "The Risks and Reconstruction Model for Resettling Displaced Populations". In *Social Development in the World Bank: Essays in Honor of Michael M. Cernea*, edited by Maritta Koch-Weser and Scott Guggenheim, 235–64. Switzerland: Springer International.

European Commission. 2020a. "Communication from the Commission to the European Parliament, the European Council, the Council, the European Central Bank, the European Investment Bank and the Eurogroup: Coordinated economic response to the COVID-19 Outbreak". Brussels, Belgium: COM.

European Commission. 2020b. "CORONAVIRUS: Emergency Response to Support the Fishing and Aquaculture Sectors". *DG for Maritime Affairs and Fisheries*. Brussels, Belgium: COM.

FAO. 2020a. "How is COVID-19 affecting the fisheries and aquaculture food systems". Rome, Italy: Food and Agriculture Organization of the United Nations.

FAO. 2020b. "How is COVID-19 outbreak impacting the fisheries and aquaculture food systems and what can FAO do". Fisheries and Aquaculture Department Information Paper. Rome, Italy: Food and Agriculture Organization of the United Nations.

FAO. 2021. "The impact of COVID-19 on fisheries and aquaculture food systems, possible responses". Fisheries and Aquaculture Department Information Paper. Rome, Italy: Food and Agriculture Organization of the United Nations.

Folke, C., T. Hahn, P. Olsson, and J. Norberg. 2005. "Adaptive governance of social-ecological systems". *Annual Review of Environment and Resources* 30: 441–73.

Giannakis, Elias, Louis Hadjioannou, Carlos Jimenez, Marios Papageorgiou, Anastasis Karonias, and Antonis Petrou. 2020. "Economic Consequences of Coronavirus Disease (COVID-19) on Fisheries in the Eastern Mediterranean (Cyprus)". *Sustainability* 12.

IPCC. 2007. "Climate Change 2007: Impacts, Adaptation and Vulnerability". Contribution of Working Group II to the Fourth Assessment Report of the Intergovernmental Panel on Climate Change. Cambridge, UK: Cambridge University Press.

Kattungi Vijaya Sekhar, A. Irin Sutha, R. Uma Devi. 2020. "Impact Of COVID-19 on the Livelihoods of Fishermen Community in Yanam, Puducherry: An Analysis". *European Journal of Molecular & Clinical Medicine* 7 (8): 869-880.

C.J. Knight, T.L.U. Burnham, E.J. Mansfield, L.B. Crowder, F. Micheli. 2020. "COVID-19 reveals vulnerability of small-scale fisheries to global markets". *Lancet Planet Health* 4 (6).

Lopez-Ercilla, Ines, Maria Jose Espinosa-Romero, Francisco J. Fernandez Rivera-Melo, Stuart Fulton, Rebeca Fernandez, Jorge Torre, Araceli Acevedo-Rosas, Arturo J. Hernandez- Velasco, Imelda Amador. 2021. "The voice of Mexican small-scale fishers in times of COVID-19: Impacts, responses, and digital divide". *Marine Policy* 131104606.

Pattaratjit Kaewnuratchadasorn, Malinee Smithrithee, Akito Sato, Worawit Wanchana, Nualanong Tongdee, and Virgilia T. Sulit. 2020. "Capturing the Impacts of COVID-19 on the Fisheries Value Chain of Southeast Asia". *Southeast Asian Fisheries Development Center* 18 (2).Smith, E. 2020. "Lunenburg lobster captain sells directly to consumers to stay afloat during COVID-19". CBC News, 6 April.

Smith, S. L., A. S. Golden, V. Ramenzoni, D. R. Zemeckis, O. P. Jensen. 2020. "Adaptation and Resilience of Commercial Fishers in the Northeast United States During the Early Stages of the COVID-19 Pandemic". *PLoS ONE* 15 (12): e0243886.

Sultana, R., H. M. Irfanullah, S. A. Selim, S. T. Raihan, J. Bhowmik, and S. G. Ahmed. 2021. "Multilevel Resilience of Fishing Communities of Coastal Bangladesh Against Covid-19 Pandemic and 65-Day Fishing Ban". *Front. Mar. Sci.* 8:721838.

Thein, A. K., R. Gregory, M. Akester, F. Poulain, and R. Langeard. 2019. *Participatory rural appraisal- Vulnerability study of Ayeyarwady Delta fishing communities in Myanmar and social protection opportunities.* FAO Fisheries and Aquaculture Circular No.1177. Rome, Italy: FAO.

United Nations (UN News). 2020. "UN working to avert dual crises as COVID-19 hits hunger hotspots". *United Nations.*

Yin Nyein, R. Gregory, and Aung Kyaw Thein. 2020. "Ten Years of Fisheries Governance Reforms in Myanmar (2008-2018)". In *Living with Myanmar,* edited by Justine Chambers, Charlotte Galloway, and Jonathan Liljeblad, 183–206. Singapore: ISEAS-Yusof Ishak Institute.

10

THE DESTABILISATION OF MYANMAR: THE COUP AND ITS IMPACT ON ECONOMIC CONDITIONS AND INTERNATIONAL BUSINESS INVESTMENT

Htwe Htwe Thein and Michael Gillan

At the turn of the new decade, Myanmar was on a pathway towards a more robust economy with prospects for sustained aggregate growth, increased employment opportunities in labour-intensive sectors such as manufacturing, and further economic policy and institutional reforms under an elected civilian government.[1] In 2020 and 2021, this trajectory was disrupted by two profoundly destabilising crises that caused immense economic damage and human misery. First, in early 2020, the COVID-19 pandemic hit hard, with workers and the poor especially hurt by lockdowns, enterprise closures and job losses. Then, in February 2021, the misery caused by the pandemic was compounded and intensified by a coup staged by the Myanmar military (Tatmadaw), which has profoundly destabilised both politics and economic life.

The political implications of these events are explored elsewhere in this volume, whereas in this chapter, we will provide a summation and perspective on the economic damage done. Nonetheless, the military's brutal and violent suppression of pro-democracy protests, persistent violations of fundamental human rights, and disruption of Myanmar's incomplete journey towards democratic governance demonstrate that politics cannot be separated from economics because damage to the latter has clearly flowed from the destabilisation of politics after the coup.

The coup, as we will explore in a later section of this chapter, may have a profound and long-term impact on Myanmar's international investment environment and economic integration, inclusive of the effects of international sanctions. However, the most significant and immediate economic impacts were driven by internal rather than external factors. Widespread protests and the civil disobedience movement (CDM) impacted both public and private sector industries, with government, healthcare, finance, banking, and transport workers participating in great numbers to push for a restoration of democracy. They rejected the legitimacy of the military junta to govern and effectively shut down most sections of the domestic economy in the early phase of resistance. The military junta, largely via coercion, pushed for a resumption of economic and industrial activity over the course of 2021. Still, most sectors have continued to be impacted by ongoing CDM activity, protest actions, financial crisis, and later by armed resistance and conflict. The economy never recovered and continues to be characterised by reduced mobility, financial instability, supply and production disruptions and weak business and consumer confidence.

In this chapter, we first provide a summative overview of economic conditions in Myanmar after the coup tracing sectoral impacts on general conditions of employment and economic security. In the next section, we then consider the impact of the coup and the reversion to military rule on international investment and businesses, with particular reference to the choice that now confronts international businesses as to whether to persevere in or exit from a destabilised business environment. The choices of international investors will be significant in shaping Myanmar's economic prospects. Arguably, however, its economy will be shaped even more so by the outcomes of the ongoing conflict between the Tatmadaw and the citizens of Myanmar, who demand a restoration of democracy and an end to the historic economic and political domination of military elites.

ECONOMIC CONDITIONS AFTER THE COUP

The economic damage associated with the coup and its aftermath — persistent and sustained conflict, political disruption, and institutional disorder — was severe and immediate. By April 2021, the United Nations Development Program warned of the risk of "economic collapse" and a "worst case scenario" of declining incomes, a doubling of the rate of poverty and serious difficulties related to "access to food, basic services and social protection" (UNDP 2021, 3). The World Bank, meanwhile, issued an update on the post-coup economy which observed "reductions in mobility, incomes, and employment, ongoing security concerns, and the disruption of banking, transport, and telecommunications services" as well as interrupting public services and significant increases in the cost of essential commodities (World Bank 2021a, 22). By mid-2021, the Bank projected an 18 per cent decline in GDP in the 2021 financial year, with severe sectoral effects in manufacturing, transport, wholesale and retail trade, construction, and agriculture (World Bank 2021b).

The economic shock of the coup and its aftermath threatened the livelihood and food security of the citizens of Myanmar with spiralling costs of essential commodities and food. Near to one year after the coup, a United Nations (UN) report identified 14 out of 15 states and regions to be at heightened risk of malnutrition and some 14.4 million people — from a total population of 54 million — to be in need of urgent and direct humanitarian assistance (United Nations Office for the Coordination of Humanitarian Affairs 2021). At the same time, the ability of international donors to provide humanitarian assistance is hindered by the intransigence of the military regime, limited access to conflict zones where there is the greatest need and the legitimate concerns of donors to avoid the military junta capturing or controlling aid resources (International Crisis Group 2022).

The overall impact on employment and the Myanmar labour market was equally stark. The International Labour Organization reported the loss of an estimated 1.6 million jobs and an eighteen per cent decline in total working hours during 2021 (ILO 2022). These impacts were "disproportionately greater for women", who "accounted for an overwhelming majority of job losses" in industries such as garment manufacturing, hospitality and tourism that were especially hard hit by the coup and its associated disruptions (ILO 2022, 1). One of the important gains for Myanmar in the transition to quasi-civilian governance after 2011 was the creation of industrial relations and labour market institutions, including independent trade unions (Gillan and Thein 2016). Still, here, again, the reversion to military rule ensures the rapid disintegration of these reforms and organisations in practice.

The coup also compounded the damage already done to the economy by the COVID-19 virus. In 2020 the virus impacted the economy in two severe infection waves (April–May and then September–October), which led to regulatory and policy interventions by the National League for Democracy (NLD) government to manage social distancing, introduce health and safety protocols for workplaces, and to extend limited support measures to workers and businesses impacted by the virus. When the third wave of infection hit in June and July 2021, it was both more widespread and serious and exacerbated by the institutional and political disruptions associated with the coup. Access to supplies of vaccines and oxygen was limited and, allegedly, directed towards military personnel. The third wave also occurred in the context of a health system in crisis and a country in conflict, with hospitals and clinics dealing with "insufficient beds, human resources, and critical inputs such as oxygen" and an estimated fifty per cent decline in healthcare workers in the public system as a consequence of the civil disobedience movement (World Bank2021b, 12). The terrible human suffering of this third wave inevitably also represented another macro-economic shock that reduced mobility, economic activity, and exchange and disrupted the production and supply of goods and services.

Sectoral Impacts

The coup impacted all sectors of the Myanmar economy. In the early months of 2021, the strength of the CDM led to the nationwide suspension of public services. The CDM was especially impactful in the health and education sectors. The disruption to schools and universities may have a lasting impact on human capital and skills for years to come (San 2021). The first phase of the CDM also had a substantial impact on transport and logistics which then transferred to limiting international trade (exports and imports) and domestic distribution of goods (Frontier 2021a), although by May–June 2021, transport systems and the movement of goods through ports had begun to normalise (World Bank 2021b).

In banking and financial services, the initial shocks associated with the coup segued into ongoing disorder and a general loss of confidence in the integrity of the system (Frontier 2021b). In the months following the coup, banks were impacted by a run of consumer withdrawals and limited openings and staff availability because of the CDM. These disruptions then led most households to encounter difficulties in accessing cash and businesses to service debt and even to pay wages for their employees. In this context, some firms sought to rely on alternate and informal systems of banking, credit or digital banking.

At the core of the post-coup crisis in banking was an absence of trust in the effectiveness of the policy interventions of the regime government, the State Administration Council (SAC). Despite various interventions throughout 2021 to stabilise the system, the kyat's value continued to decline alarmingly, and inflation spiked, which eroded the value of saving deposits and encouraged the hoarding of US dollars and gold (Win 2021b). In 2022 the SAC regime sought a policy fix for the declining value (and use) of the kyat and their own need to secure access to foreign currency by mandating the compulsory exchange of foreign currency holdings to the local currency (Strangio 2022) and import restrictions (Nikkei Asia 2022). However, these heavy-handed interventions have failed to restore confidence and arrest the combination of rising prices and the declining kyat. As noted by the World Bank, the regime's economic management was akin to a reversion to the failed economic policies of the past, which were characterised by a black-market exchange system because of a fixed "official reference exchange rate at an overvalued level, not reflective of market supply and demand", "deficit financing by the Central Bank", and import controls (World Bank 2022, 16).

In labour-intensive manufacturing, including garment manufacturing, many migrant workers returned to their villages at the height of the military's violent crackdown against dissent in industrial zones. While most of these workers subsequently returned to the industrial zones, a swathe of factories has reduced production or shut down permanently as a consequence of rising costs of imported production inputs, rising inflation, cash shortages, logistical and transportation challenges and, in the garment manufacturing industry, the reputational and human rights risks for global brands in contracting from suppliers in Myanmar operating in a country under military rule. According to survey research, even garment manufacturing workers who did not lose jobs because of factory closures were faced with increased use of casual and piece rate employment, growing personal debt in the context of price inflation and "reduced take-home pay, including reduced over-time and attendance bonuses" (EuroCham Myanmar 2022, 6). In 2022, however, garment manufacturing exports from Myanmar recovered significantly, a trend that was attributed to the rapid depreciation of the kyat, which increased the cost competitiveness of the country as a sourcing destination (World Bank 2022). Nonetheless, in the context of the aforementioned risks and operational difficulties, the pre-coup trajectory of rapid growth in the industry had certainly been disrupted.

The hotels and tourism sector in Myanmar has also been impacted severely by both the COVID-19 virus and the coup and is unlikely to rebound for the foreseeable future. Before these events, tourism was estimated to account for fourteen per cent of export revenues and over five hundred thousand jobs. A survey of tourism and hospitality businesses in the months following the coup reported that 39 per cent had suspended or ceased their usual operations (World Bank 2021b).

In agriculture, Myanmar's farmers also faced a bleak scenario because of difficulties accessing cash and credit to buy seeds and production equipment. The weakening *kyat* and difficulties with transport and trade created additional costs and bottlenecks for the importation of fertilizers, and prices for agricultural output remained volatile. All of these factors, in addition to the disruptions associated with the spread and intensification of armed conflict across the nation, led to serious concerns for a significant decline in agricultural production outputs and the heightened risk of food insecurity (Tun 2022).

The post-coup period has also been characterised by problems in the electricity supply and the telecommunication sector. A popular and widespread boycott encouraged consumers not to pay electricity bills to government-controlled entities, and the fall in revenue led to the reduced generation and cuts and rationing of electricity supply (The Irrawaddy 2021a). In the telecommunications sector, periodic shutdowns and limits on internet connections were imposed by the regime to limit political opposition to the coup. Again, this has created both practical operational difficulties for businesses but also grave concerns as to data security and human rights impacts linked to military monitoring of internet usage and data flows.

In summation, while the SAC regime has sought to make economic policy announcements to restore business, investor and consumer confidence (Liu 2021; Win 2021a), their attempts to 'normalise' the economy of Myanmar after the coup has been a dismal failure. While some sectors have stabilised or resumed functioning after a near complete shutdown in the first phase of the CDM, including transport and retail trade in major urban areas, resistance to the military regime throughout the country remains widespread and significant in its economic impact. Domestic businesses confront a "squeeze" on their profits in the context of the rising cost of imports, limited access to foreign currency, inflation, and weak domestic demand (World Bank 2022), which has led to business closures, suspensions, or contractions across sectors (Frontier 2022). Because of the coup, the people and businesses of Myanmar face a bleak economic scenario of a deflating currency, spiralling costs, a banking and financial system in disarray, weakened infrastructure, electricity supply, the risk of a crisis in agricultural production, and the loss of formal sector employment in industries such as manufacturing.

INTERNATIONAL INVESTMENT AND BUSINESSES AFTER THE COUP

Myanmar's partial and incomplete transition to democratic governance was interrelated with an expansion and opening of the economy to international business investment and integration with global value chains in industries such as garment manufacturing. It intensified international technical and donor assistance to promote economic development. The coup, amidst its many other consequences, has disrupted the internationalisation of Myanmar's economy. In particular, it has led to a dilemma for international businesses present in the nation, especially those domiciled in Europe or the United States, regarding whether they can maintain their business operations in a destabilised nation under military rule.

The economic interests of the military came to the fore *prior* to the 2021 coup. In 2019, a UN Fact-Finding Mission report on this subject drew global attention to the presence of military-owned or controlled enterprises across most sectors of the Myanmar economy. The report detailed how military-owned conglomerates (MEHL and MEC) provide revenues to the Tatmadaw and funding for its operations against Rohingya ethnic minorities (UN Independent International Fact-Finding Mission on Myanmar 2019). It called for international businesses in joint venture relationships with military-controlled enterprises to discontinue these partnerships with the military and for all businesses to carry out heightened due diligence to avoid any direct investment or indirect association with the military businesses (UN Independent International Fact-Finding Mission on Myanmar 2019). In the wake of the report and public campaigns from civil society organisations, there was indeed heightened attention to international businesses such as Kirin (Japan) and Adani Ports (India) that were connected to the military via business partnerships (Thein 2021a).

In this context, there was increasing pressure on international businesses across all sectors to discontinue a 'business as usual' response as human rights abuses intensified in the months following the coup. Most of this pressure emanated from international human rights and advocacy non-government organisations, but also civil society organisations based in Myanmar. At a minimum, international businesses operating in Myanmar were urged by a cross-section of these organisations to 1) formally and publicly condemn the coup and associated military-instigated violence; 2) sever any investment ties, business partnerships or revenue flows with military-owned enterprises or the SAC regime; and 3), for those firms not working directly with the military, to heighten due diligence to identify possible complicity in human rights violations. With the exception of businesses in direct joint ventures with military-owned enterprises or providing a large revenue stream to the SAC regime, most advocacy organisations did not call for all international businesses to suspend their operations or exit the market.

The coup may have been driven by politics, the results of the 2020 election and the desire of the Tatmadaw to retain a grip on different domains of state power, but it also served to protect the economic interests of military elites (Thein 2021b). After the coup, international businesses were especially pressed to demonstrate that they were not involved in direct partnerships with military-controlled enterprises or, via funds transfers or investment relations, linked to the financing of military operations and violent repression directed at the opposition and the CDM against the coup. Among many others, these included POSCO (South Korea), Adani (India) and investment funds based in Australia, Norway and the Netherlands (Thein and Gillan 2021; Dziedzic 2021). We consider some instances of business responses to this pressure further below. But first, we will turn to the emergence of international economic and trade sanctions after the coup.

SANCTIONS POLICIES

A number of civil society and advocacy organisations expressed their support for international economic sanctions to be 'targeted' at the business interests of the military in Myanmar and the revenue streams supporting the SAC regime. For example, the Special Advisory Council on Myanmar (SAC-M) called for the international community to "cut the cash" flowing to the regime by means of "coordinated international sanctions on the junta's extractive industry so-called State-owned enterprises — including Myanmar Timber Enterprise, Myanmar Gems Enterprise, and of course, Myanmar Oil and Gas Enterprise." (SAC-M 2021). In also supporting targeted sanctions, Human Rights Watch suggested that appropriately designed sanctions by the European Union, the United Kingdom and the United States were especially needed because their financial services are so widely used. Doing so had the potential to expand the reach of sanctions because "banks or financial institutions with no direct ties to sanctioning jurisdictions may prohibit sanctioned persons from accessing accounts or use of wire services" (HRW 2021). Similarly, an analysis developed by an independent group of economists with Myanmar-specific expertise drew attention to the significance of targeting state-owned banks and state or military-controlled enterprises in extractive industries, with sanctions on oil and gas especially significant as a means of depriving the regime of a valuable source of foreign exchange holdings after the coup (Robinson and Wallace 2021).

Targeted sanctions are intended to maximise pressure on the military while limiting impacts on the economic livelihoods of the people of Myanmar (Thein and Gillan 2021). However, there are also other voices that have called for comprehensive economic sanctions as a painful but necessary means of escalating pressure on the regime government (Brown 2021). A coalition of Myanmar-based civil society organisations and local and international trade unions have demanded comprehensive sanctions (Khaing Zar Aung and Brighi 2022) and that all international businesses withdraw from the market on the basis that "there is no ethical way to do business in the country" (IndustriALL Global Union 2021). A broader sanctions regime could include removing or adjusting Myanmar's inclusion in trade preference schemes such as the European Union's "Everything but Arms" (EBA) scheme which has provided Myanmar with tariff-free access to the European Union for exported goods. Removing this concession could be potentially harmful to the employment and livelihoods of workers in the manufacturing sector, but it has been supported by some international organisations (Clean Clothes Campaign 2021; IndustriALL Global Union 2021) and trade unions in Myanmar. The call for a comprehensive sanctions regime is based on the logic that, for all of the collateral damage associated with general sanctions, where all foreign businesses are urged to withdraw from Myanmar, "there is no greater danger to our lives and our futures than the military dictatorship" (Khaing Zar Aung 2021).

Meanwhile, the National Unity Government (NUG), a parallel government in exile comprised of elected Parliamentarians and opponents of the coup, requested foreign investors to suspend the payment of taxes or other sources of revenue to the SAC regime government until democracy is restored. This demand was focused on extractive industries which are an important source of revenue for the regime. In November 2021, the NUG issued a policy on sanctions favouring targeted measures directed at three priority sectors: oil and gas, mining, and banking. Revenues from oil and gas production were identified as a crucial economic lifeline for the regime government, whereas mining was seen as a sector where "profits directly flow to the military and their corrupt associates" (Republic of the Union of Myanmar, National Unity Government 2021). Sanctions directed at restricting SAC regime access to the international banking and financial system were necessary because these were thought to have the potential to "hurt the military's ability to buy weapons and also to misappropriate the country's revenues" (Republic of the Union of Myanmar, National Unity Government 2021). The policy did not call for comprehensive sanctions but rather for sanctions on state-owned enterprises such as the Myanmar Oil and Gas Enterprise (MOGE); military-controlled business conglomerates Myanmar Economic Corporation (MEC) and Myanmar Economic Holdings Ltd (MEHL); "private businesses owned by individual members of the junta or by senior military officers"; and "business partners and associates assisting the junta, including private sector firms owned by individuals that are known 'cronies' of the military" (Republic of the Union of Myanmar, National Unity Government 2021).

The international response to these demands has been uneven and has lacked the required breadth and coordination to amplify their economic and political impact on the regime. Nonetheless, the European Union and the United States, in addition to allies such as Canada and the United Kingdom, introduced significant economic sanctions after the coup. These were rolled out in a phased manner, typically as a means of responding to unfolding events in Myanmar, and most especially, the persistent human rights violations of the military and the failure of the SAC regime to take any action to restore democracy or even to follow the five-point consensus plan promoted by the ASEAN.

U.S. and E.U. sanctions have especially targeted military-owned enterprises and business conglomerates, and individuals associated with the regime. The United States, for instance, initially targeted senior military personnel and their family members via travel bans, asset freezes, and generally prohibiting them from engaging with U.S. nationals. These measures were later extended to a plethora of individuals serving in or associated with the SAC regime. Both the United States and the European Union have sanctioned military-owned or military-controlled companies in profitable industries such as gem mining and trading, and two massive conglomerates — the Myanmar Economic Corporation (MEC) and Myanmar Economic Holdings Ltd (MEHL) — which have extensive economic holdings and a presence in many sectors of the Myanmar economy. In 2022, the European Union escalated its sanctions measures by targeting more regime officials, 'crony' conglomerates (Htoo Group; IGE) and state-owned enterprises in revenue-generating sectors (Council of the European Union 2022). Most significantly, the European Union sanctioned MOGE, the critical state-owned enterprise and business intermediary in the oil and gas sector. These measures were "in addition to the withholding of E.U. financial assistance directly going to the government and the freezing of all E.U. assistance that may be seen as legitimising the junta" (Council of the European Union 2022). Australia was an outlier amongst its traditional allies by not imposing economic sanctions despite calls for it to introduce sanctions measures similarly targeted at military-controlled businesses (Thein and Gillan 2021).

INTERNATIONAL BUSINESS DILEMMAS: STAY OR GO?

Under adverse conditions — economic and political instability, domestic conflict and a tightening international sanctions regime — international businesses have faced dilemmas as to whether they should continue operating in Myanmar or abandon and exit the country. In general, international businesses have been caught between their publicly-stated business principles and human rights commitments and their sunk investments and commercial and economic interests in Myanmar. In a destabilised and potentially hazardous business environment, they have also acknowledged a responsibility to ensure the safety of their employees. Some have also foregrounded the significance of their role in providing essential goods and services to Myanmar citizens and consumers. Still, all have been wary of any public association, support or indirect legitimation of the military regime government.

In the immediate aftermath of the coup, a cross-section of international businesses and investors issued a collective statement to express concern and put forward a common position on the implications of these unforeseen events for the business environment and stability of Myanmar. While the statement was judicious in not directly condemning the motivations and actions of the military, it nonetheless observed that the "rule of law, respect for human rights, and the unrestricted flow of information all contribute to a stable business environment" (Statement by Concerned Businesses Operating in Myanmar 2021). However, with a few exceptions, the signatories to the statement were companies or business associations originating from Europe or North America. In contrast, investors and businesses from Asia were silent. They continued to operate their business operations as usual to the extent that this was possible in the midst of the CDM and street protests in the month following the coup (Regalado 2021).

Decisions to withdraw or not to withdraw from Myanmar's destabilised market were clearly interrelated with firm-specific characteristics such as enterprise size and the level of sunk investments. There were several factors that were clearly major drivers of exit decisions — the country of origin of the international business, the industry sector concerned and, finally, the degree of direct business association or partnership with military-owned or controlled enterprises in Myanmar. We discuss these drivers with reference to three examples that qualitatively demonstrate their salience and encapsulate the complexities and contradictions of corporate disengagement and exit under conditions of political and economic destabilisation.

Kirin

Kirin, a Japanese beer and beverage MNC, was the first major international business to take action after the coup by declaring its intention to end joint venture partnerships in brewery businesses with the military conglomerate

MEHL. In doing so, Kirin stated it was "deeply concerned by the recent actions of the military in Myanmar, which are against our standards and Human Rights Policy" and that it had entered the Myanmar market in 2015 with the belief that doing so could "contribute positively to the people and the economy of the country as it entered an important period of democratization" (Kirin Holdings 2021). It further reported that it had "no option but to terminate our current joint-venture partnership" with its local partner business because it "provides the service of welfare fund management for the military" (Kirin Holdings 2021).

Kirin's rapid decision was no doubt due to its direct links to the military in its business partnership which led to immediate international public scrutiny, activist pressure and Norway's sovereign wealth fund, the largest in the world, placing the MNC on an investment watch list for possible exclusion (Solsvik 2021). The decision to exit was undoubtedly related to the international criticism and public campaigns directed at Kirin in the years preceding the coup due to Kirin's joint-venture relationship with the military-owned company. Kirin was featured in the 2019 UN Fact-Finding Mission on the economic interests of the military but resisted public pressure on it to terminate its business relationship, even in the context of the human rights violations against the Rohingya people of Myanmar. Nonetheless, Kirin launched an investigation into how the profits generated from the brewery joint venture businesses, said to account for some eighty per cent of the local beer market, was accessed and used by the military (Oanh Ha, Khine Lin Kyaw and Jin Wu 2021). After this investigation failed to receive sufficient cooperation from the local partner business, in November 2020 Kirin suspended dividend payments to MEHL (Oanh Ha, Khine Lin Kyaw and Jin Wu 2021).

While Kirin's decision to terminate its business partnership with MEHL after the coup relieved some of its international public pressure, it subsequently proved challenging to make a clean separation nor, ultimately, for Kirin to remain in the Myanmar market. The MEHL refused to sell its stakes in the partnership to Kirin and both firms were drawn into a legal dispute over the terms and conditions of the termination of the relationship (Myanmar Now 2021). In early 2022, after failing to force the exit of MEHL, Kirin announced it would seek to sell its stakes in both brewery businesses and would exit the country (Reuters 2022a), an outcome that further pointed to Myanmar as a high-risk and uncertain business environment for international investors.

TotalEnergies

The attention to the oil and gas sector in debates over the potential impact of international economic sanctions and cutting the revenue streams supporting the military brought international firms such Chevron (United States) and TotalEnergies (France) within the spotlight after the coup. Both firms were partners in the Yadana Gas field project, which produces large volumes of gas for export to Thailand and domestic use in Myanmar. The project also involves a partnership with a Thai energy company (PTTEP, with a 25.5 per cent stake) and, within Myanmar, the state-owned MOGE (15 per cent ownership) (TotalEnergies 2022). The potential contribution of the project revenues to funding the military regime government in Myanmar attracted intense controversy in the wake of the coup, with pro-democracy and human rights organisations requesting Total and Chevron to direct any scheduled payments into an escrow account that could not be accessed by the regime.

In response, Total's Chief Executive, Patrick Pouyanné acknowledged that the company was in the midst of a business and human rights "dilemma" but also stated that Total would not suspend its gas production in Myanmar and would provide all scheduled payments as per the established arrangements of the project. Pouyanné justified Total's decision to continue payments to the military regime government because not doing so would be "a crime according to local law" and "would put those in charge of our subsidiary at risk of arrest and imprisonment" (Pouyanné 2021). Total also foregrounded the practical significance of continuing the project and maintaining production to maintain the electricity supply to Yangon and Thailand. Nonetheless, their reluctance to risk the continuity of the project was no doubt also related to its sunk investments and the profitability of the venture. However, after a year of constant pressure, Total announced its intention to exit the Myanmar market in early 2022. According to the company, it was "materially impossible" for it to prevent flows of revenues from the project to MOGE (and by extension the SAC regime) because "most of the payments for the sale of the gas are made directly by the Thai company PTT, the buyer of the exported gas" (TotalEnergies 2022). The final decision to begin a process of phased market exit was explained with acknowledgment that "human rights and more generally the rule of law, which have kept worsening in Myanmar since the coup of February 2021, has led us to reassess the situation and no longer allows TotalEnergies to make a sufficiently positive contribution in the country." (TotalEnergies 2022). Total's exit from Myanmar was premised on a phased process with associated gas sales proceeds still transferred to the junta during the withdrawal. The buyer of Total's stake was, as expected, an existing consortium partner (PTT), and the production and revenue flows are likely to continue regardless. However, the intensity of international public pressure associated with projects that fund the regime government is likely to preclude any future investments by Western nation energy firms in Myanmar.

Telenor (Norway)

While we have noted general public pressure for business disinvestment or market exit from Myanmar, the case of Telenor (Norway) in the telecommunication sector differed somewhat. Access to, and strategic use of, internet and telecommunications services have been central to resistance to the coup and the growth of the CDM. For that reason, the SAC regime has sought to periodically restrict or block access and, over time, has moved to tighten its monitoring of users and regulatory interventions in the sector. Because of its status as the only major telecommunications company in Myanmar based in the West and with a clearly stated public commitment to business and human rights principles, many local activists and citizens expressed support for Telenor to continue their operations in the country.

However, in the context of intensifying pressure from the regime government for access to data and the destabilisation of the local business environment, Telenor's assessment of the level of risk involved in remaining in the market led them to prepare for exit. By May 2021, the company announced that it had written off the full booked value (6.5 billion Norwegian Krone or US$782 million) of its business in Myanmar as the first stage of preparing for its withdrawal (Nikkei Asia 2021). Telenor subsequently announced that Lebanon's M1 Group would acquire their Myanmar business, but this led to immediate concerns about the lack of commitment of the new owner to responsible business practices, allegations of human rights concerns in their business operations in other countries and associated fears for the data security and privacy for local users in Myanmar (Ekeberg 2021). Activists called on Telenor and the Norwegian government – Telenor's biggest shareholder — to be more aware of the consequences of its pending sale to the M1 Group and to ensure the company made a responsible exit from Myanmar. These pressures and concerns have not eased with Telenor criticised again in early 2022 for the potential for the business sale and transfer leading to alleged complicity in enabling surveillance technologies and access to user data that could have harmful consequences for the human rights of Myanmar citizens (Myanmar Now 2022). The decision of Telenor to exit was linked to a publicly-stated conviction that it was no longer possible to continue doing business in Myanmar under the military regime without breaking their policy commitments to respect human rights. Yet, the terms and conditions of the exit process raised the same issues about their risks, responsibilities, and potential complicity.

The three cases described above clearly show how the heightened risk of human rights violations and associated reputational damage to corporations has facilitated significant market exits across several business sectors. It is also notable that some international companies that have exited or reduced their investments in Myanmar after the coup did not directly cite human rights concerns as a motivation, possibly to avoid provoking the military regime government (see SAC-M, undated). Aside from any such concerns, there is no doubt that the destabilised political and business environment after the coup, including the difficulty of guaranteeing the safety of investments and employees, explains many of the market exits. For those firms that have chosen to remain, inclusive of a small number of high-profile brands sourcing from Myanmar suppliers in the garment manufacturing industry, there are apparent efforts to reassure institutional investors and consumers by means of continuous operational monitoring and heightened due diligence.

CONCLUSION: FUTURE PROSPECTS

The SAC regime has sought to project an economic policy plan for reviving the economy (Win 2021a) and claims that the foreign investment environment has stabilised. In early 2022, the regime announced some US$3.8 billion in approved foreign investment in the year since the coup (Reuters 2022). This amount was largely due to the approval of a US$2.5 billion gas-fired power station to be developed and operated by a consortium of three Chinese companies in the Ayeyarwady region (Myanmar Now 2021b). While this Chinese investment clearly comprised the bulk of the FDI the other countries of origin of significant approved investments were Japan, Singapore, Thailand and South Korea (Reuters 2022). The public claim that foreign investment had returned, with the exception of China-backed projects, was received with widespread scepticism given that many projects were mere approvals rather than actually realised investments and some projects had been in development well before the coup (Reuters 2022; World Bank 2022).

Nonetheless, securing political support and economic investment from China is a clear priority for the regime. For the former, China has publicly engaged with the regime and stymied, alongside Russia, the prospects of coordinated international action against it via the United Nations Security Council (The Irrawaddy 2022). For the latter, in the context of instances of attacks on Chinese businesses and heightened security risks in Myanmar after the coup, the regime government promised to take extensive measures to secure and protect Chinese-owned enterprises and China-backed infrastructure projects (The Irrawaddy, 2021b). From 2021 onwards, China's Belt and Road infrastructure projects such as the deep sea port at Kyaukphyu and a major railway link have been fast-tracked, and these have been interpreted as crucial to Chinese concerns for the economic development and security of Yunnan Province (Banerjee and Rajaura, 2021; Tower, 2022). If the regime government is able to consolidate itself, it is likely that the economic relationship with China will be predominant in Myanmar's investment and trade. For China, a deepening political and investment nexus is also associated with the risk of a backlash if the regime should fall and, more generally, the "danger of entrusting the economic security of its southwestern provinces to a savage, illegitimate and ineffective regime" (Tower, 2022).

The regime's claims to support a conducive business environment for both domestic and international businesses have been contradicted by its own policy interventions. In particular, its desperate attempt to stabilise the kyat and the crisis in the banking and finance sector by introducing controls on the use of foreign currencies caused considerable alarm among the international businesses that remained in Myanmar. In a joint public statement issued by all major foreign chambers of commerce, it was noted that these measures would "effectively prevent the use of foreign currency in Myanmar, which disconnects Myanmar from the global economy and global financial system" and lead to "significant, and for some, insurmountable challenges to all businesses operating in Myanmar" (Joint Statement 2022). In the context of the uncertainty created by this foreign currency regulation, the SAC regime subsequently issued an exemption to international businesses. Nonetheless, the issue again provided another clear indicator that Myanmar was now a volatile and high-risk investment destination regarding markets, operations and economic policies. As observed by the World Bank (2022, 10), there was a discernible "shift away from a stable market-based system that is governed by the rule of law, and toward a system of policy making and governance that is less predictable, less clearly communicated, and characterized by more discretion in the enforcement of rules and regulations". In general, this pattern of economic management and governance also reflected a return to the interventionist, erratic and crony-based patron-client business environment that prevailed in past decades of military rule.

If the SAC regime is able to consolidate its rule, the composition of foreign investors in Myanmar will no doubt be changed by the degradation of the business environment, heightened risks and the impact of international sanctions policies. Investors from Western nations will dwindle as businesses suspend, sell or abandon their operations in Myanmar, especially companies in an early phase of market entry or an early stage of exploration in extractive industries. There could be a return to the less diverse business environment that prevailed in Myanmar before 2011, whereby various Asian investors from neighbouring nations dominated FDI in Myanmar (Meyer and Thein, 2014). Businesses originating from China and ASEAN nations would dominate foreign investment, especially in extractive industries and infrastructure development. Nonetheless, the breadth of the conflict and the depth of dysfunction in a destabilised Myanmar could even threaten the security and sustainability of these investments. Businesses require certainty and security, and these are the very things the coup has destroyed. There are also evident concerns for Asian businesses about the risks of investing in Myanmar in terms of operations, security of assets and investments, reputational damage, and the regulatory implications of international trade sanctions (Mizzima 2022).

The consolidation of the regime government would also entrench both the political power of the military but also their historical capacity, alongside a selection of favoured 'crony' private sector business oligarchs, to capture and plunder available economic rents, wealth and resources in Myanmar (Ford, Gillan and Thein, 2020). The degraded living and working conditions, risks to food security, and general impoverishment of the people of Myanmar that have occurred after the spread of the COVID-19 virus and the coup of 2021 would also be harder to reverse and, at best, any improvements in economic welfare will be incremental under military rule.

Notes

1 This chapter was supported by Australian Research Project DP180101184, entitled 'Global Production Networks and Worker Representation in Myanmar'.

References

Banerjee, S. and T. S. Rajaura (2021). "Growing Chinese investments in Myanmar post-coup." *Observer Research Foundation,* 9 November. Available at https://www.orfonline.org/expert-speak/growing-chinese-investments-in-myanmar-post-coup/ (accessed 20 February 2023).

Brown, M. (2021). "To save Myanmar, first crush its economy". *Nikkei Asia,* 18 March. Available at https://asia.nikkei.com/Opinion/To-save-Myanmar-first-crush-its-economy (accessed 20 February 2023).

Clean Clothes Campaign (2021). "Call for the EU to suspend preferential EBA trade tariffs from Myanmar". *Clean Clothes Campaign,* 22 September. Available at https://cleanclothes.org/news/2021/call-for-the-eu-to-suspend-preferential-eba-trade-tariffs-from-myanmar (accessed 20 February 2023).

Council of the European Union (2022). "Myanmar/Burma: EU imposes restrictive measures on 22 individuals and 4 entities in fourth round of sanctions". Press Release, 21 February. Available at https://www.consilium.europa.eu/en/press/press-releases/2022/02/21/myanmar-burma-eu-imposes-restrictive-measures-on-22-individuals-and-4-entities-in-fourth-round-of-sanctions/ (accessed 20 February 2023).

Dziedzic, S. (2021). "Austra'ia's Future Fund invests $150m in companies linked to Myan'ar's military, FOI documents show". *ABC News,* 29 November. Available at https://www.abc.net.au/news/2021-11-29/australia-future-fund-invest-companies-myanmar-military/100658518 (accessed 20 February 2023).

Ekeberg, E. (2021). "M1 Group offers 'best solution' for Telenor users, says CEO Brekke". *Frontier Myanmar,* 12 July. Available at https://www.frontiermyanmar.net/en/m1-group-offers-best-solution-for-telenor-users-says-ceo-brekke/ (accessed 20 February 2023).

European Chamber of Commerce in Myanmar (EuroCham Myanmar) (2022). *Myanmar Garment Sector Fact Sheet.* Online: EuroCham. Available at https://eurocham-myanmar.org/2022/01/25/myanmar-garment-sector-factsheet/ (accessed 20 February 2023).

Ford, M., M. Gillan, and H. H. Thein (2020). "Political regimes and economic policy: Isolation, consolidation, reintegration". In *Myanmar: Politics, Economy and Society*, edited by Adam Simpson and Nicholas Farrelly, 105–119). London: Routledge.

Frontier. (2021a). "'Nothing is moving': CDM freezes foreign trade, raising fears of shortages". *Frontier Myanmar*, 12 March. Available at https://www.frontiermyanmar.net/en/nothing-is-moving-cdm-freezes-foreign-trade-raising-fears-of-shortages/ (accessed 20 February 2023).

Frontier. (2021b). "As striking staff return to work, Myanmar's banks face a cash crunch". *Frontier Myanmar*, 5 May. Available at https://www.frontiermyanmar.net/en/as-striking-staff-return-to-work-myanmars-banks-face-a-cash-crunch/ (accessed 20 February 2023).

Frontier. (2022). "'We are losing while we are selling': junta policies bite businesses". *Frontier Myanmar*, 19 September. Available at https://www.frontiermyanmar.net/en/we-are-losing-while-we-are-selling-junta-policies-bite-businesses/ (accessed 20 February 2023).

Gillan, M. and H. H. Thein (2016). "Employment relations, the state and transitions in governance in Myanmar". *Journal of Industrial Relations* 58 (2): 273–288.

Human Rights Watch (2021). "Myanmar, Sanctions, and Human Rights". *Human Rights Watch*, 18 February. Available at https://www.hrw.org/news/2021/02/18/myanmar-sanctions-and-human-rights#_What_is_Human (accessed 20 February 2023).

IndustriALL Global Union (2021). "IndustriALL supports campaign for comprehensive economic sanctions against Myanmar junta". *IndustriALL*, 31 August. Available at https://www.industriall-union.org/industriall-supports-campaign-for-comprehensive-economic-sanctions-against-myanmar-junta (accessed 20 February 2023).

International Crisis Group. (2022). *Myan'ar's Military Coup: One Year On*. *International Crisis Group*, 25 January.

International Labour Organization (ILO) (2022). *Employment in Myanmar in 2021: A rapid assessment*. ILO Brief, 28 January. Online: ILO Regional Office for Asia and the Pacific. Available at https://www.ilo.org/yangon/publications/WCMS_835900/lang--en/index.htm (accessed 20 February 2023).

The Irrawaddy (2021a). "Myanmar's Electricity Sector Crippled Since Military Coup." *The Irrawaddy*, 15 July. Available at https://www.irrawaddy.com/news/burma/myanmars-electricity-sector-crippled-since-military-coup.html (accessed 20 February 2023).

The Irrawaddy (2021b). "Myanmar Coup Leader Vows to Protect China-Backed Enterprises." *The Irrawaddy*, 24 May. Available at https://www.irrawaddy.com/news/burma/myanmar-coup-leader-vows-to-protect-china-backed-enterprises.html (accessed 20 February 2023).

The Irrawaddy (2022). "Why China Is Comfortable With Myanmar's Military Rulers". *The Irrawaddy*, 1 July. Available at https://www.irrawaddy.com/opinion/analysis/why-china-is-comfortable-with-myanmars-military-rulers.html (accessed 20 February 2023).

Khaing Zar Aung (2021). "My country needs you: no cooperation, no recognition and no business with the military junta in Myanmar". *Equal Times*, 11 March. Available at https://www.equaltimes.org/my-country-needs-you-no#.YnCzvtpByUl (accessed 20 February 2023).

Khaing Zar Aung and C. Brighi (2022). "Unions call for more sanctions on anniversary of Myanmar's coup". *Open Democracy*, 14 February. Available at https://www.opendemocracy.net/en/beyond-trafficking-and-slavery/unions-call-for-more-sanctions-on-anniversary-of-myanmars-coup/ (accessed 20 February 2023).

Kirin Holdings (2021). "Statement on the situation in Myanmar". News Release. 5 February. Available at https://www.kirinholdings.com/en/newsroom/release/2021/0204_01.html (accessed 20 February 2023).

Liu, J. (2021). "Regime seeks economic recovery, but drops NLD reform agenda". *Frontier*, 17 September. Available at https://www.frontiermyanmar.net/en/regime-seeks-economic-recovery-but-drops-nld-reform-agenda/ (accessed 20 February 2023).

Meyer, K. and H. H. Thein (2014). "Business under Adverse Home Country Institutions: The Case of International Sanctions against Myanmar". *Journal of World Business* 49 (1): 156–171.

Mizzima (2022). "Two dozen foreign investors have exited in wake of Myanmar coup". *Mizzima*, 8 February. Available at https://mizzima.com/article/two-dozen-foreign-investors-have-exited-wake-myanmar-coup (accessed 20 February 2023).

Myanmar Now (2021a). "Japan's Kirin hits out at military-owned MEHL over 'unjust' legal request to dissolve partnership". *Myanmar Now*, 24 November. Available at https://www.myanmar-now.org/en/news/japans-kirin-hits-out-at-military-owned-mehl-over-unjust-legal-request-to-dissolve-partnership (accessed 20 February 2023).

Myanmar Now (2021b). "Junta approves $2.5bn power plant project backed by Chinese companies". *Myanmar Now*, 14 May. Available at https://www.myanmar-now.org/en/news/junta-approves-25bn-power-plant-project-backed-by-chinese-companies (accessed 20 February 2023).

Myanmar Now (2022). "Norway's Telenor accused of 'egregious breach' of EU sanctions with surveillance system that will allow Myanmar junta to spy on millions." *Myanmar Now*, 5 March. https://www.myanmar-now.org/en/news/norways-telenor-accused-of-egregious-breach-of-eu-sanctions-with-surveillance-system-that-will (accessed 20 February 2023).

Nikkei Asia (2021). "Norway's Telenor fully writes off Myanmar unit for $782m." *Nikkei Asia*, 4 May. Available from https://asia.nikkei.com/Spotlight/Myanmar-Coup/Norway-s-Telenor-fully-writes-off-Myanmar-unit-for-782m (accessed 20 February 2023).

Nikkei Asia (2022). "Myanmar blocks car, luxury imports amid foreign-currency crunch." *Nikkei Asia*, 23 June. Available at https://asia.nikkei.com/Spotlight/Myanmar-Crisis/Myanmar-blocks-car-luxury-imports-amid-foreign-currency-crunch (accessed 20 February 2023).

Oanh Ha, K., Khine Lin Kyaw and Jin Wu (2021). "Myanmar's Generals Run a Nearly Sanction-Proof Business Empire". *Bloomberg*, 11 May. Available at https://www.bloomberg.com/graphics/2021-myanmar-military-business/ (accessed 20 February 2023).

Pouyanné, P. (2021). "Pourquoi Total reste en Birmanie" *Le Journal du Dimanche*, 4 April. Available from https://www.lejdd.fr/International/exclusif-pourquoi-total-reste-en-birmanie-la-tribune-de-patrick-pouyanne-4035902 (accessed 20 February 2023).

Regalado, F. (2021). "Asian companies stay quiet as Western peers condemn Myanmar coup". *Nikkei Asia*, 5 March. Available at https://asia.nikkei.com/Spotlight/Myanmar-Coup/Asian-companies-stay-quiet-as-Western-peers-condemn-Myanmar-coup (accessed 20 February 2023).

Republic of the Union of Myanmar, National Unity Government (2021). *Sanction Policy*. 9 November. Online: BurmaLibrary. Available at https://www.burmalibrary.org/sites/burmalibrary.org/files/obl/2021-11-09-NUG-policy-on-sanctions-tu-en.pdf (accessed 20 February 2023).

Reuters (2022a). "Japan brewer Kirin to exit Myanmar, seek sale of two units". *Reuters*, 14 February. Available at https://www.reuters.com/business/japan-brewer-kirin-exit-myanmar-operations-nikkei-2022-02-14/ (accessed 20 February 2023).

Reuters (2022b). "Myanmar junta reports $3.8 bln FDI since coup, says stability restored". *Reuters*, 27 January. Available at https://www.reuters.com/article/myanmar-economy-idUSL4N2U721T (accessed 20 February 2023).

Robinson, G. and R. Wallace (2021). "Myanmar economists urge curbs on ju'ta's hard currency access". *Nikkei Asia*, 29 April. Available at https://asia.nikkei.com/Spotlight/Myanmar-Crisis/Myanmar-economists-urge-curbs-on-junta-s-hard-currency-access (accessed 20 February 2023).

San, S. (2021). "Beyond the Coup in Myanmar: Don't Let the Light of Education Be Extinguished." *Just Security*, 16 June. Available at https://www.justsecurity.org/76921/beyond-the-coup-in-myanmar-dont-let-the-light-of-education-be-extinguished/ (accessed 20 February 2023).

Solsvik, T. (2021). "Biggest wealth fund puts Kirin on watch list over Myanmar link". *Reuters*, 4 March. Available from https://www.reuters.com/article/us-norway-swf-idUSKBN2AV2TA (accessed 20 February 2023).

Special Advisory Council for Myanmar (SAC-M) (2021). "Tracking the Three Cuts: SAC-M Launches Live Record of Cuts to Junta's Cash". Statement, 4 June. Available at https://specialadvisorycouncil.org/wp-content/uploads/2021/06/SAC-M-PR-Cut-the-Cash-ENGLISH.pdf (accessed 20 February 2023).

Special Advisory Council for Myanmar (SAC-M) (n. d.). "Record of actions taken by private companies". Available at https://specialadvisorycouncil.org/cut-the-cash/ (accessed 20 February 2023).

Strangio, S. (2022). "Myanmar's Military Junta Tightens Control Over Foreign Currency Flows". *The Diplomat*, 5 April. Available at https://thediplomat.com/2022/04/myanmars-military-junta-tightens-control-over-foreign-currency-flows/ (accessed 20 February 2023).

Statement by Concerned Businesses Operating in Myanmar (2021). 19 February 2021 Available at https://www.myanmar-responsiblebusiness.org/news/statement-concerned-businesses.html (accessed 20 February 2023).

Thein, H.H. (2021a). "Ethical minefields: the dirty business of doing deals with Myanmar's military". *The Conversation*, 8 January. Available at https://theconversation.com/ethical-minefields-the-dirty-business-of-doing-deals-with-myanmars-military-152318 (accessed 20 February 2023).

Thein, H.H. (2021b). "Taking care of business: the coup in Myanmar is partly about protecting the economic interests of the military elite". *The Conversation*, 15 February. Available at https://theconversation.com/taking-care-of-business-the-coup-in-myanmar-is-partly-about-protecting-the-economic-interests-of-the-military-elite-154727 (accessed 20 February 2023).

Thein, H. H. and M. Gillan, M. (2021). "Sanctions against Myanmar's junta have been tried before. Can they work this time?" *The Conversation*, 22 June. Available at https://theconversation.com/sanctions-against-myanmars-junta-have-been-tried-before-can-they-work-this-time-158054 (accessed 20 February 2023).

TotalEnergies (2022). "TotalEnergies withdraws from Myanmar". Media Statement, 21 January. Available at https://totalenergies.com/media/news/press-releases/totalenergies-withdraws-myanmar (accessed 20 February 2023).

Tower, J. (2022). *China Bets Strategic Projects, Regional Stability on Myanmar Coup Regime*. United States Institute for Peace. Available at https://www.usip.org /publications/2022/07/china-bets-strategic-projects-regional-stability-myanmar-coup-regime (accessed 20 February 2023).

Tun, A. (2022). "Agriculture in a State of Woe Following Myanmar's 2021 Military Coup". *ISEAS Perspective*, 22 (2 March).

UN Human Rights Council (2019). *Economic interests of the Myanmar military*. Forty-second session, Agenda Item 4, A/HRC/42/CRP.3. 5 August 2019. Available at https://www.ohchr.org/en/hr-bodies/hrc/myanmar-ffm/economic-interests-myanmar-military (accessed 20 February 2023).

United Nations Office for the Coordination of Humanitarian Affairs (OCHA) (2021). "Humanitarian Needs Overview 2022: Myanmar". Accessed 22 November 2022. Available at https://gho.unocha.org/myanmar (accessed 20 February 2023).

United Nations Development Programme (UNDP) (2021). "COVID-19, Coup d'Etat and Poverty: Compounding Negative Shocks and Their Impact on Human Development in Myanmar". *UNDP*, 30 April. Available at https://www.undp.org/myanmar/press-releases/covid-19-coup-detat-and-poverty-compounding-negative-shocks-and-their-impact-human-development-myanmar (accessed 20 February 2023).

Win, K. (2021a). "The economics behind Min Aung Hlaing's grand delusions". *Frontier Myanmar*, 30 September. Available at https://www.frontiermyanmar.net/en/the-economics-behind-min-aung-hlaings-grand-delusions/ (accessed 20 February 2023).

Win, K. (2021b). "The currency crisis, and why we should brace for stagflation". *Frontier Myanmar*, 10 October. Available at https://www.frontiermyanmar.net/en/the-currency-crisis-and-why-we-should-brace-for-stagflation/ (accessed 20 February 2023).

World Bank (2021a). *Macro-Poverty Outlook*. Washington, D.C.: World Bank Group.

World Bank (2021b). *Myanmar Economic Monitor, July 2021: Progress Threatened; Resilience Tested*. Washington, D.C.: World Bank Group.

World Bank (2022). *Myanmar Economic Monitor, July 2022: Reforms Reversed*. Washington, D.C.: World Bank Group.

V

International Relations in Crisis

11

NEUTRALISM OR NON-ALIGNMENT? MYANMAR'S RECURRING FOREIGN POLICY DILEMMA

Andrea Passeri and Hunter Marston

Since its establishment as a sovereign state, Myanmar has demonstrated a firm commitment to a neutral and non-aligned foreign policy, capable of preventing the country's gradual tilt under the orbit of a great power or bloc of powers (Passeri 2020, 8–14). As such, the preservation of independence and freedom of action in the global arena has always embodied the paramount goal of Myanmar's diplomacy, pushing various generations of Burmese leaders to shy away from bilateral and multilateral security arrangements which could potentially jeopardise its non-aligned, "go alone" stance (Trager 1956; Silverstein 1982; Steinberg 2018; Passeri and Marston 2022). This is not to say, however, that Myanmar's diplomatic playbook has endured for more than seven decades without major twists and turns. On the contrary, even a cursory glance at the country's history reveals that Burmese diplomacy has constantly swung between two opposite archetypes of non-alignment, following an oscillating trend that has persisted up to present days. In a nutshell, this dilemma has revolved around the desire to implement a positive, dynamic, and proactive blend of non-alignment, aimed at expanding and diversifying Myanmar's international partnerships, and, on the other hand, the temptation of resorting to a more inward-looking, reactive, and torpid practice of 'negative neutralism', conducive to a gradual retrenchment from the international dimension and to the assertion of autonomy through self-aloofness.

Unsurprisingly, the same puzzle experienced by Myanmar in selecting the most appropriate prototype of non-alignment has traditionally complicated the strategic calculus of many other small powers across the globe, pushing scholars to theorise different variants of what could be considered a neutral or non-aligned behaviour in the global arena. According to Khalid I. Babaa and Cecil V. Crabb (1965, 11–12), for example, the doctrine of 'positive non-alignment' entails a clear refusal to join tight and formal alignment links (e.g. alliances, stationing of foreign troops inside the national territory) with great powers, together with a deep-felt commitment to play an independent, constructive, and cooperative role in global affairs through good offices or bridge-building efforts. As such, this positive form of neutralism is often infused with moral and ethical considerations based on an active contribution to peaceful coexistence, coupled by an equally strong rejection of colonialism, imperialism, power politics, and foreign intrusions in the domestic dimension (Goetschel 1999, 120–121). On top of that, 'positive non-alignment' also requires a dynamic, omnidirectional, and proactive diplomacy, designed to assure a somewhat equidistant position amongst competing powers. Accordingly, this concept stands at odds with the notions of disengagement or isolationism, as it prescribes the cultivation of cordial ties with a host of different interlocutors. As stated by Muhammad B. Alam (1977, 174) in one of the first seminal works on the concept of neutralism,

> positive non-alignment does not mean keeping aloof from burning international issues. On the contrary, it means a positive stand based on a non-aligned nation's own conviction and completely uninfluenced by any one of the power blocs. Thus, it ensures political independence and thereby contributes to national self-respect and integrity.

On the opposite side of the spectrum, the temptation of parochialism and isolationism might be very powerful for those who seek to pursue a negative type of neutralism. In fact, this peculiar form of neutralism differs from 'positive non-alignment' in its insular and inward-looking approach to alignment choices, which are often blended with autarchic blueprints in the economic realm. Hence, contrary to the key assumptions of 'positive non-alignment', negative neutralism postulates a reactive, defensive, and essentially diffident diplomatic mindset, capable of erecting a powerful barrier with the outside world as state authorities focus on the domestic dimension. For example, a negative form of neutralism may ensue when a small state sets aside its dynamism in attempting to mediate the dangerous quarrels of great powers, and replaces it with a sense of reprobation of the current order, an acknowledgement of the state of powerlessness experienced by secondary actors, and a refusal to even judge between competing powers (Khanna 2013, 390–391). Likewise, according to Maung Maung Gyi (1981, 10) a practice of "negative neutralism for group survival" could arise through a policy that (a) is inward-looking, xenophobic, and immature in its worldview; (b) fails to infuse dynamism into the nation's economy; and (c) lacks courage to pursue a proactive role in regional matters.

Building upon these conceptualisations, it is thus possible to differentiate between 'positive non-alignment' and 'negative neutralism' by looking at several crucial variables, such as the opposite ethical tone and underlying worldview subsumed in the two strategies; the degree of proactiveness in reaching out to a diversified range of diplomatic and economic partners; the different emphasis accorded to multilateral institutions as the key venues to adopt a bridging or mediating role amidst great power rivalries; and the ability to be flexible in fluctuating from one side to another, in order to achieve what Samir N. Anabtawi describes as "maximum benefit from a policy of play-off" (1965, 359). In the case of Myanmar, the tendency to swing between two extreme poles of neutralism as a result of domestic shocks or systemic changes, such as China's rise, has been prevalent throughout the country's history. From such a perspective, a comprehensive periodisation of Burmese practice of neutralism should consider at least five different chronological stages, characterised by a clear tilt towards one of the already mentioned archetypes of alignment behaviour. This five-phased periodisation encompasses the brief parliamentary spell experienced between 1948 and 1962; the long authoritarian era stretching from 1962 to 2010; the following opening-up achieved during Thein Sein's mandate (2011–2016); the 2016-2021 quinquennium shaped by Aung San Suu Kyi's leadership; and, finally, the aftermath of the 2021 military takeover.

Against this backdrop, the chapter examines the drivers and implications of Myanmar's shifting reliance on two opposite forms of neutralist behavior embodied by positive non-alignment and negative neutralism, by looking in particular at its foreign policy trajectory between 2011 and 2022. Accordingly, the first section provides the historical, political, and ideational background that shaped the country's conceptualisation of positive non-alignment and negative neutralism since its post-independence stage. The analysis shows that the first generation of Burmese leaders who ruled Myanmar during the brief parliamentary era (1948–1962) gave birth to a vibrant and proactive foreign policy centred on the logic of positive non-alignment, which was then followed by a swift transition towards negative neutralism in the aftermath of Ne Win's 1962 military coup. This shift largely contributed to Myanmar's progressive marginalisation in the international arena, but it also served the purpose of partially insulating its authoritarian regime from foreign scrutiny and criticism, as postulated by the concept of 'negative neutralism for group survival'. Section two sheds light on the subsequent major twist in Myanmar's alignment between positive non-alignment and negative neutralism, reflected by the country's opening-up during the Thein Sein era (2011–2016). In this case, the swing in Naypyitaw's diplomatic pendulum prompted a re-adoption of positive non-alignment as the cornerstone of its foreign policy, which nurtured a simultaneous transition away from military rule. The shift echoed the style and approach pursued by the previous civilian cabinet between 1948 and 1962. As a result, during Thein Sein's mandate Myanmar successfully reapproached the West after decades of mutual ostracism, largely stepped up its diversification efforts within the strategic triangle with China and the United States, and placed a renewed emphasis on regional and global multilateralism as key platforms to unleash a dynamic and omnidirectional foreign policy. Beginning in 2016, however, a series of events unfolded which ushered in a return to the previous isolationism and reactive policies associated with negative neutralism. Following the National League for Democracy's commanding performance in the 2015 nationwide elections, the outbreak of communal violence between Buddhists and Muslims, the military's brutal "clearance operations" against Rohingya civilians in Rakhine State in 2016–2017, the resultant deterioration of civil-military relations and interreligious strife fuelled a siege mentality sufficient to end this proactive era of global diplomacy. Under Aung San Suu Kyi's tenure, the NLD effectively stood by the military's denial of its crimes against humanity and weathered increasing international censure as a result. At the same time, with global investors leaving the country due to heightened perceptions of political risk, Myanmar once again became something of a pariah state. Ultimately, relations between the civilian government and military came to a peak in early 2021, when the armed forces launched a coup d'etat placing Commander-in-Chief Min Aung Hlaing in control of all political institutions and ending a decade of nascent democratic reforms. The State Administration Council (SAC), as the junta calls itself, has further eroded Myanmar's global standing, caused a precipitous decline in investor confidence and economic growth, and deepened the country's pariah status, by embracing a reactive and inward-looking form of negative neutralism. This chapter ends with a look at the junta's foreign policy since the 2021 coup while connecting themes of positive non-alignment and negative neutralism as throughlines across Myanmar/Burma's history since the early days of independence.

HISTORICAL BACKGROUND

Between the country's independence in 1948 and the 1962 coup staged by the army (known as the *Tatmadaw*), the Burmese government led by U Nu gave birth to one of the most vibrant, dynamic, and multidirectional foreign policy records exhibited in the developing world, which allowed the small Southeast Asian state to strike an equidistant course between the East and the West. As indicated by the conceptualisation of 'positive neutralism', this strategy was tinged with relevant ethical considerations stemming from Buddhist-infused political thought, which sought to project a 'goodwill diplomacy' in Asia and beyond (Thomson 1957, 261–265). Thanks to this activism in the international arena, Burma gained prominence as one of the leading voices within the 'Non-Aligned Movement' (NAM), while also emerging as the first non-communist country both in establishing official ties with the People's Republic of China (PRC) and concluding a peace treaty with the former Japanese oppressor. By the same token, the omnidirectional diplomacy with neighbouring countries laid the foundations for the inking of a treaty of peace and friendship with India, the adoption of a favourable border delineation with the PRC, and an overall improvement in bilateral ties with Thailand (Egreteau and Jagan 2008, 11–15). Similar achievements also paved the way for important outcomes in economic dimensions, especially in nurturing a diversified portfolio of destinations for Burma's key export commodity, namely rice

(Trager 1956, 99–102). On top of that, Burmese officials' active commitment within multilateral fora paid its dividends in 1961 when the diplomat and former counsellor of U Nu, U Thant, was elected to the prestigious post of UN Secretary General.

Yet, with the 1962 military coup that transformed Burma from a parliamentary system under a caretaker government to a praetorian and authoritarian regime led by General Ne Win, the country's foreign policy entered a new era. Progressively, the military government consolidated an inward-looking approach to diplomacy as it focused its efforts on the 'Bamarisation' of the indigenous society and the eradication of ethnic insurgencies. As a result, Burma's foreign policy proved increasingly incapable of supporting its development goals and economic performances, which had already suffered a major blow with the launch of the 'Burmese Way to Socialism', an ill-defined and essentially autarchic blueprint that set the stage for a vast program of nationalisation (Perry 2007, 26–29). By the same token, Yangon's visible tilt towards 'negative neutralism for group survival' also meant a progressive retrenchment from international venues, as epitomised in 1967 by Ne Win's refusal to stand amongst the founding members of the Association of Southeast Asian Nations (ASEAN), and, in 1979, by the withdrawal of the Burmese delegation from the NAM. The growing nationalistic and xenophobic traits entrenched in Burma's foreign policy also reverberated their disruptive effects on key bilateral ties inherited from the previous regime. With China in particular, anti-Chinese riots in 1967 triggered a major diplomatic spat. Similarly, the nationalisation without compensation of thousands of small businesses owned by Burma's Indian community pushed Indo-Burman relations to the brink (Thin Thin Aung and Soe Myint 2001, 91).

Notwithstanding a series of efforts put in place since the mid-1970s to set aside the autarchic goals of the Burmese Way to Socialism, Burma's aloofness from the outside world reached unprecedented heights between 1988 and 1990, following the regime's crackdown on pro-democracy movements and the nullification of the general elections that witnessed a landmark victory of Aung San Suu Kyi's National League for Democracy (NLD). Consequently, the new generation of military leaders who had deposed Ne Win in 1988 was forced to cope with a further sense of estrangement and isolation in the international arena, as Burma consolidated its credentials as a "pariah state" (Chow and Easley 2016, 522). With the suspension of India and Japan's engagement policies vis-à-vis the junta and the launch of economic sanctions by the United States and the European Union (EU), the regime was thus deprived of several key counterchecks to China's expanding influence inside the country, prompting diffuse fears in the military establishment that Burma's autonomous stance in the region could be jeopardised by growing overdependence on the People's Republic of China (PRC). The survival strategy sketched out by the military junta hit a crucial milestone in 1997 with the country's accession to ASEAN. The Association's membership, in fact, allowed Myanmar to avoid near-total international isolation, providing a crucial platform to kick-start an embryonic process of regional economic integration. In 2006, however, ASEAN prevented the junta from assuming its scheduled chairmanship of the organisation, further constricting the regime's international space for manoeuvre. As a result, with the country's international isolation at its peak and an endemic state of domestic political unrest, the Tatmadaw decided to ensure its own survival at the helm of Burmese politics via a completely amended strategy. The revised blueprint entailed a roadmap for the transition away from direct military rule and the establishment of a hybrid institutional architecture, centred on the creation of a civilian government and the conferment of vast veto powers to the armed forces (Passeri 2020, 947). This quasi-democratic metamorphosis, in turn, set the stage for Myanmar's rapprochement with the West and re-integration in the international community, which was seen by the Tatmadaw as a crucial pre-requisite to spur progress in the country's backward economy, minimise dissent, and balance China's growing footprint as Myanmar's main diplomatic and economic patron.

Domestically, the seven-step process towards the establishment of what the Tatmadaw labelled as a 'discipline-flourishing democracy' was ratified with the promulgation of the 2008 Constitution, which paved the way for a power-sharing agreement between military and civilian authorities. As already mentioned, the army viewed the election of the first civilian government after such a long authoritarian spell as a crucial tool to partially rehabilitate Myanmar's highly tarnished international image, weaken domestic dissent, and strengthen its shaky legitimation as the guardian of national unity. This project started to materialise in 2010 with the election of a civilian cabinet led by former General Thein Sein, who was entrusted with the task of putting an end to the country's international marginalisation through the revival of the benign and dynamic foreign policy pursued before the 1962 coup. The stage was thus set for the opening of the third stage in the history of Myanmar's neutralism, after the positive non-alignment projected during the 1950s and the progressive disengagement from the global arena initiated under military rule. Building upon the theoretical dyad between 'positive non-alignment' and 'negative neutralism', the rest of this paper sheds light on the twists and turns in Myanmar's foreign policy over the course of the last decade, looking at two additional political junctures brought about by the election of Aung San Suu Kyi in 2015 and the military putsch staged in February 2021, which pulled the plug on a decade of proto-democratic reforms.

THE RELAUNCH OF MYANMAR'S 'ACTIVE NEUTRALISM' UNDER THEIN SEIN (2011–2016)

At the dawn of the 2010s, Myanmar's relations with the outside world appeared severely undermined by almost fifty years of relentless reliance on negative neutralism, which had fuelled the country's gradual withdrawal from the international community (Egreteau and Jagan 2008, 48–49). In fact, with the Saffron Revolution (September 2007) and the disastrous response to Cyclone Nargis (May 2008), Myanmar's military regime had significantly deepened its pariah status, showcasing a further radicalisation of the draconian traits displayed during the 1988–1990 biennium. By the same token, the prolonged adoption of negative neutralism had brought the unintended yet predictable outcome of pushing Myanmar into the diplomatic orbit of its most powerful neighbour, the PRC. In 2007, China's unparalleled leverage on the junta was reconfirmed through its strenuous defence of Myanmar at the United Nation Security Council (UNSC) against a United States-led resolution condemning the regime, which was soon rewarded with a US$1 billion agreement for the construction of an oil and natural gas pipeline linking Western Myanmar to Yunnan. On top of that, during the late 2000s Beijing had also asserted itself as a key aid donor, investor, commercial partner, and provider of military hardware for Myanmar's highly unpopular junta: between 2005 and 2010, two-way trade rose from US$1.2 billion to US$4.5 billion, with Myanmar's bilateral deficit soaring from US$0.7 billion to US$2.5 billion (Hong Zhao and Mu Yang 2012, 26). For all these reasons, the imperative of mitigating such a growing overdependence on China through a more dynamic and diversified foreign policy loomed large in setting the stage for Myanmar's top-down political transformation, which hit a pivotal milestone in March 2011 with the swearing-in of a new civilian government under the leadership of retired general Thein Sein (Yun Sun 2012, 52).

Since its first weeks in office, the Thein Sein administration endeavoured to fulfil its mission in the international arena through a rapprochement with the West and an unprecedented activism within the ranks of ASEAN that would ultimately break the chains of Myanmar's isolation and burnish its global image (Maung Aung Myoe 2016, 133–134). This progressive reintegration in the international community was also accompanied by a series of sweeping domestic reforms, including the release of thousands of political prisoners, the lifting of press censorship, as well as the re-admission of Aung San Suu Kyi's NLD in the national parliament in April 2012 (Holliday 2013, 93 –95). As a result, such a far-reaching shift in Myanmar's domestic politics and international relations significantly raised Thein Sein's credentials as a reformist and proto-democratic leader, borrowing several constitutive elements of 'positive non-alignment' displayed by his predecessor U Nu between 1948 and 1962. The foreign policy re-orientation championed by the new regime was shaped by a renewed emphasis on multilateral venues such as ASEAN as key platforms to unleash a more proactive and multidirectional diplomacy; a significant push towards economic diversification as the antidote against overdependence on China; the adoption of a 'sticks and carrots' approach towards the PRC that echoed the concept of 'hedging'; and the reintroduction of an ethical dimension to foreign policy, through a clear revival of the 'goodwill diplomacy' showcased in the 1950s. With regards to the first feature of this re-orientation, Myanmar's growing activism in multilateral institutions paved the way for the conferment of Naypyitaw's first-ever ASEAN's chairmanship in 2014, which allowed the Thein Sein cabinet to present itself as a skilful convenor of 12 meetings of heads of state, 34 minister-level meetings, and 89 senior official-level meetings (Po Sone Kyu 2015). On top of that, Myanmar's chairmanship also oversaw 34 ASEAN declarations, encompassing contentious issues such as the 'ASEAN Community's Post-2015 Vision' and the maritime standoff in the South China Sea, which Myanmar handled with a firm and impartial attitude, in stark contrast with the pro-China posture exhibited by Cambodia in 2012, thus attracting numerous praises from other ASEAN member-states (Passeri and Marston 2022, 14). Likewise, during his first speech to the UN General Assembly in September 2012, President Thein Sein (2012) announced that

Myanmar was ushering in a new era, while also expressing his eagerness to participate more actively in the United Nations as a responsible and respectable international stakeholder.

The second part of Thein Sein's strategy, centred on the diversification of Myanmar's economic partnerships, largely benefitted from the country's rehabilitation both in multilateral fora and vis-à-vis the West, through the re-opening of commercial and investment relations that had been suppressed during the long era of self-aloofness in the international arena. In fact, the Thein Sein administration's adoption of political and economic reforms persuaded the United States and European partners to progressively lift their long-standing sanctions on Myanmar, which in turn prompted a surge in bilateral aid, loans, and foreign direct investment (FDI). Between 2012 and 2013, the EU suspended trade restrictions against Myanmar and reinstated its generalised system of preferences (GSP) to reward Naypyitaw's efforts aimed at political and economic liberalisation: as a result, over the course of the same period Myanmar's textile industry achieved an 18 per cent rise in global exports (Miller 2014, 93). This export-led growth centred on garment manufacturing reached its peak at the end of the 2016–17 fiscal year, as the overall value of garment exports towards the EU, Japan, and South Korea hit US$1.86 billion, with a US$1 billion increase compared to 2015–2016 (Dempsey et al. 2018, 20). Two-way trade with the United States jumped from US$9.7 million in 2010 to US$577.2 million in 2017 (Dempsey et al. 2018, 21). Further nurturing this promising growth, in 2013 the two countries inked the United States–Myanmar Trade and Investment Framework Agreement, allowing Naypyitaw to benefit from Washington's GSP since November 2016. Besides Myanmar's flourishing ties with the United States and the EU, the Thein Sein era also witnessed a positive dynamic in terms of Naypyitaw's relations with Japan. Since the start of Thein Sein's administration, Tokyo began positively engaging the new government with a significant increase in development assistance. Accordingly, in 2013 Japan stood out as Myanmar's top donor, whilst also cancelling US$2.72 billion in debt (Mahtani 2014). Additionally, Japanese private investors provided the lion's share of the capital for the Thilawa Special Economic Zone (SEZ), conceived in 2011 to rival the China-backed Kyaukphyu SEZ.

In parallel, the third imperative pursued by Myanmar's foreign policy between 2011 and 2016 revolved around the establishment of a less subordinate and dependant position vis-à-vis China, through the adoption of a 'sticks and carrots' approach signalling a relative tilt away from Beijing's shadow, while also safeguarding cordial and rewarding ties with the PRC (Fiori and Passeri 2015). This change of posture, which stood at odds with the far more deferential attitude displayed by Myanmar before the start of its political transition, came to the fore in September 2011 with Thein Sein's decision to halt the Chinese-backed Myitsone Dam megaproject. Since its genesis in 2003, a vast portion of the local population had perceived the dam as a symbol of the deprivation of Myanmar's natural resources by Chinese companies, and its suspension illustrated how Naypyitaw saw Beijing's dominant economic footprint inside the country as a potential threat to its independent and autonomous stance in the international arena. In a similar fashion, in July 2014 the Thein Sein administration broke Myanmar's decade-long silence on the South China Sea issue with a public statement that raised many eyebrows in Beijing. The document urged restraint on the claimant states, pushed for the relaunch of peaceful negotiations, and expressed its commitment to a rule-based solution of the dispute that clearly contradicted Beijing's claims to large portions of the South China Sea (Nyan Lynn Aung 2016). Similar displays of defiance, however, were rapidly followed by a series of counteracting moves, as postulated by the concept of hedging (Kuik 2008, 171). Accordingly, throughout its mandate the Thein Sein government implemented a series of measures and initiatives to show deference to the PRC, assuage its concerns, and further clarify that Myanmar was not adopting an all-out balancing shift against Beijing. In October 2011, for instance, shortly after the halt to the construction of the China-backed Myitsone Dam the two sides thus elevated the status of their bilateral ties, through the establishment of a 'comprehensive strategic cooperative partnership' rooted in the principle of good neighbourly ties (Chenyang Li 2012, 64).

Finally, Thein Sein's efforts to boost Myanmar's role in multilateral fora and nurture rapprochement with the international community were suffused by a renewed ethical tone, in stark contrast with the xenophobic and reactive worldview displayed by previous military juntas. This revised ideological outlook subsumed in Myanmar's new course sought to present it as a "responsible international citizen", committed to contributing to regional peace and friendly relations amongst states (Maung Aung Myoe 2016, 128–29). As such, this rhetoric echoed U Nu's 'goodwill diplomacy' in the 1950s and signalled that Myanmar was finally eager to drop its self-reliant approach to international relations, in favor of a more constructive role both in regional and global affairs. Arguably, Thein Sein's fervent Buddhist faith also played a role as an important consensus-building tool in shaping the benign narrative of his cabinet, and the pledge to act as a virtuous member of the global community soon became a recurring tune in the President's speeches at the UN, during Myanmar's ASEAN chairmanship, and in state visits abroad (Besheer 2012). As with U Nu, who had tinged Burma's diplomacy with religious references to the Theravada Buddhist doctrine of the 'middle path' and to the concepts of metta (all embracing love) and upekkha (equanimity), Thein Sein presented the shift towards positive non-alignment both as a rational choice to assuage Naypyitaw's security dilemma, and as a righteous path from a moral standpoint. For all these reasons, at the end of 2016 the Thein Sein cabinet could look back at its foreign policy record with a clear sense of fulfilment.

Compared to the start of its mandate, Myanmar had largely re-asserted its non-aligned stance in the international arena, as well as its centrality in Southeast Asia's changing geopolitical contours. Additionally, the relative tilt away from China had been achieved without jeopardising Naypyitaw's ties with the PRC, while the rapprochement with Western stakeholders had endowed Myanmar with a series of credible counterweights to Beijing's influence. At the start of 2016, this positive legacy was inherited by a new government led by Aung San Suu Kyi's NLD, which displayed stronger democratic credentials than its predecessor. Yet, during its tenure the NLD cabinet proved incapable of replicating the previous administration's diplomatic achievements, as the country once again swung from 'positive non-alignment' to 'negative neutralism'. The shift was largely fuelled by the 2017 Rohingya crisis, which reinvigorated deeply ingrained xenophobia within Myanmar's political establishment and the country's perception as a pariah state internationally.

THE NLD ERA: RETURN TO NEGATIVE NEUTRALISM

Unlike the Union Solidarity and Development Party (USDP) led by Thein Sein, the NLD ultimately failed to achieve much-needed domestic renewal, political reconciliation, or significant economic growth. While Aung San Suu Kyi enjoyed an outpouring of support from both jubilant voters and the international community, turbulent domestic politics gradually fostered a less proactive and dynamic foreign policy, which came to resemble 'negative neutralism'. Particularly in the second half of the NLD's term, the party adopted a more inward-looking and 'go alone' worldview, suffused with nationalism and xenophobia. This specific *weltanschauung* informed the party's approach toward MaBaTha, a popular ultranationalist Buddhist organisation that attacked the NLD for being too tolerant of Myanmar's Muslims, while pushing discriminatory legislation to protect race and religion. Despite effectively banning MaBaTha, the NLD remained beholden to the majority Buddhist, Bamar ethnic group, as demonstrated by its decision to exclude Muslim candidates in the 2015 and 2020 elections (as did the USDP) (Human Rights Watch 2016). After the assassination of Suu Kyi's adviser and prominent Muslim U Ko Ni in January 2017, the party took a harder line against Muslims, refusing to use the term Rohingya to refer to the minority Muslim group in Rakhine State, and became a staunch defender of the military and Buddhist nationalism. As Myanmar abandoned its outward-facing regional strategy, it found itself increasingly reliant on China diplomatically as well as economically. On a five-day visit to Beijing in June 2015, Suu Kyi met Xi Jinping, reassuring the Chinese leader that she would prioritise relations with China, Myanmar's largest trading partner (Forsythe 2015). A Chinese Ministry of Foreign Affairs spokesman said that the meeting would "promote the development of friendly and cooperative relations between China and Myanmar" (Ibid). If the Thein Sein years had marked a low point for Myanmar–China relations, Suu Kyi's trip thus sought to recalibrate the relationship by restoring ties with Naypyitaw's powerful neighbour.

In early 2016, the NLD issued a foreign policy manifesto, which referenced the country's "independent non-aligned policy" and neutralism during the Cold War and pledged to pursue "an active and independent foreign policy" (Maung Aung Myoe 2017, 91–94). The NLD grounded its vision in democratic values and committed "to work together for the benefit of the region on issues relating to regional organizations and programs" (Ibid, 91). In an interview with Chinese state-run media, Suu Kyi opined that "Myanmar had no enemies, but relations with neighbors were more sensitive than others and needed to be carefully handled" (Ibid, 98). Naypyitaw has been wary of China's Belt and Road Initiative (BRI), which it viewed as a risk to Myanmar's sovereignty, particularly in the sensitive northern border region where Chinese influence over insurgent groups such as the United Wa State Army has long caused distrust (Perlez 2015). However, Suu Kyi sought to increase Chinese investment, and in May 2017 the State Counsellor travelled to Beijing for the first Belt and

Road Forum.

As rapprochement with Beijing gained steam, relations with the West cooled, largely due to Myanmar's Rakhine State crisis and intercommunal violence against Rohingya Muslim minorities. The military's brutal "clearance operations" in 2016–2017, which led to the exodus of nearly 800,000 Rohingya to neighbouring Bangladesh, represented a major turning point for the party as well. Facing mounting criticism from western media and politicians, the NLD encouraged a message of self-reliance and denied atrocities carried out by the Tatmadaw. Suu Kyi claimed outsiders had failed to understand the complexities of Myanmar's internal issues. The crisis in Rakhine complicated the normalisation of ties with the United States, which peaked in 2016 with Aung San Suu Kyi's visit to the White House, when President Obama announced the suspension of remaining economic sanctions against Myanmar (Kennedy 2016). The decision was meant to signal support for ongoing political reforms, in spite of a clear lack of progress concerning the Rohingya and broader human rights abuses. Having thrown off economic constraints imposed by the West, Myanmar was free to pursue economic development and solicit foreign direct investment (FDI) from U.S. and European businesses, as the EU followed the American example by suspending its economic sanctions against Myanmar in early 2012 (Emmott and Blenkinshop 2018). In reality, things were not so simple. American companies continued to shun Myanmar, which they largely perceived as a risky investment frontier (Murphy, Kucik and Rose 2016). In the absence of Western investment, nearly 40 per cent of all FDI came from China (including Hong Kong) in 2019–2020, and more than a quarter in 2018–2019, according to Myanmar's Ministry of Investment and Foreign Economic Relations (Directorate of Investment and Company Administration 2020). While total FDI remained high throughout the NLD's first five years, it was comparatively lower than the five years of the Thein Sein administration (US$4.6 billion versus US$5.5 billion on average annually). Similarly, gross domestic product (GDP) growth fell from a high of 8.4 per cent in 2013 to 2.9 per cent in 2019 (World Bank 2020). Meanwhile, the NLD failed to address economic inequality and ignored the issue in its policy platform. Instead, party leaders championed neoliberal economic policies based on market reforms and foreign investment while preaching "individual moral revival" as the path to national unity (McCarthy 2020).

In contrast to U.S. and European condemnation of Myanmar, Beijing bolstered its relationship with Naypyitaw and voiced support for the NLD's characterisation of the military operations as a legitimate response to "terrorism". As Myat Myat Mon (2019) has observed, political pressure from western countries over conflict in Rakhine State "provided a conducive opportunity for China to negotiate BRI projects in Myanmar" and deepen Beijing's influence in the peace process given the diplomatic protection it provided Naypyitaw in the United Nations. The Chinese state-run Global Times charged that Myanmar had been "derailed" by its engagement with the West and contrasted those ties with Beijing's approach, stating that only China could "pull Myanmar from the sludge" (Li Xuanmin 2020). It went on: "After some turbulence, Myanmar realized there were double standards in the approach Western countries had taken on human rights issues and began to turn to China for diplomatic and economic help." Beijing also benefited from fluctuations in U.S. policy and Myanmar's internal dysfunction. As Yun Sun (2020) observes, "China's best relations with Myanmar usually emerge when Myanmar is facing international isolation due to domestic politics, whether it's the 1988 uprising, the 1990 elections, the Saffron Revolution of 2007 or the Rohingya crisis." When Xi Jinping travelled to Naypyitaw in January 2020, the NLD agreed to a "Sino–Myanmar community of common destiny", building on already strong bilateral relations. Myanmar and China previously elevated ties to the level of a "comprehensive strategic cooperative partnership" in 2013 (Ministry of Foreign Affairs of China). In this light, Xi's 2020 official visit was "the result of trends that have brought the two countries much closer in the past several years, and reflects the elevation of Myanmar's importance in China's foreign policy and of Sino-Myanmar relations generally" (Yun Sun 2020).

From Naypyitaw's side, China's willingness to overlook state violence against the Rohingya and eagerness to advance business and development ties perfectly suited the NLD's political agenda, which viewed economic growth as the path to sustainable peace. Beijing consistently supported the NLD government as well as the military's use of force, emphasising that the crisis was an internal affair, and that China would not seek to interfere in Myanmar's sovereignty (Joy 2018, 4). Chinese Foreign Minister Wang Yi stated that, "The Rakhine state issue is in essence an issue between Myanmar and Bangladesh. China does not approve of complicating, expanding or internationalizing this issue" (Blanchard 2018). Much to

Aung San Suu Kyi's appreciation, Beijing played a key role in blocking resolutions against Myanmar within the UN Security Council. Suu Kyi was less engaged in multilateral fora such as the United Nations, opting to skip the UN General Assembly in 2017, 2018, and 2019. While the State Counsellor was present in ASEAN gatherings, her diplomatic travel to the West was limited as a result of the country's inward turn and international condemnation following the humanitarian crisis in Rakhine. While Suu Kyi attended most ASEAN summits as Foreign Minister, notably she decided to skip the 32nd ASEAN Summit in Singapore in April 2018, not long after the violence of 2017 (Kyodo 2018). In general, despite vague pledges in its 2015 manifesto "to work together for the benefit of the region on issues relating to regional organizations", the NLD largely preferred to deal with international partners bilaterally, for instance soliciting trade and support from Japan, India, and Singapore (Moe Thuzar 2020). Bilateral diplomacy, as opposed to multilateralism, better suited the NLD's negative neutralism. Thus, Myanmar's previously proactive engagement vis-à-vis ASEAN dissipated substantially in favour of a more passive, low-profile approach.

On a rare trip to Europe in 2019, Suu Kyi visited Hungary, where she met with nationalist leader Victor Orban and voiced agreement about the challenge that migration posed to both countries' internal cohesion, particularly as a result of "continuously growing Muslim populations" (Ellis-Petersen 2019). Most infamously, Suu Kyi travelled to the Netherlands later that year to defend Myanmar against charges of genocide at the International Court of Justice in The Hague (Bowcott 2019). Her intransigence in the face of accusations of complicity in the military's crackdown on Rohingya won her plaudits among her domestic constituents, who had little sympathy for the Rohingya and largely supported the military.[1]

In addition to the massive humanitarian crisis in Rakhine, the NLD struggled to keep the stalled peace process alive. Representatives from the civilian government and ethnic armed groups held the fourth 21st Century Panglong Union Peace Conference in August 2020, the first since July 2018 (The Irrawaddy 2018). However, progress was extremely tentative, and conflict escalated in Rakhine, Kachin, and Shan states during the latter years of the NLD administration, with particularly fierce fighting between the Tatmadaw and the Arakan Army (Nyein Nyein 2020). In a speech on state media, Suu Kyi declared, "In defending the nation, we have to consider not only internal perils but external dangers as well.

There are tangible defences, such as the wall along our Western border" (Myanmar News Agency 2020). She announced that her government had approved 20 billion *kyats* (about US$15.3 million) for the project. She also warned, "More profound and challenging is the intangible, invisible task of defending our country in the international arena", pointing to external "criticism and pressure, rather than understanding, sympathy and help". It was perhaps the clearest expression of her administration's embrace of negative neutralism.

Beyond the enormous costs of the COVID-19 pandemic, numerous internal security crises, and diminished economic growth, renewed international isolation following the 2021 military coup has constrained Naypyitaw's strategic manoeuvrability and effectively ended efforts to diversify external ties to hedge against China. For the foreseeable future, Myanmar's junta appears mired by insurmountable domestic hurdles and a pessimistic, reactive view of its international environment.

RETURN TO MILITARY RULE: DEEPENING NEGATIVE NEUTRALISM AFTER THE 2021 COUP

On 1 February 2021, the Tatmadaw detained representatives of the elected government, abruptly ending Myanmar's fragile democratic experiment. The move shocked international observers and drew sharp criticism from broad swathes of Myanmar's populace, who overwhelmingly support the NLD and Aung San Suu Kyi, as well as western governments that backed the country's continued transition toward full democracy. The junta has deepened Myanmar's pariah status and returned the country to a repressive and autarchic form of negative neutralism, not seen since the SLORC/SPDC era of the 1990s–2000s. Following the coup, protests erupted across the country, with hundreds of thousands of demonstrators in the streets (Radcliffe 2021). Elected leaders quickly formed a Committee Representing Pyidaungsu Hluttaw (CRPH),[2] which subsequently established a National Unity Government (NUG) in April 2021.[3] In Washington, the new administration of Joseph Biden Jr. swiftly condemned the coup leaders and called for an immediate return to democratic rule. President Biden himself warned of consequences and soon announced new sanctions on the leaders of the coup (Washington had already sanctioned Min Aung Hlaing in 2019) and the military's state-controlled entities, such as Myanmar

Timber Enterprise and Myanmar Gems Enterprise (U.S. Department of State 2021).

While the Chinese government at first downplayed the coup as a "major cabinet reshuffle", it was clear that Beijing was apprehensive regarding the military takeover (McLaughlin 2021). Protesters attacked Chinese-owned factories in Yangon, and many blamed Beijing for its perceived support of the military coup. Yet the Chinese Communist Party (CCP) had invested billions of dollars and years of patient diplomatic support in its cooperative partnership with the NLD. Beijing was generally pleased with the working relationship with the NLD government and views the military as a fickle partner. Senior General Min Aung Hlaing quickly signalled interest in revitalising Chinese infrastructure projects such as hydroelectric dams, likely in a bid to retain Beijing's support in light of growing international isolation (Zaw Tun 2021). At the same time, officials from the State Administration Council (SAC) (as the junta refers to itself) have made several trips to Russia, meeting with Russian military leaders and Defence Minister Sergei Shoigu. Moscow has pledged to continue to support bilateral ties with the Myanmar military, especially through the sale of arms (Reuters 2021). The SAC has asserted that it is prepared to weather international isolation and that it has withstood economic sanctions in the past (Nichols 2021). As outgoing UN special envoy Christine Schraner Burgener recounted after a meeting with deputy commander-in-chief Soe Win, the junta's second-in-command told her matter-of-factly that the regime would "learn to walk with only few friends" (Ibid).

Despite Moscow and Beijing's support, the junta faces fierce, armed resistance across the country. Resistance groups claim their efforts have resulted in more than 10,000 military defections since the coup, and reports of Tatmadaw casualties accrue daily (Bociaga 2021; VOA News 2023). The World Bank reported that Myanmar's economy contracted by 18 percent in FY2021, while international investment has ground to a halt and businesses have shuttered across the country. On top of a devastating third wave of COVID-19, the military's ongoing crackdown on civil society and brutal attacks on peaceful protesters have destroyed consumer as well as investor confidence. According to Myanmar's Directorate of Investment and Company Administration (US–ASEAN Business Council 2021), FDI in Myanmar declined by over 54 per cent from 2019 through FY2020–2021.

Part of the decline was no doubt due to COVID-19, but the coup has certainly exacerbated this trend by scaring off international investors (see

Htwe Htwe Thein and Gillian this volume). Even ASEAN, which prides itself on non-interference, took the unprecedented step of barring the junta from sending representatives to the 38th ASEAN Summit in Brunei in November 2021 and subsequent high-level meetings. This move embodied a massive turning point for the Association and its integration blueprint dubbed the 'ASEAN Way', which traditionally advocates non-interference in the domestic affairs of member-states. Yet the junta has remained defiant, refusing to cooperate with ASEAN's Five Point Consensus, which calls for dialogue between all parties and an end to conflict between the military and its opponents (Connelly 2021). The military appears content to hold the Myanmar people hostage to the international community, while insisting that all international humanitarian assistance go through the SAC and not the National Unity Government nor cross-border ethnic community-based organisations. Hence, the dramatic events since February 2021 indicate that the current junta will most likely endorse a foreign policy posture reminiscent of the 'negative neutralism for group survival' exhibited during Ne Win's rule, while prioritising efforts to eradicate domestic unrest.

CONCLUDING REMARKS

Myanmar's quest for a neutral and autonomous agency in international affairs dates back to the country's independence in 1948. Various leaders have pursued non-alignment in divergent ways. Two archetypes of non-alignment emerge from this analysis. On the one hand, positive non-alignment entails the deliberate eschewal of international alliances and multilateral commitments in favour of a more omnidirectional and equidistant position toward great powers (Babaa and Crabb 1965, 11-12; Goetschel 1999, 120-21). Yet this positive form of neutralism remains proactive rather than isolationist (Alam 1977, 174). Negative neutralism, on the other hand, represents a more concerted rejection of international commitments and the embrace of autarchic economic and/or social policies domestically. Negative neutralism also manifests in state leaders' failure to inject a sense of dynamism into the national discourse, rather emphasising a more inward-focused worldview (Maung Maung Gyi 1981, 10). The case of Myanmar illustrates that non-alignment can be pursued in various, and sometimes opposite ways, by relying on different tools and worldviews. As such, the country's pendulum of neutralism has alternatively oscillated between activism and aloofness vis-à-vis the international arena. Inspired by positive non-alignment, U Nu's early post-independence foreign policy forged a new national identity in the shadow of British colonialism by embracing an active and dynamic balance between East and West and seeking to play various blocs of great powers off one another. At the same time, U Nu (1948–1962) highlighted tenets of Burma's Buddhist philosophy in order to catalyse his proactive form of positive non-alignment while promoting economic vitality at home. The result was Burma playing a lead role in the Non-Aligned Movement (NAM) globally, while cementing friendly relations with regional powers including India and China. Thanks to these efforts, the country's diplomacy gave birth to a complex balance of the external influences operating within its borders, which acted as a powerful antidote to Burma's satelisation under the shadow of a great power or bloc of powers.

Burmese positive neutralism, however, gave way to a more xenophobic and autarchic rule following General Ne Win's military coup in 1962, which paved the way for the emergence of an inward-focused and isolationist foreign policy blueprint. In line with Burma's posture of negative neutralism for the subsequent five decades, Ne Win backed away from engagement with the newly emerged Association of Southeast Asian Nations, severely reduced his country's commitment with the United Nations, and withdrew Burma from the Non-Aligned Movement in 1979. On top of that, his regime targeted ethnic minorities for persecution, especially Indian and Chinese communities, and nationalised key domestic industries, while socialist policies in the 1970s slowed economic growth and deepened Burma's isolation on the world stage. The ensuing military dictatorship, which ruled with an iron fist under the banner of the State Law and Order Restoration Council (SLORC) (1988–2010), further exacerbated the country's self-imposed isolation by alienating western partners and investors and seeding a culture of fear by fiercely cracking down on civil society and political activism. During this time, China's economic and political influence waxed as Myanmar's foreign relations frayed due to domestic repression and international pariah status (Chow and Easley 2016, 522). When Myanmar acceded to ASEAN in 1997, glimmers of hope emerged that the country would undertake necessary domestic reforms to embark on a brighter path (Passeri 2020, 947), but it would be more than a decade before it ratified a military-drafted constitution in 2008 and held multi-party elections two years later, leading to the transition to partial civilian rule with President Thein Sein's USDP administration taking the helm in 2011.

Once in power, Thein Sein implemented political and economic reforms and recalibrated Myanmar's relations with great powers, engaging the United States while pushing back on Chinese influence (Fiori and Passeri 2015). When Myanmar successfully chaired ASEAN in 2014, it became clear that Naypyitaw had once again embraced positive neutralism. The Thein Sein administration also saw a surge in foreign direct investment, successfully brokered ceasefires with eight of 15 major armed groups in 2015 before leaving office, and effectively rebranded Myanmar's image as a proactive global player that was once again open for business (Maung Aung Myoe 2017, 128–29).

In 2015, Aung San Suu Kyi's NLD competed in national elections, which it won with a resounding majority, eliciting an overwhelming positive response from the international community and even drawing support from Beijing, which had been caught off guard by Thein Sein's independent foreign policy. However, the outbreak of violence between Buddhists and Muslims in Rakhine State in 2016 and 2017, and the military's central role in what it termed "clearance operations" targeting the Rohingya with genocidal violence, led to international outcry and the return of targeted U.S. sanctions. Trade and investment declined as the global business community reassessed the risks of operating in Myanmar. At the same time, Aung San Suu Kyi's denials of military atrocities and resistance to criticism from ASEAN as well as other partners created frictions in Naypyitaw's external relations — particularly with the West — and triggered international opprobrium. As State Counsellor, Suu Kyi vocally advocated Myanmar's self-reliance and decried international criticism, projecting a return to Cold War-era negative neutralism. Meanwhile, she relied on Beijing's diplomatic protection within the United Nations to shield Naypyitaw from censure and deepened economic dependence on Chinese capital.

Following the 2021 military coup, which initiated a protracted political crisis as well as sharp economic contraction, a nationwide civil disobedience movement (CDM), ongoing conflicts with ethnic armed groups, as well as efforts to mitigate the COVID-19 pandemic, have compounded the country's numerous internal divisions. For the time being, Myanmar's pendulum of neutralism has once again swung from the positive side of the ledger to the negative. Whether it swings back to a positive direction depends on the collective ability of Myanmar's protest movement, the National Unity Government and CRPH, to stand up a diverse and inclusive coalition capable of supplanting the military regime that has held power since February and establishing a genuine federal union with a proactive international agenda.

Notes

1 Public sentiments have shifted dramatically since the February 2021 military coup. Protesters held signs to apologise for ignoring the plight of Rohingya, and public animosity against the Tatmadaw for its subversion of Myanmar democracy is now nearly universal with widespread opposition to military rule and support for the National Unity Government (NUG).
2 *Pyidaungsu Hluttaw* is the Burmese term for Myanmar's Union Parliament.
3 The NUG includes representatives from a variety of ethnic minority parties in addition to the NLD.

References

Alam, Muhammad B. (1977). "The Concept of Non-Alignment: A Critical Analysis". *World Affairs* 140 (2): 166–85.
Anabtawi, Samir N. (1965). "Neutralists and Neutralism". *The Journal of Politics* 27 (2): 351–61.
Babaa, Khalid I. and Cecil V. Crabb (1965). "Nonalignment as a Diplomatic and Ideological Credo". *The Annals of the American Academy of Political and Social Sciences* 362: 6–17.
Besheer, Margaret (2012). "Thein Sein: Burma 'Now Part of Family of Nations.'" *VOA News*, 27 September. Available at: https://www.voanews.com/a/thein-sein-burma-is-experiencing-amazing-changes/1516096.html (accessed 19 May 2022).
Blanchard, Ben (2018). "China Says Rohingya Issue Should Not Be 'Internationalized'". *Reuters*, 28 September. Available at https://www.reuters.com/article/us-myanmar-rohingya-china/china-says-rohingya-issue-should-not-be-internationalized-idUSKCN1M8062 (accessed 1 April 2021).
Bociaga, Robert (2021). "Can Defections Take Down Myanmar's Military?" *The Diplomat*, 5 November. Available at https://thediplomat.com/2021/11/can-defections-take-down-myanmars-military/ (accessed 15 November 2021).
Bowcott, Owen (2019). "Aung San Suu Kyi Pleas with Court to Dismiss Genocide Claims". *The Guardian*, 13 December. Available at https://www.theguardian.com/world/2019/dec/12/myanmar-military-incapable-of-looking-into-abuses-court-told2019 (accessed 1 April 2021).

Carroll, Joshua (2019). "Myanmar Nationalists Look to Stoke Anti-US Anger over Travel Bans against Military". *Voice of America*, 8 August. Available at https://www.voanews.com/east-asia-pacific/myanmar-nationalists-look-stoke-anti-us-anger-over-travel-bans-against-military (Accessed 1 April 2021).

Chenyang Li (2012). "China–Myanmar Comprehensive Strategic Cooperative Partnership: A Regional Threat?" *Journal of Current Southeast Asian Affairs* 31 (1): 53–72.

Chow, Jonathan T. and Leif-Eric Easley (2016). "Persuading Pariahs. Myanmar's Strategic Decision to Pursue Reform and Opening." *Pacific Affairs* 89 (3): 521–42.

Connelly, Aaron (2021). "Why ASEAN's Rebuke of Myanmar's Top General Matters". *International Institute for Strategic Studies* (blog), 21 October. Available at https://www.iiss.org/blogs/analysis/2021/10/why-aseans-rebuke-of-myanmars-top-general-matters (accessed 15 November 2021).

Dempsey, Harry, Ann Listerud, Hiroyuki Nakashima, Shin Oya, and Daniel Remler (2018). "The Article II Mandate. Forging a Stronger Economic Alliance between the United States and Japan". *Center for Strategic and International Studies*, 28 November. Available at https://www.csis.org/analysis/article-ii-mandate-forging-stronger-economic-alliance-between-united-states-and-japan (accessed 17 November 2022).

Directorate of Investment and Company Administration (2020). "Foreign Investment by Country". Available at https://www.dica.gov.mm/en/taxonomy/term/38 (accessed 1 April 2021).

Egreteau, Renaud and Larry Jagan (2008). *Back to Old Habits. Isolationism or the Self-Preservation of Burma's Military Regime.* Bangkok: Institut de Recherche sur l'Asie du Sud-Est Contemporaine.

Ellis-Petersen, Hannah (2019). "Aung San Suu Kyi Finds Common Ground with Orbán over Islam". *The Guardian*, 6 June. Available at https://www.theguardian.com/world/2019/jun/06/aung-san-suu-kyi-finds-common-ground-with-viktor-orban-over-islam2019 (accessed 1 April 2021).

Emmott, Robin and Philip Blenkinshop (2018). "Exclusive: EU Considers Trade Sanctions on Myanmar over Rohingya crisis". *Reuters*, 4 October. Available at https://www.reuters.com/article/us-myanmar-rohingya-eu-exclusive-idUSKCN1MD28E (accessed 1 April 2021).

Fiori, Antonio and Andrea Passeri (2015). "Hedging in Search of a New Age of Non-Alignment. Myanmar between China and the USA". *The Pacific Review* 28 (5): 679–702.

Forsythe, Michael (2015). "Aung San Suu Kyi of Myanmar Meets with Xi Jinping in Beijing". *New York Times*, 12 June. Available at https://www.nytimes.com/2015/06/12/world/asia/aung-san-suu-kyi-of-myanmar-meets-with-xi-jinping-in-beijing.html (accessed 1 April 2021).

Goetschel, Laurent (1999). "Neutrality, a Really Dead Concept?" *Cooperation and Conflict* 34 (2): 115–39.

Holliday, Ian (2013). "Myanmar in 2012: Toward a Normal State". *Asian Survey* 53 (1): 93–100.

Hong Zhao and Mu Yang (2012). "China-Myanmar Economic Corridor and its Implications." *East Asian Policy* 4 (2): 21–32.

Human Rights Watch (2016). "Burma: Events of 2015." *ReliefWeb*, 2 February. Available at https://reliefweb.int/report/myanmar/burma-events-2015 (accessed 11 May 2022).

Joy, Adrienne (2018). *Understanding China's Response to the Rakhine Crisis*. Special Report No. 419. Washington, D.C.: United States Institute of Peace. Available at https://www.usip.org/sites/default/files/2018-02/sr419-understanding-chinas-response-to-the-rakhine-crisis.pdf (accessed 1 April 2021).

Kennedy, Merrit (2016). "U.S. Lifts Economic Sanctions Against Myanmar". *National Public Radio*, 7 October. Available at https://www.npr.org/sections/thetwo-way/2016/10/07/497070188/u-s-lifts-economic-sanctions-against-myanmar (accessed 1 April 2021).

Khanna, V.N. (2013). *International Relations*, 5th ed. New Delhi: Vikas Publishing.

Kuik, Cheng Chwee (2008). "The Essence of Hedging: Malaysia and Singapore's Response to a Rising China". *Contemporary Southeast Asia* 30 (2): 159–85.

Kyodo (2018). "Myanmar's Suu Kyi to Skip ASEAN Summit in Singapore". *South China Morning Post*, 23 April. Available at https://www.scmp.com/news/asia/southeast-asia/article/2142992/myanmars-suu-kyi-skip-asean-summit-singapore (accessed 1 April 2021).

Li Xuanmin (2020). "Xi to Make First Visit in New Year to Myanmar". *Global Times*, 10 January. Available at https://www.globaltimes.cn/content/1176359.shtml (accessed 1 April 2021).

Mahtani, Shibani (2014). "Japan Pledges $96 Million to Reduce Conflicts in Myanmar". *Wall Street Journal*, 7 January. Available at https://www.wsj.com/articles/japan-pledges-96-million-to-reduce-conflicts-in-myanmar-1389077331 (accessed 1 April 2021).

Marston, Hunter (2020). "Has the US Lost Myanmar to China?" *The Diplomat*, 20 January. Available at https://thediplomat.com/2020/01/has-the-us-lost-myanmar-to-china/ (accessed 15 November 2021).

Maung Aung Myoe (2017). "The NLD and Myanmar's Foreign Policy: Not New, but Different". *Journal of Current Southeast Asian Affairs* 36 (1): 89–121.

--- (2016). "Myanmar's Foreign Policy under the USDP Government: Continuities and Changes". *Journal of Current Southeast Asian Affairs* 35 (1): 123–50.

Maung Maung Gyi (1981). "Foreign Policy of Burma since 1962. Negative Neutralism for Group Survival". In *Military Rule in Burma since 1962*, edited by Frederic K. Lehman. Hong Kong: Maruzen Asia.

McCarthy, Gerard (2020). "Class Dismissed? Explaining the Absence of Economic Injustice in the NLD's Governing Agenda". *Journal of Current Southeast Asian Affairs* 38 (3): 358–80.

McLaughlin, Timothy (2021). "China Is the Myanmar Coup's 'Biggest Loser'". *The Atlantic*, 23 February. Available at https://www.theatlantic.com/international/archive/2021/02/what-myanmars-coup-means-china/618101/ (accessed 15 November 2021).

Miller, Meredith (2014). *Myanmar's Emerging Role in the Regional Economy*. Special Report No. 45. Washington, D.C.: National Bureau of Asian Research.

Ministry of Foreign Affairs of the People's Republic of China. "China and Myanmar". Available at https://www.fmprc.gov.cn/mfa_eng/wjb_663304/zzjg_663340/yzs_663350/gjlb_663354/2747_663498/ (accessed 1 April 2021).

Moe Thuzar (2020). "What to Expect from Myanmar's Post-Election Foreign Policy". *The Strategist*, 3 November. Available at https://www.aspistrategist.org.au/what-to-expect-from-myanmars-post-election-foreign-policy/ (accessed 1 April 2021).

Murphy, Erin, Peter Kucik, and Eric Rose (2016). *US–Myanmar Commercial Relations: The Next Phase*. Washington, D.C.: U.S. Chamber of Commerce. Available at https://www.uschamber.com/sites/default/files/us_-_myanmar_commercial_relations_-_the_next_phase_-.pdf (accessed 1 April 2021).

Myanmar News Agency (2020). "National League for Democracy (NLD) Presents Its Policy, Stance and Work Programmes". *Global New Light of Myanmar*, 18 September. Available at https://www.gnlm.com.mm/national-league-for-democracy-nld-presents-its-policy-stance-and-work-programmes/ (accessed 1 April 2021).

Myat Myat Mon (2019). "Trends in China-Myanmar Relations: 2018 Year in Review". *Tea Circle Oxford*, 31 January. Available at https://teacircleoxford.com/2019/01/31/trends-in-china-myanmar-relations-2018-year-in-review/ (accessed 1 April 2021).

Nichols, Michelle (2021). "Myanmar Army Tells U.N. It Is Ready to Weather Sanctions, Isolation, Envoy Says". *Reuters*, 4 March. Available at https://www.reuters.com/article/us-myanmar-politics-un-idUSKCN2AV2CJ (accessed 15 November 2021).

Nyan Lynn Aung (2016). "Myanmar Wades in to South China Sea Ruling with a Balancing Act". *Myanmar Times*, 19 July. Available at https://www.mmtimes.com/national-news/21447-myanmar-wades-in-to-south-china-sea-ruling-with-a-balancing-act.html (accessed 15 November 2021).

Nyein Nyein (2020). "Myanmar Govt Declares Arakan Army a Terrorist Group". *The Irrawaddy*, 24 March. Available at https://www.irrawaddy.com/news/burma/myanmar-govt-declares-arakan-army-terrorist-group.html2020 (accessed 1 April 2021).

Passeri, Andrea (2020). "A Tender Gourd among the Cactus. Making Sense of Myanmar's Alignment Policies through the Lens of Strategic Culture". *The Pacific Review* 33 (6): 931–57.

Passeri, Andrea and Hunter Marston (2022). "The Pendulum of Non-Alignment: Charting Myanmar's Great Power Diplomacy (2011–2021)". *Journal of Current Southeast Asian Affairs*: 1–26.

Perry, Peter J. (2007). *Myanmar (Burma) Since 1962. The Failure of Development*. New York: Routledge.

Perlez, Jane (2015). "With Aung San Suu Kyi's Rise, China and Myanmar Face New Relationship". *New York Times*, 12 November. Available at https://www.nytimes.com/2015/11/13/world/asia/aung-san-suu-kyis-china-and-myanmar-relations.html (accessed 1 April 2021).

Po Sone Kyu (2015). "ASEAN Community with Opportunities". *Myawaddy Newspaper*, 20 August.

Psaledakis, Daphne and Simon Lewis (2019). "U.S. Slaps Sanctions on Myanmar Military Chief over Rohingya atrocities". *Reuters*, 11 December. Available at https://www.reuters.com/article/us-usa-myanmar-sanctions/us-slaps-sanctions-on-myanmar-military-chief-over-rohingya-atrocities-idUSKBN1YE1XU (accessed 1 April 2021).

Radcliffe, Rebecca (2021). "Myanmar: More Than 100,000 Protest in Streets Against Coup". *The Guardian*, 18 February. Available at https://www.theguardian.com/world/2021/feb/17/suu-kyi-myanmar-trial-protests-military (accessed 15 November 2021).

Reuters (2021). "Russia Says to Boost Military Ties With Myanmar as Junta Leader Visits". *Reuters*, 23 June. Available at https://www.reuters.com/world/asia-pacific/russia-says-boost-military-ties-with-myanmar-junta-leader-visits-2021-06-23/ (accessed 15 November 2021).

Silverstein, Josef (1982). "The Military and Foreign Policy in Burma and Indonesia". *Asian Survey* 22 (3): 278–91.

Steinberg, David I. (2018). "The World". In *Routledge Handbook of Contemporary Myanmar*, edited by Adam Simpson, Nicholas Farrelly, and Ian Holliday. Abingdon: Routledge.

Storella, Mark (2017). "The Rohingya Crisis: U.S. Response to the Tragedy in Burma". Testimony delivered to the House Foreign Affairs Committee, Washington, DC, 5 October. Available at https://2017-2021.state.gov/the-rohingya-crisis-u-s-response-to-the-tragedy-in-burma/index.html (accessed 1 April 2021).

The Irrawaddy (2021). "Myanmar Military Regime Removes Arakan Army From List of Terrorist Groups". *The Irrawaddy*, 11 March. Available at https://www.irrawaddy.com/news/burma/myanmar-military-regime-removes-arakan-army-list-terrorist-groups.html (accessed 30 November 2021).

--- (2018). "Our Coverage of the 3rd Union Peace Conference". *The Irrawaddy*, 17 July. Available at https://www.irrawaddy.com/news/burma/our-coverage-of-the-3rd-union-peace-conference.html (accessed 1 April 2021).

Thein Sein (2012). "Speech at the United Nations (UN) General Assembly, 27 September". *The New Light of Myanmar*, 28 September.

Thin Thin Aung and Soe Myint (2001). *Challenges to Democratization in Burma: Perspective on Multilateral and Bilateral Responses*. Stockholm, Sweden: International Institute for Democracy and Electoral Assistance.

Thomson, John S. (1957). "Burmese Neutralism". *Political Science Quarterly* 72 (2): 261–83.

Trager, Frank N. (1956). "Burma's Foreign Policy, 1948–56: Neutralism, Third Force, and Rice". *Journal of Asian Studies* 16 (1): 89–102.

U.S. Department of State (2021). "Burma Sanctions". Available at https://www.state.gov/burma-sanctions/ (accessed 15 Novembe 2021).

VOA News. 2023. "Junta Defections Drop Two Years After Myanmar Coup." *VOA News*, 30 January. Available at https://www.voanews.com/a/junta-defections-drop-two-years-after-myanmar-coup/6940032.html accessed 12 May 2023.

World Bank (2020). *Myanmar*. Washington, D.C.: The World Bank Group. Available at https://data.worldbank.org/country/myanmar (accessed 1 April 2021).

Yun Sun (2020). "A New Era for China and Myanmar, but Old Constraints Still Hold". *Frontier Myanmar*, 20 January. Available at https://frontiermyanmar.net/en/a-new-era-for-china-and-myanmar-but-old-constraints-still-hold (accessed 1 April 2021).

--- (2012). "China and the Changing Myanmar". *Journal of Current Southeast Asian Affairs* 31 (4): 51–77.

Zaw Tun (2021). "Hydropower Plants and Electrification Projects to Carry On". *Myanmar Times*, 16 February. Available at https://www.mmtimes.com/news/hydropower-plants-and-electrification-projects-carry.html (accessed 15 November 2021).

12

BETWEEN CONTACT AND LEGITIMATION: INTERNATIONAL RESPONSES TO MYANMAR'S COUP

Nicholas Coppel

The 1 February 2021 coup in Myanmar prompted a diverse range of responses from foreign governments and intergovernmental organisations, revealing considerable misunderstanding within Myanmar on the scope of feasible international responses. This chapter describes these responses and discusses the challenges in navigating tensions between contact and legitimation. It discusses the utility of condemnations, calls for accountability, the release of detainees and recognition of the National Unity Government, and the handling of competing claims to represent Myanmar in international organisations. In the context of calls on the international community to "save Myanmar", this chapter also considers whether the United Nations Responsibility to Protect concept could be invoked and discusses attempts by the Association of Southeast Asian Nations (ASEAN) to encourage dialogue between the parties.

I argue that while there is a performative dimension to the post-coup diplomatic response, it is also important for the international community to articulate its understanding of what constitutes acceptable conduct. Since the coup there has been a growing discourse and anxiety amongst people from Myanmar that, with the passage of time, nations, international organisations and businesses will increasingly become engaged with the military council. This anxiety is reflected in condemnation of contact, criticism of ASEAN efforts to find a pathway out of the political crisis and the calling out of all contact as "legitimising" the regime (Forum Asia 2021; Oo and Liu 2021). This tactic attempts to deny the military council any form of legitimacy. This chapter argues that some contact is necessary and useful and should not be stigmatised. To move on from the current situation to a restoration of democracy requires more than hope that the military council, on the basis of international opprobrium and a denial of international recognition, will eventually and voluntarily admit defeat and seek a return to parliamentary democracy.

The analysis in this chapter is based on observations of the first 18 months following the coup. Responses by advocacy groups — such as fundraising, lobbying for referral to the International Criminal Court, and other activities — and responses by the international donor and business communities, while important, are beyond the scope of this chapter. I bring to these issues the perspective of a career diplomat who served as Australia's Ambassador to Myanmar over the four years 2015–2018, when I met on a number of occasions the key protagonists — State Counsellor Aung San Suu Kyi and Commander-in-Chief Min Aung Hlaing — and many other citizens.

INITIAL RESPONSES

On 1 February 2021, Commander-in-Chief Min Aung Hlaing mounted a coup detaining President Win Myint, State Counsellor Aung San Suu Kyi, and numerous other National League for Democracy (NLD) politicians who were scheduled to convene later that day to elect a new president. Rumours of a coup in Myanmar are often assessed as unlikely on the basis that the military was committed to the 2008 Constitution which preserved a role for it in Myanmar's political life (Selth 2018, p.12-13; Callahan 2016; Huang 2020, p. 152; Kyaw Phyo Tha 2021). But the Commander's remarks that there was nothing he would not dare do and his threat to repeal the Constitution generated fresh alarm (Frontier 2021a; Myanmar Now 2021). Diplomatic missions in Yangon issued a joint statement urging the military to adhere to democratic norms and opposing any attempt to alter the election outcome (US Embassy 2021).

The initial international responses to the coup came not only from Western democracies but also from countries with large Muslim populations such as Turkey and Malaysia already unhappy with Myanmar's military for the forced exodus of Rohingya Muslims. Statements expressed concern at developments in Myanmar and called for peace and the restoration of democracy. The then-Australian Foreign Minister expressed deep concern at reports the Myanmar military "is once again seeking to seize control of Myanmar and has detained State Counsellor Daw Aung San Suu Kyi and President U Win Myint" and called for their immediate release (Payne 2021a). Malaysia expressed "serious concern over the latest developments" and called on the military "and all relevant parties" to give priority to the maintenance of peace and security (Malaysia 2021a). Turkey similarly expressed deep concern, strongly condemning the military takeover, saying that they expected the immediate release of all detainees and for parliament to be convened (Turkey 2021). The ASEAN statement did not condemn the military leaders directly and instead encouraged the pursuance of "dialogue, reconciliation and the return to normalcy in accordance with the will of the people". In an early indication of what was to emerge as an adjustment to the way ASEAN views and responds to adverse internal developments in a member state, the statement recalled "the purposes and principles enshrined in the ASEAN Charter, including, the adherence to the principles of democracy, the rule of law and good governance, respect for and protection of human rights and fundamental freedoms" (ASEAN 2021a). The consequences of this adjustment are discussed below (see 'ASEAN-led Engagement').

These early statements were followed by the G7 Foreign Ministers (Canada, France, Germany, Italy, Japan, the United Kingdom and the United States) and the High Representative of the European Union issuing on 3 February a Joint Statement condemning the coup and expressing deep concern at the detention of political leaders and civil society activists, and at the targeting of the media. It called for an immediate end to the state of emergency, the release of those unjustly detained, and for the election results to be upheld (United Kingdom Government 2021). These international outpourings of concern in the early days after the coup revealed both a concern for what had taken place, but also the view that these were matters that would need to be resolved within Myanmar.

There was not, and has never been since, any suggestion of international intervention: this was a Myanmar crisis, not a global one.

On 4 February, the United Nations Security Council called for the release of Aung San Suu Kyi and other political detainees and stressed the need to uphold democratic institutions and processes, to refrain from violence, to fully respect human rights, fundamental freedoms and the rule of law — but, blocked by Russia and China (Han 2021), it stopped short of condemning the coup (UNSC 2021). This was followed on 14 February by a statement reaffirming "the unwavering support of the United Nations to the people of Myanmar in their pursuit of democracy, peace, human rights and the rule of law" and urging the military authorities to allow the UN Special Envoy, Ms Christine Schraner Burgener, to visit Myanmar (UNSG 2021). She was to be denied entry to Myanmar before concluding her appointment at the end of 2021. Other statements followed, including a joint statement by the UN Special Representative of the Secretary-General for Children and Armed Conflict and the UN Special Representative of the Secretary-General on Violence Against Children (United Nations 2021) and from the 29th Special Session of the Human Rights Council on Myanmar which decided "to remain seized of this matter" (OHCHR 2021).

On 11 February the White House announced that ten individuals, including the Commander-in-Chief Min Aung Hlaing, and three entities had been sanctioned for their association with the military apparatus responsible for the coup. It also announced that it was taking immediate action to limit exports of sensitive goods to the military and other entities associated with the coup and steps were being taken to prevent the military from improperly accessing more than US$1 billion in Myanmar Government funds held in the United States. Finally, it said USAID would redirect US$42.4 million of development assistance away from work that benefited the government of Myanmar to programs that support and strengthen civil society and the private sector. The Rohingya and other vulnerable populations would continue to be supported (United States Government 2021).

Within Myanmar, reaction to the coup was stronger and different from that seen in the protests of 1988 and 2007 which had taken place mostly in Yangon and were led by university students and Buddhist monks respectively (Charney 2009, p. 148-150; Holliday 2011, p. 54-55, 65-66). Myanmar had become a different country after a decade of economic and political reform, including widespread and affordable access to the internet through mobile telephony. The telecommunications revolution had a profound impact on the ability of citizens to exchange and disseminate information and to organise themselves (Chang and Coppel 2020). Within hours of the coup, a Facebook post issued by the National League for Democracy, and ostensibly drafted by Aung San Suu Kyi in anticipation of her arrest, called on her supporters to protest the coup. Hundreds of thousands of citizens took to the streets in a spontaneous outpouring of opposition to the detention of President Win Myint, State Counsellor Aung San Suu Kyi, and other NLD politicians and civil society activists. The first open use of lethal force came on 9 February with the ultimately fatal shooting of a 19 year-old woman in Naypyitaw. Then, on 20 February, live ammunition was used to disperse a group of striking workers, killing two in Mandalay. Images of the army crackdown were captured on smartphones and shared widely, rousing citizenry throughout the country.

The military's use of force against peaceful protestors prompted the diplomatic missions of the United Kingdom, the United States, Canada, the twelve European Union member states present in Myanmar and, a day later, Australia to issue a joint statement calling on the military to refrain from violence, condemning the growing number of arrests and the interference with communications. As the violence and intimidation increased, further statements were issued.

On 7 March the then-Australian Foreign Minister Marise Payne issued another statement expressing grave concerns about the military coup and escalating violence against civilians and called again for the release of Australian academic Professor Turnell and others arbitrarily detained since the onset of the coup. The Minister announced that Australia's small defence cooperation program would be suspended and Australia's development assistance program would be re-directed and delivered through non-government organisations. Payne said Australia would continue to review its sanctions regime (Payne 2021b), but in the 18 months since the coup no additional sanctions were introduced (ACFID 2022). Countries, and not just Western countries, continued to issue statements (see for example Japan 2021; Malaysia 2021b; Turkey 2021). The statements increasingly came to be seen by the people of Myanmar as formulaic and performative.

It is not common practice for military chiefs in democratic states to comment on political developments in other places, as this might be seen as threatening. Notwithstanding this custom, on 27 March the Chiefs of Defence of Australia, Canada, Germany, Greece, Italy, Japan, Denmark, the

Netherlands, New Zealand, the Republic of Korea, the United Kingdom and the United States issued a joint statement. The statement condemned the use of lethal force by the Myanmar armed forces and noted how a "professional military follows international standards for conduct and is responsible for protecting – not harming – the people it serves". It urged the Myanmar armed forces "to cease violence and work to restore respect and credibility with the people of Myanmar that it has lost through its actions" (US Defense 2021). The comment was all the more unusual for being from such a diverse range of militaries. Its focus on military professionalism and community respect and support differentiates it from the rest of the international chorus. The peer judgment, especially with the inclusion of Japan and Korea, would have rankled the senior echelons of the Myanmar military. If there were to be an internal challenge to Commander-in-Chief Min Aung Hlaing, then this joint statement might well be used by a challenger to justify insubordination. However, 18 months after the coup Min Aung Hlaing remains the Commander-in-Chief of the country and the armed forces, the military continue to deny human rights and democracy, and to detain politicians, journalists, protestors and academics.

Several observations can be drawn from the various statements following the coup. First, they are mostly but not exclusively from Western and other liberal democracies and international institutions constituting the rules-based international order. Second, the international response (or lack thereof) has been consistent with the responses to developments of concern usually seen from these respective countries. Third, they have not been successful in bringing about change. And fourth, the countries and institutions expressing concern do not expect that they will have an impact on the military. This leads those among them who feel most strongly about developments to call for further action, such as targeted sanctions.

TARGETED SANCTIONS

There have been no calls for economy-wide sanctions. Most studies show that these fail to achieve their stated objectives (Pape 1997; Marinov 2005), have negative humanitarian consequences, and worsen both human rights (Peksen 2009) and democratic freedoms (Peksen and Drury 2010). Unilateral sanctions previously applied to Myanmar were largely ineffectual and did more harm than good (Nyun 2008; David and Holliday 2012). Economy-wide sanctions are widely regarded as a "blunt instrument" (Boutros-Ghali

1995) leading policy-makers and academics alike to favour so-called smart or targeted sanctions (Weiss 1999; Tostensen and Bull 2002; Cortright and Lopez 2003; Drezner 2011).

After the coup, sanctions targeted at senior members of the Myanmar military and the business interests owned by them or under their control were imposed by European and North American countries. Australia was criticised for not following these countries and imposing sanctions in response to the coup, although it has maintained existing sanctions on five members of the military (but not Commander-in-Chief Min Aung Hlaing) imposed in response to the Rohingya crisis (ACFID 2022).

At an Australian parliamentary inquiry, the Department of Foreign Affairs and Trade argued that Australia's approach was consistent with like-minded countries in the region with whom the government was in close contact. It said Australia did not simply follow the steps taken by other countries. Each country had its own relationships, levels of influence and levers. The government argued that what mattered was Australia's ability to have influence in Myanmar, even if that was only at the margins. It argued that to sanction more military officers would send a message, but would not have a substantial impact on the ground. Furthermore, it might limit Australia's influence and ability to provide assistance in Myanmar. This approach was consistent with all other countries in the region, including Japan, India, South Korea and all the members of ASEAN (Australian Parliament 2021a; 2021b).

A number of countries have long-standing restrictions on the export of weapons and ammunition to Myanmar, and other countries re-imposed restrictions following the Rohingya crisis in 2017. Owing to the veto power of China and Russia, the UN Security Council has been unable to mandate a general arms embargo. However, on 18 June 2021 the United Nations General Assembly did vote in favour of a non-binding resolution calling on Member States to prevent the flow of arms into Myanmar (UNGA 2021). In a signal of his contempt and disregard for the UN, two days later Senior General Min Aung Hlaing visited Russia where he met the Defence Minister and a Director General of Rosoboronexport, a state-run weapons export firm (Frontier Myanmar 2021c). In addition to Myanmar's ongoing military links to Russia and China, the UN arms embargo faces "intractable impediments" to success including because "the Myanmar military produces almost all of the light arms and ammunition it needs to kill civilians and put down urban uprisings" (Mathieson, 2021a).

Myanmar's recent history suggests that targeted sanctions will not bring about regime change and are unlikely to have a direct impact on the behaviour of the military. In the assessment of the International Crisis Group, "sanctions may have hardened Myanmar's military leaders against diplomatic entreaties from the West, at the same time rallying Asian neighbours to the junta's side" (ICG 2021). The sanctions imposed on the military following the Rohingya crisis in 2017 have had no observable impact and around one million Rohingya remain in refugee camps in Bangladesh with no prospect of returning to Myanmar any time soon. Writing about a previous period, Myanmar specialist David Steinberg said, "Although sanctions provide the moral high ground to those imposing them, they have been proven to be ineffectual" (Steinberg 2010, 174-175). Myanmar's military is well-practised in thriving despite sanctions and the opprobrium of much of the rest of the world.

China, however, is a special case in that it does have levers to put pressure on Myanmar's military (Nilsen et al 2021). Its support for a range of armed groups within Myanmar (including the United Wa State Army, the largest and most powerful of the ethnic armed organisations), its sale of military hardware (China supplied 41 per cent of Myanmar's arms imports over 2009-2019 (Nilsen et al 2021)) and the protection it provides to Myanmar in the United Nations Security Council are all powerful levers. But China has no history of active diplomacy in the pursuit of regional or international security. As has been seen in other crises, unless there is a direct threat to China or China's interests, China does not act in the interests of democratic or human rights (Tan 2021, 8). The Chinese Communist Party refers to this as a policy of non-interference, but it could also be called indifference beyond the protection of its own interests which include the Belt and Road Initiative (especially road and rail infrastructure linking China's Yunan Province to the deep seaport at Kyaukpyu and the Bay of Bengal); border security and stability; and Myanmar's continued non-alignment. The coup has resulted in incidents of anti-Chinese violence, internal instability, increased armed conflict and a weakened ability to govern the state and the economy. None of these developments are desirable or in China's interests, and yet China has not shown an appetite for brokering a solution or putting pressure on the parties to encourage them to find one.

The military council continued to ignore the views of all countries, both those imposing targeted sanctions and those calling for dialogue.

Most foreign ministries outside of ASEAN do not realistically expect that their statements of concern, on their own, will produce change within Myanmar and they hold other reasons for expressing their views. Foremost among these is consideration of how their response will be received by the people of Myanmar, their own populations and by other countries. Similarly, those states imposing targeted sanctions do not expect to restore democracy. Statements and sanctions send a signal of discontent at developments and can be an articulation of values and expected norms for international behaviour. The people of Myanmar, however, continue to look to the international community for support, and the imposition of targeted sanctions is one way of showing that support, even if they are an imperfect response. Countries also consider the possible consequences of their actions or inactions on their reputation and ability to influence a future democratic government. The actions taken in response to the coup will have an impact on the way a restored democratic government and the people of Myanmar might view and deal with them. Both statements and targeted sanctions can give hope and encouragement to the people of Myanmar and help them sustain their struggle. On the whole, however, Myanmar people feel abandoned by the international community and the United Nations, particularly since witnessing the international response to the war in Ukraine. People from Myanmar have also been dismissive of the role played by ASEAN and its ongoing attempts to facilitate a dialogue with the military's State Administration Council (SAC).

ASEAN-LED ENGAGEMENT

The role of ASEAN in relation to adverse developments within a member state is widely regarded as constrained by its core principle of non-interference in other member states' internal affairs (Suzuki 2019, 158), although in addressing non-traditional security challenges (such as pandemics, climate change, illegal migration and transnational crimes) and trade agreements, ASEAN has deviated from this principle (Caballero-Anthony 2008, 522; Suzuki 2021, 401). It is not surprising that with its diversity of political systems and perspectives, ASEAN's pursuit of accommodation and consensus results in a limited response to political crises (Dosch 2008, 542). It is also argued, in the alternative, that the process of reaching consensus pulls outliers closer to a median position (Connelly 2021).

Since Myanmar's joining ASEAN in 1997, the Association has often faced criticism over its inability to go beyond issuing statements and for its failure to influence Myanmar's military (Haacke 2008, 353). However it is also credited with successfully brokering an agreement enabling ASEAN, the United Nations and other sources of humanitarian assistance to be delivered after Cyclone Nargis hit Myanmar in 2008 (Suzuki 2021, 406).

ASEAN's response to the 2021 coup did not deviate far from its reputation: it sought accommodation and consensus in calling for dialogue towards a peaceful solution and it sought a role for ASEAN in facilitating humanitarian access. The March 2021 Informal ASEAN Ministerial Meeting expressed concern at the situation in Myanmar and called on all parties to refrain from instigating further violence and exercise utmost restraint and flexibility. It called on the parties to seek a peaceful solution through constructive dialogue and practical reconciliation, and expressed ASEAN's readiness to assist Myanmar. The Chair's Statement said, somewhat lamely, that the meeting "heard some calls for the release of political detainees and for the United Nations Secretary-General's Special Envoy on Myanmar to engage the parties concerned" (ASEAN 2021b).

This was the median position. Several outliers — Singapore, Indonesia, Malaysia and the Philippines — wanted more from ASEAN while others wanted less. Singapore Foreign Affairs Minister Vivian Balakrishnan spoke about the importance of the principles enshrined in the ASEAN Charter including adherence to democracy, rule of law, good governance and respect for human rights, and threatened to speak unilaterally which would be to the detriment of the Association if it failed to act. He also called for the immediate release of all political detainees (Singapore MFA 2021). This is a significant departure from ASEAN's tradition of displaying unity and signals an important recalibration of ASEAN principles which previously had privileged the non-interference in the internal affairs of member states principle to the exclusion of all others.

At the April 2021 ASEAN Leaders' Meeting, Commander-in-Chief Min Aung Hlaing attended in person but was denied the courtesies and symbolism usually extended to a head of government. The meeting produced five points of consensus (ASEAN 2021c):

1. Immediate cessation of violence
2. Commencement of constructive dialogue among all parties concerned
3. A special envoy of the ASEAN Chair who will facilitate mediation of the dialogue, with the assistance of the ASEAN Secretary-General

4. ASEAN provision of humanitarian assistance through the ASEAN Coordinating Centre for Humanitarian Assistance on Disaster Management
5. A visit to Myanmar by the Special Envoy and delegation to meet all parties concerned

There was strong international recognition of and support for a role for ASEAN in ending the Myanmar crisis. The United Nations, United States, European Union, China, Russia and other countries expressed support for the Five Point Consensus (UNGA 2021; EU 2021; China 2021; Aljazeera 2021). Shortly after the meeting, Australia commended ASEAN, welcomed the five points of consensus and committed A$5 million to the ASEAN Coordinating Centre for Humanitarian Assistance on Disaster Management (Payne 2021c). However, within Myanmar and among human rights groups there was less enthusiasm for the Consensus and the Special Envoy (Reuters 2021a; Reuters 2021b; Mathieson 2021b). Commentators were quick to point out what was not in the Five-Point Consensus, notably no call for the release of political detainees, no condemnation of the coup, no participation in the meeting by the Committee Representing Pyidaungsu Hluttaw (CRPH)/National Unity Government (NUG) or National League for Democracy (NLD), and no timeline for implementation. Compared with a plethora of statements from governments and UN agencies, ASEAN's response was seen as relatively weak. The majority of articles on ASEAN's response to the coup, from within and outside Myanmar, have been highly critical of the association and even derided those who have expressed support for ASEAN centrality and efforts to encourage a dialogue among the parties as "claptrap" (Mathieson 2021b). Scepticism seemed well-placed when the military council quickly announced that it would consider ASEAN's "suggestions" only after the situation stabilised (Frontier Myanmar 2021b). Nevertheless, it has been argued that ASEAN is better positioned than Western states to shape the international response to the coup (Decker 2021).

In the months following the Five-Point Consensus, ASEAN's Special Envoy was unable to visit Myanmar on acceptable terms including opportunities to meet all parties as agreed in the Five-Point Consensus (Brunei 2021). While the violence had eased it had not ceased, as had been agreed, and the distribution of humanitarian assistance faced restrictions and other difficulties (Kamal 2021). ASEAN Parliamentarians for Human Rights concluded that the Myanmar military had "displayed a flagrant lack of respect for ASEAN, and in fact since the coup, it appears to have used the bloc to try to gain legitimacy while at the same time increasing its brutal reprisals" (APHR 2021). Frustrated by the lack of progress, the United States sent a delegation to Indonesia, Thailand and Singapore in advance of the October Emergency ASEAN Foreign Ministers' Meeting with the public message that there are political and economic levers that can be pulled by the United States and other governments to "pressure the regime to try to give them the kinds of incentives to change their behaviour" (ABC News 2021). Reaching a similar conclusion, and perhaps not wishing the United States to pull those levers, ASEAN foreign ministers agreed to not invite a political representative (i.e., Senior General Min Aung Hlaing) to the October ASEAN Summit and related meetings, including the East Asia Summit. The National Unity Government had requested an invitation but "in view of the competing claims…and to allow Myanmar the space to restore its internal affairs and return to normalcy", the meeting decided to invite an un-named "non-political representative" to the summits (Brunei 2021). However, Myanmar chose to leave its seat empty rather than accept the humiliation of downgraded representation.

While a small step in terms of international pressure on the regime, it was a giant leap for ASEAN. The unprecedented decision to uninvite the person who purported to be the leader of a member state from an ASEAN leaders' meeting is a judgment and action by ASEAN on the internal affairs of a member state (Bland 2021). It represents the elevation of other values and principles embodied in the ASEAN Charter and ASEAN Human Rights Declaration, including the principles of democracy, the rule of law and good governance, and respect for and protection of human rights and fundamental freedoms. These principles were included in ASEAN's statement issued on the day of the coup, which was considered weak at the time, and would become the basis for an unprecedented decision saying, in effect, that these principles are not subservient to the more frequently espoused principles of non-interference and consensus decision-making. Malaysian Foreign Minister Saifuddin Abdullah is reported as saying ASEAN should do some "soul-searching" on its non-interference policy and that ASEAN "cannot use the principle of non-interference as a shield to avoid issues being addressed" (Reuters 2021c). The exclusion of Min Aung Hlaing from high level ASEAN meetings was sustained with his non-invitation, at the insistence of Malaysia, Indonesia, Singapore and Brunei, to the ASEAN-China summit on 22 November 2021 (Irrawaddy 2021b).

ASEAN has shown that it is prepared to not invite political representation from Myanmar to its leader-level meetings, but Myanmar is participating in other ministerial-level meetings and there has been no open discussion among ASEAN members about a next possible step such as suspending or expelling Myanmar from the Association. The ASEAN Charter, the legally-binding framework that underpins ASEAN, contains no explicit provision for the suspension or expulsion of a member and in this sense, it has no obvious coercive power over Myanmar. Article 20 of the Charter provides a process for deciding how to deal with a recalcitrant member: "In the case of a serious breach of the Charter or non-compliance, the matter shall be referred to the ASEAN Summit for decision" (ASEAN 2020). The process that is provided for is unbounded and one could contemplate that the measures open to leaders extend to suspension of a member. However, suspension would weaken ASEAN's ability to engage Myanmar and its diplomatic efforts would be seen to have failed. ASEAN's standing in the eyes of its community and those of the international community would be reduced. Consultation and consensus are likely to remain ASEAN's preferred and overriding principles and it is unlikely there will be an appetite to suspend Myanmar from all meetings while these avenues have not been fully exhausted. ASEAN will continue to rely on persuasion supported by any lingering attachment among Myanmar's military to ASEAN camaraderie and the feelings of comfort and protection that come from being part of the ASEAN family. The tone of shock and feeling of hurt in Myanmar's press statements (Myanmar MFA 2021b; 2021c) reveal a sensitivity to ASEAN action, and perhaps a fear of being ostracized from the bloc. If this is indeed the case, then further exclusion of Myanmar from the plethora of ASEAN ministerial-level meetings might achieve an outcome, even if that is no more than a preparedness by the military to fulfil the undertakings in the Five Point Consensus.

CALLS FOR INTERNATIONAL INTERVENTION AND THE RESPONSIBILITY TO PROTECT

While many in Myanmar rejected a role for ASEAN in facilitating a dialogue between the parties, they called on the United Nations to 'save Myanmar'. This is somewhat surprising as there was widespread antipathy and animosity towards the UN within Myanmar following UN-led efforts to investigate and report on allegations of human rights abuses and the forced exodus of over 700,000 Rohingya into Bangladesh. No doubt the three decades of UN General Assembly resolutions expressing concern at Myanmar's human rights situation and mandating the Secretary-General to promote, amongst other things, democracy encouraged Myanmar's citizens to believe the UN would be on their side this time and able to assist them. The UN Secretary General's statement of "unwavering support of the United Nations to the people of Myanmar" (UNSG 2021), would have raised expectations among Myanmar's citizenry that the international community could and would take action to end the coup. With little understanding of the processes and limitations of the UN they called for the despatch of peacekeepers and by early March were invoking the international community's 'Responsibility to Protect'. On placards, t-shirts and on social media citizens sent the message: "We need R2P – Save Myanmar". They were joined in their calls by 45 former country leaders from the Global Leadership Foundation who implored Secretary-General António Guterres to invoke the Responsibility to Protect (GLF 2021).

Responsibility to Protect (R2P) is the international doctrine guiding responses to mass atrocity situations that was included in the 2005 World Summit Outcome document adopted as a General Assembly resolution at the level of Heads of State and Government. It is characterised as having three pillars: the first is that each state has a responsibility to protect its own population through appropriate and necessary means. The second pillar encourages the international community to assist a country in the exercise of the responsibility to protect. And under the third pillar the international community:

> ...has the responsibility to use appropriate diplomatic, humanitarian and other peaceful means...to help protect populations from genocide, war crimes, ethnic cleansing and crimes against humanity... In this context, we are prepared to take collective action, in a timely and decisive manner, through the Security Council...should peaceful means be inadequate and national authorities manifestly fail to protect their populations (UNGA 2005, 30).

With Security Council permanent members China and Russia unwilling to support collective action against Myanmar, action under the Responsibility to Protect doctrine is not possible. The pleas from within Myanmar for the world to invoke the responsibility to protect, to impose an arms embargo and to put in place a no-fly zone reveal a misplaced faith in the decision-making capacity of the United Nations and its power to intervene with military force. An all-out kinetic conflict with Myanmar's 300,000-plus strong state military would likely be opposed by China (not wanting either conflict or foreign troops in a neighbouring country) and likely ASEAN nations too, fearful of a humanitarian crisis in the region. The "peaceful means" in the third pillar of the R2P offer more realistic options for the international community, in addition to diplomatic efforts and targeted sanctions as discussed above.

The calls to the international community to 'save Myanmar' soon turned into feelings of "intense anger, betrayal, and despair at the United Nations, and the international community more broadly, for doing too little to help the country" (McLaughlin 2021b). In a commentary in *The Irrawaddy*, Naing Khit said, "After two and a half months, however, their condemnations and diplomatic actions, including sanctions on the coup leaders, have had no impact at all" (Naing Khit 2021). On social media signs began to read, "Hello UN, How many dead bodies needed for UN to take action against the military coup. Please Save Myanmar". Another said sarcastically "Just '700' people killed in '70' days. Take your time UN. We still got 'millions' left".[1] These and many other protestor signs, mostly in English and written for an international audience, attempted to achieve what polite requests had failed to do and sought to shame the United Nations and the international community into a more muscular intervention.

Despite China having a strong military capability along its 2,185 km land border with Myanmar, there were no signs requesting help from China. From the perspective of many ordinary people and pro-democracy activists, it was perceived that China was involved in the coup, was supplying technicians and equipment to build an internet firewall and was even deploying soldiers to assist the military's operations. Chinese factories were targeted by arsonists and anti-Chinese protestors gathered in front of the Chinese Embassy in Yangon (McLaughlin 2021a).

Before long, the people of Myanmar came to a more informed and sober understanding of the nature and limits of international responses to the military coup and concluded that it would be up to the people of Myanmar to challenge the military. On 5 March the newly established Committee Representing the Pyidaungsu Hluttaw (CRPH), composed primarily of elected members of the NLD who had managed to flee or were in hiding, published a four-point vision which called for the 2008

Constitution to be rescinded and a new constitution based on principles of federalism to be drafted. These steps, if eventually implemented, would constitute a remaking of the government of Myanmar and its political foundations. In the words of an opinion piece in Mizzima, "It has become quite obvious that 'watching and worrying' strategy by the international community is obviously not working" (Saw Kapi 2021). On 31 March the first draft of a Federal Democracy Charter (Part I) was released, stipulating the fundamental principles and roadmap to address the grievances of all the peoples of Myanmar through a federal democracy, with interim constitutional arrangements (Committee Representing the Pyidaungsu Hluttaw, 2021). On 16 April the Interim National Unity Government was replaced by a 26-member National Unity Government and, two weeks later, it announced the establishment of People's Defence Forces as a forerunner to Federal Democratic Armed Forces (NUG 2021). The protest movement had become a revolutionary cause complete with manifesto and armed acolytes. However, the international community remained reluctant to formally recognise the NUG or to provide weapons in support of the armed resistance.

CONTESTED REPRESENTATION ABROAD: CALLS TO NOT 'LEGITIMISE' THE MILITARY COUNCIL

Since March 2021, people from the revolutionary movement have been pushing foreign governments and various international and regional bodies to formally recognise the NUG as the legitimate representative of the people of Myanmar (AMI 2021). They base their calls on the fact that the majority of leaders that make up the NUG were formally elected in the November 2020 national elections. In parallel, efforts to pursue dialogue with Senior General Min Aung Hlaing and the SAC are condemned as legitimising what is often described as a "terrorist regime". Indeed, there have been numerous statements that any dealing with the military regime helps it to achieve legitimacy and therefore should be resisted (Lee 2021).

On the whole, many countries are reluctant to engage with the SAC due to the growing list of atrocities against civilians. Three powerful countries — Russia, China and India — have publicly sought relationships with the SAC and (not accidentally) conveyed legitimacy to the coup. However, most countries have sought a balancing act: trying to maintain some kind of presence in Myanmar to get an informed understanding of the situation as it unfolds, but also careful not to confer any kind of legitimacy on the military leaders through public acts of support. The calls to recognise the NUG as the legitimate government have not been successful because the calls are for something that isn't generally practised. Most countries recognise states with the requirements for statehood being a defined territory, a government, a permanent population and a capacity to enter into relations with other states (Bergin 1988, 150). The prior policy of recognising governments has fallen from practice. Australia's 1988 switch from recognising both states and foreign governments to recognition of states only was done to avoid conveying (through recognition) either approval or disapproval of a regime (Evans and Grant 1995, 64-65). However, formal recognition is not the only policy option. Foreign governments can and do indicate their attitude to regimes which come to power through unconstitutional means. Indicators of attitude to a new regime are found in ministerial statements (especially statements congratulating a new government or condemning a coup), the conduct of diplomatic relations, and the nature and extent of any ministerial contact and other contacts (for example economic, aid or defence arrangements, technical and cultural exchanges) (Bergin 1988, 151).

There have been occasions when the urge to say or do something has resulted in the policy being ignored. In 2019, in concert with more than 50 countries (Urribarri 2019), the Australian Government took a unique approach to relations with Venezuela, conferring recognition and support for the President of the National Assembly, Juan Guaidó, in assuming the position of interim President (Payne 2019).

While no *government* has officially recognised either the junta or the CRPH/NUG (the French Senate, the upper house of the French parliament, has adopted a resolution calling on the French Government to recognise the National Unity Government (French Senate 2021)), governments have indicated their attitudes through statements condemning the coup, expressing concern at the detention of political leaders or calling for a return to democracy, and also by meeting with CRPH and NUG representatives. The approach has allowed diplomats to engage with all parties and to do so with a degree of political detachment. The Malaysian Foreign Minister, members of the Australian Parliament, Czech Foreign Ministry officials, the US National Security Advisor, amongst others, have all been open about their meetings with the NUG (Nikkei Asia 2022; NUG MFA 2021b). In the United Kingdom, a House of Commons Foreign Affairs Committee report said the National Unity Government should be treated as a government-in-waiting and recommended the UK Government support the NUG by working with its representatives but was silent on the calls for recognition (UK House of Commons 2021).

Similarly, on 7 October 2021 the European Parliament adopted a resolution which, in addition to strongly condemning the coup, declared it "Supports the CRPH and the NUG as the only legitimate representatives of the democratic wishes of the people of Myanmar". It also called on ASEAN and the international community "to include and involve them in genuine and inclusive political dialogue and efforts aimed at the peaceful resolution of the crisis based on respect for the rule of law" (European Parliament 2021). This was seized upon by opponents of the military regime as "the first international legislative body to officially endorse the organisations behind the fight against the military rule" (Irrawaddy 2021a). The EU parliament's resolution prompted the SAC's Ministry of Foreign Affairs to issue a press statement asserting that contact with the CRPH and NUG "could give rise to abetting terrorism" and "lead to the interference in the internal affairs of a sovereign state" (Myanmar MFA 2021a). Despite these warnings, many foreign governments continue to engage with representatives of the NUG, including through Myanmar's Permanent Representative to the United Nations, Kyaw Moe Tun, who was one of the first Myanmar diplomats to join the resistance against the military and pledge his support to the NUG.

Like most states, the United Nations does not have a policy or procedures for the recognition of governments. The UN is concerned instead with membership and the acceptance of credentials from a recognised state. By their very nature international organisations are a collection of government representatives and the question of who represents a country, when there is more than one claim to be the government, is not an uncommon situation. Here we are talking about representation, not membership which is the recognition of the State itself. However, the United Nations was suddenly presented with a dilemma on 26 February 2021 when Kyaw Moe Tun, told the General Assembly, after denouncing the coup, that he would remain loyal to the democratically-elected government. The next day the military council dismissed him and the Ministry of Foreign Affairs advised the UN through a diplomatic note that his deputy would be Myanmar's chargé d'affaires (i.e., acting permanent representative). Kyaw Moe Tun wrote to the President of the General Assembly and to Secretary General António

Guterres to advise that he remained Myanmar's permanent representative to the United Nations (CNN 2021). Recognition of a representative is not the same as recognition of a government, but it is often interpreted as such.

The rules of the UN's Credentials Committee are silent on situations where representation is contested, and different criteria have been invoked over time to address cases of contested representation. Prior to 1991, the Committee put more emphasis on which of the competing claimants was in a position to use state resources in fulfillment of the obligations of membership, that is, which claimant had effective control of the state. Since 1991 more emphasis has been placed on the protection of democracy, especially in jurisdictions where the UN has invested in bringing peace and democracy to a country (Griffin 2000, 746-769).

The silence of the Charter of the United Nations on governments that have come to power through unconstitutional means, and the absence of legal rules on competing claims to representation before the Credentials Committee, mean that the views of the major powers who are members of the Credentials Committee decide who represents Myanmar. Its decision has consequences also for the numerous subsidiary bodies of the United Nations, such as UNDP, UNESCO, UNICEF, UNAIDS and the World Food Program. The General Assembly's decision on credentials is not binding on the other UN bodies but in practice those bodies invariably follow the decision of the General Assembly (Griffin 2000, 732).

In the lead-up to the 76th Session of the General Assembly, there was a concerted campaign in support of allowing the National Unity Government representative to represent Myanmar (SAC-M 2021). The campaign faced an uncertain outlook. The world's enthusiasm for democracy evident in the 1990s had waned in the 21st century and the UN's relationship with the National League for Democracy, which denied most UN agencies access to Rakhine State during and following the forced exodus of over 700,000 Rohingya into Bangladesh, did not augur well. On the other hand, accepting NUG representation would be a stand for democracy and against a regime that had come to power by unconstitutional means and shown little regard for UN commitments, including to human rights. The Credentials Committee postponed a decision on Myanmar's diplomatic representation and, in the meantime, allowed Kyaw Moe Tun to continue to occupy Myanmar's seat (Foreign Policy 2021; Reuters 2021d).

DIALOGUE AND CHANNELS OF COMMUNICATION

It has been argued that the strident international condemnation that followed the 1988 coup "served to solidify the military leadership in a bunker-style mentality against foreigners", making it even harder for humanitarian agencies to work inside the country (Steinberg 2010, 182). The inability of the former UN Special Envoy Christine Schraner Burgener to get approval to travel to Myanmar to talk to all stakeholders is reminiscent of this former bunkering-down approach, rather than engaging in dialogue, in the face of external criticism. Christine Schraner Burgener was able to meet the Senior General in Jakarta on the margins of the April 2021 ASEAN Leaders' Meeting but was denied the opportunity to meet other stakeholders in Myanmar. Similarly symptomatic of the regime's international withdrawal is the six-week delay between ASEAN's five-point consensus and the visit of ASEAN's Secretary-General to discuss, inconclusively, nothing more than who might be the ASEAN Special Envoy (one of the five points), and then when the Special Envoy was eventually appointed, the refusal to allow the envoy to meet all the parties (also as agreed in the Five Point Consensus) (Brunei 2021).

In an example of the necessity and utility of communication, the President of the International Committee of the Red Cross, Peter Maurer, met Senior General Min Aung Hlaing in a bid to resume ICRC prison visits, have more humanitarian access to conflict areas, and to urge an end to violence (Nikkei Asia 2021). Far from legitimising the regime such contacts, by their very nature, are a refusal to accept the status quo. They convey messages of condemnation and they seek to explore options to reduce violence, allow humanitarian access and improve the prospects for a return to democracy. They have no resemblance to Russia and China's engagement which in their content and character convey some legitimacy to the military council — especially when supplying arms to the military in their ongoing campaign of violence against the resistance and ordinary civilians.

Despite the difficulties and notwithstanding the risks of misrepresentation and the appearance of conferring legitimacy, channels of communication with the military council are necessary — whether that be through the auspices of ASEAN, through diplomatic channels or through direct senior military-to-military communications. An open channel of communication provides the insight into the state of mind of the coup leaders and can be used to propose and broker solutions.

While channels of communication are necessary, they might not be sufficient. A willingness on the part of the military leadership to engage is also required and such a willingness is not yet evident. From the military council's point of view, there is little incentive to engage and, on the contrary, a fear that any eventual settlement would involve a new constitution with a reduced role for the military in the government of the country. A return to the status quo ante would expose the pointlessness of the coup and leave Commander-in-Chief Min Aung Hlaing and the military with a tarnished image and legacy. Furthermore, a return to pre-coup partial democracy is no longer accepted by the Civil Disobedience Movement and the CRPH/NUG.

CONCLUSION

Myanmar continues to languish under military rule and the military shows no sign of turning or letting up on the use of whatever force they assess as necessary to stay in power, including execution of opposition actors. The people have not acquiesced to military rule and there are daily incidents of low-level violence against ward administrators, police posts and suspected informants. The situation in Myanmar is by no means settled and the international community is not resigned to accept the status quo, believing there remains a chance to contribute to a peaceful resolution. However, the international community as a whole, as embodied by the United Nations, is unable to make much of a contribution beyond the issuing of statements and the provision of humanitarian assistance. The United Nations Security Council has not managed to adopt a resolution relating to the coup. It was 18 months before a UN Special Envoy was able to visit Myanmar, though she was not permitted to meet Aung San Suu Kyi or other political prisoners. Hope from activists and ordinary civilians that the international community might somehow "save Myanmar" has been replaced by a sobering realisation that, if change is to come, it will have to come from within Myanmar.

Contact for the purpose of expressing opposition to the coup, calling for a return to democracy and the release of political detainees, or facilitating dialogue is useful and necessary. It is the minimum that can be expected from the international community. The junta's bristling at the downgrading of Myanmar's representation at the October 2021 ASEAN Summit reveals a sensitivity to non-inclusion in the grouping. It remains to be seen whether ASEAN has the appetite to be more determined in its dealings with Myanmar and how Myanmar might respond to further exclusion from ASEAN. The UN's troubled relationship with Myanmar's military leadership, still evident in the inability of its Special Envoy to meet Aung San Suu Kyi, combined with its need to maintain humanitarian operations in Myanmar, constrain its ability to broker a peaceful outcome.

International pressure has a poor track record in terms of changing the mindset of Myanmar's military and this has led to calls for the international community to adopt bolder policies and back a national uprising (Marciel, 2022). Neither side, 18 months after the coup, appear to believe that dialogue and a negotiated settlement is preferable to armed confrontation. Nevertheless, as seen with the August 2022 visit to Naypyitaw of the new Special Envoy of the UN Secretary-General, Noeleen Heyzer, international responses, even if imperfect and lacking immediate effect, are likely to continue with the related goals of facilitating dialogue between the parties and averting further loss of life and a humanitarian crisis. Ultimately, though, Myanmar's future will be determined by the people of Myanmar and not by the international responses seen so far.

Notes

1 Links to the Facebook posts have not been included to protect the identity of individuals.

References

ABC News (2021). "Official: US at turning point in dealing with Myanmar crisis". *ABC News*, 22 October. Available at https://abcnews.go.com/US/wireStory/official-us-turning-point-dealing-myanmar-crisis-80701893 (accessed 23 October 2021).

ACFID (2022). "Australia continuing to avoid direct sanctions on the Myanmar military". *Australian Council for International Development*, media release, 2 May. Available at https://acfid.asn.au/media-releases/australia-continuing-avoid-direct-sanctions-myanmar-military (accessed 12 September 2022).

Aljazeera (2021). "Russia backs ASEAN consensus on Myanmar crisis". *Aljazeera News*, 6 July. Available at https://www.aljazeera.com/news/2021/7/6/russia-backs-asean-consensus-on-myanmar-crisis (accessed 26 July 2021).

AMI (2021). "Open Letter to Governments around the World". *Australia Myanmar Institute*, media release, 15 June. Available at https://scholarsformyanmar.eu/letter.html (accessed 28 July 2021).

APHR (2021). "Open Letter to ASEAN Leaders Re: Myanmar's presence at the ASEAN Summit". *ASEAN Parliamentarians for Human Rights*, 13 October. Available at https://aseanmp.org/wp-content/uploads/2021/10/Open-Letter-Myanmars-presence-at-the-ASEAN-Summit.pdf (accessed 17 October 2021).

ASEAN (2020). *The ASEAN Charter*. Jakarta: Association of Southeast Asian Nations, 28th reprint. Available at https://asean.org/storage/November-2020-The-ASEAN-Charter-28th-Reprint.pdf (accessed 19 June 2021).

-----(2021a). "ASEAN Chairman's Statement on The Developments in The Republic of the Union of Myanmar". *Association of Southeast Asian Nations Secretariat*, 1 February. Available at https://asean.org/asean-chairmans-statement-on-the-developments-in-the-republic-of-the-union-of-myanmar-2/ (accessed 21 October 2021).

-----(2021b). "Chair's Statement on the Informal ASEAN Ministerial Meeting (IAMM)". Jakarta: Association of Southeast Asian Nations. Available at https://asean.org/chairs-statement-informal-asean-ministerial-meeting-iamm/final-chairmans-statement-on-the-iamm/ (accessed 19 June 2021).

-----(2021c). "Chairman's Statement on the ASEAN Leaders' Meeting, 24 April 2021 and Five-Point Consensus". *Association of Southeast Asian Nations*, 24 April. Available at https://asean.org/chairmans-statement-asean-leaders-meeting-24-april-2021-five-point-consensus/ (accessed 4 August 2021).

Australian Parliament (2021a). *Official Hansard*. Joint Standing Committee on Foreign Affairs, Defence and Trade, 13 April. Available at https://parlinfo.aph.gov.au/parlInfo/download/committees/commjnt/310c8f82-55bc-4002-983e-40a8e4e29ac7/toc_pdf/Joint%20Standing%20Committee%20on%20Foreign%20Affairs,%20Defence%20and%20Trade_2021_04_13_8658_Official.pdf;fileType=application%2Fpdf#search=%22committees/commjnt/310c8f82-55bc-4002-983e-40a8e4e29ac7/0000%22 (accessed 21 July 2021).

Australian Parliament (2021b). *Official Hansard*. Joint Standing Committee on Foreign Affairs, Defence and Trade, 13 May. Available at https://parlinfo.aph.gov.au/parlInfo/download/committees/commjnt/8b22a686-a11a-4a21-bda8-d03e67baf414/toc_pdf/Joint%20Standing%20Committee%20on%20Foreign%20Affairs,%20Defence%20and%20Trade_2021_05_13_8756_Official.pdf;fileType=application%2Fpdf#search=%22worthaisong%20DFAT%20committees%22 (accessed 22 June 2021).

Bergin, Anthony (1988). "The New Australian Policy on Recognition of States Only". *Australian Journal of International Affairs* (December).

Bland, Ben (2021). "ASEAN muddles through on Myanmar". *The Interpreter*, Lowy Institute for International Affairs, 22 October. Available at https://www.lowyinstitute.org/the-interpreter/asean-muddles-through-myanmar (accessed 24 October 2021).

Boutros-Ghali, Boutros (1995). "Statement to an agenda for peace: Position paper of the Secretary-General on the occasion of the fiftieth anniversary of the United Nations". United Nations General Assembly A/50/60, 25 January.

Brunei (2021). "Statement of the Chair of the ASEAN Foreign Ministers' Meeting". Brunei Ministry of Foreign Affairs, 16 October. Available at http://www.mfa.gov.bn/Lists/Press%20Room/news.aspx?id=947&source=http://www.mfa.gov.bn/site/home.aspx (accessed 17 October 2021).

Caballero-Anthony, Mely (2008). "Non-traditional security and infectious diseases in ASEAN: going beyond the rhetoric of securitization to deeper institutionalization". *The Pacific Review* 21 (4): 507-525.

Callahan, Mary (2016). "Fears of a military coup in Myanmar are exaggerated". *Nikkei Asia*, 14 December. Available at https://asia.nikkei.com/Politics/Fears-of-military-coup-in-Myanmar-are-exaggerated (accessed 2 May 2022).

Chang, Lennon Y.C. and Nicholas Coppel (2020). "Building cyber security awareness in a developing country: Lessons from Myanmar". *Computers & Security* 97.

Charney, Michael W. (2009). *A History of Modern Burma*. Cambridge: Cambridge University Press.

China (2021). "Wang Yi talks about the Situation in Myanmar". *Ministry of Foreign Affairs of the People's Republic of China*. 8 June. Available at https://www.fmprc.gov.cn/mfa_eng/zxxx_662805/t1882086.shtml (accessed 28 July 2021).

CNN (2021). "A fight is brewing over Myanmar's seat at the United Nations", *CNN news report*, 3 March. Available at https://edition.cnn.com/2021/03/02/world/myanmar-united-nations-ambassador-intl-latam/index.html (accessed 19 June 2021).

Committee Representing the Pyidaungsu Hluttaw (2021). *Federal Democracy Charter*. Available at https://crphmyanmar.org/wp-content/uploads/2021/04/Federal-Democracy-Charter-English.pdf (accessed 19 June 2021).

Connelly, Aaron (2021). "Why ASEAN's rebuke of Myanmar's top general matters". *International Institute for Strategic Studies*, 21 October 2021. Available at https://www.iiss.org/blogs/analysis/2021/10/why-aseans-rebuke-of-myanmars-top-general-matters (accessed 12 September 2022).

Cortright, David and George A. Lopez (2002). *Smart Sanctions: Targeting Economic Statecraft*. New York: Rowman & Littlefield.

David, Roman and Ian Holliday (2012). "International sanctions or international justice? Shaping political development in Myanmar". *Australian Journal of International Affairs*, 66 (2): 121-138.

Decker, Barry (2021). "ASEAN's Myanmar dilemma". *East Asia Forum*, 23 May. Available at https://www.eastasiaforum.org/2021/05/23/aseans-myanmar-dilemma/ (accessed 12 September 2022).

Dosch, Jörn (2008). "ASEAN's reluctant liberal turn and the thorny road to democracy promotion". *The Pacific Review* 21 (4): 527-545.

Drezner, Daniel W. (2011). "Sanctions Sometimes Smart: Targeted Sanctions in Theory and Practice". *International Studies Review*, March 2011 13 (1): 96-108.

EU (2021). "Myanmar: Statement by High Representative Josep Borrell on the outcome of the ASEAN Summit". *European Commission*, Brussels, 24 April. Available at https://eeas.europa.eu/headquarters/headquarters-homepage/97200/myanmar-statement-high-representative-josep-borrell-outcome-asean-summit_en (accessed 28 July 2021).

European Parliament (2021). "Resolution on the human rights situation in Myanmar, including the situation of religious and ethnic groups". Resolution 2021/2095 (RSP). Available at https://www.europarl.europa.eu/doceo/document/TA-9-2021-0417_EN.html (accessed 16 October 2021).

Evans, Gareth and Bruce Grant (1995). *Australia's Foreign Relations in the World of the 1990s*, 2nd ed, Melbourne: Melbourne University Press.

Foreign Policy (2021). "US and China Reach Deal to Block Myanmar's Junta From U.N.". *Foreign Policy*, 13 September. Available at https://foreignpolicy.com/2021/09/13/myanmar-united-nations-china-biden-general-assembly/ (accessed 18 October 2021).

Forum Asia (2021). "ASEAN: Failure to meet with all parties neglects ASEAN's own five-point consensus". *Forum Asia*, 7 June. Available at https://www.forum-asia.org/uploads/wp/2021/06/Statement-by-419-organisation-on-the-visit-of-ASEAN-Delegations.pdf (accessed 19 June 2021).

French Senate (2021). *"Resolution portant sur la nécessité de reconnaître le Gouvernment d'unité nationale de Birmanie"*. Senat: 647 (2020-2021), 5 octobre 2021. Available at http://www.senat.fr/leg/tas21-002.html (accessed 23 October 2021).

Frontier Myanmar (2021a). "Min Aung Hlaing's constitutional crisis". *Frontier Myanmar*, 12 February. Available at https://www.frontiermyanmar.net/en/min-aung-hlaings-constitutional-crisis/ (accessed 12 September 2022).

Frontier Myanmar (2021b). "Frontier Fridays". *Frontier Myanmar*, 30 April. Available at https://mailchi.mp/frontiermyanmar.net/general-walks-back-asean-agreements?e=90549c231c (accessed 22 June 2021).

Frontier Myanmar (2021c). "Frontier Fridays". *Frontier Myanmar*, 25 June. Available at https://mailchi.mp/frontiermyanmar.net/clashes-in-urban-mandalay-ytfbme52j5?e=90549c231c (accessed 26 June 2021).

GLF (2021). "GLF Letter to UN Secretary General on Myanmar". *Global Leadership Foundation*, 29 March. Available at https://www.g-l-f.org/glf-letter-to-un-secretary-general-on-myanmar/ (accessed 28 July 2021).

Griffin, Matthew (2000). "Accrediting Democracies: Does the Credentials Committee of the United Nations Promote Democracy Through its Accreditation Process, and Should It?". *New York University Journal of International Law and Politics* 32 (3): 725-786.

Haacke, Jürgen (2008). "ASEAN and Political Change in Myanmar: Towards a Regional Initiative?". *Contemporary Southeast Asia*, 30 (3): 351-78.

Han, Enze (2021). "China does not like the coup in Myanmar". *East Asia Forum*, 6 February. Available at https://www.eastasiaforum.org/2021/02/06/china-does-not-like-the-coup-in-myanmar/?utm_source=newsletter&utm_medium=email&utm_campaign=newsletter2021-02-07 (accessed 10 March 2022).

Holliday, Ian (2011). *Burma Redux: Global Justice and the Quest for Political Reform in Myanmar*. New York: Columbia University Press.

Huang, Roger Lee (2020). *The Paradox of Myanmar's Regime Change*. Routledge: London.

ICG (2021). "Responding to the Myanmar Coup". *International Crisis Group*, Asia Briefing No. 166, 16 February.

Irrawaddy (2021a). "European Parliament Throws Support Behind Myanmar's Shadow Government". *The Irrawaddy*, 8 October. Available at https://www.irrawaddy.com/news/european-parliament-throws-support-behind-myanmars-shadow-government.html?__cf_chl_jschl_tk__=pmd_E6lJqg5zScBK_GQgWdbTmuUMffpisXXjm6xlD.pz6_I-1634334992-0-gqNtZGzNAmWjcnBszQm9 (accessed 16 October 2021).

Irrawaddy (2021b). "Myanmar Coup Leader Min Aung Hlaing Barred From China-ASEAN Summit". *The Irrawaddy*, 19 November. Available at https://www.irrawaddy.com/news/burma/myanmar-coup-leader-min-aung-hlaing-barred-from-china-asean-summit.html (accessed 10 March 2022).

Japan (2021). *Ministry of Foreign Affairs* website. Available at https://www.mofa.go.jp/region/asia-paci/myanmar/index.html (accessed 21 June 2021).

Kamal, Adelina (2021). "An inconvenient ASEAN-led approach to Myanmar crisis". *The Jakarta Post*, 24 October.

Kyaw Phyo Tha (2021). 'A Military Coup in Myanmar Is Unlikely, But....'. *The Irrawaddy*, 27 January. Available at https://www.irrawaddy.com/opinion/commentary/military-coup-myanmar-unlikely.html (accessed 13 May 2022).

Lee, Chen (2021). "ASEAN's huge gamble on Myanmar". *The Interpreter*, Lowy Institute, 24 May. Available at https://www.lowyinstitute.org/the-interpreter/asean-s-huge-gamble-myanmar (accessed on 16 October 2021).

Malaysia, Government of (2021a). "Latest Situation in Myanmar", Embassy of Malaysia in Yangon, 1 February. Available at https://www.kln.gov.my/web/guest/-/latest-situation-in-myanmar (accessed 21 June 2021).

Malaysia, Government of (2021b). "The adoption of the United Nations General Assembly resolution on the situation in Myanmar, 18 June 2021". Ministry of Foreign Affairs Malaysia Press Release, 19 June 2021. Available at https://www.kln.gov.my/web/guest/-/the-adoption-of-the-united-nations-general-assembly-resolution-on-the-situation-in-myanmar-18-june-2021 (accessed 10 March 2022).

Marciel, Scot (2022). "It's Time to Help Myanmar's Resistance Prevail". *United States Institute of Peace*, 22 August. Available at https://www.usip.org/publications/2022/08/its-time-help-myanmars-resistance-prevail (accessed 7 September 2022).

Marinov, Nikolay (2005). "Do Economic Sanctions Destabilize Country Leaders?". *American Journal of Political Science* 49(3): 564-576.

Mathieson, David Scott (2021a). "Can a UN Arms Embargo on Myanmar Work?". *The Irrawaddy*, 24 August. Available at https://www.irrawaddy.com/opinion/guest-column/can-a-un-arms-embargo-on-myanmar-work.html?__cf_chl_jschl_tk__=pmd_aXbOjLsexAR1qHgGMExnf5b14PGDEQDIh17u.wlnl1Q-1634251747-0-gqNtZGzNAlCjcnBszQll (accessed 15 October 2021).

Mathieson, David Scott (2021b). "ASEAN Diplomatic Deftness on Myanmar is Claptrap". *The Irrawaddy*, 6 August. Available at https://www.irrawaddy.com/opinion/asean-diplomatic-deftness-on-myanmar-is-claptrap.html?fbclid=IwAR3hSPAtiTjPp0Lpu9zru0Te0EaG37GEsAPWa7yV4OgfnS_Lp2riFBoGP5o (accessed 23 October 2021).

McLaughlin, Timothy (2021a). "China is the Myanmar Coup's 'Biggest Loser'". *The Atlantic*, 23 February. Available at https://www.theatlantic.com/international/archive/2021/02/what-myanmars-coup-means-china/618101/ (accessed 19 June 2021).

McLaughlin, Timothy (2021b). "No One is Saving Myanmar", *The Atlantic*, 24 April.

Ministry of Foreign Affairs (2021a). *Ministry of Foreign Affairs Press Statement*. Naypyitaw: Myanmar Ministry of Foreign Affairs, 9 October. Available at https://www.mofa.gov.mm/press-statement-9/ (accessed 23 October 2021).

Myanmar MFA (2021b). Ministry of Foreign Affairs Press Release, Nay Pyi Taw, 16 October 2021. Available at https://www.mofa.gov.mm/press-release-6/ (accessed 23 October 2021).

Myanmar MFA (2021c). Ministry of Foreign Affairs Press Release, Nay Pyi Taw, 22 October. Available at https://www.mofa.gov.mm/press-release-7/ (accessed 23 October 2021).

Myanmar Now (2021). "Commander-in-Chief says 'Constitution can be repealed'", Available at Commander-in-chief says 'constitution can be repealed' | Myanmar NOW (myanmar-now.org), Myanmar Now, 28 January (accessed 20 April 2022).

Naing Khit (2021). "How Many Mass Killings Are Enough Before the World Helps Myanmar?", *The Irrawaddy*, 14 April. Available at https://www.irrawaddy.com/opinion/commentary/many-mass-killings-enough-world-helps-myanmar.html (accessed 19 June 2021).

Nikkei Asia (2021). "International Red Cross head meets Myanmar junta chief in Naypyitaw". *Nikkei Asia*, 3 June. Available at https://asia.nikkei.com/Spotlight/Myanmar-Crisis/International-Red-Cross-head-meets-Myanmar-junta-chief-in-Naypyitaw (accessed 28 July 2021).

Nikkei Asia (2022). "Malaysia foreign minister meets counterpart from Myanmar shadow government". *Nikkei Asia*, 15 May. Available at https://asia.nikkei.com/Spotlight/Myanmar-Crisis/Malaysia-foreign-minister-meets-counterpart-from-Myanmar-shadow-govt (accessed 29 May 2022).

Nilsen, Marte, Amara Thiha, Ilaria Carrozza and Oystein H. Rolandsen (2021). "China in Myanmar: Complex Engagements, Complicated Relations". PRIO Policy Brief 06/2021, Peace Research Institute Oslo. Available at https://legacy.prio.org/Publications/Publication/?x=12766 (accessed 9 March 2022).

NUG (2021). "Announcement of the Establishment of People Defence Forces, Notification 1/2021, 5 May". National Unity Government. Available at https://www.burmalibrary.org/en/announcement-of-the-establishment-of-peoples-defence-force-national-unity-government-notification (accessed 19 June 2021).

NUG MFA (2021). National Unity Government Ministry of Foreign Affairs website. https://mofa.nugmyanmar.org/latest-news/ (accessed 27 October 2021).

Nyun, Thihan Myo (2008). "Feeling Good or Doing Good: Inefficacy of the U.S. Unilateral Sanctions Against the Military Government of Burma/Myanmar". *Washington University Global Studies Law Review* 7 (3): 455-518.

OHCHR (2021). "Human rights implications of the crisis in Myanmar". Resolution adopted by the Human Rights Council on 12 February 2021, A/HRC/RES/S-29/1. United Nations Human Rights Council. Available at https://undocs.org/A/HRC/RES/S-29/1 (accessed 21 October 2021).

Oo, Dominic and Liu, John (2021). "Investors Spooked by Myanmar Crisis as Economy Braces for Free Fall". *The Diplomat*, 20 October. Available at https://thediplomat.com/2021/10/investors-spooked-by-myanmar-crisis-as-economy-braces-for-free-fall/ (accessed 22 October 2021).

Pape, Robert A., (1997). "Why Economic Sanctions Do Not Work". *International Security* 22 (2): 90-136.

Payne, Marise (2019). "Statement on Venezuela", 28 January. Available at https://www.foreignminister.gov.au/minister/marise-payne/media-release/statement-venezuela (accessed 7 March 2022).

Payne, Marise (2021a). "Statement on Myanmar", 1 February. Available at https://www.foreignminister.gov.au/minister/marise-payne/media-release/statement-myanmar (accessed 21 June 2021).

Payne, Marise (2021b). "Statement on Myanmar", 7 March. Available at https://www.foreignminister.gov.au/minister/marise-payne/media-release/statement-myanmar-0 (accessed 21 June 2021).

Payne, Marise (2021c). "Statement on ASEAN Leaders' Meeting", 25 April. Available at https://www.foreignminister.gov.au/minister/marise-payne/media-release/statement-asean-leaders-meeting (accessed 12 September 2022).

Payne, Marise (2021d). "Joint Statement of Support for the Special Envoy of the ASEAN Chair on Myanmar". Media Release, 15 October. Available at https://www.foreignminister.gov.au/minister/marise-payne/media-release/joint-statement-support-special-envoy-asean-chair-myanmar (accessed 23 October 2021).

Peksen, Dursun (2009). "Better or Worse? The Effect of Economic Sanctions on Human Rights". *Journal of Peace Research* 46 (1): 59-77.

Peksen, Dursun and A. Cooper Drury (2010). "Coercive or Corrosive: The Negative Impact of Economic Sanctions on Democracy". *International Interactions* 36 (3): 240-264.

Reuters (2021a). "Myanmar activists deride ASEAN-junta consensus, vow to continue protests", 26 April. Available at https://www.reuters.com/world/asia-pacific/myanmar-people-slam-asean-junta-consensus-end-violence-no-immediate-protests-2021-04-25/ (accessed 19 June 2021).

Reuters (2021b). "Myanmar civil society groups reject regional envoy". *Reuters*, 6 August. Available at https://www.reuters.com/world/asia-pacific/myanmar-civil-society-groups-reject-regional-envoy-2021-08-06/ (accessed 17 October 2021).

Reuters (2021c). "ASEAN should re-think non-interference policy amid Myanmar crisis, Malaysia FM says". *Reuters*, 21 October. Available at https://www.reuters.com/world/asia-pacific/asean-should-rethink-non-interference-policy-amid-myanmar-crisis-malaysia-fm-2021-10-21/ (accessed 25 October 2021).

Reuters (2021d). "U.N. committee agrees Taliban, Myanmar junta not allowed in U.N. for now". *Reuters*, 2 December. Available at https://www.reuters.com/world/asia-pacific/taliban-myanmar-junta-unlikely-be-let-into-un-now-diplomats-2021-12-01/ (accessed 9 March 2022).

SAC-M (2021). "SAC-M Briefing Paper: Recognition of Government". Special Advisory Council for Myanmar, 23 August. Available at https://specialadvisorycouncil.org/wp-content/uploads/2021/08/SAC-M-Briefing-Paper-Recognition-of-Governments-ENGLISH.pdf (accessed 18 October 2021).

Saw Kapi (2021). "Myanmar's potential solution from within". *Mizzima Myanmar News*, 21 March. Available at https://www.mizzima.com/article/myanmars-potential-solution-within?fbclid=IwAR3chwQcF9bQWMjS6VwzQxmH6oRN5OcGOk4MoWYlOOc4X4HLvE4zguyYPeI (accessed 19 June 2021).

Selth, Andrew (2018). "All Going According to Plan? The Armed Forces and Government in Myanmar". *Contemporary Southeast Asia* 40 (1).

Singapore MFA (2021). "Minister for Foreign Affairs Dr Vivian Balakrishnan's Intervention at the Informal ASEAN Ministerial Meeting on 2 March 2021 at 1600 hours". Singapore Ministry of Foreign Affairs, 2 March. Available at https://www.mfa.gov.sg/Newsroom/Press-Statements-Transcripts-and-Photos/2021/03/02032021-IAMM (accessed 18 October 2021).

Steinberg, David I. (2010). *Burma/Myanmar – What Everyone Needs to Know*. Oxford: Oxford University Press.

Suzuki, Sanae (2019). "Why is ASEAN not intrusive? Non-interference meets state strength". *Journal of Contemporary East Asia Studies* 8 (2): 157-176.

Suzuki, Sanae (2021). "Interfering via ASEAN? In the Case of Disaster Management" *Journal of Current Southeast Asian Affairs* 40 (3): 400-417.

Tan, Anna (2021). "China and the Myanmar dilemma". Lau China Institute, King's College London, Policy Series 2021 – China in the World. Available at https://www.kcl.ac.uk//lci/assets/lci-policy-paper-china-and-the-myanmar-dilemma.pdf (accessed 15 October 2021).

Tostensen, Arne and Beate Bull (2002). "Are Smart Sanctions Feasible?". *World Politics* 54 (3): 373-403.

Turkey, Republic of (2021). Ministry of Foreign Affairs. Press Releases No.45, 79, 102, and 124, issued on 1 February, 28 February, 15 March and 27 March respectively. Available at https://www.mfa.gov.tr/sub.en.mfa?fd9f46da-96b0-4a85-89a8-aaad5f5bb833 (accessed 21 June 2021).

UK House of Commons (2021). "The UK Government's Response to the Myanmar Crisis". *House of Commons Foreign Affairs Committee*. Available at https://committees.parliament.uk/publications/6773/documents/72101/default/ (accessed 21 July 2021).

UNGA (2005). "Resolution adopted by the General Assembly on 16 September 2005 – 2005 World Summit Outcome", United Nations General Assembly A/RES/60/1. Available at https://documents-dds-ny.un.org/doc/UNDOC/GEN/N05/487/60/pdf/N0548760.pdf?OpenElement (accessed 9 March 2022).

UNGA (2021). "The situation in Myanmar". United Nations General Assembly Resolution A/RES/75/287. Available at https://undocs.org/en/A/RES/75/287 (accessed 16 October 2021).

United Kingdom Government (2021). "Condemning the coup in Myanmar: G7 Foreign Ministers' statement". 3 February. Available at https://www.gov.uk/government/news/condemning-the-coup-in-myanmar-g7-foreign-ministers-statement (accessed 22 July 2021).

United Nations (2021). "Myanmar: Joint Statement by UN Special Representative of the Secretary-General for Children and Armed Conflict & the UN Special Representative of the Secretary-General on Violence Against Children", 1 April. Available at https://violenceagainstchildren.un.org/news/myanmar-joint-statement-un-special-representative-secretary-general-children-and-armed-conflict (accessed 21 June 2021).

United States Government (2021). "Biden-Harris Administration Actions in Response to the Coup in Burma". *White House Fact Sheet*, 11 February. Available at https://www.whitehouse.gov/briefing-room/statements-releases/2021/02/11/fact-sheet-biden-harris-administration-actions-in-response-to-the-coup-in-burma/ (accessed 21 June 2021).

UNSC (2021). "Security Council Press Statement on Situation in Myanmar", *United Nations Security Council*, SC/14460, issued 4 February. Available at https://news.un.org/en/story/2021/02/1083852 (accessed 18 June 2021).

UNSG (2021). "Violence, Intimidation, Harassment by Myanmar Security Personnel Unacceptable, Secretary General Says, Also Expressing Concern over Restrictions on Internet". *United Nations Secretary-General*, statement issued by the Spokesperson for UN Secretary-General on 14 February, SG/SM/20581. Available at https://www.un.org/press/en/2021/sgsm20581.doc.htm (accessed 21 June 2021).

Urribarri, Raul Sanchez (2019). "Australia's Recognition of Juan Guaidó as Venezuela's Interim President". Australian Outlook, 24 March. Available at https://www.internationalaffairs.org.au/australianoutlook/australia-recognition-venezuela-interim-president-guaido/ (accessed 14 January 2022).

US Defense (2021). "Joint Statement of Chiefs of Defense Condemning Military-Sponsored Violence in Myanmar". *US Department of Defense*, media release, 27 March. Available at https://www.defense.gov/Newsroom/Releases/Release/Article/2552778/joint-statement-of-chiefs-of-defense-condemning-military-sponsored-violence-in/ (accessed 21 June 2021).

US Embassy in Myanmar (2021). Joint Statement by Diplomatic Missions in Myanmar, 29 January. Available at https://mm.usembassy.gov/joint-statement-by-diplomatic-missions-in-myanmar/ (accessed 7 September 2022).

Weiss, Thomas G. (1999). "Sanctions as a Foreign Policy Tool: Weighing Humanitarian Impulses". *Journal of Peace Research* (36) 5: 499-509.

VI
Epilogue

13

ON DISAPPOINTMENT AND HOPE: MYANMAR STUDIES AND THE MULTIPLE CRISES

Michael R. Dunford and Dinith Adikari

We are in an era of both crisis and disappointment: the hopes and plans of millions have been ruined by the myriad political-economic problems caused by COVID-19, but mostly by the impact of Myanmar's military coup. However, within disappointment, there is generative potential. Amidst the chaos and despair caused by the coup, a revolutionary movement has grown, pointing towards new and innovative political possibilities for Myanmar. This revolutionary turn has been indexed by a radical decolonial turn in Myanmar-focused academia: even in the "ivory tower", many desire a fundamental shift in the terms of engagement. We view this decolonising movement as part of a revolutionary zeitgeist in Myanmar right now, a historical conjuncture in which the terms of political engagement are being renegotiated across the board. In this contested historical moment, we see potential for disappointment and frustration to drive a kind of paradoxical optimism. Much of the work being done now, in politics as in academia, is being done under the assumption that the future will be better than the present, that there is something worth working toward both in the politics of Myanmar itself and in Myanmar-focused research. The purpose of this concluding chapter is to trace a line from disappointment to revolution, and to consider what directions Myanmar research might be able to take in the future.

We will begin with a meditation on disappointment and frustration, with a particular focus on people who grew up during the "transition" (people born between the late 1990s and the 2010s — so-called Generation Z), who came of age during the peak of Myanmar's recent international research engagement. Unlike older generations, who have seen cycles of liberalism and military authoritarianism, Generation Z has never really had to contend directly with military dictatorship in Myanmar. They are disappointed, and they are angry. From there, we will examine how this anger has produced not only a revolutionary political movement within Myanmar, but also a radical shift towards decolonial praxis in Myanmar studies (see for example, Chu May Paing and Than Toe Aung 2021; Tharaphi Than 2022) — a shift that is still somewhat nascent, but undeniably an important feature of contemporary Myanmar research. This radical shift has productively combined with ongoing debates about research ethics in Myanmar (see Brooten and Metro 2014), producing research on Myanmar that foregrounds ethical conduct and careful attention to the politics of social research itself (see for example, Toomey 2022). These shifts, we argue, are hopeful: they demonstrate a "fidelity to the future" (Thompson 2016) of Myanmar as a country and to Myanmar studies as an academic field. We will finish by exploring possible avenues for future research on Myanmar in light of all the aforementioned considerations.

DISAPPOINTMENT: A NEW GENERATION AGAINST THE GENERALS

Disappointment is as much a concrete, bodily feeling as it is an abstract notion about the present state of affairs. It signals a changed way of relating to the world: places and processes that once brought excitement can suddenly bring pain. Imagined futures — hopeful ones, or even neutral ones — disappear, and unease sets in. It is something that one feels in the gut, an instantaneous clench-release discomfort in the pit of one's stomach. At the same time, disappointment is political. Disappointment is "a space where moral compasses and political righteousness are troubled by a world that is not what it should be" (Greenberg and Muir 2022, 308). Disappointment is the space of failed potentials, weak returns on investment, and the anger that comes when someone or something falls short of one's expectations. Whether visceral or political, disappointment is always accompanied by questions: How did we get here? How has it come to this? Can anything be done to reverse this course of events? At first glance, "disappointment" almost seems like too weak a word to describe the affective consequences of Myanmar's 2021 military coup and the subsequent political, economic and social crises the country finds itself in. Much stronger, more active emotions have also been at play: rage, against the military and the Bamar establishment; pride, in the CDM, the street protestors, and the revolution's martyrs; and above all, dogged perseverance, the will to keep living and keep imagining a future. However, we have chosen to meditate on disappointment because of its specific orientation toward the world "as it once was," or as it could have been. Disappointment considers the present in light of the past.

Myanmar, right now, is certainly "not what it should be" (ibid.). The current state of play can easily be imagined otherwise: as of 2022, anyone under the age of 30 will have grown up and entered adulthood during Myanmar's "transition", a period of massive political-economic liberalisation (Chachavalpongpun, Prasse-Freeman, and Strefford 2020; Jones 2014; Rhoads and Wittekind 2018; Stokke and Aung 2020). Some will have voted in two, or even three elections; they will have witnessed the reduction of foreign sanctions on Myanmar and an enormous influx of foreign capital. They will have read relatively open and free newspaper articles, scrolled Facebook, and listened to music on mobile phones made possible by a liberalised media sector that would have been utterly unimaginable under the former dictator, Than Shwe. For anyone born after about 1995, the coup is an aberration, an abnormality, and a massive political rupture. It is hugely disappointing. For Generation Z, the coup is not a return to normal: it is a disaster, and they are angry about it. To make matters worse, the coup came on top of the COVID-19 pandemic, which stalled this generation's education, destroyed many burgeoning careers, forced many into debt and insecurity and threw their entire world into uncertainty. The social consequences of the pandemic were only made more severe by the virus itself, killing thousands during the delta wave outbreak in mid-2021. And as the pandemic raged on, the political problems associated with the coup only deepened, forcing hundreds of thousands to flee — not only violence, but also an inability to make ends meet. The generation who came of age in a politically liberalising and economically booming Myanmar feels as though their future has been stolen. As they navigate post-coup Myanmar, they are repeatedly confronted with the foreclosing of possibility, with "the ruins of the future" (Aung 2019, 199).[1]

Myanmar's university students have been especially disappointed by COVID-19 and the coup. In Myanmar, university students are considered archetypal political activists, and symbols of the cutting edge of national political and economic progress. During the transition period, many students were seen as key participants in the burgeoning civil society sector and were already building connections to a global world. Study abroad programs and foreign-sponsored research programs exploded at Yangon University and Mandalay University. Myanmar's universities had long been symbols of cosmopolitanism, flattened and suppressed by military regimes; it looked like they were once again becoming lively sites of (relatively) open discourse. For Generation Z, the transition period signified the emergence of educational opportunities not available to their parents' (or even older siblings') generations, and the palpable sense that — with a civilian government in power — there might be a way for ordinary people to have a stake in the future of Myanmar. International engagement stalled in late 2017, when the Rohingya genocide caused many international partners to suddenly become skittish of bilateral partnerships in Myanmar; however, this setback, from the perspective of many students, was temporary rather than definitive. The fact that the Rohingya genocide or the wars in Kachin and Shan states could be publicly critiqued at all was taken by many to be a sign of the success of the liberalising movement of the transition period.

In some ways, the conference that produced this volume — the "Myanmar Update", hosted bi-annually by the Australian National University's Myanmar Research Centre (ANU-MRC) — is a product of the transition period.[2] When the Myanmar Research Centre was established in 2015, it sought to engage more openly and allow for more exchange with politicians, students, researchers and activists from Myanmar. The conference was conceived (and still strives to be) an event that specifically targets students and researchers within Myanmar and brings them into dialogue with the global Myanmar studies community. The conference conveners began planning the 2021 Myanmar Update in 2020 — before the coup, but after the COVID-19 outbreak. They were thus fully prepared for a largely online, COVID-safe conference. However, the fact of the coup, and the chaos that it caused, meant that many Myanmar researchers were suddenly not in a position to participate. Distance-participation technologies double as surveillance technologies: in the wake of the coup, anything said over the airwaves was assumed to be compromised. Some scholars asked to present their conference papers anonymously; others pulled out altogether. Some still participated, and chose to show their face (including some of the authors in this volume) — they chose to do so at significant personal risk, and did so in defiance of the Sit Tat's vast surveillance apparatus. The lively intellectual community that boomed during the "transition" years appeared to have been shuttered, and the opportunities for Myanmar scholars to connect to the outside world seemed to have collapsed.

The point here is that the disappointments caused by COVID-19 and the coup, felt viscerally by millions in Myanmar, have been indexed by similar frustrations and disappointments even in the relatively rarified context of academia. However, socio-political shifts happening in Myanmar have been indexed in the Myanmar research community in other, more positive ways as well. For some, the disappointments of the early 2020s— and the rage, the disbelief, the sadness—have been channeled into calls for radical change. The street protestors and the CDMers call their movement the "Spring Revolution"; in Myanmar studies, this revolutionary energy has been indexed by calls for fundamentally restructuring the political, methodological, and ethical stakes of Myanmar-focused research. We now turn to those calls, and their consequences for this field.

NEW DIRECTIONS IN MYANMAR RESEARCH: CHANGING THE TERMS OF ENGAGEMENT

One of the goals of this conclusion is to point out how disappointment — and rage, and heartbreak — can be generative. The popular political movement that has exploded in response to the February 2021 coup has been astounding, and has sparked a political interest in revolution that has even reached the relatively conservative and slow-moving domain of academia. There is a movement amongst Myanmar scholars to decolonise Myanmar studies, a movement that is tightly indexed to the revolutionary movement in the country at large. In this section, we will briefly highlight some of the notable voices in this movement, and the impacts that their work has had on the academic community. Although the work we discuss here has generally not been written in explicit alignment with the Spring Revolution or the responses to the coup, we think that the timing is not coincidental. The Spring Revolution's calls for a fundamental reworking of Myanmar politics and society have unleashed a revolutionary zeitgeist that could rewrite the script not only of Myanmar studies, but — if the projects we outline below continue apace — of area studies more broadly. We also note that this revolutionary and decolonial ethos will be especially potent if it can be brought into dialogue with conversations about research risk and ethics that began during the "transition" period (cf. Brooten and Metro 2014), which we will also mention below. If taken together, these interventions stand to have a major impact on the field of Myanmar studies, especially in the way that foreign researchers engage with local researchers and local research collaborators — that is, if the calls to decolonise Myanmar studies are taken seriously.

We will begin with the most radical intervention and proceed towards more incremental ones. In mid-2021, Chu May Paing and Than Toe Aung published an article critiquing the "pervasive whiteness" of Myanmar studies. Although their frustrations (and the genesis of the article) began long before the coup, the coup exacerbated the split they identify between white academics (who are assumed to be foreigners and outsiders) and Myanmar people (both academics and "ordinary" people). Disappointment — and especially disappointment with Myanmar studies establishment — is a major theme for Chu May Paing and Than Toe Aung. As they point out, research carries very different risks for foreign researchers compared to local researchers: many of the activities that constitute safe and benign "research methods" for outsiders — collecting screenshots, news articles, and evidence of military brutality — would induce punishment, jail time, or worse if they were carried out by people inside Myanmar. From their view, foreign (especially white) researchers should begin their research from this premise. Their vision for the impacts of their essay is very explicit: white researchers should feel "guilt and shame" for their orientialisation, gatekeeping, and reliance on colonial tropes; "Local and Native" (to Myanmar) researchers should "come together, create initiatives, and brainstorm plans to create ethical and decolonial research culture in Burma Studies circles" (ibid.). Put differently, the terms of Myanmar studies should be decided by people who actually live in Myanmar. Inasmuch as conducting research is a political act, the politics of research should be dictated by researchers with subaltern identities who have active family and social ties to Myanmar. Chu May Paing and Than Toe Aung are calling for a fundamental change in the terms of engagement in Myanmar studies — if not the abolition of "Myanmar studies" as an entire disciplinary domain. "Talking Back to White 'Burma Experts'" is part of a post-2021 boom of scholarly writing aimed at reframing the cultural politics of Myanmar studies, and prying open space for non-white voices in scholarly discourse about Myanmar. This boom indexes a wider shift, which is at least coeval with (if not caused by) the Spring Revolution.

For Chu May Paing and Than Toe Aung, the starting point for moving forward is dismantling the "neocolonial" structures that produce knowledge about Myanmar. For others, the starting point should be a focus on the interests and values of scholars local to Myanmar, whose ideas about what constitutes meaningful research do not necessarily align with white, western (i.e., colonial) rubrics. Cultural historian Tharaphi Than (2021) has lamented how her colleagues in Myanmar universities are often "self-Orientalised" when they must cite and perform mastery of (very dated!) Western-written ethnography of Myanmar. They feel they have to do this to be taken seriously as social scientists, but their interests lie elsewhere — for example, they are more interested in understanding daily life and lived experience in Myanmar *right now*. This leads to a kind of paradox: Myanmar scholars of Myanmar cannot study the topics that are close to their hearts, because there is no precedent for research on those topics. Only when a white scholar ratifies these topics as legitimate do they begin to carry weight. From Tharaphi Than's perspective, decolonisation of the academy has already begun in Myanmar, but it has begun "at the margin" (ibid), and is being done by students more than those who have institutional power (faculty and administrators). She does not cite Chu May Paing and Than Toe Aung, but her piece is clearly addressing a problem directly related to the one that they raise; it is possible that they are counted among the scholars and students who Tharaphi Than identifies as already engaged in decolonial work. The call for decolonisation here is less of a critique of white (and "outsider") scholars than it does as a meditation about what decolonisation will mean for the scholarly community already inside Myanmar itself (her piece grew out of her reflections on a workshop held in Yangon). The common thread is that these are both injunctions about what Myanmar studies can and should do *for Myanmar people*.

Tharaphi Than argues that the movement to decolonise Myanmar studies is part of a "global" shift (2021) currently taking place in the academy. There is some reason to believe that she is correct, even outside of the social sciences and humanities. A related (albeit much less radical) discussion is even happening in the natural sciences: Myanmar scholars have recently argued that "parachute research" (Zin-Maung-Maung-Thein and Khin Zaw, 2021) — research conducted by fly-in/fly-out scholars who do not go through formal academic channels — is damaging to the scientific community within Myanmar. Zin-Maung-Maung-Thein and Khin Zaw are focused less on fundamental changes in the academy, and more on how foreign researchers ought to build lasting connections to Myanmar institutions and use Myanmar-focused scientific research as a way to build a global research network that is *inclusive* of Myanmar researchers. Their criticisms have been taken seriously by the amber paleontology community, and the aforementioned Burmese authors also joined a more recent study on the ethics of Myanmar-focused paleontological research (Dunne et al. 2022), which highlights the importance of collaborative (rather than extractive) scientific research. Neither Khin-Maung-Maung-Thein and Khin Zaw nor Dunne et al. employ theoretically-inflected language like "decolonise" or "anticolonial," but their serious reflections on the ethical stakes of Myanmar-focused research are evidence in favor of Tharaphi Than's hypothesis about the political shift already underway in academic research.

By some accounts, the Myanmar studies community has been "particularly attentive to issues of decolonisation and neo-coloniality", not only in the wake of the coup, but since at least the 2010s (Fumagalli and Kemmerling 2022). However, for authors like Chu May Paing and Than Toe Aung, Myanmar studies clearly has not gone far enough. Given the efflorescence of works like those mentioned in the previous paragraphs of this section, it is clear that the "decolonial turn" has not yet gone far enough in Myanmar studies, and it has become part of the zeitgeist of the Spring Revolution. For scholars like Chu May Paing, Than Toe Aung, and Tharaphi Than, the people's revolution will be coterminous with a revolution in the way people conduct scholarship about Myanmar. Their calls are not for a "transition," but for a fundamental change in the way that outside (especially white, Western) researchers approach Myanmar studies, and how researchers local to Myanmar conceptualise their work. Some scholars have already begun to adopt explicitly decolonial approaches to Myanmar, and combine them with ethical considerations already taking place within Myanmar Studies. For example, education scholar Nisha Toomey, whose research focuses on Myanmar migrants in the Mae Sot area, has drawn on Black and Indigenous scholarly practices to assess her research participants' comfort with and interest in her work. She has developed methodological tools for this: she has generated a list of topics that she will explicitly *avoid*, about which she (as a white outsider) is not "entitled" to speak (Toomey 2022, 137); she also actively asked research participants to self-assess their interest in her project. The purpose of the former intervention is to declare, openly, that her ability to speak on certain issues is circumscribed not only by her training but also by her personal identity and experiences. By acknowledging these gaps, she intended to create a more equitable environment for conducting her research. It seems to have worked, as her interlocutors — mostly leaders of Community Based Organisations (CBOs) in the Mae Sot area — were very open with her: they expressed deep cynicism towards academic researchers in general, and Myanmar political experts in particular. Her interlocutors also expressed a desire for research to "go back" (Toomey 2022, 133) to the communities who provided the data for it.

The above interventions all consist of published scholarly research. Alongside these relatively public interventions, there is a movement amongst Indigenous organisations and Indigenous researchers[3] to call for direct, visible, and explicit collaboration between foreign (or even Bamar) researchers and Indigenous groups. It has not been well-documented in scholarly literature, but both authors of this conclusion have encountered it in academic research settings and consultancy settings. Indigenous-led organisations in Myanmar are already staffed by highly capable researchers, and should be useful starting points for collaborations in either academic or applied research.[4] However, engaging these groups is politically and ethically complex, and even fraught. Indigenous activist organisations are politicised within their own communities and in Myanmar writ large: when researchers choose to work with one group or another, they are not making neutral decisions, but political ones. Direct collaboration with Indigenous organisations thus requires careful ethical considerations. However, based on conversations with multiple researchers who do identify as Indigenous, there is increasing frustration that foreign researchers do not rely on partnerships with Indigenous researchers (or at least researchers local to Myanmar). Foreign and local researchers would both benefit if local partners within Myanmar were given the space to lead the research process from the beginning — in other words, if people historically in the role of "fixers" and "research assistants" were viewed instead as "collaborators" with parallel skills and equal (or even deeper) insights. Even a relationship between individual researchers is rife with ethical complications: there is a massive power imbalance between foreign researchers coming from wealthy institutions with global reach, who do not have to live with the day-to-day political pressures inside Myanmar, and local researchers inside Myanmar who could (and likely would) come under scrutiny for making public comments about contentious political, social, or environmental issues.

Some of these ethical considerations have been at the forefront of Myanmar Studies for years already. In 2014, the *Journal of Burma Studies* released a special issue on the particular complexity of ethical issues in the Myanmar context (Brooten and Metro 2014). From the perspective of 2021, it seems worth revisiting this scholarship in light of the revolutionary energy currently surging through Myanmar politics writ large, and the Myanmar research community on a smaller scale. To some extent, Toomey's work could be read as pushing that 2014 conversation from *Burma Studies* in a new direction, more suitable to the post-coup context. The future of Myanmar studies will benefit greatly if these conversations about ethics can be brought into dialogue with the more revolutionary calls we outlined above (Toomey's work is already a step in this direction). Even as calls for the decolonisation of Myanmar studies become more urgent, scholarly research runs an ever-increasing risk of working as a form of surveillance: all online activity, especially when it is politically sensitive, can very easily fall into the wrong hands and "double" as intelligence material, aiding hostile states in tracing dissidents (Driscoll and Schuster 2018). Some work is already being done to counteract the surveillance-like aspect of online research: scholars like Courtney Wittekind (Wittekind and Faxon 2022) have developed online research methods that center an ethical approach; others, like Matthew Venker (2022), have turned to historical anthropology and archival research so that their work will not interfere with people's daily lives in crisis-stricken Myanmar. We hope that these are the beginnings of a renewed focus on research ethics in Myanmar, which will be applicable to a wide variety of situations where research is being carried out amidst political conflict.

FIDELITY TO THE FUTURE: ACTING NOW, FOR THE LONG HAUL

We find *hope* in these critiques of Myanmar studies, in this desire to fundamentally change the terms of Myanmar-focused research. Hope can be about reading disappointment in reverse. Disappointment comes from the distance between the present condition of the world and an enduring idea about what the world should be: it centers past goals, past ideals, and brings them to bear on an unsatisfactory present. Hope, on the other hand, is mainly concerned with a world that is yet-to-be. Hope has a futurity that disappointment lacks. Summarising the politics of Ernst Bloch, political theorist Peter Thompson describes a politics of hope as a politics based on "fidelity to an event that has not yet happened" (Thompson 2016 p. 442). This "event" is the formation of a "utopia", which — for Bloch — is "not a programmatic [utopia] laid down in any blueprint but...processual and autopoietic: it would emerge out of the process of its own becoming" (ibid.). Bloch's politics of hope is thus not aimed at the creation of a millenarian utopia — a "heaven-on-earth", as it were — but a pragmatic one: a world that is better than the one we live in, a world made better by constant and incremental actions in the present. Pragmatic, but not programmatic. This kind of pragmatic utopia — this politics of hope, in other words — is roughly what Myanmar political activists are claiming when they self-describe the 2021 uprising as the "Spring Revolution". The broad activist consensus around the word "revolution" is important for understanding the general political direction of this particular moment. In calling the post-coup uprising a "revolution", activists are signaling their dissatisfaction with the liberalising 2010 and 2015 governments: where the "transition" failed to deliver a sustainable new form of democratic governance, the "revolution" is poised to provide *something* better than Myanmar's current crisis, even if the specifics of this revolutionary future are still undecided.

In this post-coup period, old hopes are competing with (and being replaced by) new hopes, and ever more radical demands (see also Pedersen, this volume). In the so-called "transition period," the timeline of hope was protracted, and the people of Myanmar were essentially asked to have faith in a slow process. Hope was parsed incrementally. The coup cast "transition" rhetoric in a new light, and raised new question: was the transition discourse made in bad faith? If the slow transition amounted to nothing, why not speed up the process? The temporal orientation of hope was compressed, away the from the future, towards the present: by labeling the anti-coup action the Spring Revolution, the protestors and anti-coup activists began operating as though the movement was their cause (evident in the popular chant, *"doe ayei, doe ayei!"*),[5] an active movement, not a reactive one. By emphasising "revolution" as the "cause" of the grassroots political movements of 2021, activists and protestors de-emphasise the coup, and redirect attention to political possibility (rather than political foreclosure). We view this shift in emphasis as evidence of a proleptic temporal orientation within the Spring Revolution. "Prolepsis" refers to behaving as though a future condition has already arrived: when a story's narrator begins with events that happen at the chronological end of the story, they are engaging in prolepsis; likewise, labeling the street protests and the Spring Revolution as *"doe ayei"* is an act of declaring that, through protest, the people have already started to win — rather than merely rejecting the military coup, protestors make active claims to establish an alternative political future.

The future of Myanmar is uncertain, and the prognoses are mostly pessimistic. However, we maintain that this pessimistic outlook should not preclude continuing research engagement with the country. If anything, academic and development researchers are particularly well-positioned to funnel resources and work or training opportunities into the hands of people in and outside the country at a time when many programs and sources of external funding are rapidly drying up. The Myanmar studies community spent the transition years building projects, developing research networks, and collaborating with local experts within Myanmar itself; abandoning these relationships would be a terrible mistake. We hope that the Myanmar research community feels the same sense of urgency that we do to maintain these networks and relationships and find a way for researchers within Myanmar itself to keep doing their work and continue Myanmar's lively academic traditions. There are barriers to these collaborations, some of which we have already mentioned: surveillance of academics and public figures of all kinds is at its most intensive since the pre-transition years; Internet access is spotty, and the living situation of almost everyone directly involved in politics is extremely precarious. We also acknowledge that the power dynamic (and disproportionate burden of risk) between outside researchers and local researchers within Myanmar can lead to exploitation without recourse: developing Myanmar-focused social science methodologies that are attentive to these risks and power relations should be a top priority for Myanmar studies going forward.

This is also not to exaggerate the role that social research can play in the day-to-day lives of anyone in Myanmar. The catastrophic social problems exacerbated by the coup will not go away, regardless of how much economic or sociological research is done. However, what Myanmar research can do is twofold. First, as mentioned above, Myanmar researchers located outside of Myanmar can funnel resources and opportunities back into the country, to those researchers whose lives have been made immeasurably more difficult by the coup. Furthermore, the Myanmar studies community can focus our research towards political possibilities, economic interventions, and social changes that might be able to mitigate the damages of the coup. This is not to say that Myanmar research must be "applied" research, but that it can be attuned to the socio-political consequences of writing, researching, and even reading. The massive social changes that took place during the "transition period" are still ongoing: social media has reshaped markets (Faxon and Wittekind 2022) and reorganised the politics of language (Myat The Thitsar 2022); according to friends inside Myanmar, privately-funded educational initiatives are still appearing even in junta-controlled Yangon and Mandalay. The Myanmar studies community can play a positive role in providing tools for making sense of these changes. However, this role will be most beneficial if research begins from careful methodological consideration of the risks and benefits involved to people on the ground in Myanmar. Careful attention to ethical and methodological risks is especially important in the post-coup world, when affiliation with foreign institutions is all the more risky and people's lives and livelihoods are at stake.

ACKNOWLEDGEMENTS

The authors would like to thank Justine Chambers and Samuel Hmung for their helpful reviews of this piece, as well as all of the participants in the Myanmar Update conference.

Notes

1 Geoffrey Aung, in the article cited above (2019), is arguing for a reworking of the futures imagined by historical radical movements within Myanmar. Stephen Campbell (Campbell 2021) and Aung Kaung Myat (Aung Kaung Myat 2022) have also joined Aung in redirecting attention towards movements and individuals who have imagined more emancipatory or more inclusive versions of Myanmar politics. Elliott Prasse-Freeman has also followed this line of research, with a greater focus on grassroots movements and "daily" politics (Prasse-Freeman 2012; 2015). As these scholars argue, Myanmar politics have already been imagined otherwise: put into the context of this edited volume, Generation Z have grown up not only amongst liberalisation and transition, but amongst the ghosts of even more radical political possibilities.
2 A bi-annual Myanmar Update was hosted by the Department of Political and Social Change at the ANU beginning in 1999. When the Myanmar Research Centre was established in 2015, it assumed responsibility in hosting the update.
3 The English term "Indigenous" is contested in Myanmar (Dunford 2019), and comprehensive coverage of the debates surrounding it is outside the scope of this paper (Baird 2016; Thawnghmung 2016; Cheesman 2017; Morton 2017). Here, we use "Indigenous" because it is the term of self-identification used by the groups we mention.
4 Examples of Indigenous-led research organisations include, but are not limited to (listed alphabetically): Chin Human Rights Organisation (CHRO), Kachin Development Networking Group (KDNG), Kachinland Research Centre (KRC), Karen Environmental and Social Action Network (KESAN), Karenni Independence Through Education (KITE), among many others; there are also many organisations led by ethnic groups who do not self-identify as "Indigenous" but would nonetheless provide similar starting points for local collaborations, including Oamyeal Development Institute for Highland Communities (ODIHC), Shan Women's Action Network (SWAN), Ta'ang Women's Organisation (TWO), and many more.
5 The oft-repeated protest slogan "doe ayei, doe ayei" literally means "our cause, our cause!" or "our business, our business!" It is an old slogan, not a new one, and has been part of Myanmar's protest lexicon for decades.

References

Aung, Geoffrey. 2019. "Reworking Bandung Internationalism: Decolonization and Postcolonial Futurism in Burma/Myanmar." *Critical Asian Studies* 51 (2): 198–209.

Aung Kaung Myat. 2022. "The Machine That Went Rogue." *Himal Southasian*. June 28, 2022. Available at https://www.himalmag.com/the-machine-that-went-rogue-third-force-myanmar-2022/ (accessed 15 March 2023).

Baird, Ian G. 2016. "Indigeneity in Asia: An Emerging but Contested Concept." *Asian Ethnicity* 17 (4): 501–5.

Brooten, Lisa, and Rosalie Metro. "Thinking about Ethics in Burma Research." *Journal of Burma Studies* 18, no. 1 (2014): 1–22.

Campbell, Stephen. 2021. "Negotiating Antifascist Solidarity across Ethnic Difference in Myanmar: Bhamo Tin Aung's *Yoma Taikbwe*." *Critical Asian Studies*, June, 1–21.

Chachavalpongpun, Pavin, Elliott Prasse-Freeman, and Patrick Strefford. 2020. *Unraveling Myanmar's Transition: Progress, Retrenchment, and Ambiguity Amidst Liberalization*. 京都大学学術出版会.

Cheesman, Nick. 2017. "How in Myanmar 'National Races' Came to Surpass Citizenship and Exclude Rohingya." *Journal of Contemporary Asia* 47 (3): 461–83.

Chu May Paing and Than Toe Aung. 2021. "Talking Back To White 'Burma Experts.'" *AGITATE! Journal*. Available at https://agitatejournal.org/talking-back-to-white-burma-experts-by-chu-may-paing-and-than-toe-aung/ (accessed 16 March 2023).

Driscoll, Jesse, and Caroline Schuster. "Spies like Us." *Ethnography* 19, no. 3 (September 1, 2018): 411–30.

Dunford, Michael R. 2019. "Indigeneity, Ethnopolitics, and Taingyinthar: Myanmar and the Global Indigenous Peoples' Movement." *Journal of Southeast Asian Studies* 50 (1): 51–67.

Fumagalli, Matteo, and Achim Kemmerling. 2022. "Development Aid and Domestic Regional Inequality: The Case of Myanmar." *Eurasian Geography and Economics* 0 (0): 1–30. https://doi.org/10.1080/15387216.2022.2134167.

Greenberg, Jessica, and Sarah Muir. 2022. "Disappointment." *Annual Review of Anthropology* 51 (1): 307–23.

Jones, Lee. 2014. "The Political Economy of Myanmar's Transition." *Journal of Contemporary Asia* 44 (1): 144–70.

Morton, Micah F. 2017. "Indigenous Peoples Work to Raise Their Status in a Reforming Myanmar," May. Available at https://think-asia.org/handle/11540/7021 (accessed 15 March 2023).

Myat The-Thitsar. 2022. "Empowering or Endangering Minorities? Facebook, Language, and Identity in Myanmar." *Asian Ethnicity* 23, no. 4: 718–40.

Prasse-Freeman, Elliott. 2012. "Power, Civil Society, and an Inchoate Politics of the Daily in Burma/Myanmar." *The Journal of Asian Studies* 71 (2): 371–97.

———. 2015. "Grassroots Protest Movements and Mutating Conceptions of 'the Political' in an Evolving Burma." In *Metamorphosis: Studies in Social and Political Change in Myanmar*, edited by Renaud Egreteau and François Robinne, 69–100. Singapore: NUS Press.

Rhoads, Elizabeth L., and Courtney T. Wittekind. 2018. "Rethinking Land and Property in a 'Transitioning' Myanmar: Representations of Isolation, Neglect, and Natural Decline." *Journal of Burma Studies* 22 (2): 171–213.

Stokke, Kristian, and Soe Myint Aung. 2020. "Transition to Democracy or Hybrid Regime? The Dynamics and Outcomes of Democratization in Myanmar." *The European Journal of Development Research* 32 (2): 274–93.

Tharaphi Than. 2022. "Why Does Area Studies Need Decolonization?" Critical Asian Studies Commentaries. Available at https://criticalasianstudies.org/commentary/2021/11/20/commentary-tharaphi-than-why-does-area-studies-need-decolonization (Accessed 16 March 2023).

Thawnghmung, Ardeth Maung. 2016. "The Politics of Indigeneity in Myanmar: Competing Narratives in Rakhine State." *Asian Ethnicity* 17 (4): 527–47.

Thompson, Peter. 2016. "Ernst Bloch and the Spirituality of Utopia." *Rethinking Marxism* 28 (3–4): 438–52.

Toomey, Nisha. 2022. "Researcher's Refusals: Ethical Dilemmas, Ethical Practices in Qualitative Research. Interviews on the Thailand-Myanmar Border." In *Handbook of Qualitative Cross-Cultural Research Methods: A Social Science Perspective*, edited by Pranee Liamputtong, 121–41. Cheltenham, United Kingdom: Edward Elgar Publishing Limited.

Venker, Matthew. 2022. "An Anthropologist in the Archives: Colonial Sources, Contemporary Resonances, and Studying Myanmar from Afar". (Lecture, the Inya Institute, Yangon, Myanmar, and online, 23 September 2022).

Wittekind, Courtney T., and Hilary Oliva Faxon. 2022. "Networks of Speculation: Making Land Markets on Myanmar Facebook." *Antipode* n/a, no. n/a. Accessed November 7, 2022.

INDEX

A
Academic sector
 18-21, 323-24, 326-27, 327-35
Agricultural sector
 8, 9, 15, 240
Arakan Army (AA)
 49, 100, 114-115, 276
Armed Resistance
 5, 6, 7, 46, 57-61, 107-109, 116, 129, 142, 172, 278
Association for Southeast Asian Nations (ASEAN)
 10, 16, 17, 38, 193, 245, 266, 267, 269, 272, 276, 279, 280, 281, 289, 290, 291, 295, 297-301, 303, 306, 308, 310
Aung San Suu Kyi
 3, 4, 7, 12, 13, 16, 33, 34, 36, 38, 42, 44, 47, 53, 54, 63, 97, 104, 263, 264, 266, 268, 269, 272-77, 281, 290, 291, 292, 293, 309, 310
Australia
 10, 193, 197, 242, 245, 290, 291, 293, 295, 299, 305

B
Business sector
 15, 51, 194-95, 201, 241-3, 245-50, 251-52

C
Chin National Front (CNF)
 6, 49, 128, 146
Chin State
 37, 46, 49, 60, 110, 137, 143, 145-46, 147
China
 7, 8, 16, 34, 38, 62, 97, 140, 141, 187-90, 191-92, 195, 250-52, 263, 264, 265-67, 268-77, 280, 292, 296, 296, 299, 300, 302, 303, 304, 308
Civil Disobedience Movement (CDM)
 General
  4, 6, 14, 19, 37, 45, 50, 74, 99, 111, 115, 128, 141, 143, 144, 159-61, 236, 238, 242, 246, 249, 281, 309, 325
 Political positionality
  165-68
 Solder defections
  7, 57, 60-2, 171, 278
 Tactical creativity
  14, 160, 163-65, 167-70, 175
Civil-Military Relations
 34, 37, 41, 48, 53-6, 97, 103, 149, 264, 267

Civil Society
    63, 99, 102, 114, 242, 243, 278, 293
Committee Representing the Pyidaungsu Hluttaw (CRPH)
    7, 47, 48, 112, 277, 282, 299, 303, 305, 306, 309
Constitutional matters
    General
        44, 54, 55, 97, 98, 104, 147, 151, 290
    2008 Constitution
        11, 34, 43, 54, 56, 97, 98, 104, 107, 136, 267, 280, 290, 303
Coup d'etat (2021)
    Causes of
        51-53, 97-8
    Economic consequences
        198-201, 204-205, 237-41
    General
        4, 8, 12, 14, 35, 41-42, 45, 63, 95, 105, 114, 127, 159, 199, 216, 235-36, 263, 265, 277-79, 281-82, 289, 292-94, 298, 323, 325, 327, 335
COVID-19
    Economic consequences
        186, 190-97, 203-04, 214, 222-23, 228, 230-31, 235, 238-9, 277
    General
        3, 9, 12, 13, 14, 15, 17, 19, 69, 72-4, 111, 113, 115, 141, 213, 216-19, 281, 323, 325-26, 327
    Health crisis
        69, 72, 74, 224
    Lockdown restrictions
        3, 15, 72, 213-15, 220, 224, 226, 229
    Military handling
        73, 80-4, 102, 238, 278
    NLD's handling
        15, 52, 72, 76, 77, 238
    Prisoners' experiences
        69-71, 74-87,
    Vaccines
        72, 73, 82, 140, 238
Crisis
    Terminology
        17-21, 31-32, 71, 85-87
Cyclone Nargis
    97, 268, 298

D
Death penalty
    9, 102
Debt
    9, 11, 190, 196
Drug trafficking
    51, 188, 194

E
Economic Crisis
    3, 14, 50-51, 194-95, 197, 199-200, 216, 236, 281
Education sector
    11, 101, 113, 143, 146, 165, 238, 325, 335
Elections
    2015 elections
        34, 52, 54, 106, 264, 273, 281
    2020 elections
        3, 4, 41, 44, 52, 56, 73, 97, 106, 107, 242, 273, 304
    Military planned elections
        17, 43, 44-45, 98
Environmental matters

8, 10, 15, 18, 141, 203-4, 227, 229-31, 244, 271
Ethnic activism
10, 166-167
Ethnic Armed Organisations (EAOs)
See "Ethnic Resistance Organisations (EROs)"
Ethnic Resistance Organisations (EROs)
ERO governance
109, 113-115, 125-6, 127, 132, 139-42, 149
General
6, 7, 10, 12, 13, 32-3, 34, 46, 47, 48-50, 51, 59, 61, 96, 99, 100, 104, 108-09, 111, 116, 125-27, 128, 129, 142, 147-49, 150
Ethno-national conflict (long-term)
11, 32, 34, 36, 49, 58, 103-104, 116, 127, 129
European Union (EU)
10, 187, 188, 190, 196-97, 200, 243, 245, 267, 270, 274, 275, 291, 293, 295, 299, 306
Extraction initiatives/activities
12, 51, 139, 141, 192, 244, 248-49, 251, 270

F
Federal army
47, 48, 49, 304
Federalism
12, 37, 50, 95, 99, 100, 102-06, 116, 117, 127, 135-37, 150-51
Federal Democracy Charter (FDC)
6, 10, 13, 47, 128, 129, 136, 147, 150, 304

Fishing communities
General
15, 215, 223-29
Illegal, Unreported and Unregulated (IUU) fishing
15, 215, 217, 220, 226-30
Foreign investment
15, 16, 185, 189, 191, 194-95, 200, 241-42, 245-53, 270, 274, 278, 281
Foreign affairs
Diplomacy
16, 43, 261-63, 308-309
Negative neutralism
262-65, 266-68, 272-79, 280, 281
Positive non-alignment
262-65, 269-72, 280
Recognition of NUG
99, 106, 304-307

G
Gender equality
5, 10, 11, 163, 197, 198, 202-3, 214, 226, 230
General Administration Department (GAD)
44, 54, 99, 110, 132, 138, 139
General Strike Committee (GSC)
6, 99, 103, 166-68
Governance:
Subnational
14, 95-6, 99, 110-15, 117, 137-38, 148
ERO
109, 113-15, 125-26, 127, 132, 139-42, 147, 148
Literature
133-35

H
Health sector
    3, 18, 74, 101, 143, 145, 159, 238
Humanitarian crisis
    9, 18, 41, 147, 237, 276

I
India
    8, 37, 62, 187, 266, 276, 280, 295, 304
Indigenous concerns/activism
    10, 141, 150, 331
Interim Chin National Consultative Council (ICNCC)
    126, 144, 146
International Criminal Court (ICC)
    52, 59, 290
International Response (to the coup)
    General
    16-17, 38, 54-5, 149, 244-45, 289-90, 309-10
    Initial Responses to the coup
    290-94
    Responsibility to Protect
    301-04

K
Kachin Independence Organisation (KIO)
    6, 49, 100, 128, 141
Kachin State
    12, 34, 110, 276, 326
Karen National Union (KNU)
    6, 49, 100, 114, 128, 139, 140, 141
Karen State
    34, 37, 110, 114

Karenni National Progressive Party (KNPP)
    6, 128, 140, 141, 144
Karenni (Kayah) State
    37, 46, 49, 60, 110, 137, 143-45, 147, 149
Karenni State Consultative Council (KSCC)
    126, 144-45

L
Labour rights/movement
    10, 160, 167

M
Majority-minority relations
    10-12, 36, 49, 61, 100, 103-07, 114, 129, 135-37, 280
Magway Region
    6, 46, 107, 142, 147
Mandalay
    107, 110, 142
Migration
    10, 14, 186, 190, 196
Military rule
    General
    101, 150, 280, 309-310
    1962-1988
    33, 36, 102, 263, 264, 266, 280
    1988-2010
    33-34, 97, 98, 263, 264, 266-68, 280, 308
    2021 Coup d'etat
    See separate entry for "2021 Coup d'etat"
    Sit Tat
    See separate entry for "Sit Tat"

Militias
  Pro military
    62
  People's Defence Forces (PDFs)
  See separate entry for "People's Defence Forces"
Min Aung Hlaing
  4, 42, 43, 52-55, 57, 58, 63, 97, 98, 265, 277-79, 290, 292, 294, 295, 298, 300, 304, 308, 309
Myanmar Economic Holdings Limited (MEHL)
  10, 241, 244, 245, 247
Myanmar Economic Cooperation (MEC)
  10, 241, 244, 245
Myanmar National Democratic Alliance Army (MNDAA)
  114

N
National League for Democracy (NLD)
  4, 7, 10, 11, 12, 13, 16, 33, 36, 37, 38, 41, 42, 44, 47-8, 52, 54, 55, 74, 97, 98, 104-05, 107, 127, 144, 166, 201, 238, 264, 266, 272-77, 278, 290, 293, 299, 303, 307
National Unity Consultative Committee (NUCC)
  6, 13, 47, 64, 99, 103, 105, 107, 128-29, 144, 147, 150
National Unity Government (NUG)
  7, 10, 13, 37, 47, 48, 49, 50, 60, 95, 99, 100, 102, 103, 106, 109, 110, 112, 113, 115, 116, 125, 126, 127, 135, 142-43, 147, 148, 150, 166, 244, 277, 279, 282, 289, 299, 300, 304-07, 309
New Mon State Party (NMSP)
  140
Non-violent resistance
  14, 47, 47, 104, 112, 160-64

P
Peace process (2011-2020)
  11, 43, 103-04, 276, 281
People's Defence Forces (PDFs)
  General
    6, 7, 48, 70, 99, 100, 106, 108-109, 112, 126, 129, 172, 304
  Governance
    126, 135, 142-43, 149
  Women's participation
    100
Political prisoners
  10, 13, 69-70, 80-84, 107, 269, 292, 298
Poverty
  3, 9, 201-02
Protests
  1988
    33, 59, 292
  2021
    4-5, 45, 98, 100, 159-60, 161, 163-65, 169, 277, 292-93
Pyithu Aochoteye a'Pweh (PAPs)
  112, 126, 142-43

R
Rakhine State
  12, 34, 96, 114-115, 264, 274, 276, 281, 307
Refugees
  8, 9, 38

Remittances
    15, 190, 196
Restoration Council of Shan State (RCSS)
    140
Revolution
    10, 12, 13, 17, 21, 37, 47, 61-63, 95, 100, 107, 116, 127-29, 130, 147-52, 167-68, 304, 323-24, 327, 332-34
Rohingya
    12, 16, 35, 36, 52, 54, 58, 97, 115, 241, 264, 272, 274, 275, 276, 281, 291, 292, 295, 296, 302, 307, 326
Rule of Law
    9, 44, 82, 292
Russia
    7, 8, 38, 62, 251, 278, 292, 295, 299, 302, 304, 308

S

Sagaing Region
    6, 8, 15, 46, 49, 60, 96, 107, 112-13, 142, 147
Sanctions
    10, 16, 17, 97, 236, 243-45, 274, 281, 292, 294-97
Self-reliance
    115, 137
Shan State
    12, 34, 96, 114, 276, 326
Sit Tat
    General
        43, 53-56, 58-61, 62, 150, 236, 241, 266-68, 274, 276, 277-79
    Legacies of colonialism
        172-175
    Defections
        7, 57, 60-2, 171, 278
    Leadership
        45, 53
Spring Revolution
    6, 13, 31, 128, 327-28, 333-34
State Administration Council (SAC)
    4, 10, 43, 49, 50, 53, 63, 70, 95, 98, 125, 126, 139, 148, 149, 239-40, 242, 243-45, 249, 250-52, 265, 277-79, 297, 304, 306
Sustainable Development Goals (SDGs)
    221, 229

T

Ta'ang National Liberation Army (TNLA)
    100
Tatmadaw
    See "Sit Tat"
Territorial control
    7, 46, 61, 114, 116, 125, 129, 139, 149
Thailand
    8, 38, 140, 187, 189, 190, 192,193, 194, 196, 248-49, 251, 265, 300
Than Shwe
    52, 98, 325
Thein Sein
    16, 34, 53, 102, 103, 263, 264, 267, 268, 269-72, 273, 281
Torture
    5, 8, 9, 70, 86
Transition years
    11, 12, 34, 36, 53-55, 76, 97, 103-5, 238, 263, 264, 269-272, 273-77, 326, 333, 335

U

Union Election Commission (UEC)
43, 44, 56, 72

Union Solidarity and Development Party (USDP)
34, 43, 97, 98, 103, 110, 272, 273, 281

United Kingdom
10, 190, 197, 200, 243, 244, 291, 293, 294, 305

United Nations
10, 32, 58, 79, 128, 251, 268, 270, 272, 275, 276, 278, 280, 281, 289, 292, 295, 296, 297, 298, 299, 301-3, 306-7, 309

United States
10, 38, 52, 190, 192, 197, 200, 241, 243, 244, 245, 264, 267, 268, 270, 274, 275, 277, 281, 291, 293, 294, 299, 300

United Wa State Army (UWSA)
49, 100, 139, 273, 296

Urban Warfare
6, 107, 110, 111-12, 149

W

Weapons technology
8, 13, 59

Women
5, 163, 198, 230

Ward and Village Tract Administrators (WVTAs)
43, 128, 137

Y

Yangon
107, 110, 111-112, 159, 167, 168-69, 172

Youth
4, 18, 48, 100, 102, 111, 113, 129, 165, 175, 324, 325-26

www.ingramcontent.com/pod-product-compliance
Lightning Source LLC
Chambersburg PA
CBHW072120290426
44111CB00012B/1718